THE CA:

The
Case for God

PETER S. WILLIAMS

MONARCH
BOOKS

First published by Monarch Books 1999

ISBN 1 85424 454 X

Editorial Office: Monarch Books,
Broadway House, The Broadway, Crowborough,
East Sussex TN6 1HQ

British Library Cataloguing Data
A catalogue record for this book is available
from the British Library.

Designed and produced for the publishers by
Bookprint Creative Services
P.O. Box 827, BN21 3YJ, England
Printed in Great Britain.

God is more truly imagined than expressed, and He exists more truly than He is imagined.

Augustine (*De Trinitate*)

CONTENTS

ACKNOWLEDGEMENTS

The material presented here has evolved through several incarnations, in which many people have played a part. I'd like to take this opportunity to thank them all. However, I would like to express particular thanks to the following people and organisations:

Some of the following resembles material which appeared in the *Stirling Christian Pages* of Stirling University, on the Web, during the academic year 1996–97.

A version of my discussion of William James' argument in his paper 'The Will To Believe' appeared in *The Philosopher's Magazine*, Volume One (Winter 1997), pp.49–51 as 'The Right To Believe' (which is the title James later wished he had given his paper). My thanks to the editor, Dr Julian Baggini.

Most closely associated with the following were several of a series of apologetics pamphlets I produced for the Christian Union at the University of East Anglia during the academic year 1997–98. My thanks to my Christian brothers and sisters at UEA for their prayers and warm-hearted encouragement; especially those who served on the CU executive between 1997 and 1998, the members of my Bible-study group for 1997–1998, and of 'The Word' Christian reading-group for the same period.

Thanks to the UEA chaplaincy's Rev. Garth A. Barber, MSc (London), LTh (St John's Nottingham), FRAs, SOSc, for his encouragement and input. Thanks also to Strahan Spencer.

I'd like to thank the many philosophers from whose tutelage

I have benefited, in particular Michael Durrant and Dr Steven Moller at Cardiff University, and Professor Christopher Hookway at Sheffield University. Thanks to Nicholas Everitt, my research tutor at UEA, for his comments on thesis material bearing a close relationship to part of the following.

Grateful thanks to David Bacon, BA, MSc (Jesus College, Cambridge) for faithful Christian friendship and discussion, and for being involved in the roots of this project.

Love and thanks to my parents for their support and proof-reading. Thanks to Thelma and Susan Maunsell for hospitality and lifts while I visited Monarch. A big thank you to Simon Ghafur and Stella Whittenham for their proof-reading and textual suggestions.

Last but not least, thanks to Tony Collins, editor at Monarch, and to Professor Ian Malcolm at Liverpool Hope University, who reviewed the first draft of this volume, for his balanced and constructive critique. Of course, any inadequacies remain my own.

Peter S. Williams, BA (Cardiff), MA (Sheffield)

Portsmouth, Summer 1998

NOTE

Every effort has been made to contact the copyright holders of material used in this book, but this has not always been successful. Full acknowledgement will gladly be made in any future editions.

INTRODUCTION

In the words of the Apostles' Creed: 'I believe in God, the Father almighty, creator of heaven and earth.' As a Christian, I both believe that God exists, and have faith in him. Why do I believe that God exists? Why should anybody believe that God exists?

I was born into a Christian family. I attended a Baptist church, and went to a Church of England school. That's how I came to believe in God. But if you ask how I can intellectually justify believing in God's existence, that's a different question altogether. This book is my attempt to answer that question from a Christian viewpoint.

Interesting times

There is an ancient Chinese curse that runs, 'May you live in interesting times.' The twentieth century has certainly been an 'interesting time' for those concerned with the question of God's existence, believers and non-believers alike.

Interesting times for the believer

For the majority who believe in God, 'interest' has been provided by a combination of factors. For the first time in history, secular atheism (as opposed to religious atheism such as Buddhism) became a significant minority world-view.[1] The reasons for this drift away from belief are many and complex, but I would single out: 1) The intermixing of world-views caused by globalisation. 2) The West's increased material affluence. 3) The emergence of young adults as a distinct social group with their own sub-culture; a sub-culture often in rebellion against the values of the previous generation.

Intellectually, atheism has drawn comfort from two pillars of the establishment—philosophy and science (or rather, from non-believing philosophers and scientists).

Philosophically, there was a time when God was almost banished from the intellectual scene by the idea that talk about God either said nothing about reality, or else was meaningless. This view was based on the now infamous 'verification principle' of the 'logical positivist' school of philosophers. This strand of philosophy held that the meaning of any statement that was not true by definition (such as $2 + 2 = 4$) lay in its ability to be verified (in practice or at least in principle). To 'verify' something simply means to check it out with the senses. In other words, the statement, 'This is a book', is meaningful because you can verify it by touching and reading the book; but the statement, 'God exists', is not meaningful because you can't verify it by touching or looking at God.

Scientifically, increased knowledge of the physical universe has fed massive technological growth, which has contributed to the illusion of human independence from nature and from nature's creator. Why pray to God when taking penicillin has a greater likelihood of resolving the situation to your own satisfaction?

Science has also clashed with a literal interpretation of the biblical picture of human origins, persuading many that a scientific world-view can and must replace the traditional religious outlook.

The reality of human suffering was brought home to us in the twentieth century as in no other. Two world wars and the Nazi genocide presented humanity with tragic incarnations of the problem of evil.

Interesting times for the non-believer

The believer is not the only one to have had an 'interesting time' in the past century; far from it. The latter half of the twentieth century has seen growing dissatisfaction with secular existence. The barrenness of materialism, the realisation that science doesn't hold all the answers (especially when it comes to the morality of research and application), the partial collapse of Communism as a political power, and the world-weariness of 'Generation X' are a few of the factors contributing to a reawakening of the search for life's spiritual dimension.

Things soon unravelled for the verification principle. Most importantly, it was pointed out that the principle itself was neither true by definition (it was merely an arbitrary rule) nor open to verification—even in principle. The verification principle ruled itself to be meaningless!

While the scientific theory of evolution has been taken by some to undermine belief in God, the scientific theory of a cosmic origin in the so-called 'big bang' has replaced the ancient Greek idea of a beginningless universe and supported the biblical view of a cosmic beginning (Genesis 1:1). Astrophysicist Robert Jastrow writes that, for the non-believing scientist, 'the story ends like a bad dream';[2] for, having scaled the mountains of ignorance, 'he is greeted by a band of theologians who have been sitting there for centuries'.[3]

The intellectual resurrection of Theism

In the mid 1960s, *Time Magazine* ran a cover story which asked, 'Is God Dead?' about the then current 'death-of-God' movement in theology. A few years later, *Time* carried a similar cover story asking 'Is God coming back to life?' Interest in the philosophy of religion grew to the point where, in 1980, *Time* found itself running a story about 'Modernizing the case for God', describing the contemporary movement among philosophers putting new life into the arguments for God's existence. *Time* reported that:

> In a quiet revolution in thought and argument that hardly anybody could have foreseen only two decades ago, God is making a comeback. Most intriguingly, this is happening not amongst theologians or ordinary believers, but in the crisp intellectual circles of academic philosophers, where the consensus had long banished the Almighty from fruitful discourse.[4]

According to the same article, noted American philosopher Roderick Chisholm believes that while the brightest philosophers a generation ago were atheists, today most of the brightest philosophers believe in God. This shift in attitude prompts another noted philosopher, Professor William Lane Craig, to write: 'I think it is clear . . . that philosophical theism is very much alive and well today indeed, when one recalls the bleak days of the "Death of God" movement in the sixties, it is not unfair to speak of a veritable resurrection of theism.'[5]

An increasing number of philosophers and scientists are prepared to stand up and be counted as believers willing and able, as Craig writes, to use 'a tough-minded intellectualism in defence of that theism'.[6] Christianity is experiencing something of an intellectual rebirth. As the American philosopher J.P. Moreland says, 'In recent years there has been a noticeable increase in the number of intellectuals who embrace historic Christianity as a rational worldview.'[7] For example, at least seven philosophy journals are produced by Christians. The Society of Christian Philosophers was formed in 1978, and now has a membership of several hundred professionally trained philosophers who embrace some form of the Christian faith.

On the scientific front there are organisations such as Christians in Science, which has a membership of over 700 academics, and the Society of Ordained Scientists:

A significant and growing number of scientists, historians of science, and philosophers of science see more scientific evidence now for a personal creator and designer than was available fifty years ago. In the light of this evidence, it is false and naïve to claim that modern science has made belief in the supernatural unreasonable.[8]

When respected philosophers and scientists of the undoubted calibre of William P. Alston, Ian Barbour, William Lane Craig, Peter Geach, J.P. Moreland, Arthur Peacocke, Alvin Plantinga, John Polkinghorne, Richard Swinburne and Keith Ward believe in God, no one can say that such belief is only for the uneducated. These men follow on the heels of the likes of G.K. Chesterton, A.E. Taylor, C.S. Lewis, F.C. Copleston and Francis A. Shaeffer. This academic revival looks set to carry the intellectual representation of Christianity through into the twenty-first century after Christ, confounding those sceptics who once saw Christianity as a dying religion.

Joining the debate

These are certainly 'interesting times'. Despite the fact that around sixty per cent of people believe in the existence of a god, this percentage is lower in academic circles (for example, around forty per cent of scientists believe in a personal god). There are enough critics of belief in God to make for a good debate in which the believer need not always invent criticisms of their own views in order to ensure that those views withstand the fires of reason. Thinking up your own counter-arguments is a useful approach that allows one to follow through a line of thought, but debating with someone else introduces new perspectives which the lone armchair philosopher might not consider. Christianity cannot afford to ignore its detractors. I have therefore sought to interact with the arguments and opinions of non-believers (past and present). As to whose arguments are best, I leave that to my reader to judge.

Apologising for apologetics?

Christian pastor Dr Roy Clements notes that many people disapprove of controversy and are frustrated by the endless debates
in which opposing factions indulge. Concern increases as frus-
tration turns to fear, for verbal quarrelling can lead to physical
violence. All in all, suggests Dr Clements, many people conclude that we would all be better off without controversy: 'That
is one reason why Christianity is sometimes an unpopular religion today. For, as everybody knows, Christians love a good argument. They have been arguing for two thousand years. They
argue both among themselves, and with everybody else.'[9]

Debate about issues of religious belief can generate more heat
than light. However, that is no more of an argument against
debate than the argument that food can choke people to death
is an argument against eating! Disagreeing with a person's views
does not necessarily mean finding them disagreeable. Christians
argue because they are passionate about truth, and they believe
that Christianity is true.

Apologetics without apology

Some Christians question the possibility, legitimacy and practical benefits of engaging in rational debate about God's existence. To answer this concern, I will first look at the broader
question of the relationship between faith and reason, and at
the basis for debate, before considering the Bible's attitude
towards these matters.

All argument rests upon trust in the truth of basic principles.
While these principles cannot be called into question without
(at least implicitly) being assumed, neither can they be ultimately justified in a way that does not also assume their truth.
One cannot doubt that 'nothing can both be and not be in the
same way at the same time' (the law of non-contradiction)
without assuming that one's doubt is the case in contrast to its

not being the case. However, nor can one give a justification for this basic principle that does not itself depend upon the very principle in question. To do this would be an exercise in what philosophers call 'begging the question'.

Commitment to the laws of reason is an act of 'fundamental trust'. To give a proof for a conclusion ultimately requires trust in something which cannot itself be 'proved', but which must be assumed. Such an ultimate assumption is a 'basic' belief. The assumptions reason requires us to make are few in number, and to qualify as 'basic' a belief must be a belief that cannot be questioned without being assumed. It seems impossible for anyone but a mad person to live as if these basic assumptions were not true; but assumptions they are.

Surely, it may be said, if we cannot doubt these assumptions, then they must be true. I agree that basic assumptions are true. However, pointing out that we cannot doubt these assumptions does not amount to saying anything other than that there are things we cannot help believing. The assertion that 'if a belief cannot be doubted without assuming that it is true, then it must be true on pain of self-contradiction' begs the question. It relies upon the very principle that it invokes. Pointing out that an argument begs the question says nothing about the truth or falsity of that argument's conclusion, but it does show that the conclusion is not justified by that argument. Beliefs within the 'game' of reason may be supported or discredited to one degree or another, but we cannot turn logic upon itself.

This view of the basic principles of reason finds a happy home with the seventeenth-century French philosopher and mathematician Blaise Pascal, who wrote that: 'We know the truth not only by means of the reason but also by means of the heart. It is through the heart that we know the first principles.'[10] Modern-day philosopher Thomas Nagel is nevertheless correct when he writes:

> Certain forms of thought can't be intelligibly doubted because they force themselves into every attempt to think about anything . . .

There just isn't room for scepticism about basic logic, because there is no place to stand where we can formulate or think it without immediately contradicting ourselves by relying on it.[11]

While the truth of basic principles are ultimately logically unjustifiable, we nevertheless 'see' that they are true, and are justified in holding to their truth.

There are then certain basic beliefs without which argument, and so rational debate, cannot take place. I have already mentioned the law of non-contradiction, which is one of three basic assumptions traditionally singled out as of particular note:

1. X is X (the law of identity)
2. X is not both X and non-X (the law of non-contradiction)
3. Every declarative sentence is either true or false (the law of the excluded middle)

The basic notion is that something cannot both be and not be at the same time. This can be endlessly illustrated.[12]

For example: 1. An elephant is an elephant. 2. An elephant is not both an elephant and not an elephant (an elephant is not both an elephant and a mouse). 3. The assertion 'An elephant is standing on my foot' either is, or is not, true. There are other 'laws of reason', but these three are traditionally chosen as representative examples. Nevertheless, the most fundamental law is the law of non-contradiction, because the most basic distinction is that between something rather than nothing existing, between something of this nature rather than any other being the case (since to be is to be a something of some determinate sort). Bertrand Russell made the following observations about the 'laws of thought':

Some at least of these principles must be granted before any argument or proof becomes possible. When some of them have been granted, others can be proved, though these others, so long as they are simple, are just as obvious as the principles taken for granted . . . for instance . . . that what follows from a true premise is true.[13]

Russell notes that the name 'laws of thought' is misleading, 'for what is important is not the fact that we think in accordance with these laws, but the fact that things behave in accordance with them',[14] so that when we think in accordance with them 'we think truly'.[15]

Common ground

If a question is asked, or an objection to some belief is raised, the person asking or objecting makes assumptions. These assumptions certainly include the above laws of reason, whether they hold them implicitly or explicitly. These universal assumptions are the common ground on which rational debate takes place.

Sometimes a person may need to recognise in an explicit way their previously implicit trust in these principles before fruitful debate can take place. Nevertheless, whether this common ground needs to be dusted off a little, or lies waiting in eager anticipation of the next 'game' of reason, common ground exists.

The metaphor of rational debate as a 'game' is not meant to imply that arguments necessarily have winners and losers. If both sides have a greater commitment to *the* truth than to *their* truth, then even if one side's arguments crumble and the other side's arguments triumph, both 'sides' will emerge as winners. One side will be pleased to have been freed from ignorance and delusion, and the other side will be glad they could help, and will respect the 'loser' for having the courage to admit they were wrong. Rational debate is one 'game' where everyone can be a winner, if they stick to the rules. Arguments attack assertions, not people, even when people make the assertions under attack.

Playing by the rules

Some readers may benefit from a quick brushing up on the rules for the 'game':

The inherent structure of human reason manifests itself in three acts of the mind: 1) understanding, 2) judging and 3) reasoning. These three acts of the mind are expressed in 1) terms, 2) propositions and 3) arguments. Terms are either clear or unclear. Propositions are either true or untrue. Arguments are either logically valid or invalid. A term is clear if it is intelligible and unambiguous. A proposition is true if it corresponds to reality, if it says what is. An argument is valid if the conclusion follows necessarily from the premise. If all the terms in an argument are clear, and if all the premises are true, and if the argument is free from logical fallacy, then the conclusion must be true.

These are the essential rules of reason, in apologetics and in any other field of argument. They are not rules of a game we invented and can change. They are rules of reality . . . To disagree with the conclusion of any argument, it must be shown that either an ambiguous term or false premise or logical fallacy exists in the argument.[16]

Christians are committed to rationality, because they view the cosmos as the creation of a rational God, and believe human beings are made in God's 'image' (Genesis 1:27, Acts 17:27–28). In the Bible, God says 'Come now, let us reason together' (Isaiah 1:18). The apostle Paul wrote of 'defending and confirming the gospel' (Philippians 1:7), and 'reasoned . . . from the scriptures, explaining and proving' (Acts 17:2–3). Jesus said that the greatest commandment was to 'love the Lord your God with all your heart and with all your soul *and with all your mind*' (Matthew 22:37, my italics). Christians are commanded to 'always be prepared to give an answer to everyone who asks you to give the reason for the hope that you have . . . with gentleness and respect' (1 Peter 3:15). The Greek word translated here as 'reason' is the word '*apologia*', which means 'a reasoned defence', and from which we get the word 'apologetics'. Christian apologetics is the art of giving a reasoned defence for Christian beliefs.

The task of apologetics can be divided into the negative task of defending Christian beliefs against objections, and the positive task of offering reasons for Christian beliefs. For the Christian, apologetics is a part of 'spiritual warfare' wherein we 'demolish arguments and every pretension that sets itself up against the knowledge of God, and we take captive every thought to make it obedient to Christ' (2 Corinthians 10:5). This spiritual warfare 'is against unbelief, not unbelievers . . . The goal of apologetics is not victory but truth. Both sides win.'[17]

Apologetics involves scholarship of many kinds: scientific, historical, archaeological, textual, all of which involve an essential commitment to the 'laws of reason' which lie at the heart of philosophy. Christians therefore have a particular interest in and responsibility to study philosophy. As C.S. Lewis once wrote:

> To be ignorant and simple now—not to be able to meet the enemies on their own ground—would be to throw down our weapons, and to betray our uneducated brethren who have, under God, no defence but us against the intellectual attacks of the heathen. Good philosophy must exist, if for no other reason, because bad philosophy needs to be answered.[18]

Norman L. Geisler and Paul D. Feinberg note that some Christians are suspicious of philosophy. Having heard stories of Christians who have lost their faith through studying it, some well-meaning believers advise others to stay away from the subject. However, say Geisler and Feinberg, this is not wise advice: 'Christianity *can* stand up to the intellectual challenge mounted against it. The result of such a challenge should not be the loss of faith, but the priceless possession of a well-reasoned and mature faith.'[19] They go on to note that the failure to be aware of contemporary thought patterns can have serious consequences for the Christian who avoids philosophy, for 'the Christian most likely to fall prey to false philosophy is the ignorant Christian'.[20]

I am sometimes asked whether anybody ever arrived at belief

in God through the arguments for His existence. No argument can make you believe in God in the sense of trusting in Him; but arguments can and do play a role in people's decision whether or not to believe that there is a God to be trusted or rejected. After all, 'Theists have not usually come to believe that there is a God because they think this is the most unreasonable view they could hold!'[21] And yes, there are examples of people being convinced by arguments that God exists, and going on to place their faith in God. The moral argument for God's existence played a role in the conversion of C.S. Lewis, and philosopher Norman L. Geisler arrived at his belief in God's existence through studying philosophy:

> If one is unwilling to look at a proof, unwilling to accept any proof, unwilling to accept the validity of a proof as applied to God, or unwilling to accept the God the proof concludes, then one will not be persuaded by theistic arguments. On the other hand, persons of good will who are seeking the truth will be persuaded by good reasoning. And it is up to the theist to supply these good reasons.[22]

For those who doubt the practical usefulness of apologetics, perhaps the following illustration will encourage a more positive attitude. On 27 June, 1993, a crowd of thousands gathered at Willow Creek Community Church in South Barrington, Illinois, America. An audience listening to the over one hundred radio stations that broadcast the evening's events joined those who attended. The occasion? A debate. The subject of this debate? 'Atheism versus Christianity—Where does the evidence point?'

Frank Zindler, a former professor of geology and biology who writes for American Atheists Inc. spoke for the atheists' case. Advocating the case for God was Dr William Lane Craig, Professor of Philosophy of Religion at Trinity Evangelical Divinity School, and author of several notable books defending Christian beliefs.[23]

At the end of the evening, Lee Strobel, Pastor of the Willow Creek Church and one-time award-winning journalist at the *Chicago Tribune*, asked the audience for their verdict: 'I stressed to everyone that they should set aside their personal beliefs and vote only for which side had laid out the most compelling evidence that night.'[24] The result? Ninety-seven per cent declared that the Christian case had prevailed. Moreover:

> Of the 632 people who said they were definitely not Christians, an overwhelming eighty-two per cent of them concluded that the evidence offered for Christianity was definitely the most compelling. And—get this!—Forty-seven of the people who had walked in as unbelievers walked out as believers! The evidence for Christ was so strong.[25]

No one became an atheist.

Faith and reason

But what has all this to do with faith? Isn't faith the very opposite of reason?

> Many think that faith is a substitute for reason and that the important thing about belief is that you believe it for yourself and are helped by accepting the belief. It really doesn't matter if the belief is true . . . faith and religion are nothing more than relativistic, privatized placebos.[26]

Such a view seems to me to be a travesty of both faith and reason. The only good reason to believe something is because you think it is true; not merely 'true for me', but True with a capital T. Perhaps my earlier discussion of the necessity for ultimately unprovable basic assumptions within logic itself will indicate to the reader why I see no conflict between faith and reason.

C.S. Lewis was puzzled by the fact that Christians regard

faith as a virtue, asking what could be moral or immoral about believing or failing to believe certain statements. Lewis solved this puzzle to his own satisfaction when he realised that he was assuming 'that if the human mind once accepts a thing as true it will automatically go on regarding it as true, until some real reason for reconsidering it turns up'.[27] But the human mind is not so completely ruled by reason. The virtue of faith is not believing something you know isn't true, or believing something despite a considered judgement that the evidence points to the opposite conclusion. Rather, the virtue of faith is continuing to believe something you have judged to be true, when your feelings of belief and certainty let you down.

Michael J. Langford, Professor of Philosophy at The Memorial University of Newfoundland, Canada, makes the distinction between 'blind faith' and 'heroic faith': 'In the former case, one is resisting the onslaught of reason; in the latter, the onslaught of weariness or pain or temptation.'[28] Christian faith should be heroic, but never blind.

To illustrate this point, C.S. Lewis tells us that his reason is perfectly convinced by good evidence that anaesthetics will not smother him and that a well-trained surgeon doesn't start operating until the patient is unconscious. Nevertheless, 'that does not alter the fact that when they have me down on the table and clap their horrible mask over my face, a mere childish panic begins inside me'.[29] He may think he is going to choke, or be afraid that they will start operating before he has been knocked out: 'In other words, I lose my faith in anaesthetics. It is not my reason that is taking away my faith: on the contrary, my faith is based on reason . . . The battle is between faith and reason on one side and emotion and imagination on the other.'[30]

Like Lewis, I wouldn't dream of asking anyone to believe that God exists, or to accept Christianity, if their reason concludes that the evidence is against it. No, faith is 'the art of holding onto things your reason has once accepted, in spite of your changing moods'.[31] I agree with Michael J. Wilkins and

J.P. Moreland who write that 'the modern view of faith as something unrelated or even hostile to reason is a departure from traditional Christianity and not a genuine expression of it'.[32] Rather, we should follow the Bible's advice to 'test everything. Hold on to the good' (1 Thessalonians 5:21).

Where I'm heading and how I plan to get there

The aim of this book is the simple one of arguing *The Case for God*. The God I have in mind is, of course, the God of Christianity, but much of what I have to say will be of equal support to Jewish and Muslim belief. Nevertheless, the God whose existence the following arguments testify is fully compatible with those additional Christian beliefs about God's action in history, the incarnation, and God's triune nature (Christians believe God is three divine persons in one divine personal being).

My approach to God's existence will be as follows: First, I will consider the main argument against the existence of God, the argument from evil. I point out that all this argument can claim to rule out is the existence of a God who is all-good, all-powerful and all-knowing. That is, even were this argument to succeed, it would still allow for the existence of a god who had two out of three of these attributes to a maximal degree, and the remaining attribute to an almost maximal degree. Then I will show that there simply is no contradiction involved in holding that there is an all-good, all-powerful and all-knowing God, and that evil exists. In fact, I will show how the recognition of evil actually supports the case for God's existence by granting the most important premise of the moral argument for the existence of God. After concluding my discussion of the 'problem of evil' with some theological perspectives upon the issue, I will therefore move into a defence of the moral argument for God's existence.

The moral argument, I claim, establishes the existence of an all-good, personal, eternal and transcendent creator. In the light of the failure of the argument from evil, we can conclude that this god may also possess the traditional qualities of maximal power and knowledge attributed to God by the Bible (whether this is restricted to Old Testament Judaism, or inclusive of New Testament Christianity). The task of the remaining arguments is therefore twofold: to reinforce the conclusions of the moral argument, and to defend the belief that God has maximal power and knowledge.

My second positive argument is a version of the so-called 'cosmological argument'. After a brief look at the apologetic value of the argument from the evidence of a cosmic beginning, I argue for the existence of an un-caused cause, or independent being, upon which all caused or dependent things depend for their existence. It is further argued that, as the source of our moral intuitions, we cannot think of this independent being as anything other than good—a contention which supports, and is supported by, the moral argument.

I then turn to design arguments. Design arguments are a growth area in the current literature, and I will therefore devote two chapters to this most popular of subjects. The arguments for design often proceed by way of analogy between human artefacts and nature—an analogy which, I will argue, is not at all undermined by the evidence for evolution, as is popularly thought. In the second of these chapters I will consider just one recent argument for design which proceeds by way of seeking the best explanation for the scientific data of universal 'fine tuning' which has been dubbed 'the anthropic principle'.

Then I give my attention to more personal arguments: from common consent, authority and religious experience, from desire and from the absurdity of the universe if God does not exist. These arguments round off the positive case for belief in the existence of God.

Continuing the more personal theme, I then move on to a discussion of Pascal's notorious Wager arguments, and William

James' argument in his important paper of 1897: 'The Will To Believe'. I will defend a sober view of what James is saying in 'The Will To Believe', and show how his arguments complement those of the earlier Pascal.

Last, but not least, I provide a summary of the kind of God to which the preceding arguments point, concluding with some thoughts on the meaning and import of God's existence and some suggestions on resolving the question of God's existence or non-existence at the personal level. Before launching into the arguments, I have a few things to say about belief and disbelief.

Three views

Broadly speaking there are three views about the existence of God. The first view is theism. Theism is a word taken from ancient Greek, and it literally means 'god-ism'—belief in God. Theism is the belief that God exists, where the term 'God' means a personal, supernatural being who is all-good, all-powerful and all-knowing, and by whose will everything apart from the divine being exists. Judaism, Christianity and Islam are all forms of theism. In this book I will present reasons for believing that theism is true, and therefore that other points of view on the question of God's existence are false.

The opposing view to theism is the view that God does not exist. This view is called atheism. Atheism adds the negative alpha 'a' to 'theism' to get 'no-god-ism'. Atheism is the belief that there is no God. The atheist is 'a person who maintains that there is no God; that is, that the sentence "God exists" expresses a false proposition'.[33]

It has sometimes been argued that atheism is self-contradictory because, in affirming the absolute universal negative 'There is no God', the atheist claims the sort of infinite knowledge that only God could possess. In order to know for certain that God does not exist, it is suggested, you would have to be God—in which case God exists! For example, the Indian apologist

Dr Ravi Zacharias writes that: 'Having quickly recognised the inherent contradiction of affirming god's non-existence, which absolutely would at the same time presuppose infinite knowledge on the part of the one doing the denying, a philosophically convenient switch was made [by some Atheists] to agnosticism.'[34] I agree with Dr Zacharias on many things, and I highly recommend his books, which focus on the existential dimensions of theism and atheism. However, on this occasion I must seek to correct what I believe to be a serious mistake.

Making an absolute universal denial simply does not require infinite knowledge on the part of the denier. A 'negative universal absolute' may indeed be the hardest kind of proposition to defend. Defending the proposition 'There is no mouse in this building' is far harder than defending the proposition 'There is a mouse in this building'. The one requires a knowledge of the whole building excluding the presence of any mice, while the other merely requires that we have spotted one mouse in one room at one time. However, saying 'There is no God' is not like saying 'There is no mouse'. If, for example, the traditional 'problem of evil' were a sound argument against the existence of God, then all the atheist would need to know in order to defend, and indeed prove, the proposition 'There is no God' would be just that argument from the existence of evil.

Atheism cannot be defeated by so brief an argument. Although it is enticingly simple, it is inadequate. The atheist must be convinced that they have no sound argument against the existence of God, and more reason to believe in his existence than to believe that he does not exist. This process of argumentation is far less simple, but far more adequate.

A third view of God's existence is called agnosticism, again from the Greek, meaning 'one who doesn't know'. ('*Ginosko*' means 'to know' and the alpha 'a' again means the negation of its subject.) The uncomplimentary Latin equivalent is 'ignoramus'! Strictly speaking, an agnostic is someone who says that we *cannot* know (or prove) whether or not God exists; but it is also used to mean someone who says they *do not* know whether or not God exists.

The first thing I'd say to the agnostic is that, whether or not we have proof or disproof of God's existence, we will inevitably end up living either as if God existed, or as if God did not exist. As Somerset Maugham wrote: 'I remain an agnostic, and the practical outcome of agnosticism is that you act as though God did not exist.'[35] How refreshing it would be to find an agnostic who lived as though God did exist, just in case He does! Pascal's Wager arguments (which I shall discuss towards the end of this work) suggest, at the very least, that we should take great care into which 'as if' we fall. William James, in 'The Will To Believe' (at which we'll take a close look later on), assures us that there is nothing irrational in following a desire to believe in God in the absence of proof either way.

The second thing I'd say to the agnostic is that, like the atheist, they should not ignore purported evidence for God's existence (or, indeed, non-existence). If any of the arguments provide evidence for the existence of God, then we cannot shirk the task of judging whether belief in God's existence seems to us to be reasonable, or even compelling. Nor can we avoid the decision as to what effect we will allow this judgement to have upon our lives.

'Agnosticism' is popularly used to mean 'sitting on the fence' as regards God's existence. However, sitting on the fence is not an option here. We all live as if God exists, or as if God does not exist. The question is, in which camp are we, and which camp is living under a delusion? Either God exists, or God does not exist. Theists are either living under an illusion, or they are right. The same holds true for atheists.

The spirit of inquiry

Some readers may be wondering what room I leave in all that I have said for the 'work of God's Spirit'. Everywhere! I do not believe that God coerces belief or disbelief; but I am sure He can be very persuasive if the unbeliever will allow himself or herself to 'listen' to Him. It is entirely appropriate, as we begin to look at the arguments, that we begin with a prayer. The atheist has nothing to fear in such a prayer, because they will see it as talking to empty space; and many would admit that God might exist, although they think it unlikely. The agnostic should welcome prayer, because they must admit that God might be there; and if God is there, then He can surely 'hear' our prayers. The theist will welcome prayer, as another chance to touch base with their wonderful creator. Anthony Kenny, an agnostic philosopher, agrees:

> There is no reason why someone who is in doubt about the existence of God should not pray for help and guidance . . . Some find something comic in the idea of an agnostic praying to a God whose existence he doubts. It is surely no more unreasonable than the act of a man adrift in the ocean . . . who cries for help though he may never be heard.[36]

Therefore, whatever your beliefs as you begin this voyage of discovery, I urge you to mean this prayer: 'Dear God, if you are truth, then I seek to know you. Travel with me as I seek the truth and help me to seek the truth, whatever it may be, in preference to all else.' After all, God promises in the Bible that those who truly seek will find (Matthew 7:7).

On quoting authorities

I have truly 'stood on the shoulders of giants', and credit is due where credit is due. Quotations are gems which embellish the text, highlighting this or that point by virtue of their being material of a different quality and radiance. While we shouldn't give special consideration to someone's words simply because they are famous, there is a legitimate use of supporting quotations:

It would be a . . . mistake to suppose that every appeal to authority is illegitimate, for the proper use of authority plays an indispensable role in the accumulation and application of knowledge . . . The appeal to reliable authority is legitimate, for the testimony of a reliable authority *is* evidence for the conclusion.[37]

On recommended reading

Each chapter ends with a recommended reading list, graded for readability and sophistication. Books marked (1) are easy to read, basic entry-level material. Books labelled (2) are more sophisticated than books marked (1), but should still be accessible to the non-specialist. Books marked (3) are not for the beginner, being fairly sophisticated treatments of their subject. Books marked (4) are only for the advanced reader looking for a sophisticated treatment of the subject matter. To give you a benchmark for comparison, I'd mark this book as a (2).

Occasionally I recommend an illustrative film to view (these films would make for excellent launch pads for group discussion of the relevant issues), or even some music to listen to.

I have also included as an appendix a 'Resources Library' with an annotated book list, addresses for useful organisations, journals and Web pages to visit.

Recommended reading

World-views, religion and the history of ideas

David Cook, *Blind Alley Beliefs* (IVP). (2)

Dean C. Halverson, ed., *The Compact Guide To World Religions* (Bethany House, 1996). (1)

Josh McDowell and Don Stewart, *Concise Guide To Today's Religions* (Scripture Press, 1992). (1)

Francis A. Shaeffer, *Trilogy* (IVP). (2)

James W. Sire, *The Universe Next Door*, third edition (IVP, 1997). A classic analysis and assessment of world-views. (2)

Merve Jones, *The Universe Upstairs* (Frameworks–IVP, 1991). A cartoon-strip version of Sire's *The Universe Next Door*. (1)

Logical positivism and the verification principle

Brian Davies, *An Introduction to the Philosophy of Religion*, second edition (Oxford, 1993), chapter 1. (2)

Expositions of atheism

J.J. Mackie, *The Miracle of Theism* (Oxford, 1982). (4)

Michael Martin, *Atheism—a Philosophical Justification* (Temple University Press, 1990). (3)

Robin Le Poidevin, *Arguing for Atheism—An Introduction to the Philosophy of Religion*, (Routledge, 1996). (3)

Bertrand Russell, *Why I Am Not A Christian* (Routledge, 1996). (1)

Debates between atheists and theists

Bertrand Russell and F.C. Copleston, 'A debate on the existence of God', in John Hick, ed., *The Existence of God* (Macmillan, 1964). (1)

J.J.C. Smart and J.J. Haldane, *Atheism and Theism* (Blackwell, 1996). (4)

J.P. Moreland and Kai Nielsen (with Peter Kreeft, Antony Flew, William Lane Craig, Keith Parsons and Dallas Willard), *Does God Exist? The Debate between Theists and Atheists* (Prometheus Books, 1993). (3)

Christian critiques of atheism

Norman L. Geisler, *Christian Apologetics* (Baker, 1995). (3)

James W. Sire, *The Universe Next Door*, third edition (IVP, 1997). (2)

Ravi Zacharias, *Can Man Live Without God?* (Word, 1994). (1)
Also available on two audio cassettes, the lectures upon which the book is closely based, *Can Man Live Without God?* (Word Audio, 1994). (1)

Ravi Zacharias, *A Shattered Visage—The Real Face of Atheism* (Baker, 1995). (1)

Introduction to Philosophy, Truth, Knowledge and Argument

Clive Calver, *Thinking Clearly about Truth* (Monarch, 1995). (1)

F.C. Copleston, *A History of Philosophy*—in nine volumes (Image Books). (3)

Jostein Gaarder, *Sophie's World—A Novel about the History of Philosophy* (Phoenix, 1994). (1)

Norman L. Geisler and Paul D. Feinberg, *Introduction to Philosophy—A Christian Perspective* (Baker, 1997), chapters 1–17. (2)

Norman L. Geisler, *Christian Apologetics* (Baker, 1995), Parts One and Two. (3)

Arthur F. Holmes, *All truth is God's truth* (IVP, 1979). (3)

Peter Kreeft, *The Best Things In Life* (IVP, 1984). (1)

Peter Kreeft, *The Journey* (IVP, 1996). (1)

Peter Kreeft and Ronald Tacelli, *Handbook of Christian Apologetics* (Monarch, 1995), Chapters 1, 2, and 15. (1)

C.S. Lewis, 'De Futilitate' in *Christian Reflections* (Fount, 1980). (1)

Thomas Nagel, *The Last Word* (Oxford, 1997). An influential secular philosopher defends objectivity in language, logic, science and ethics. (3)

Bertrand Russell, *The Problems of Philosophy* (Oxford, 1980). (2)

James W. Sire, *Why Should Anyone Believe Anything at All?* (IVP, 1994). (2)

Ravi Zacharias, *Can Man Live Without God?* (Word, 1995). (1)

Ravi Zacharias, *Deliver Us from Evil* (Word, 1996), appendix B. (1)

Faith and reason

William J. Abraham, 'Soft Rationalism', in Michael Peterson *et al* eds, *Philosophy of Religion—Selected Readings* (Oxford, 1996). (3)

Arthur F. Holmes, *All truth is God's truth* (IVP, 1979). (3)

Peter Kreeft and Ronald Tacelli, *Handbook of Christian Apologetics* (Monarch, 1995), Chapters 1, 2 and 15. (1)

C.S.Lewis, *Mere Christianity* (Fount, 1986), pp.119–129. (1)

C.S.Lewis, 'Learning in War Time' in *Fern-seed and Elephants* (Fount, 1975). (1)

Michael Peterson *et al*, *Reason and Religious Belief—An Introduction to the Philosophy of Religion* (Oxford, 1991), chapter 3. (3)

James W. Sire, *Discipleship Of The Mind—Learning to love God in the ways we think* (IVP, 1990). (2)

Faith and science

Ian G. Barbour, *Religion in an Age of Science* (SCM, 1990). (4)

R.J. Berry, ed., *Real Science, Real Faith, Sixteen leading British scientists discuss their science and their faith* (Monarch, 1995). (1)

Kitty Ferguson, *The Fire In The Equations—Science, Religion and The Search For God* (Bantam Books, 1995). (2)

Nicky Gumbel, *Searching Issues*, chapter 6 (Kingsway, 1995). (1)

John Houghton, *The Search For God—Can Science Help?* (Lion, 1995). (2)

A.R. Peacocke, *Creation and the World of Science* (Oxford, 1979). (4)

John Polkinghorne, *Quarks, chaos and christianity* (Triangle, 1994). (1)

John Polkinghorne, *Serious Talk—Science and Religion in Dialogue* (SCM, 1995). (2)

John Polkinghorne, *Scientists as Theologians—A comparison of the writing of Ian Barbour, Arthur Peacocke and John Polkinghorne* (SPCK, 1996). (3)

John Polkinghorne, *Beyond Science—The wider human context* (Cambridge, 1996). (2)

John Polkinghorne, *Belief in God in an Age of Science* (Yale University Press, 1998). (2)

W. Mark Richardson and Wesley J. Wildman eds, *Religion and Science—History, Method, Dialogue* (Routledge, 1996). (4)

Russell Stannard, *Science and Wonders—Conversations about Science and Belief*, (Faber and Faber, 1996). (2)

Keith Ward, *God, Faith and The New Millennium—Christian Belief in an Age of Science* (OneWorld, 1998). (3)

The art of apologetics

William Lane Craig, *Reasonable Faith—Christian Truth and Apologetics* (Crossway, 1994), introduction and chapter 1. (3)

C.S. Lewis, 'Christian Apologetics' in *Timeless At Heart* (Fount, 1987). (1)

Alister McGrath, *Explaining Your Faith* (IVP, 1995). (1)

Alister McGrath, *Bridge-Building—Communicating Christianity effectively* (IVP, 1992). (2)

Peter C. Moore, *Disarming The Secular Gods—Sharing your faith so that people will listen* (IVP, 1989), chapter 1. (1)

Nick Pollard, *Evangelism made slightly less difficult* (IVP). (1)

Notes

1. A world-view is 'a set of presuppositions (assumptions which may be true, partially true or entirely false) which we hold (consciously or subconsciously, consistently or inconsistently) about the basic makeup of our world'. (James W. Sire, *The Universe Next Door*, third edition [IVP, 1997], p.16.)

2. Robert Jastrow, *God and the Astronomers* (W. W. Norton: New York, 1978).

3. *Ibid.*

4. 'Modernizing the case for God', *Time Magazine*, 7 April 1980, pp.65–66.

5. William Lane Craig, 'The Resurrection of Theism', *Truth Journal*, updated 8 August 1997: http://www.leaderu.com/truth/3truth01.html

6. *Ibid.*
7. J.P. Moreland, *Scaling the Secular City* (Baker, 1987), p.11.
8. Michael J. Wilkins and J.P. Moreland, *Jesus Under Fire* (Paternoster Press, 1995), p.10.
9. Roy Clements, *Introducing Jesus* (Kingsway, 1986), p.83.
10. Blaise Pascal, Honor Levi, trans., *Pensées and other writings* (Oxford, 1995), *Pensées* 142.
11. Thomas Nagel, *The Last Word* (Oxford, 1997), pp.61–62.
12. James W. Sire, *Why Should Anybody Believe Anything At All?* (IVP, 1994), p.84.
13. Bertrand Russell, *The Problems of Philosophy* (Oxford, 1980), p.40.
14. *Ibid.*, pp.40–41.
15. *Ibid.*, p.41.
16. Peter Kreeft and Ronald Tacelli, *Handbook of Christian Apologetics* (Monarch, 1995), pp.17–18.
17. *Ibid.*, p.22.
18. C.S. Lewis, quoted by Norman L. Geisler in the Foreword to J.P. Moreland's *Scaling the Secular City* (Baker, 1987).
19. Norman L. Geisler and Paul D. Feinberg, *Introduction to Philosophy—A Christian Perspective* (Baker, 1997), pp.21–22.
20. *Ibid.*, pp.22, 74.
21. Norman L. Geisler and Winfried Corduan, *Philosophy of Religion*, second edition (Baker, 1988), p.87.
22. *Ibid.*, p.88.
23. William Lane Craig's books include: *The Kalam Cosmological Argument* (Barnes and Noble: New York, 1979); *The Cosmological Argument from Plato to Leibniz* (Barnes and Noble: New York, 1980), and *Reasonable Faith* revised edition (Crossway Books, 1994).
24. Lee Strobel, *What Jesus Would Say . . .*, p.131.
25. *Ibid.*
26. Michael J. Wilkins and J.P. Moreland, *op cit.*, pp.7–8.
27. C.S. Lewis, *Mere Christianity* (Fount, 1986), p.120.

28. Michael J. Langford, *Unblind Faith* (SCM, 1982), p.3.
29. C.S. Lewis, *op cit.*, p.120.
30. *Ibid.*
31. *Ibid.*, pp.121–122.
32. Michael J. Wilkins and J.P. Moreland, *op cit.*, p.8.
33. Paul Edwards, ed, *Encyclopaedia of Philosophy*.
34. Ravi Zacharias, *Can Man Live Without God?* (Word, 1995), p.334.
35. Somerset Maugham, quoted by Colin Chapman, *Christianity on Trial* (Lion, 1981), p.198.
36. Anthony Kenny, *The God of The Philosophers* (Oxford, 1979), p.129.
37. Wesley C. Salmon, *Logic*, Foundations of Philosophy Series (Prentice-Hall: Englewood Cliffs, NJ, 1963), pp.63–64.

CHAPTER ONE

THE PROBLEM OF EVIL

> For I have the desire to do what is good, but I cannot carry it out. For what I do is not the good I want to do; no, the evil I do not want to do—this I keep on doing (Romans 7:18–19)

This chapter aims to show that the existence of evil does not disprove the existence of God. I argue that there is no contradiction between the existence of God and the existence of evil. Moreover, any argument from the existence of evil against the existence of God depends upon the recognition of objective moral values, which point to God as their source. (The argument for the existence of God from the existence of objective moral values will be examined in greater detail in Chapter Two.) I propose a justification of the existence of evil, taking into account what the scientific picture of nature can say about natural evil, and discussing some of the goods that can arise from the existence of evil. I also examine the implications for the 'problem of evil' on Christian beliefs about Jesus, heaven and hell.

If you are currently facing the problem of evil in your life, or in the life of someone you know, then reading philosophy is probably the last thing you need to do. So don't. (You may, however, find some of the thoughts towards the end of this chapter more relevant to your situation.) The person in pain needs love more than metaphysics. The time for philosophy is either before you hit one of life's rough patches, or a long time afterwards.

God and evil

The famous atheist and philosopher Lord Bertrand Russell once asked the following rhetorical question about God and evil: 'Do you really think that, if you were granted omnipotence and omniscience and millions of years in which to perfect your world, you could produce nothing better than the Ku-Klux-Klan or the Fascists?'[1] ('Omnipotence' means 'all-powerful', and 'Omniscience' means 'all-knowing'.) He had, of course, picked upon some of the world's worst features. God has done better! Did Bertrand Russell really think that, if he were all-powerful and all-knowing, and had millions of years in which to perfect a world, he could do better than music, art, the Brazilian rain-forest or the Rocky Mountains? Better than friendship, sex and love?

The real question is, 'How can the existence of God be reconciled with the existence of the Ku-Klux-Klan and the Fascists? How can there be evil in a world created by an all-good, all-powerful and all-knowing God?' As modern-day atheist, Robin Le Poidevin writes, 'The fact of suffering faces theists with a truth that is both undeniable and apparently incompatible with their belief.'[2] From the depths of our personal and shared pain comes the question, 'Why?' We know at a gut level that some things are Wrong, and we have trouble accepting that both God and Wrong exist in the same world. Nevertheless, 'It is important to distinguish a cry of agony in the face of what we cannot comprehend from the recognition of contradiction at the heart of theistic belief.'[3]

There is something odd about the claim that the millions of people who live and suffer without abandoning faith in God are all somehow inconsistent. We might use the words of C.S. Lewis to ask Bertrand Russell a question of our own: 'If the universe is so bad, or even half so bad, how on earth did human beings ever come to attribute it to the activity of a wise and good creator? Men are fools, perhaps; but hardly so foolish as that.'[4] The Christian religion, springing from the brutal crucifixion of its founder, might be expected to cope rather well with the problem of pain and suffering.

What is wrong?

At first glance it may be tempting to define Wrong as anything that frustrates human desires. Bertrand Russell defined bad desires as 'those which tend to thwart the desires of others, or more exactly, those which thwart more desires than they assist'.[5] Given this definition, pain, sickness, murder and cruelty are all clearly bad. However, once we ask whether the desires frustrated by Wrong are desires we *ought* to have, we realise that this definition is inadequate.

Suppose I aspire to the accumulation of great wealth at the

expense of my relationships. Suppose further that I am temporarily struck down with a disease that frustrates my dream of wealth, forcing me to depend upon the loving care of my family and friends. Through this experience I become a humbler and ultimately more contented person. I give up my single-minded pursuit of riches in preference for a simple life. Was my disease a bad thing or a good thing? I think most people would agree that, as the disease frustrated a bad aspiration, and resulted in my coming to possess right aspirations, it was probably a good thing that I was ill.

Augustine and Aquinas said that evil has no reality of its own, but is parasitic upon good. As Augustine wrote, 'Evil has no positive nature; but the loss of good has received the name "evil".'[6] In the words of Aquinas: 'Evil is privation; in this sense blindness means the privation of sight . . . a thing is called evil for lacking a perfection it ought to have; to lack sight is evil in man, but not in a stone . . .'[7] It follows that 'every evil is based on some good . . . Evil cannot exist but in good; sheer evil is impossible.'[8]

I feel attracted to the definition of evil as the lack of good. However, I wonder whether hate, for example, is merely the lack of love. Lack of love would result in indifference, but hate is something else again. But perhaps hate is the lack of both love and indifference.

Whether or not the definition of evil as 'the privation of good' is a good one, I agree with Augustine and Aquinas that whatever evil is, it is parasitic upon good. This definition of evil contradicts the popular view that good and evil are equal opposites. Some say that good and evil need each other, each existing only in contrast with the other. However, as C.S. Lewis asked, 'If a taste for cruelty and a taste for kindness were equally ultimate and basic, by what common standard could the one reprove the other?'[9] Christianity says that ultimate reality, God, is all-good, and that everything else is dependent upon God. It follows that 'evil cannot exist at all without the good [whereas] the good can exist without evil'.[10]

The argument from evil

Some people think that the existence of evil proves that God does not exist. Here is a prime example of an argument to this effect given by Robin Le Poidevin:

> If [God] is all-knowing, he will be aware of suffering; if he is all-powerful, he will be able to prevent suffering; and if he is perfectly good, he will desire to prevent suffering. But, clearly, he does not prevent suffering, so either there is no such deity, or, if there is, he is not all-knowing, all-powerful and perfectly good, though he may be one or two of these.[11]

If God doesn't know about the existence of Wrong, or knows but can't do anything about it, or knows and could do something but doesn't care enough to do so, then the existence of Wrong, so the argument goes, would be understandable. However, any God worthy of the name would know, would care and would have the power to do something. Yet Wrong exists. It would seem then, that no God worthy of the name exists. Let's lay this argument out nice and neatly so we can get a good look at it (I will use 'Wrong' as a covering term for both 'suffering' and 'evil'):

Premise 1) If God existed there would be no Wrong (because God would be aware of Wrong, he would desire to prevent Wrong, and he would be able to prevent Wrong).
Premise 2) Wrong exists.
Conclusion. Therefore, God does not exist.

The argument from evil says that it is contradictory to hold that the statements 'God is all-knowing', 'God is all-good', 'God is all-powerful' and 'Wrong exists' are all true. As H.J. McCloskey alleges, 'Evil is a problem for the theist in that a *contradiction* is involved in the fact of evil, on the one hand,

and the belief in the omnipotence and perfection of God on the other.'[12] My task is to show that (correctly understood) there is no contradiction in holding all four beliefs, and that William Lane Craig is right when he says that 'there is no contradiction between the two statements "God exists" and "Evil exists"'.[13]

The scope of the argument

The above argument claims to rule out the existence of a being that is all-knowing and all-powerful and all-good. As Le Poidevin admits, it does not attempt to rule out belief in the existence of a god. Rather, it attempts to rule out belief in any god with all three qualities of ultimate power, knowledge and goodness. As far as the argument from evil is concerned, there could exist a god who has any two of the above qualities to an infinite degree, and the remaining quality to a very great degree. For example, the argument cannot rule out the existence of a god who is all-good, all-knowing and extremely powerful. All the argument claims is to rule out the existence of a god who is all-good *and* all-knowing *and* all-powerful. Of course, this is just the sort of God Christians believe in.

Is Wrong an illusion?

If God exists, there must be a flaw in the argument from Wrong. One possibility would be to deny that there is Wrong in the world (premise 2). Believe it or not, some people do make such a denial. Some believe that evil is an illusion, and so does not really exist. However, if evil is an illusion, then the illusion of evil exists, and the illusion of evil is no less evil for being an illusion. Moreover, to paraphrase Freud, 'It would be nice if it were true that no evil existed, but the very fact that men wish it to be so makes this belief very suspect.'[14] Christian belief in God includes the belief in God's forgiveness. If there is no Wrong to forgive, Christianity is a delusion. As a Christian, I cannot deny the reality of evil.

Is Wrong subjective or objective?

The Christian cannot deny that evil exists. To define evil as a lack is not to call it an illusion. If evil is the lack of good, that lack is just as real as the lack of being which is the hole in a mint: 'Evil is not a thing but it is a real lack in things.'[15] The second premise of the argument from evil must remain. However, it is with the claim that some things are Wrong that the argument meets a crucial problem.

The argument from Wrong depends upon the judgement that objective Wrong exists. No objective Wrong, no argument. The atheist says, 'This is Wrong; if God existed this Wrong would not exist, so God doesn't exist'; but if the Wrong that the atheist points to is merely a subjective 'Wrong for me', or 'Wrong in the eyes of my society', then the argument falls apart. How can we condemn God on the basis of a moral standard if that standard doesn't apply to everyone, everywhere and at all times?

Facts come in two varieties, subjective and objective. Both subjective and objective facts are equally real, but they differ in what makes it the case that they are facts. Something is a subjective fact if its definition requires reference to the mental states of finite minds. Something is subjective if it depends upon some finite person (or collection of persons) having a mental state. The pain of a toothache is a subjective fact. An objective fact, on the other hand, is a fact the existence of which does not depend upon the mental state of any finite person (or collection of persons). The tooth-decay that causes your toothache is an objective fact. An objective fact 'is true regardless of how anyone thinks or feels about the matter'.[16]

The truth of the statement 'It is raining', given that it is raining, is an objective fact. It would still be raining, and still true to say so, even if you, or I, or any number of people didn't believe it was raining. No one, singly or collectively, can make it the case that it is or is not raining simply by believing that it is or is not raining. However, the truth of the statement, 'I believe it is raining', is a subjective truth. The truth of the statement that I believe it is raining depends upon my having the belief that it is raining. If it is raining, and I believe it is raining, and I say so, both my belief that it is raining, and the truth of my assertion that I believe it to be raining, are subjective facts; but that it is raining is an objective fact.

Are moral values subjective or objective? Is the distinction between good and evil a subjective fact, or an objective fact? If moral values are subjective facts, and subjective facts are reducible to facts about individual or collective people's mental states, then moral values must be reducible to facts about actual or possible individual or collective people's mental states. Wrongness would consist in the existence of facts such as, 'Murder makes me feel sick', or 'I don't want people to commit murder', or 'Society disapproves of murder', or 'If people agreed on a set of rules to live by, and came to that agreement in a situation where they didn't know what station in the resulting society they would occupy, then they would outlaw murder.' However, if moral values are objective, then the fact that murder is wrong does not depend upon my belief that it is wrong, or my dislike of murder, or my society's disapproval, or what people would agree in some situation or another. If the wrongness of murder is objective then that wrongness would not vanish if I liked murder, or if murdering people made me feel happy, or if my society stopped disapproving of it.

Here is the crucial question: Where, apart from God, can we find an objective standard of right and wrong? Not in our own beliefs, feelings or desires. Not in our collective beliefs, feelings or desires. Not in our social or cultural disapproval. Not in the establishment of laws or taboos. I therefore believe that the existence of Wrong is actually a bigger problem for the atheist than it is for the theist.

All anyone can say on the basis of a subjective moral standard is that they, or some group of people, don't like something; or that something isn't useful in achieving some pragmatic end. Imagine Bertrand Russell using the argument from Wrong: 'Look at the Nazis,' he might say, 'that was wrong, and if God existed then he wouldn't have let it happen; but it did happen, so God doesn't exist.' Then we ask what he means by 'wrong' and he says, 'anything I don't like' or 'anything my culture dislikes'. So we point out that Hitler and the Nazi Party didn't like the Jews, and that they thought it was a good thing that six million Jews were murdered. If there is no objective moral standard, a standard that's out there and independent of us, then we cannot judge between our condemnation of the Holocaust and Hitler's approval. All we can say is that Hitler approves and we disapprove. If there is no privileged opinion about what's good and what's bad, then all opinions are equally valid, and hence equally invalid. If we are to make objective moral judgements we must recognise the existence of an objective moral standard: 'All injustice presupposes a standard of justice by which it is judged to be not-just. And an ultimate injustice demands an ultimate standard of justice.'[17]

The argument from Wrong can't pretend to rule out the existence of a god; and when we take a close look it seems to presuppose the existence of an objective moral standard, a standard I believe can only find a home in the existence of God. However, the defence of this claim must wait until Chapter Two.

Russell v. Copleston

In 1946 Bertrand Russell debated about the existence of God with fellow philosopher F.C. Copleston. This classic debate was broadcast by BBC Radio's *Third Programme* and a transcript was published. Their discussion of moral judgements (which centred on the then recent Holocaust), is worth quoting at some length:

Russell: I feel that some things are good and that other things are bad. I love the things that are good, that I think are good, and I hate the things that I think are bad. . . . [Notice how Russell catches himself making the objective assertion that some things 'are good', and corrects himself to make the subjective statement that he 'loves the things that . . . I think are good'.]

Copleston: Yes, but what's your justification for distinguishing between good and bad . . ?

Russell: I don't have any justification any more than I have when I distinguish between blue and yellow. . . .

Copleston: You distinguish blue and yellow by seeing them, so you distinguish good and bad by what faculty?

Russell: By my feelings.

Copleston: . . . You think that good and evil have reference simply to feeling?

Russell: Well, why does one type of object look yellow and another blue? I can more or less give an answer to that thanks to the physicists, and as to why I think one sort of thing good and another evil, probably there is an answer of some sort, but it hasn't been gone into in the same way and I couldn't give it to you.

Copleston: Well, let's take the behaviour of the Commandant of Belsen. That appears to you as undesirable and evil and to me too. To Adolf Hitler we suppose it appeared as something good and desirable. I suppose you'd have to admit that for Hitler it was good and for you it is evil.

Russell: No, I shouldn't go quite so far as that . . . I think people can make mistakes in that as they can in other things. If you have jaundice you see things yellow that are not yellow. You're making a mistake.

Copleston: Yes, one can make mistakes, but can you make a mistake if it's simply a question of reference to a feeling or emotion? Surely Hitler would be the only possible judge of what appealed to his emotions.

Russell: It would be quite right to say that it appealed to his emotions, but . . . that sort of thing . . . makes quite a different appeal to my emotions.

Copleston: Granted. But there's no objective criterion outside feeling then for condemning the conduct of the Commandant of Belsen, in your view?

Russell: No more than there is for the colour-blind person . . . Why do we intellectually condemn the colour-blind man? Isn't it because he's in the minority?

Copleston: . . . I don't approve of [the actions of the Commandant of Belsen], and I know you don't approve of them, but I don't see what ground you have for not approving of them, because after all, to the Commandant of Belsen himself, they're pleasant, those actions.

Russell: Yes, but . . . There are some people who think everything is yellow . . . and I don't agree with these people. I can't prove that the things are not yellow, there isn't any proof, but most people agree with me that the Commandant of Belsen was making mistakes.

Copleston: Well, do you accept any moral obligation?

Russell: . . . Practically speaking—yes. Theoretically speaking I should have to define moral obligation rather carefully . . . I think right conduct is that which would probably produce the greatest possible balance in intrinsic value of all the acts possible in the circumstances. . . .

Copleston: Well, I brought in moral obligation because I think that one can approach the question of God's existence in that way . . . I think, in fact, that those modern atheists who have argued in the converse way 'there is no God; therefore, there are no absolute values and no absolute law', are quite logical.

Russell: I don't like the word 'absolute'. I don't think there is anything absolute whatsoever.

Copleston: . . . I can't help feeling . . . that you regard the conduct of the Commandant of Belsen as morally reprehensible, and that you yourself would never under any circumstances act in this way, even if you thought . . . that possibly the balance of the happiness of the human race might be increased through some people being treated in that abominable manner . . . I suppose some of the Nazis of the better type would have held that although it's lamentable to have to act in this way, yet the balance in the long run leads to greater happiness. I don't think you'd say that, would you? I think you'd say that this sort of action is wrong—and in itself, quite apart from whether the general balance of happiness is increased or not. Then, if you're prepared to say that, then I think you must have some criterion of right and wrong, that is outside the criterion of feeling, at any rate.

To me, that admission would ultimately result in the admission of an ultimate ground of value in God.

Russell: . . . It is not direct feeling about the act by which I should judge, but rather a feeling as to the effects [which only pushes the problem a step down the line]. And I can't admit any circumstances in which certain kinds of behaviour, such as you have been discussing, would do good . . . But if there were circumstances in which they would have a beneficial effect, then I might be obliged, however reluctantly, to say—'Well, I don't like these things, but I will acquiesce in them.' [In other words, Russell's answer to Copleston's question is a yes].[18]

I think it is pretty clear that Copleston shows up Russell's position for the house of cards that it is. Either the Commandant of Belsen was making an objective moral 'mistake'—judged with reference to an objective moral law, just as the colour-blind person's 'mistake' in seeing two different colours as the same colour is judged according to the differing frequency of light-waves—or else he was making a subjective 'moral' decision for which Russell has no reason to condemn him.

Does might make right?

What does Russell mean when he talks about 'intrinsic value'? Certainly not what he might at first seem to mean. In his own words, he means: 'a feeling as to the effects' of actions. But as Copleston said, 'One can make mistakes, but can you make a mistake if it's simply a question of reference to a feeling or emotion? Surely Hitler would be the only possible judge of what appealed to his emotions . . . to the Commandant of Belsen himself, they're pleasant, those actions.' Russell is forced to admit that he acknowledges no standard by which to make objective moral judgements. As he says in the debate (and this is my favourite example of a self-contradiction), 'I don't think there is anything absolute whatsoever.' Or as he says elsewhere:

Everything . . . can be appraised by us, and there is no outside standard to show that our valuation is wrong. We are ourselves the ultimate arbiters of value . . . On such a matter no argument is possible.
I cannot, therefore, prove that my view of the good life is right . . .
All moral rules must be tested by examining whether they tend to
realise ends that we desire . . . not ends that we ought to desire.[19]

For Russell then, the actions of the Commandant of Belsen concentration camp are condemned, 'because he's in the minority'.
We only condemn him because we happen to be in the majority
to whose emotions mass-murder 'makes quite a different
appeal'. And that's all there is to it. If the Nazis had won the
Second World War and indoctrinated everyone into believing
what the Commandant of Belsen presumably believed, then, on
Russell's account of moral values, the Holocaust would have
been right. Not objectively right, but 'right' in the subjective
sense that it would be an action for which 'the majority' had a
'feeling' of approval.

There is, on the subjective view to which Russell subscribed,
no logical contradiction involved in saying, 'Mass-murder is a
good thing.' No 'outside standard' exists to show that this
judgement is false. Such a statement is merely factually correct
or incorrect depending upon the feelings of the majority—feelings that can be manipulated by the minority. In other words,
'might makes right', for, 'Whoever has the power makes the laws
defines justice and good and evil.'[20]

In Hitler's Germany, mass-slaughter was defined as 'good' by
those in power; and if might makes right, then mass-slaughter
was 'good'—for Nazis. Only in the belief that there exists an
objective, independent moral standard can saying, 'Mass-
murder is a good thing,' be logically contradictory—like saying,
'A square is circular.' Only if we acknowledge a moral ideal over
and above our individual and social lives can we condemn
Hitler's actions as really Wrong: 'If . . . there is no higher law of
good and evil than the State, then the individual or group is

never right in rebelling or changing it. If the State creates the right, it can never be right to oppose the State.'[21] As Father Copleston said in the debate: 'The possibility of criticising the accepted moral code presupposes that there is an objective standard, that there is an ideal moral order.'

If, like Bertrand Russell, you admit no standard by which to make objective moral judgements, then you cannot use the argument from Wrong. The argument presupposes the existence of objective moral values in the light of which some things are not merely 'wrong for me/my culture', but wrong for everyone, everywhere and at all times. As Copleston argued, the admission that the Holocaust was objectively wrong leads to the admission that there must be some standard beyond ourselves in the light of which we know this to be so. The attempt to use the argument from Wrong to disprove the existence of God leads us to the moral argument for the existence of God! This is just what C.S. Lewis, who for many years was an atheist, discovered:

> My argument against God . . . depended on saying that the world was really unjust not simply that it did not happen to please my fancies. Thus in the very act of trying to prove that God did not exist—in other words, that the whole of reality was senseless—I found I was forced to assume that one part of reality—namely my idea of justice—was full of sense. Consequently atheism turns out to be too simple.[22]

The atheist must buy into the existence of objective moral values in order to use the existence of Wrong as an argument against the existence of God. If Wrong is not objective, then it can only be subjectively 'wrong' in some sense, and the problem of evil becomes no more serious than a lack of agreement between cards in a game of 'snap'. The cards must match before there is to be any disagreement over who called 'snap' first. The atheist must mean the same thing by 'wrong' as the objectivist means if the problem of evil is to carry any weight.

However, once objective moral values are admitted, the

atheist is faced with the moral argument for the existence of God. This argument does not require that God have all three qualities of total goodness, power and knowledge—but it does undermine pure atheism. Hence Lewis' comment that 'atheism turns out to be too simple'.

Suppose that, like C.S. Lewis, an atheist was convinced by the argument from objective morality that there is an all-good god who is the independent source of moral standards. Even so, they could still ask, 'Doesn't the argument from evil show that it can't also be all-knowing and all-powerful?' At this point we must turn our attention from the second premise of the argument from Wrong, to the first.

If I can show that the first premise is flawed, this will 'disarm' the argument and open the way to looking at arguments for the existence of a God who is all-knowing and all-powerful as well as all-good. We should note that there would be nothing irrational in believing God to have these qualities in the absence of proof, just as long as we can further defuse the argument from evil. It is to this task that I now turn—seeking to show that we can affirm with Robin Le Poidevin that God is aware of Wrong, desires to prevent Wrong, and is able to prevent Wrong, without having to conclude that God does not exist. This is possible because, as I shall argue, Le Poidevin and his fellow atheists fail to qualify what they say about God's nature in certain necessary respects.

How can God be all-good, all-knowing and all-powerful in a world containing evil?

An answer to the above question is called a theodicy. In the words of John Milton, a theodicy is an attempt to 'justify the ways of God to man'. A theodicy is not only an attempt to prove that no contradiction is involved in asserting that God exists in a world containing Wrong, but it is also an attempt to explain why no contradiction is involved.

The basis of the following theodicy has been traced back to St Irenaeus (AD 120–202). Irenaeus began with a picture of God's purpose for humanity, from which flows an understanding of moral and natural evils. His basic idea was that God made us with genuine freedom in relation to our maker so that we are able to enter into a personal relationship with him. With this end in mind, we have been brought into being as imperfect creatures. As a home for imperfect creatures, the universe is not intended to be a paradise, but a 'vale of soul-making'. In a sense, our world is God's green-house where human souls are grown and shaped before they can be transplanted (only by their own free will in accepting what they perceive of God) into the true garden of Eden, which is heaven. This theodicy begins with what is known as the 'free-will defence' for the existence of moral evil. Then it enlarges in scope to argue that a world in which moral choices between good and evil can be made must be a world containing natural evils.

Moral and natural evils

I had better explain the distinction between moral and natural evils. Moral evil is all the evil caused by people deliberately doing what they ought not to do, or allowed to exist by people negligently failing to do what they ought to do. Premeditated murder, and failing to provide the police with information about the murderer, are both examples of moral evil. Natural evil is all the evil that isn't moral evil. Unaptly named 'acts of God' such as earthquakes and tornadoes are examples of natural evils. These two classes can overlap. For example, human mistreatment or neglect of the environment might cause so-called 'natural disasters' through climate change. Of course, things like germs, earthquakes and floods are not considered evil in themselves, but only when they cause suffering.

The interconnectedness of nature

Science shows us that only very small changes in the structure of the universe and its physical laws would result in a totally different universe, one devoid of intelligent life (I will be returning to this scientific data when I discuss the argument for design). The evolution of rational creatures with free will requires a universe free to make itself according to laws similar to those of our own universe. What we call physical evils are simply the result of a universe operating according to certain physical laws:

> Yet this fact prompts the following question. Even if some bodily suffering is inevitable within the structure of our world could not God have modified the structure so that the worst forms of suffering would have been averted? It is very doubtful whether he could have done so. The components of nature are so closely interlocked . . . that even a slight change could cause large-scale effects; so that to ask for even a slight change could entail asking for a very different kind of world.[23]

Everything is linked. For example, without the natural disaster that wiped out the dinosaurs, we would not be here to complain about natural disasters (perhaps intelligent dino-descendants might be!). Modern physics shows us how the cost of suffering caused by natural disasters is necessary for the gain of our existence, for the basic constants of nature are so interconnected that even small changes in a single law would have a catastrophic knock-on effect. For example, 'The organic . . . conflicts with the functioning of the inorganic world. This mutual conflict is indigenous to any world of genuine natural forces. Ridding the world of this conflict would eliminate the natural world altogether.'[24]

The connection between human freedom to accept or reject God, and an environment generally free to carry on in its own sweet way is supported by science; but the basic concept I am drawing upon was expounded by Paul in one of his New Testament letters over nineteen-hundred years ago!

> The creation waits in eager expectation for the sons [inc. daughters] of God to be revealed. For the creation was subjected to frustration,

not by its own choice, but by the will of the one who subjected it [ie by God], in hope that the creation itself will be liberated from its bondage to decay and brought into the glorious freedom of the children of God. We know that the whole creation has been groaning as in the pains of childbirth right up to the present time. Not only so, but we ourselves . . . groan inwardly as we wait eagerly for our adoption . . . the redemption of our bodies. For in this hope we were saved (Romans 8:19–24).

The outline of a Christian theodicy

Nature as it is now, substantially free to be itself without regard for human suffering, is a temporary evil necessary for the evolution of people free to choose between good and evil over a lifetime at one step removed from the presence of God. The creation of beings such as ourselves is a package deal, as it were, with certain natural laws, and the attendant likelihood of suffering that they bring, an integral part of the bargain.

Christians believe that God will eventually wrap-up creation, transforming those who love him into a state without evil. This new state will be made out of the old state, the ultimate in recycling! Christians hold that the resurrected Jesus gives us a sample of this 'new creation' state, a foretaste of God's promise of an eternal destiny both to those who trust in him and for the matter of the universe. John Polkinghorne writes that:

the soul is the immensely complex 'information-bearing pattern' in which the ever-changing atoms of our bodies are arranged. It is surely a coherent hope that the pattern that is me will be remembered and re-embodied by God . . . The 'matter' of that universe, [will be changed] by God . . . It will have new properties, consistent with the end of transience, death and suffering, because it will be part of a new creation, now no longer standing apart from its creator . . . and so paying the necessary cost of an evolutionary world's making itself. [25]

Jesus' empty tomb announces that his resurrected body is the transformation of his earthly body and that God has a destiny not only for the human soul, but for matter as well.[26] Our choices for or against God made, it will no longer be necessary for God to play 'hide-and-seek' with us. For, 'in keeping with his promise we are looking forward to a new heaven and a new earth, the home of righteousness' (2 Peter 3:13).

The basic Christian answer to the problem of evil is that the existence of Wrong is justified by the greater good to which it is the sadly unavoidable means: 'The Free Will Defence maintains that it is necessary for God to allow evil in order that human beings should be free to enter into a love relationship with him.'[27] That 'greater good' includes love shared between God and morally perfect finite beings for a limitless duration: 'Humankind's freedom ... can lead eventually to a consummation of limitless value which could never be obtained without that freedom, and which is worth any finite suffering in the course of its creation.'[28] This cosmic consummation is heaven, where 'the dwelling of God is with men, and he will live with them. They will be his people, and he will be with them and be their God. He will wipe every tear from their eyes. There will be no more death or mourning or crying or pain, for the old order of things has passed away' (Revelation 21:3–4). The free-will defence is summarised by Alvin Plantinga:

> A world containing creatures who are significantly free ... is more valuable, all else being equal, than a world containing no free creatures at all ... To create creatures capable of moral good ... [God] must create creatures capable of moral evil; and He can't give these creatures the freedom to perform evil and at the same time prevent them from doing so.[29]

Is a world of people free to choose between good and evil more valuable than a world of people without such freedom? Such a world would be a world without hate, but it would also be a world without the distinctive value of chosen love. The existence of beings with such freedom, is both good in itself, and necessary to the end of creating heaven. We may define heaven as 'the chosen communal existence with God of morally perfected people'. In heaven there is no moral or natural evil. Heaven's citizens have freely chosen to allow God to transpose them into a state of being wherein they cannot choose evil, although they remain free to choose between goods. Our present freedom is the precondition of the existence of people who have chosen to be incapable of evil:

> A sinless heaven is better than an evil earth, but there was no way for God to achieve a sinless heaven unless he created beings who would sin and did sin in order that out of their sin he could produce the best world where beings would not sin. An imperfect moral world is the necessary precondition for achieving the morally perfect world.[30]

I will return to the Christian hope of heaven towards the end of this chapter, where I will also consider the existence of hell.

Premises, premises

Having outlined a possible explanation of how God can be all-good, all-knowing and all-powerful in a world containing evil, let's take another look at the first premise of our original argument from evil. Even if we don't buy the explanation just offered, we might still be able to convince ourselves, as a matter of unexplained or even inexplicable fact, that there is no contradiction involved in believing in God and the existence of Wrong:

1) If God existed there would be no Wrong (because God would be aware of Wrong, he would desire to prevent Wrong, and he would be able to prevent Wrong).

It is obviously meant that God would know about all Wrong, desire to prevent all Wrong, and be able to prevent all Wrong. I will not dispute that God knows about all Wrong. (The question of whether or not God knows the future is relevant here. Someone who thinks that God exists in time might argue that he couldn't have foreseen the amount of suffering that would result from creation, and so can't be held responsible in quite the same way as if he did know.) I will take issue with the other two assertions, in reverse order.

Is it right that God, as an all-powerful being, would be able to prevent all Wrong? Atheist J.L. Mackie certainly thought so:

> According to traditional theism, there is a god who is both omnipotent (and omniscient) and wholly good, and yet there is evil in the world . . . It is true that there is no explicit contradiction between the statements that there is an omnipotent and wholly good god and that there is evil. But if we add the at least initially plausible premises that good is opposed to evil in such a way that a being who is wholly good eliminates evil as far as he can, and that there are no limits to what an omnipotent being can do, then we do have a contradiction.[31]

I agree that 'good is opposed to evil in such a way that a being who is wholly good eliminates evil as far as he can', but I do not agree that 'there are no limits to what an omnipotent being can do'. To be more technical, I do not agree that God is omnipotent; at least, not in the sense that Mackie means the term.

Is God omnipotent?

> All confess that God is omnipotent; but it is difficult to explain in what His omnipotence precisely consists. For there may be a doubt as to the precise meaning of the word 'all' when we say God can do all things. (Thomas Aquinas, *Summa Theologica*)

Strictly speaking, being omnipotent means 'being able to do all things'. It comes from the Latin *omni* meaning 'all' and '*potens*' meaning 'powerful' or 'able'. It's also linked to *Pati* meaning 'Lord', and to 'potentate' as in 'ruler'. It is this side of the word that is drawn out by the Greek *Pantokrator* which means 'Lord over all', 'God's having power over all things'.[32] There are, in other words, at least two distinct meanings of 'omnipotent'. The first sense means having absolutely no limitations, to be 'all-able'. The second sense means being 'Lord over all', being maximally powerful.

I do not believe that God is omnipotent in the first sense of the word; but then I believe it to be impossible for anything to be omnipotent in this way. If anything exists there must be limits to what it can do. Nothing can both exist and not exist at one and the same time. Nothing can be both square and circular, totally blue and wholly yellow. Meaningless sentences don't gain meaning simply because someone sticks 'God can . . .' on the beginning.

For something to have absolutely no limitations is for it to have no characteristics that distinguish it as a particular thing. For something to exist is for it to be 'a something', and so to have at least one defining, essential characteristic. A 'something' without any characteristics is a nothing! Even to say 'this thing exists without limitations', is actually to assert that it has a limitation, namely, that of existing without any limitations! The notion of so-called 'absolute omnipotence' is therefore the notion of something impossible. Mackie agrees that 'omnipotence does not include the power to do what is logically impossible'.[33]

I take God's omnipotence to mean that he can do anything that doesn't contradict his essential characteristics (characteristics such as independent and personal being, rationality, ultimate goodness, knowledge and power). If God exists, he can do anything he wants. As Psalm 115 says, 'He does whatever he pleases.' However, God can't do anything that would contradict his own divine character. 'God can do what he likes, but God wills only what is in accordance with his nature.'[34] God is by definition totally good (and we have seen that God is at least this). Whatever he wills to do is therefore good, and God cannot cause a self-contradictory or logically impossible state of affairs to exist, because it is God's essential nature that defines what is and is not logical.

God's inability to be other than he is does not contradict his omnipotence; it defines it. God cannot be said to do anything that he doesn't want to do, as if he could be forced to do something against his will, or as if he could 'absent-mindedly' do something he didn't intend to do! That would, as St Anselm said, be powerlessness indeed. Rather, 'The freedom of God consists in the fact that no other cause other than himself produces his acts and no external obstacle impedes them.'[35]

God is omnipotent in the second sense of the word, the only sense that makes any sense. He is almighty, having 'power over all things', such that 'there is no question of God's trying to do anything and failing'.[36] As Job says to God in the Bible, 'no plan of yours can be thwarted' (Job 42:2). This is what I mean by saying that God is all-powerful.

So, there are things that even God cannot do, and Mackie is wrong to claim that there would be 'no limits' to what God can do. This means that the first premise of the argument from evil is flawed. I agree with Robin Le Poidevin that God can prevent Wrong, but the argument from evil requires that God be able to prevent all Wrong in all circumstances, and this is not the case. As Mackie says, 'it may be argued that there are limits—and limits that matter in this context—to what even an omnipotent being can do'.[37] The question is, 'Can God justify the creation of a world in which Wrong plays an unavoidable role? Is the pain worth the gain?'

Is the pain worth the gain?

If we answer 'No', we must be prepared to consent to our own non-existence. We must wish that we had never been born: 'If we take with full seriousness the value of human freedom and responsibility, as essential to the eventual creation of perfected children of God, then we cannot consistently want God to revoke that freedom when its wrong exercise becomes intolerable to us.'[38] For, 'When we see that, if God did not have this goal, we would not exist at all, we may think twice before blaming God for having this goal.'[39]

This might seem like a rather selfish reason not to condemn God. However, to recognise our value as beings who can choose to love, and to judge that this value outweighs any 'disvalue' in our existence, is to make the unselfish decision that we would rather the universe contain the value that we embody, even if that means we must suffer, than that the universe be without that value.

What is more important, to say 'No' would be to think that God did something that contradicted his goodness. But God is good by definition. As an all-good being, God must prevent all the Wrong that he can prevent without contradicting his character. Therefore, it must be the case that God either morally need not, or metaphysically cannot, eliminate the Wrong that exists without contradicting his character. An all-good God would not cause any state of affairs that, all things considered, wasn't worth any Wrong it contained.

An argument for the compatibility of God and wrong

It is my suggestion that God allows the existence of Wrong in order to achieve the greater goods of free will, love and heaven. But if we discount this suggestion, and even if we can't find any explanation that satisfies us as to why God would allow the existence of Wrong, it remains the case that, if God exists, there must be a reason which means that the existence of Wrong is compatible with the existence of God. Knowing this to be so, the atheist can't point to the existence of Wrong as proof that God does not exist. Here's a summary of the argument that I'm putting forward:

1) If God exists He knows about any Wrong that exists (because God is all-knowing).

2) If God exists He is opposed to Wrong in such a way that He would eliminate it unless to do so would contradict His nature or is morally unnecessary (because God is an all-good being).

3) If God exists He can do anything that doesn't contradict His own nature (because God is Almighty).

4) Wrong exists.

5) Therefore, if God exists, He is an all-good being who knows about the Wrong that exists, but eliminating it would contradict His nature or is morally unnecessary.

Now we know Mackie's assertion that there are 'no limits to what an omnipotent being can do' to be nonsensical, we see that there is no contradiction here. God can be all-knowing, all-powerful and all-good, and exist in a world containing Wrong, without this entailing any contradiction whatsoever. The pain must be worth the gain, and it must be unavoidable given that gain—or else God would not have created this world. Augustine was right when he wrote that 'God . . . would not allow any evil in his works, unless in his omnipotence and goodness . . . he is able to bring forth good out of evil.'[40]

It is then little wonder that there is a growing realisation in the philosophical community that the classical 'argument from evil' against the existence of God is a flop. As Alvin Plantinga reports:

Now, as opposed to twenty or twenty-five years ago, most [atheists] have conceded that in fact there isn't any inconsistency between the existence of an omnipotent, omniscient and wholly good God and the existence of the evil the world contains.[41]

Some atheists have switched from trying to argue that the existence of evil contradicts the existence of God, to arguing that the existence of evil merely makes the existence of God unlikely.

My response to this weaker version of the argument from evil is to point out that it still assumes the notion of objective moral value, and therefore grants the first premise of the moral argument for God's existence. As even J.L. Mackie admitted, 'If . . . there are objective values, they make the existence of a god more probable than it would have been without them.'[42]

Can you kick a football?

If someone asked me whether I could kick a football I might well answer them, 'Yes.' If I were asked to kick a football now, I would probably say something like, 'But I haven't got a football to hand.' My ability to kick a football is not the same thing as my being able to kick a football. My being able to kick a football depends upon my having a football to kick. In a world without footballs no one would be able to kick a football, even if everyone had the ability to kick a football. In the same way, God's being able to prevent the existence of Wrong depends upon the context. If God didn't create anything, then there would certainly be no Wrong. In as much as God has created, it is clear that he is 'to blame' for the existence of Wrong. However, Wrong obviously can't be something that, as an all-good being, God desires for its own sake.

The above football kicking example shows us that we need to distinguish, as did Aquinas, between desires that are 'before' and 'after-the-fact'. A before-the-fact desire is a desire I have about some sphere of activity I enter into. The desire to play football is a before-the-fact desire. It involves the desire to play by the rules of football. An after-the-fact desire is a desire I have about anything within that sphere of activity. Wanting to score a goal, or wanting to touch the ball with my hands, are both after-the-fact desires. I can only have these after-the-fact desires because before-the-fact I wanted to play football. After-the-fact desires may, or may not, be in-line with my before-the-fact desire. The after-the-fact desire to score a goal is in-line with my before-the-fact desire to play football. My after-the-fact desire to touch the ball with my hands (presuming that I'm not a goal-keeper), is against the rules of football, and so contradicts my before-the-fact desire to play football.

Imagine that I have a before-the-fact desire to take part in a game of Snakes and Ladders. When the dice are thrown, I have a before-the-fact desire the results to be random. It wouldn't be a game of chance otherwise. However, every time the dice are thrown, I actually have an after-the-fact desire that a particular personally advantageous number results. If the random result of throwing the dice means I have to slide down a snake, then that's the result I want before-the-fact, because before-the-fact I want the generated numbers to be random. Nevertheless, I have an after-the-fact desire for numbers that mean I avoid the snakes and land on the ladders: 'So it is that I may want this game to be played as it is, but I do not want some of the events in it to happen as they do. Nevertheless, I must accept them, if I will the game.'[43]

Similarly, we can suppose that, before-the-fact, God wants there to be a world where what happens depends in part upon the free choices of rational creatures. If so, many things may happen after-the-fact that God does not, before-the-fact, intend, since He might wish we had chosen otherwise, just as I might wish the dice had generated a seven and not a nine. Using this analogy we can see how it could be that even God would have to accept after-the-fact outcomes he does not desire before-the-fact if these outcomes are the result of an overall context He desires before-the-fact. Thus God 'can properly be said to desire the existence of a world containing many particular events that he does not desire'.[44]

Before-the-fact, God desires the existence of the universe, for the sake of goods that only a universe such as ours can realise. Those goods include the evolution of rational creatures with free will, capable of entering into relationship with the God in whose image they are made. However, as a result of the free will of these creatures (who, as John Hick argues, must begin in moral imperfection), and of the natural order necessary to the evolution and existence of such beings, any such universe is bound to contain Wrongs which God does not desire before-the-fact: 'From that system arise evils of many sorts, and though God foresees that and indeed sustains them in being, as a condition of maintaining the system which is necessary to so many goods, he neither desires nor intends them.'[45]

God is therefore as much to blame for the existence of Wrong as is the field-surgeon who has to amputate a soldier's leg in order to save their life, for, 'Approval of large context does not necessarily mean . . . Approval of everything that appears in that context.'[46] The existence of Wrong is something that even God could not prevent if He is to create a world which includes creatures with free will. This is precisely what is claimed by the free-will defence: 'The possibility of humans bringing about significant evil is a logical consequence of their having . . . free and responsible choice. Not even God could give us this choice without the possibility of resulting evil.'[47]

God could not create us with the freedom to choose, over an extended period of time, to love Him and each other, without consequently allowing the existence of moral evil. Nor could He allow for the existence of such freedom without creating a world that was, as it were, 'once removed' from His presence, and which consequently contains natural evils. In a world where God sustains the underlying laws of nature which sustain our existence, we need not be confronted with our dependency, and thus with God's being, in a blatant fashion:

> The mode of human creation involved the setting of man in an environment where he was removed from the immediate presence of the divine glory. If he had been placed in the full light of the unveiled majesty of God, it is hardly conceivable that he would have any freedom to choose to sin.[48]

Presumably when an angel considers its existence (if angels go in for that sort of thing), it immediately perceives the raw will-power of God upon which its existence depends. This dependency would be a most terrible thing for a person to behold if they did not want to admit their dependency, because it would force them to make such an admittance. As Richard Swinburne, with dry wit, puts it: 'God would be too evident a member of the community.'[49] C.S. Lewis hit the nail on the head when he pointed out that, 'Merely to over-ride a human will (as His felt presence in any but the faintest and most mitigated degree would certainly do) would be for Him useless. He cannot ravish. He can only woo.'[50]

God created us for a perfect and eternal relationship of freely chosen love with Him, with ourselves and with our fellow God-loved God-lovers. Freedom to choose to love God (and so to love ourselves and others as God loves us), requires the existence of some moral evil. Unless we are able to reject God we cannot genuinely accept Him; and unless we are initially less than perfect, it would be impossible for us to reject Him. Morally perfect beings cannot do morally imperfect things. Rejecting God, the source and standard of all good, is as morally an imperfect act as can be imagined. Since we can do such a thing, we cannot be morally perfect beings. We must initially be morally imperfect beings:

> if the end state which God is seeking to bring about is one in which finite persons have come in their own freedom to know and love God, this requires creating them initially in a state which is not that of their already knowing and loving God. For it is logically impossible to create beings already in a state of having come into that state by their own free choices.[51]

No initial imperfection, no freedom to reject God; no freedom to reject God, no freedom to accept God. Some may wonder how this fits with the biblical view that, in the beginning, 'God saw all that he had made, and it was very good' (Genesis 1:31). God did not say that everything was perfect, he said everything was 'very good'. We go beyond the text if we say that Genesis requires the belief that God created humans in a state of moral perfection. Furthermore, I believe that God's seal of approval in Genesis applies to creation *as a whole*. The overall result of creation was 'very good', but that does not mean that nothing in creation was less than perfect.

It is common sense that morally perfect creatures would not rebel against God. As Leibniz wrote, 'we must consider that there is an *original imperfection in the creature* before sin, because the creature is limited in its essence; whence it follows that it cannot know all, and that it can deceive itself and commit other errors.'[52] Without this initial imperfection, I believe God could only have made people incapable of choosing to love Him. As John Hick argues, God's children must choose to come to Him from a far-off land (though prompted by their need and drawn by His love). This means that human sinfulness, and the suffering it causes, has a necessary and integral role to play in the divine purpose:

> The contribution which sin and its attendant suffering make to God's plan does not consist in any value intrinsic to themselves but, on the contrary, in the activities whereby they are overcome, namely redemption from sin . . . sin plus redemption is of more value in the sight of God than an innocence that permits neither sin nor redemption.[53]

Even J.L. Mackie wrote that, 'It would be coherent to argue that sin . . . is logically necessary for repentance and redemption, and that "joy shall be in heaven over one sinner that repenteth, more than over ninety and nine just persons, which need no repentance." (Luke 15v7) Sin followed by repentance and redemption would then be [an evil which is explained and justified].'[54]

Should God prevent all Wrong?

Although I consider the argument from the existence of evil to have been successfully defused, it's still worth taking a brief look at the remaining proposition of the first premise: 'If God existed . . . he would desire to prevent [all] Wrong.'

Is it necessarily true that an all-good being would desire to prevent all Wrong? I do not think so. Good people sometimes allow suffering for the sake of some higher good, so it is not necessarily the case that an all-good God must desire to prevent all Wrong. Indeed, a good person might allow the existence of more suffering than a bad person who was insensitive to the greater goods this suffering permitted.

It does not really matter whether or not we can imagine exactly what these 'greater goods' might be. Just as long as we believe that God is all-good, the fact that good people need not always abolish all the suffering they can means that God can be all-good even if He does not abolish all the suffering He can.

God should desire to prevent Wrong, and I am sure He does, but Le Poidevin's argument requires that God desires to prevent all Wrong in all circumstances, and this need not be the case. Le Poidevin himself admits that 'suffering may be part of the divine design, in so far as suffering is an essential consequence of some greater good'.[55] Besides, if God did eliminate all Wrong, who of us would be left?

All you need is love

> If God is love, he is by definition something more than mere kindness. And it appears, from all the records, that though he has often rebuked us and condemned us, he has never regarded us with contempt. He has paid us the incredible compliment of loving us in the deepest, most tragic, most inexorable sense. (C.S. Lewis)

Love is the essential component of God's goodness. We often have too sentimental a picture of God's love, because we often misunderstand the full portent and meaning of love. True love has no truck with the unthinking indulgence of the beloved's desires, but asks whether those desires are innocent or destructive, and if they are destructive, sets itself against them absolutely. God's love involves our personal transformation, and that can hurt. As C.S. Lewis (whose mother, father and wife all died from cancer) asked with sharp-edged humour, 'What do people mean when they say, "I am not afraid of God because I know He is good?" Have they never even been to a dentist?'[56] Hence, 'The more we believe that God hurts only to heal, the less we can believe that there is any use in begging for tenderness.'[57]

The Scottish writer George MacDonald, a formative influence upon C.S. Lewis, provides this awesome description of God's love:

> Nothing is inexorable but love . . . For love loves unto purity. Love has ever in view the absolute loveliness of that which it beholds. Where loveliness is incomplete . . . it spends itself to make more lovely, that it may love more; it strives for perfection . . . Therefore all that is not beautiful in the beloved, all that comes between and is not of love's kind, must be destroyed . . . God is a consuming fire . . . that only that which cannot be consumed may stand forth eternal. Such is the mercy of God that he will hold his children in the consuming fire of his distance . . . until they drop the purse of selfishness . . . and rush home to the Father . . . rush inside the centre of the life-giving fire whose outer circles burn. A man might flatter, or bribe, or coax a tyrant; but there is no refuge from the love of God.[58]

Christians believe that God loves us enough to suffer death on a cross for us. But in return He demands, for our own good, that, 'If anyone would come after me, he must deny himself and take up his cross and follow me' (Matthew 16:24).

Pain as God's megaphone

Suffering reminds us that we are not God; for while God can only suffer if He chooses to suffer, we do not. Suffering is often beyond our control, however advanced medical science becomes. Remembering that we are not God spurs us to seek God. Having our need pointed out to us causes us to search for something that answers our need. As C.S. Lewis wrote: 'God whispers in our pleasures, speaks in our conscience, but shouts in our pain: it is His megaphone to rouse a deaf world.'[59]

I am not knocking medical science or, heaven forbid, attempting to justify the Holocaust by pointing out that it serves to remind us of our own mortality. But that suffering does serve this purpose means that some good can arise from even the worst atrocity—and this is better than nothing. Suffering brings about the funeral of the myth of present immortality. Our life in this world must pass and end; but God will live on, and we can live on with Him if we will only cast off the bonds which tie us to this dying world, and reach out to embrace God's will for us. 'Suffering, though tragic, is not pointless. It is the pin which bursts the balloon of our delusions, and opens the way to an urgent and passionate wrestling with the reality of death and the question of what lies beyond.'[60]

This truth is born out in the lives of many who have found God, or a deeper relationship with God, through suffering. It is no mere coincidence that many of the greatest 'saints' have been men and women well acquainted with suffering. God is concerned with our happiness, but He is much more concerned with our wholeness. Wholeness is a broader, deeper and therefore more important thing than mere happiness. Sometimes the unhappiness of suffering is our path to greater wholeness. As Christian writer, David Watson, wrote shortly before his death from cancer, it is often those who experience most of God's love who have also endured most suffering:

An agnostic Professor of Philosophy at Princeton University became a Christian when he studied carefully the lives of some of the great saints of God throughout the history of the Church . . . Often they suffered intensely, far more than most other people, yet through all their agony their spirits shone forth a glorious lustre that defied extinction. This philosopher became convinced that some power was at work within them, and this discovery eventually brought him to Christ.[61]

If millions can suffer and yet still believe in God—indeed, if millions can suffer and come to a deeper love of God than they might otherwise have had—doesn't this indicate that the existence of suffering cannot count against the existence of God?

Evil and the cross

Welsh philosopher H.P. Owen makes two very important points, both of which centre on the incarnation of the second 'person' of the Trinity:

> The incarnation solves the problem created by the fact that God is responsible for evil in the sense that he created a world in which it was either certain . . . or probable . . . that evil would arise. I do not think it is too much to say that by becoming man God acknowledged this responsibility. At the same time he justified himself by revealing the full extent of his love for his human creatures and by enabling them to acquire a supernatural mode of existence.[62]

Owen's first point is that God has not remained remote from His creation. He is not like a well-to-do general playing at soldiers while, on His orders, men in their thousands die in the mud. God got stuck in on the front line, suffering in the world and thereby earning the moral right to affirm that the pain is worth the gain of existence. Dorothy L. Sayers summarises this point forcefully:

> For whatever reason God chose to make man as he is—limited and suffering and subjected to sorrows and death—He had the honesty and the courage to take His own medicine. Whatever game He is playing with His creation He has kept His own rules and played fair . . . He was born in poverty and died in disgrace, and felt it worthwhile.[63]

God's intimate involvement in the suffering of creation is discussed by the late Hugh Silvester, one time theology lecturer at Oak Hill Theological College in London, in his book *Arguing with God*. Silvester's discussion focuses on 'a very suggestive phrase that comes in one of Jesus' parables of the last judgement (Matthew 25:31–46).'[64] When the king confronts his subjects who have led self-centred lives he accuses them of failing to help him when he was hungry, thirsty, naked, sick or in prison. Indignant, the subjects object that they have never seen the king in such circumstances. The king replies, 'I tell you the truth, whatever you did not do for one of the least of these, you did not do for me' (Matthew 25:45). As Silvester says, 'there is no kind of suffering where God is not there in person . . . '[65] If you get close to a rough stone, if you hold it in your hand, it will cut you. Analogously, for God even to allow our existence is painful for him. Silvester says that 'The implications of this teaching for theodicy are tremendous.'[66] For a start, when people ask why God doesn't do something about evil, the Christian answer is that He has. 'For God so loved the world that he gave his one and only Son, that whoever believes in him shall not die but have eternal life' (John 3:16).

> God has done everything possible, short of un-making man and depriving him of his free will . . . The most fundamental concept we have of God is of love. But in that love there is contained deep suffering . . . the truly tremendous cost that God himself undertook when he decided to create 'in his own image' . . . Who will argue with such a God as this?[67]

The Jewish writer Elie Wiesel describes the hanging of three inmates of a concentration camp charged with sabotage. They are two adults and a child. The other inmates were paraded to watch the executions. The two adults died quickly, but the child (being lighter than the men) struggled between life and death for half an hour:

And we had to look him full in the face. He was still alive when I
passed in front of him. His tongue was still red, his eyes were not
glazed. Behind me, I heard a man asking: 'Where is God now?' And
I heard a voice within me answer him: 'Where is He? Here He is—
He is hanging here on this gallows.'[68]

Is Wiesel describing a loss of faith? Is this a declaration that
'God is dead'? I believe so; but if we look at things a little differently, Wiesel's words may be more literal than he knew. This is
not looking at the world through 'rose-tinted' spectacles, but
through eyes tinted red with the blood of Jesus Christ, hung out
to die on a Roman 'gallows'.

Following the death of his wife, C.S. Lewis prefigured H.P.
Owen's thought that, in dying as a man, God somehow
acknowledged responsibility for creating and sustaining our
world: 'Sometimes it is hard not to say "God forgive God".
Sometimes it is hard to say so much. But if our faith is true, He
didn't. He crucified Him.'[69]

The glory that will be revealed

The second point made by Owen is that the ultimate, justifying
purpose of this world is the creation of heaven, where, in the
words of Sam the Hobbit, everything sad will 'come untrue'.[70] I
define heaven as 'the chosen communal existence with God of
morally perfected people'. This moral perfection is not achieved
by human effort, but received from God. Heaven is a world
without natural or moral evil, consisting in the limitless existence of value.

Peter Kreeft argues that there are at least six earthly activities
which continue in heaven: 'These six things are the reason we are
here on earth in the first place. They are our fundamental task,
the meaning of life.'[71] What are these six activities? They are to
understand and know God, others and ourselves. That's two
categories of action (understanding and loving) applied to three

subjects of activity (God, neighbour and self). I would add a fourth subject to understand and love, nature (or in terms of heaven, supernature).

Heaven will not be boring, as some people fear, because every subject of love and understanding mentioned above is inexhaustible: there will always be more reality, more of other people and of self, and most especially more of God, to know and love.

John Polkinghorne, a Cambridge physicist who retired to become a member of the clergy, writes of the recreated universe having 'new properties, consistent with the end of transience, death and suffering . . . no longer standing apart from its Creator . . . and so paying the necessary cost of an evolutionary world's making itself, but fully integrated with the divine life through the universal reconciliation brought about by . . . Christ.'[72]

A good analogy for the 'new creation' is to be found in cartoons. In a cartoon, the laws of nature are more flexible than they are 'in the real world', without being chaotic. The cartoon world has a 'higher logic' all of its own, a logic that has been called 'the plausible impossible'. It is a world in thrall to the mental, or the spiritual. Bugs Bunny can come and go at will despite physically inescapable traps, just as the resurrected Jesus appeared in the locked upper room where his frightened disciples hid themselves (John 20:26).

In the world of cartoons, there is no evil. Don't cartoons depict greed and hate? What of all that cartoon violence? Cartoon evil is play-acting. Cartoon violence is not evil, it's funny. Tom and Jerry can go from deadly enemies to best buddies in the space of five minutes. It's like the Viking vision of Valhalla, where warriors fight and slaughter each other by day, but feast together all night. No one really gets hurt in a cartoon; no one really suffers or dies (anyone who 'dies' will be back in the next episode). The new creation, like a cartoon, will be a wholly good supernatural reality more responsive to the desires of the purified heart than the demands of its own nature. Physicality will be closer to spirituality: 'The body that is sown is perishable, it is raised imperishable; it is sown in dishonour, it is raised in glory; it is sown in weakness, it is raised in power; it is sown a natural body, it is raised a spiritual body' (1 Corinthians 15:42–44).

Every miracle reveals that we already live in a lesser 'cartoon reality'. The divine director is free to suspend the normal course of events in the interests of a 'higher logic'. The laws of science tell us what must happen in the natural course of events, but there is no reason that events have to take their natural course if God's will demands that they take a supernatural one. If it is asked why God does not perform more miracles to save people from suffering, or to prove His existence, I answer that doing so is either not required by, or would contradict, God's essential character; and that my previous arguments prove that this apparent lack of action in no way disproves God's existence, goodness, power or knowledge.

At present, God's 'higher logic' demands 'enough light for those whose only desire is to see, and enough darkness for those of the opposite disposition'.[73] Consequently, the current cosmic plot is largely one of 'gritty realism', but Christians (unlike atheists) have good reason to believe in a happy ending. Out of the present world, God will make 'a new heaven and a new earth' (Revelation 21:1). In that new creation, God's 'higher logic' will enter a new phase. The documentary film of life will become a heavenly cartoon reality. Nature will be 'taken up' into God's 'higher logic' to become a spiritual nature. As John Polkinghorne says, 'The 'matter' of that world-to-come must be such that it will not enforce recapitulation of the deadly raggedness and malfunctions of the present universe.'[74] All this talk of 'cartoon reality' is only an analogy; but if these analogies are not very close to the reality, 'something better will be'.[75]

St Paul (a man not unaccustomed with hardship), wrote, 'I consider that our present sufferings are not worth comparing with the glory that will be revealed' (Romans 8:18). And Jesus, using an analogy that could be applied to God's suffering as much as to our own, said:

> A woman giving birth to a child has pain because her time has come; but when her baby is born she forgets the anguish because of her joy that a child is born into the world. So with you: Now is your time of grief, but I will see you again and you will rejoice, and no-one will take away your joy. (John 16:21–22)

Hell

Of course, as well as the Christian belief in heaven, there is hell. I am well aware that the Christian doctrine of hell is a contro-versial one, often misunderstood, which will raise many issues in readers' minds. Hell concerns me here only in as much as it touches upon the problem of evil, and I urge readers to consult the recommended reading on this subject for a more adequate treatment of the subject that I can give here.

Whatever sort of reality hell is (and Christians differ in what sort of reality they ascribe to hell), its existence follows from belief in the love of God which will not force anyone to love Him. I certainly believe that 'no one is sent to hell against his or her will'.[76] In the end, as C.S. Lewis said, there are two sorts of people, those who say to God, 'Your will be done,' and those to whom God says, 'Your will be done.'

The Christian doctrine of hell means that evil will not triumph. God forgives anyone who will receive forgiveness, and all who receive forgiveness enter heaven. Anyone who will not accept God's forgiveness thereby chooses hell. Indeed, we might suggest that heaven would be hell for anyone who rejected God's love: 'the very love of God for the sinner . . . would threaten and torture that egotism that the damned . . . insist on and cling to . . . So the fires of hell may be made of the very love of God, or rather by the damned's hatred of that love.'[77]

Hell is not an arbitrary punishment for disbelief or evil, as a jail sentence is an arbitrary punishment for theft. Hell is the natural consequence of unrepentant evil, as a hangover is the natural consequence of getting drunk:

> Perhaps it can be said that hell begins in this life in the same sense that heaven does: its seed is planted here. Perhaps when we reach eternity we will look back and see this life as the beginning of eternity; . . . the blessed will say they have always been in heaven and the damned will say they have always been in hell.[78]

We pull back at the thought of hell because we imagine people in hell as people, with all the attendant value the concept of a person contains. However, hell is essentially the lack of heaven, eternal separation from communion with God (2 Thessalonians 1:9), the privation of the supreme good. Those who cast themselves 'outside, into the darkness' (Matthew 8:12) therefore cut themselves off from the root and source of all good, from God himself, and have no salvageable value. As C.S. Lewis wrote:

> In all our experience . . . the destruction of one thing means the emergence of something else. Burn a log, and you have gases, heat and ash. To have been a log means now being those three things. If souls can be destroyed, must there not be a state of having been a human soul? . . . What is cast (or casts itself) into hell is not a man; it is 'remains'.[79]

I see hell as something God has to accept after-the-fact. Jesus says that 'it is not the will of my Father [before-the-fact] . . . that one of these little ones should perish' (Matthew 18:14). Free will, once granted, is not revoked. To do so would defeat the whole point of human existence. Hence, 'The cause of hell is not divine vengeance or cruelty or mercilessness. The cause of hell is our free choice to refuse God's forgiveness and kindness and mercy.'[80]

If there is no hell, then one of three options must be the case.

Option one is that God never eliminates evil from creation, old or new. The idea that God would let evil into heaven is neither appealing nor reasonable. This option amounts to giving up heaven, for no reality worthy of the name could include the existence of evil. Option two is that hell is a temporary reality where people, as a matter of fact, eventually give in to God's love and graduate to heaven. In other words, hell is in fact a sort of purgatory, a temporary half-way house between the old and new creation. However, not even God can guarantee that everyone will accept Him, unless He over-rides their freedom of will, which is option three: 'If God is to remain consistent with the divinely established desire for human beings to be free, God has no choice but to "give them up" (Rom. 1:24, 26, 28) . . . In this sense, we can view hell as an expression not only of divine justice but of divine love.'[81]

Hell is the other side of the coin marked 'heaven': 'If a game is to be taken seriously, it must be possible to lose it.'[82] To exclude the possibility of hell, God would either have to allow evil into the new creation, or revoke free will. Either way, heaven becomes a lost cause. Either way, there would no longer be much point to creation.

Conclusion

I have sought to show that the existence of Wrong does not rule out the existence of God. Neither the claim that God can prevent the existence of all Wrong in every circumstance, nor the claim that He necessarily ought to prevent all Wrong, stands up to investigation. Consequently, I believe that the argument from the existence of Wrong fails to prove its point. Indeed, in drawing attention to the existence of Wrong, it actually draws us towards a knowledge of God as the source and standard of our moral feelings and judgements.

The ground should now be clear for us to move ahead to further examination of whether or not God exists; beginning with the moral argument. Even if you haven't been convinced by the theodicy provided here, it is right to move on to such an examination, for you might find the arguments for God's existence compelling enough to outweigh any remaining doubts based upon the existence of evil.

Recommended reading

M. Adams and R. Adams eds, *The Problem of Evil* (Oxford, 1996). (4)

Thomas Aquinas, *Selected Philosophical Writings* (Oxford, 1993), chapters 29–32. (3)

Brian Davies, *An Introduction to the Philosophy of Religion*, second edition (Oxford, 1993). (2)

C. Stephen Evans, *Why Believe?* (IVP, 1996). (1)

John Hick, *Evil and the God of Love*, second edition (Macmillan, 1977). (4)

Peter Kreeft and Ronald Tacelli, *Handbook of Christian Apologetics* (Monarch, 1995). (1)

C.S. Lewis, *The Problem of Pain* (Fount, 1977). (2)

C.S. Lewis, *Mere Christianity* (Fount, 1986). (1)

C.S. Lewis, 'Evil and God' in *Christian Reunion and Other Essays* (Fount, 1990). (1)

C.S. Lewis, *A Grief Observed* (Faber and Faber, 1966). (1)

Alister McGrath, *Suffering* (Hodder and Stoughton, 1992). (1)

H.P. Owen, *Christian Theism* (Allen and Unwin, 1965). (3)

Michael Peterson *et al*, *Reason and Religious Belief—An Introduction to the Philosophy of Religion* (Oxford, 1991). (3)

Michael Peterson *et al*, eds, *Philosophy of Religion* (Oxford, 1996). (3/4)

John Polkinghorne, *Scientists as Theologians* (SCM, 1996). (3)

Hugh Silvester, *Arguing with God* (IVP, 1996). (1)

Richard Swinburne, *Is There A God?* (Oxford, 1996). (3)

Richard Swinburne, *Providence and the Problem of Evil* (Oxford, 1998). (3)

Keith Ward, *God, Chance and Necessity* (OneWorld, 1996). (3)

Keith Ward, *God, Faith and The New Millennium* (OneWorld, 1988). (3)

On heaven and hell

Stephen T. Davies, 'Resurrection and Judgement' in *Risen Indeed—Making Sense of the Resurrection* (SPCK, 1993). (3)

Peter Kreeft and Ronald Tacelli, *Handbook of Christian Apologetics* (Monarch, 1995). (2)

C.S. Lewis, *The Problem of Pain* (Fount, 1977). (2)

C.S. Lewis, *The Great Divorce* (Fount, 1991). (1)

C.S. Lewis, 'The Weight of Glory' in *Screwtape Proposes a Toast—and other pieces* (Fount, 1979). (1)

C.S. Lewis, *Prayer—Letters to Malcolm* (Fount, 1977), esp. letters XXI and XXII. (1)

John Polkinghorne, *Science and Christian Belief* (SPCK, 1994), chapter nine. (3)

Richard Swinburne, *Responsibility and Atonement* (Oxford, 1989). (3)

David Winter, *Where Do We Go From Here?—The Case for Life Beyond Death* (Hodder and Stoughton, 1996). (1)

On miracles

R. Douglas Geivett and Garry R. Habermas, eds, *In Defence of Miracles—A Comprehensive Case For God's Action In History* (Apollos, 1997). (3)

C.S. Lewis, *Miracles* (Fount, 1974). (2)

Films to watch

From Dusk Till Dawn (Dir. Robert Rodriguez). Evil points to God as objective moral standard.

The Fifth Element (Dir. Luc Besson). Is the pain worth the gain?
Time Bandits (Dir. Terry Gillam). The free-will defence.

Notes

1. Bertrand Russell, *Why I Am Not A Christian* (Routledge, 1996), p.18.
2. Robin Le Poidevin, *Arguing for Atheism* (Routledge, 1996).
3. Keith Ward, *Holding Fast to God* (SPCK).
4. C.S. Lewis, *The Problem of Pain* (Fount, 1977), p.12.
5. Bertrand Russell, 'What I Believe' in *Why I Am Not A Christian*, p.62.
6. Augustine, *City of God* (Penguin), 11.9
7. Thomas Aquinas, *Compendium of Theology*, 114, in T. Gilby, ed., *St Thomas Aquinas: Philosophical Texts* (Oxford, 1951).
8. Thomas Aquinas, *Summa Contra Gentiles*, 3.7 and 11.
9. C.S. Lewis, 'Evil and God' in *Christian Reunion* (Fount, 1990), p.49. See also *Mere Christianity* (Fount, 1986), pp.42–47.
10. Augustine, from *Confessions and Enchiridion*, trans. and ed., Albert C. Outer, (Westminster Press: Philadelphia, 1955), in Michael Peterson *et al* eds, *Philosophy of Religion—Selected Readings* (Oxford, 1996), p.234.
11. Robin Le Poidevin, *op. cit.*, p.88.
12. H.J. McCloskey, 'God and Evil' in *The Philosophical Quarterly*, 10 (1960), p.97.
13. Willliam Lane Craig, *The Craig-Jesseph Debate—Does God Exist?*, 'Craig's Opening Arguments'.
14. Norman L. Geisler and Winfried Corduan, *Philosophy of Religion*, second edition (Baker, 1988).
15. *Ibid.*, p.330.
16. Paul Chamberlain, *Can we be Good without God?* (IVP, 1996), pp.27–28.
17. Norman L. Geisler, *Christian Apologetics* (Baker, 1976), chapter 12.

18. Bertrand Russell and F.C. Copleston, 'The Existence of God', *Humanitas*, Autumn 1948.

19. Bertand Russell, 'What I Believe', *op cit.*, pp.48, 51.

20. Peter Kreeft, *The Journey* (IVP, 1996), p.69.

21. *Ibid.*, p.70.

22. C.S. Lewis, *Mere Christianity* (Fount, 1986).

23. H.P. Owen, *Christian Theism* (Allen and Unwin, 1965).

24. Norman L. Geisler and Winfried Corduan, *op cit.*, p.369.

25. John Polkinghorne, *Scientists as Theologians* (SPCK, 1996), pp.54–55.

26. For readers who want to follow up Christian thought about soul and resurrection, I recommend: Stephen T. Davies, *Risen Indeed—Making Sense of the Resurrection* (SPCK, 1993) (4); Peter Kreeft, *The Best Things in Life* (IVP, 1984) (1); John Puddefoot, *God and the Mind Machine—Computers, Artificial Intelligence and the Human Soul* (SPCK, 1996) (3); Richard Swinburne, *The Evolution of the Soul* (Oxford) (4); and Keith Ward, *Defending the Soul* (OneWorld) (3). See also the recommended reading for Chapter Six.

27. Peter Vardy, *The Puzzle of Evil* (Fount, 1992).

28. John Hick, 'Soul-Making Theodicy' in Michael Peterson *et al* eds, *Philosophy of Religion—Selected Readings* (Oxford, 1996).

29. Alvin Plantinga, 'The Free Will Defence' in Basil Mitchell, ed., *The Philosophy of Religion*, Oxford readings in Philosophy (Oxford, 1971).

30. Norman L. Geisler and Winfried Corduan, *op cit.*, p.313.

31. J.L. Mackie, *The Miracle Of Theism* (Oxford, 1982), p.150.

32. Peter Geach, 'Omnipotence'.

33. J.L. Mackie, *op cit.*, p.160.

34. John Polkinghorne.

35. C.S. Lewis, *The Problem of Pain*.

36. Peter Geach, *op cit.*

37. J.L. Mackie, *op cit.*, p.151.

38. John Hick, 'Soul-Making Theodicy' in Michael Peterson *et*

al eds, *Philosophy of Religion—Selected Readings* (Oxford, 1996).

39. Keith Ward, *God, Chance and Necessity* (OneWorld, 1996), p.193.

40. Augustine, *Confessions*, Henry Chadwick, trans., (Oxford, 1992).

41. Alvin Plantinga, 'Tooley and Evil: A Reply', *Australasian Journal of Philosophy*, 60 (1981): 74.

42. J.L. Mackie, *op cit.*, pp.115–116.

43. Keith Ward, *Divine Action*.

44. *Ibid.*, p.52.

45. *Ibid.*

46. Hugh Silvester, *Arguing with God, The Problem Of Evil* (IVP, 1996), p.21.

47. Richard Swinburne, *Is There A God?* (Oxford, 1996).

48. John Wenham, *The Enigma of Evil*, p.37.

49. Richard Swinburne, *The Existence of God*, second edition (Oxford, 1991), p.212.

50. C.S. Lewis, *Screwtape Letters* (Macmillan, 1952), p.46.

51. John Hick, 'Soul-Making Theodicy' in Michael Peterson *et al* eds, *Philosophy of Religion—Selected Readings*.

52. Leibniz, *Theodicy*, quoted by F.C. Copleston in *A History of Philosophy, Volume 4, Modern Philosophy: Descartes to Leibniz* (Image, 1963), p.331.

53. John Hick, *Evil and the God of Love* (Macmillan, 1977).

54. J.L. Mackie, *op cit.*, pp.159, 154.

55. Robin Le Poidevin, *op cit.*, p.89.

56. C.S. Lewis, *A Grief Observed*, (Faber and Faber), p.38.

57. *Ibid.*, p.38.

58. C.S. Lewis, ed., *George MacDonald, An Anthology* (Geoffrey Bles, 1946).

59. C.S. Lewis, *The Problem of Pain* (Fount, 1977).

60. Alister McGrath, *Suffering* (Hodder and Stoughton, 1992), pp.30–31.

61. David Watson, *Fear No Evil* (Hodder and Stoughton).

62. H.P. Owen, *op cit.*

63. Dorothy L. Sayers, *The Man Born to be King.*

64. Hugh Silvester, *op cit.*

65. *Ibid.*

66. *Ibid.*

67. *Ibid.*

68. Elie Wiesel, *Night.*

69. C.S. Lewis, *A Grief Observed*, p.25.

70. J.R.R. Tolkien, *The Lord of the Rings* (Unwin Paperbacks, 1979).

71. Peter Kreeft and Ronald Tacelli, *Handbook of Christian Apologetics*, p.263.

72. John Polkinghorne, *op cit.*

73. Blaise Pascal, *Pensées*, 274, Honor Levi, trans. (Oxford, 1995), p.81.

74. John Polkinghorne, *Science and Christian Belief* (SPCK, 1994), p.167.

75. C.S. Lewis, *Prayer—Letters to Malcolm* (Fount, 1977), p.124,

76. Stephen T. Davies, 'Resurrection and Judgement' in *Risen Indeed* (SPCK/C.S. Lewis Centre, 1993), p.155.

77. Peter Kreeft and Ronald Tacelli, *op cit.*, p.289.

78. *Ibid.*, p.286.

79. C.S. Lewis, *The Problem of Pain*, chapter eight, 'Hell'.

80. Peter Kreeft and Ronald Tacelli, *op cit.*, p.304.

81. Stephen T. Davies, 'Resurrection and Judgement' in *Risen Indeed—Making Sense of the Resurrection* (SPCK/C.S. Lewis Centre, 1993), p.156.

82. C.S. Lewis, quoted by Peter Kreeft and Ronald Tacelli, *op cit.*, p.283.

CHAPTER TWO

THE MORAL ARGUMENT

The law of the LORD is perfect,
reviving the soul.
The statutes of the LORD are trustworthy,
making wise the simple.
The precepts of the LORD are right,
giving joy to the heart.
The commands of the LORD are radiant,
giving light to the eyes.
The fear of the LORD is pure,
enduring for ever.
The ordinances of the LORD are sure
and altogether righteous.

(Psalm 19:7–10)

In Chapter One I claimed that the argument from evil against the existence of God depends upon the recognition of objective Wrong. I suggested that the recognition of objective Wrong required the existence of objective moral values, which granted the first premise of the moral argument for God's existence. In this Chapter I will present and defend a moral argument for the existence of God from the existence of objective moral values. At the close of the chapter I will return to the problem of evil to show how the existence of evil actually demands the existence of an all-good God.

The moral argument for the existence of God finds its most popular expression to date in the writings of C.S. Lewis, although it has found favour with a number of other philosophers.[1] The most basic form of the argument has been given as follows:

Premise 1) 'Morality is an objective feature of our universe.'
Premise 2) 'Naturalistic explanations of the objectivity of morality are inadequate.'
Conclusion. Therefore, 'there must be a universal personal authority that is the source of morality.'[2]

Both premises are doubted by some people, and need defending if the argument is to convince them. Allow me first of all to expand the above argument into the form I shall defend:

Premise 1) There are objective moral values.
Premise 2) Objective moral values either require the existence of 'a personal ground', or not.
2i) If objective moral values do not require the existence of a personal ground, then they must be explicable in non-personal terms.

2ii) Objective moral values are not explicable in non-personal terms.

2iii) Objective moral values therefore require explanation in terms of 'a personal ground'.

2iv) This personal ground of objective moral values must be the independent creator who has always existed and is ultimate goodness personified.

2v) Such a being can appropriately be called 'God'.

Conclusion. Therefore God exists.

The importance of the issue

The philosophy of moral value that we hold, as individuals or as a society, has great implications for our lives. As R.M. Hare put it, the question, 'What shall I do?' cannot be avoided for long, for 'the problems of conduct, though sometimes less diverting than crossword puzzles, have to be solved in a way that crossword puzzles do not. We cannot wait to see the solution in the next issue, because on the solution of the problems depends what happens in the next issue.'[3] Hence C.S. Lewis' warning:

> If [moral] Truth is objective, if we live in a world we did not create and cannot change merely by thinking, if the world is not really a dream of our own, then the most destructive belief we could possibly believe would be the denial of this primary fact. It would be like closing your eyes while driving, or blissfully ignoring the doctor's warnings.[4]

Defining moral goodness

Richard Swinburne's book *Responsibility and Atonement* (*Oxford*, 1989), is a masterful account of Christian beliefs about the moral status of humanity—particularly the concepts of sin, atonement, salvation, heaven and hell. Swinburne begins with a discussion of goodness in general, and of moral goodness in

particular. Although I do not agree with Swinburne on everything, I find his analysis of moral value, and his insistence on the
objectivity of moral value, a useful starting point:

> Our moral beliefs are beliefs that objectively certain things matter,
> whether or not we admit it . . . we believe that actions have objective
> properties of mattering which exist independently of our recogniz-
> ing them. Our moral beliefs are not mere principles which we decide
> to follow; but convictions which nag at us . . . We who believe it
> wrong to torture children, believe it would still be wrong if we had
> been brought up to think otherwise. We who believe it our duty to
> help the starving, feel the force of a moral obligation from without.[5]

Swinburne's definition of objective moral values is clearly cap-
tured by my criteria that an objective fact is a fact that does not
depend upon any finite mental state (or collection thereof).
Swinburne says that 'Our moral beliefs are beliefs that *objectively* certain things matter, whether or not we admit it' (my
italics), and as such hold 'independently of our recognizing
them', because they are not merely principles which we 'decide'
upon, and could in principle change.

I believe that Swinburne's analysis of objective moral values
as facts 'which nag at us', and are felt as a 'force . . . from
without', captures something irreducibly true about goodness.
Moral goodness matters. There is an emotional content to our
understanding of moral values, both good and bad; but these
values cannot be reduced to, or explained away as 'nothing but'
subjective facts about ourselves or our communities.

Dividing up the field

Theories about the status of moral values can be divided in the
following way. The first division is between theories which say
that moral utterances express propositions (and so are either
true or false), and theories which say that moral utterances do
not express propositions (and so are neither true nor false). A

proposition is simply a sentence that makes a factual claim. The sentence 'It is raining' is a proposition. The sentence 'Take an umbrella with you' is not.

Theories which say that moral utterances are not propositions, and have no truth-value, are called non-propositional theories, for obvious reasons. Let's look at non-propositional moral theories first.

Non-propositional theories

Prescriptivism

Prescriptivism, as expounded by R.M. Hare, asserts that moral utterances are universal prescriptions; in other words, they are orders or demands that the utterer thinks should apply to everyone. As such, moral utterances have no propositional content, and no truth conditions, being on a par with sentences like 'Shut that door'. On this theory the utterance, 'Child pornography is evil' means something like, 'No one engage in child pornography!'

Ayer's emotivism

Emotivism, as expounded by A.J. Ayer, asserts that moral utterances merely express the attitude of the speaker. According to emotivism, moral utterances do not even claim that the speaker has the attitude in question, but simply express their attitude much as my saying 'Ow!' when someone stamps on my foot expresses my pain. Moral utterances have no propositional content, and no truth conditions. On this theory, the utterance, 'Child pornography is evil' means something like, 'Child pornography? Yuck!'

Stevenson's emotivism

Charles L. Stevenson gave the world a more sophisticated emotivism by distinguishing between 'disagreement in belief' and 'disagreement in attitude'[6]. The first kind of disagreement 'involves an opposition of beliefs, both of which cannot be true', while the second 'involves an opposition of attitudes, both of which cannot be satisfied'.[7]

Stevenson concludes that 'ethical arguments usually involve disagreement in belief; but they also involve disagreement in attitude'.[8] However, Stevenson gives an example of a moral disagreement from which it is clear that he sees 'disagreement in attitude' as the defining characteristic of moral arguments, and sees any 'disagreement in belief' within moral arguments as disagreement about non-moral facts only.

Stevenson's example is of a union urging a company, against its will, to increase wages. Stevenson says that 'such an argument clearly represents a disagreement in attitude. The union is for higher wages; the company is against them, and neither is content to let the other's attitude remain unchanged.'[9] So far so good, but when Stevenson turns to the factual disagreements involved in this dispute, he lists only non-moral facts:

> Perhaps the parties disagree over how much the cost of living has risen and how much the workers are suffering under the present wage scale. Or perhaps they disagree about the company's earnings and the extent to which the company could raise wages and still operate at a profit.[10]

It would seem from this example, that the 'disagreement in belief' couldn't be about the recognition or failure to recognise the existence or application of a moral value such as fairness.

Stevenson says that 'disagreement in attitude plays a unifying and predominating role in [moral] argument'. In other words, there are no factual moral values to be correctly or incorrectly invoked in the course of moral arguments. The only facts relevant to moral arguments are non-moral facts. Resolving disagreements of belief is relevant to moral argument only because 'attitudes are often functions of beliefs', and so 'agreement in belief may lead people, as a matter of psychological fact, to agree in attitude'.[11] But the beliefs in question are not, according to Stevenson, moral beliefs (or at least, anyone who thought so would presumably be thought mistaken by Stevenson). The beliefs in question are beliefs about matters of fact, 'open to the usual methods of the sciences', which Stevenson takes to be 'the *only* rational methods for supporting beliefs'.[12]

Stevenson admits that there is no reason to say that the meaning of ethical terms 'is *purely* emotive, like that of "alas" or "hurrah"'.[13] But this is because ethical arguments include expressions of factual belief, 'and the rough rules of ordinary language permits us to say that some of these beliefs are expressed by an ethical judgement itself'.[14] The important thing for Stevenson is that ethical terms 'are so habitually used to deal with disagreement in attitude' that 'they have acquired a strong emotive meaning', which 'makes them serviceable in initiating changes in a hearer's attitudes'.[15]

Just feelings and commands?

From this brief survey we can see that non-propositional moral theories analyse moral language into commands and/or expressions of feelings:

> acts with certain natural properties (e.g. the deliberate taking of human life) tend to cause in us feelings of revulsion, pity, etc., and thus lead us to condemn the act. Saying 'this is wrong' is simply an expression of that feeling.[16]

Moral judgements are seen, at best, as being the same as our subjective judgements of taste. 'Apples are nice' and 'Apples are horrible' appear to be contradictory statements. Not so. They are shorthand for, 'I like apples', and, 'I don't like apples'. They are reports of subjective facts. Similarly, so it is argued, 'Murder is wrong', and, 'Murder is right', appear to be contradictory statements, but this is merely because we misinterpret them as assertions of objective facts when they are reports of subjective facts. This is the line that A.J. Ayer took:

> the function of the relevant ethical word is purely 'emotive' . . . Thus the sentence 'it is your duty to tell the truth' may be regarded both as the expression of a certain sort of ethical feeling about truthfulness and as the expression of the command 'Tell the truth'.[17]

Non-propositional theories say that our moral language is just an expression of subjective facts, perhaps combined with a demand. Thus the statement, 'Murder is wrong' actually means something like, 'Murder? Yuk! Don't do it!' A moral objectivist might agree with this, but would want to add to it. This is surely not all we do in fact mean by our moral language. When I say 'Murder is wrong', I do not mean merely that I feel murder to be wrong, or that I do not desire murder as an end, and do not want others to commit murder. What I mean is that even if I personally (or my society) felt that murder was right, or desired murder as an end, it would nevertheless be Wrong. I mean that people genuinely ought not to commit murder, and ought not to desire murder as an end, whether they actually do or not. As Bernard Williams writes:

> Moral judgements . . . mean what we take them to mean; and what we take them to mean, the way we use them, is such that they do not merely make autobiographical claims, but a sort of claim which is being rejected by someone who utters a contrary moral judgement. Thus they do not merely describe the speaker's own attitude.[18]

Why do we feel the way we feel?

Emotivism grounds ethics in feelings: 'ethical judgements are mere expressions of feelings, and [there is] no way of determining the validity of any ethical system, and . . . no sense in asking whether any such system is true.'[19]

A.J. Ayer and R.M. Hare suggest two routes by which we get these all-important moral feelings. The first, advocated by Ayer, is by some irrational process (he favours social conditioning). The second, advocated by Hare, is by rational choice: 'To become morally adult,' says Hare, 'is . . . to learn to use 'ought' sentences in the realisation that they can only be [meaningful] with reference to a standard or set of principles which we have by our own decision accepted and made our own.'[20]

We either choose our moral feelings, or some irrational process places them within us. The third option, rejected or passed over by Ayer and Hare, is that our moral feelings are placed in us by a rational source, whether directly or through a directed natural process. This is the option advocated by theism.

If the possession of moral feelings is the result of rational choice, as Hare thinks, what standard of good and bad do we use in making that choice? Suppose someone decides to become a utilitarian (someone who tries to act so as to maximise happiness). They cannot choose to become a utilitarian on the basis of utilitarian principles, because they have not yet adopted utilitarianism! To use utilitarian principles in making a rational choice to adopt utilitarian principles amounts to begging-the-question.

Hare assumes that people can stand in a sort of moral vacuum while choosing their moral feelings; but if they did this, why would they bother about morality at all? There could be no moral reason for the adoption of any morality if morality must be chosen from within a 'morality-free zone'. As Bernard Williams says, 'this mid-air place . . . is not a place in which anyone can have a moral thought.'[21] Even if we could invent our own 'set of principles', as Hare suggests, there would be nothing to stop us changing our principles when it suited us. If we bind ourselves we can loose ourselves, because the power of self-made principles rests in the self that made them.

On the other hand, if we do not decide upon our moral feelings, but inherit them from society, as Ayer suggests, then how did society arrive at its ethical feelings? All Ayer does is to push the question of how we come to possess our moral feelings back a step from the individual onto society. But society is a collection of individuals; so how did the first individuals of any society come by their moral feelings?

If we do not choose our moral feelings, then they must be given to us. The ultimate source of these feelings can only be either rational (and therefore personal) or non-rational (and therefore impersonal). That is, moral propositions must be definable either in naturalistic (non-rational and impersonal) or supernatural (rational and personal) terms. If the source of our moral feelings is non-rational, the only candidate is the purposeless nature described so well by atheists like Bertrand Russell. If this is the source of our moral feelings, then I do not see how to escape the conclusion that life is without purpose. If we are the product of a purposeless, meaningless universe, how can we have or create meaning?

Moreover, if our ability to reason comes from nature—the product of impersonal matter, plus time, plus chance—then why should we trust the reasoning that brought us to such a conclusion?

> So long as the ultimate reality of things is regarded as purely material, so long as material process is regarded as the sole cause or source or ground of mind and all its contents, there is always the possibility of scepticism as to the knowledge of which this material world has somehow delivered itself. Our knowledge may be conceived of as representing, not the real truth of things, but the way in which it is most conductive to the survival of the race that we should think of them. [22]

As Nietzsche put it: 'All our organs of knowledge and our senses are developed only as a means of preservation ... Trust in reason and its categories, in dialectic, therefore the valuation of logic, proves only their usefulness for life, proved by experience—not that something is true.'[23] Pragmatist Richard Rorty says that,

> From the post-Darwinian perspective there is no such thing as 'how things really are'. There are simply various descriptions of things, and we use the one which seems most likely to achieve our purposes.[24]

Any philosophy that attempts to ground reason in the non-rational, meaning in the meaningless, purpose in the purposeless, morality in the a-moral, is doomed. (I will return to the question of reason and naturalism in Chapter Four.)

If we should give up the objectivity of moral values because a non-rational process forms our moral feelings, then we should jettison the objectivity of truth for the same reason. If, on the other hand, the source is rational (and therefore personal and purposeful), then the same question applies to it, unless it is God. If the source is God, then our moral feelings are a reflection of God's character, and are absolute, objective and binding. God's desires, formed against the background of his essential and necessary nature, and expressed in creation, constitute the context of cosmic meaning and purpose. Whether by means direct or indirect, the moral feelings of humans made in the image of God match (although imperfectly) with the objective transcendent all-good character of the divine. As Paul wrote: 'God's law is not something alien, imposed on us from without, but [is] woven into the very fabric of our creation. There is something deep within [humans] that echoes God's yes and no, right and wrong' (Romans 2, *The Message*).

Propositional theories

In contrast to such non-propositional theories as prescriptivism and emotivism are what we might call, naturally enough, propositional theories. Propositional theories hold that moral utterances have a propositional content, and so a truth value. Propositional theories see moral utterances as making factual claims, although they may also express attitudes and make demands. Clearly, if moral utterances have a truth-value, then that truth-value must either be objective or subjective.

Propositional theories lend themselves to further sub-division. The first division to be made is between theories which hold that moral truths are knowable (cognitive theories), and those which hold that moral truths are not knowable (non-cognitive theories). The latter class is moral scepticism. Moral sceptics believe that moral utterances are propositions with an unknowable truth-value. The moral sceptic is willing to admit that moral utterances are propositions which are either true or false, but unwilling to admit that we know the truth-value of any given moral utterance.

Cognitive theories can be further divided along the following lines: On the one hand it might be claimed that moral propositions are equivalent to (ie definable in terms of) non-moral propositions. On the other hand it might be claimed along with Kant that moral propositions are not equivalent to non-moral propositions (ie are not definable in terms of non-moral propositions). This view describes the autonomy of morality.

Kant held that morality is based on a 'categorical imperative', a matter of absolute duty, which is not equivalent to any other facts. Kant believed that this categorical imperative obliged us to seek the greatest good, that an obligation to seek the greatest good implied that the greatest good is achievable ('should', he argued, implies 'can'), and that since the greatest good was only (as he believed) achievable if both God and the afterlife existed, morality requires us to believe in the existence of each. I will return to this type of practical moral argument in a later chapter.

Naturalism or supernaturalism

Those who claim that moral propositions are equivalent to non-moral propositions will either claim that moral propositions are definable in naturalistic terms (eg in terms of the state of your mind as determined by evolutionary programming, or in terms of the agreement of a human society), or that moral propositions are definable in non-naturalistic, supernatural terms.

I believe that naturalistic theories are inevitably subjective theories; the truth of moral propositions depending upon facts about the actual or possible states of one or more finite minds (although these states may be accounted for through naturalistic explanations such as evolutionary programming).

Supernatural theories include the following three accounts: 1) The 'finite-godism' of Plato (there exists an eternal, supernatural but non-divine 'form' of 'the good' in accordance with which the world has been fashioned by a finite god). 2) The 'divine command theory' (the truth condition of moral propositions is the will of God, perhaps as revealed in some divine revelation). 3) 'Essentialism' (the truth condition of moral propositions depends upon God's essential character).

I am an essentialist. I believe that moral utterances express propositions, and so have a truth-value. I believe that the truth-value of moral utterances is objective and knowable. I believe that moral propositions are equivalent to non-moral propositions; and that those non-moral propositions are truths about God (my theory is therefore a supernaturalist theory).

Objectivism v. relativism

Moral relativism is a theory about ethics which alleges that 'There are no objective values'[25]; there are only subjective 'morality opinions'. Different societies can have different opinions about what is right and wrong, without implying any absolute contradiction. The 'moral' thing to do is 'whatever the society you align yourself with holds is right': 'The moral principles that govern our behaviour are rooted in habit and custom, feeling and fashion.'[26] Moral relativism contradicts moral objectivism, which asserts that there are objective moral values:

> relativists often couple this account of morality with the belief that, because morality is relative, we should never interfere with the customs of other societies on the ground that there is no neutral standpoint from which to judge . . . When moral relativism has this added component . . . it is usually known as normative relativism.[27]

There is an obvious link between moral relativism and moral subjectivism. Moral subjectivism carries moral relativism to its logical extreme, asserting that moral values are relative to the individual. Since 'society' is made up of individuals, these two theories go hand in hand. Moral relativism points out that there is a natural 'peer-pressure' that arises when individuals live in community. This peer-pressure constrains behaviour within broadly defined limits, 'averaging out' the moral subjectivist's assumed individual relativism. In this way moral subjectivism underlies moral relativism. Both moral relativism and moral subjectivism are moral non-objectivisms. Each, as we shall see, comes in various 'flavours', but both agree that there are no objective moral values.

Moral relativism asserts that morality is not the sort of thing that can be objectively right or wrong, true or false. For the moral relativist there can be no objective moral ought about ethics. In matters of morality there is no absolute standard beyond our own standards. As J.L. Mackie believed: 'Morality is not to be discovered, but to be made: we have to decide what moral views to adopt, what moral stands to take.'[28]

Moral objectivism, on the other hand, asserts that a theory of morality can be objectively true, or false, in accordance to what objectively ought to be the case: 'Objective morality is simply there for us to discover and measure our actions against. Certain ones conform to it; these we call morally good acts. Others, the immoral ones, do not.'[29] Moral objectivists believe that there are objective moral values, 'a moral law', independent of the knower. Moral judgements are either true or false, and this truth or falsity is independent of human thought or belief or desire: 'Just so, if a certain line is crooked, it is crooked, and though I may possibly not remark this, or may even think that the line is straight, or may wish that it were straight, it is none the less crooked for all that.'[30] Moral values are discovered, not invented.

The wrong end of the stick

Some atheists, such as Jean-Paul Sartre, have argued that: 'Only if God exists would there be an objective moral law. God does not exist. Therefore there is no objective moral law.' As Sartre put it, 'everything is permissible if God does not exist.'[31] The argument from objective morality agrees with atheists like Sartre that objective moral values require the existence of God. Even J.L. Mackie conceded that 'if the requisite theological doctrine could be defended, a kind of ethical prescriptivity could be thus introduced'. However, he went on to say: 'Since I think that Theism cannot be defended, I do not regard this as any threat to my argument [for moral scepticism].'[32]

Faced with the argument from objective morality we cannot say, 'God does not exist so morality cannot be objective.' That would be question-begging. We must be prepared to show that the argument itself is flawed. To do otherwise would be like saying to someone who came to us with what they claimed to be high quality videotape of the Loch Ness Monster, 'There is no Monster, so your tape must be a fake.' However sceptical we were, we should at least examine the evidence, testing it for forgery. If the evidence stands up, and if the evidence is strong enough to outweigh our previous reasons for disbelief, then we ought to change our mind. (Is our obligation to change our mind objective or subjective?) If we look honestly at the evidence and remain unconvinced, then, until next time, we will have done all that we can do.

A.E. Taylor warns that 'the systematic disregard of all "moral" arguments would only be possible to one who frankly takes the line that there are no moral facts, that is, that right and wrong are pure illusions'.[33] It is to the defence of this crucial premise that we now turn.

I will begin by looking at some common arguments advanced in defence of moral non-objectivism (I have summarised objections in my own words where I have not quoted from objectors themselves). I suggest that moral non-objectivism is so counter-intuitive that if the following arguments in its defence can be defeated, moral objectivism will win by default. However, I will go on to give reasons to be suspicious of moral non-objectivism, and reasons to believe moral objectivism.

Objections raised against moral objectivism

1. Values are relative to different cultures. Ignorance blinded humanity to this truth until recently, when anthropologists discovered that there are cultural exceptions to every moral value.

How is the term 'values' used here? Objectivists and non-objectivists mean different things by 'moral values'. The term 'values' is ambiguous. The term 'values' is used in its non-objective sense in this argument, and so it begs the question. This argument is meant to be opposing moral objectivism, where 'values' means 'objective moral laws', but it disregards this use of the term from the start.

Not only does this objection beg the question, but its premises are faulty: 'The first premise is false because cultures can err just as individuals can . . . what is culturally relative is opinions about what is really right and wrong, not right and wrong themselves. The word values fudges this distinction.'[34] While the moral objectivist accepts that different cultures have different values in the subjective sense of the word, this does not prove the non-existence of an objective moral law: 'Though value-opinions may be relative to different cultures and subjective to individuals, that does not necessarily mean that real values are.'[35] Naturally, some people may be wrong about what the moral law actually is; we could hardly have disagreements about moral issues if everyone agreed! The fact that not everyone agrees about what actually is right or wrong, does not show that there is no ultimate standard. As F.C. Copleston replied when Bertrand Russell raised this objection: 'Let's assume for the moment that there are absolute moral values. Even on that hypothesis it's only to be expected that different individuals and different groups should enjoy varying degrees of insight into those values.'[36]

The second premise, that cultures differ about values, does not carry the weight that the non-objectivist intends, for no culture ever existed which held a totally different set of values. As C.S. Lewis pointed out: 'If anyone will take the trouble to compare the moral teaching of, say, the ancient Egyptians, Babylonians, Hindus, Chinese, Greeks and Romans, what will really strike him will be how very like they are to each other and to our own.'[37] We can scarcely imagine, wrote Lewis, how a totally different morality would work. The very thought of a country where people were admired for cheating on those closest to them is absurd: 'You might just as well try to imagine a country where two and two made five.'[38] There is no avoiding the fact that 'Men have differed as regards what people you ought to be unselfish to . . .'.[39] Nevertheless, 'they have always agreed that you ought not to put yourself first'.[40]

Sometimes differing beliefs make it look as if different cultures have different values. For example, there was a society in which people had the custom of killing their parents when they began to get old. To Western eyes, such a practice appears immoral. We employ the standard that parents should be honoured. It may seem that the society in question did not employ the same standard, but they did. These people thought that we spend the afterlife in the physical state in which we die. Allowing someone to grow old and decrepit would not be honouring them, because they would be like that for ever. One and the same moral principle may be employed, but different beliefs can lead to a different application of that principle. Many differences in action can be explained in this way, without postulating different ethical standards.

That people disagree about ethics indicates, not that moral values are subjective, but that they are objective. What do people disagree about? They disagree about matters of objective truth such as how old the universe is and whether there are objective moral values or not (there either are or are not objective moral values). When it comes to subjective truths, people do not disagree. Whether or not I am in pain is a subjective truth. Unless you had reason to think I was only pretending to be in pain you would not disagree with me when I say, 'I'm in pain.' 'So disagreement about something is a reason not for thinking that something is subjective, but rather for thinking that it is objective.'[41]

Normative relativists using this argument deplore the 'crude importation of Western values' (in the subjective sense) to non-western cultures. However, to do this they must acknowledge the existence of an objective value of cultural sensitivity; for if they do not, they are crudely importing their own subjective 'Western' values into a non-western culture!

J.L. Mackie acknowledged that 'Such variation is in itself merely . . . a fact of anthropology which entails neither first order nor second order ethical views.'[42] However, he thinks that the variation of moral values between cultures 'may indirectly support second order subjectivism: radical differences between first order moral judgements make it difficult to treat those judgements as apprehensions of objective truths'.[43] This difficulty is made worse because disagreement about moral codes is apparently reflected in people's participation in different ways of living: 'people approve of monogamy because they participate in a monogamous way of life rather than that they participate in a monogamous way of life because they approve of monogamy.'[44]

Mackie admits that this argument can be countered in part at least by pointing out that objective validity may be claimed primarily for basic general principles of morality acknowledged by almost everyone, which result in different specific rules when married to different circumstances. The specific rules would then be 'objectively valid or true, but only derivatively and contingently'.[45]

It seems to be a simple truism that people will tend to endorse subjective moral values that support what they actually want to do. Besides:

> Different groups of men, living under different conditions and in different ages, may disagree widely on the question whether a certain thing belongs to the first or the second of these classes [things which they ought to do and other things which they ought not to do]. They may draw the line between right and wrong in a different place, but at least they all agree that there is such a line to be drawn.[46]

And the existence of this line is all that the moral argument for the existence of God requires. The argument does not depend upon the recognition of particular ethical rules. Rather, it depends upon the existence of an objective distinction between right and wrong, and an objective obligation to pursue goodness and shun evil.

2. Moral subjectivism produces tolerance. Moral objectivism produces intolerance; if you believe your moral values are objective, you will try to impose them on people.

It is not true that belief in objective values necessarily produces intolerance. In fact, the value of tolerance is something the objectivist can take more seriously than the relativist, for if values are subjective, then the value of tolerance is subjective. Besides which, the very meaning of 'tolerance' requires moral objectivity, 'For we tolerate only real evils, in order to prevent worse evils. We do not tolerate good; we promote it.'[47]

In condemning intolerance, the relativist appeals to an objective, universal moral law, by saying that we ought to be tolerant:

> those who advocate ethical relativism often do so on the grounds that moral relativism promotes tolerance . . . But this only reintroduces objective moral values, for unless some values are better than others—tolerance better than intolerance . . . there is no ground for praising these virtues, other than that we approve them.[48]

As W. David Beck writes, 'To assert that those who pass judgement on the slaughter of the innocent are just being intolerant is ridiculous. The claim is even self-defeating, for tolerance is itself assumed to be an objective, unexceptionable moral value.'[49] Such post-modern 'tolerance' is exemplified by *Star Trek*'s 'prime directive' of non-interference; but this is a directive that Captain Kirk is forever breaking, with the full support of the viewers, in order to do the right thing.

If a moral value is objective, it can no more be imposed upon someone than can the law of gravity. Of course, believers in objective moral values may wrongly attempt to force others to act in accordance to what they believe those standards to be, but moral relativists are just as likely to impose their views upon others as are moral objectivists. Normative moral relativists are very keen to impose their view that no one should be 'intolerant' by presuming to question the rights and wrongs of any value-opinions that differ from their own.

The tolerance argument is self-defeating, for most cultures in the past did not value tolerance:

Should we tolerate this intolerance? If the subjectivist answers no, he is either appealing to the objective value of tolerance or being intolerant in imposing his personal value of tolerance on other cultures. If his answer is yes—if we should tolerate intolerance—then the subjectivist has no reason to quarrel with the supposed intolerance of objectivists.[50]

3. Doing the right thing for the wrong reason is wrong, but you can't blame people for doing the wrong thing for the right reason. Morality is a matter of the heart, and that's clearly relative to the individual.

You might accidentally do something that is in itself not good, and remain beyond reproach for what happened. However, to say that 'since motives are relative to individuals, therefore moral values must be relative', is a non-starter. There must be objective criteria by which motives can be recognised as being moral or not. The standard cannot be relative because then one person's 'good' could be another person's 'bad'. To say that someone's motive was good is not merely to say that their motive is what my society and/or I happen to consider to be a good motive. Rather it is to say that their motive, and my moral assessment of that motive, are both in line with an objective standard beyond both of us and our society or respective societies. To say otherwise is to admit that if everyone on earth were brainwashed to believe that rape was a good thing, and that the desire to rape was a good motive, then rape and the desire to rape would indeed be good. Trying to amend the argument by adding in an 'unless people are all brainwashed' clause, would be *ad hoc*.

4. No moral rule can be universal. We can always imagine a situation where it would be right to lie, or even to kill. The right thing to do is conditioned by the situation, and that's relative.

The moral objectivist may accept all of the above without concluding that moral values are relative: 'it would still be objectively right to lie to the Nazis about hiding Jews, or to kill in self-defence, or to steal a maniac's weapon.'[51]

> Love is never caught on the horns of a dilemma. There are levels and spheres of love, and one is always higher than another. Each love command is absolute in its area. But when that area overlaps with another area, then the lower responsibility of love should be subordinated to the higher . . . We must always opt for the greater good.[52]

5. If objective values existed, humans would not be free to create their own values. To preserve human dignity we must preserve human freedom, and to preserve human freedom we must preserve our ability to create values. As Kai Nielson says, 'if God exists, you were made for a purpose. And that itself poses problems about your autonomy.'[53]

While we are not 'free' to create our own moral law, we are free to reject the moral law, and we may choose to elevate some part of it out of proportion to its context. In order to have freedom we must have rules; not to break in order to assert our freedom, but within which to exercise our freedom. I am only free to play chess if I play within the 'limits' of the rules. If I do not stay within the 'limitations' of the rules then I am not playing chess. Certain 'limitations' are necessary for making chess a possible, worthwhile, and enjoyable past-time. Within the rules I am free; but without the rules I would not be free to play chess, because the rules define what chess is. Similarly, within the moral law I am free to play the 'game' of life however I want, but without the moral law I would not be free to play the 'game' of life, because the moral law defines what 'life' is.

The freedom valued by this objection is rather hard to swallow. It is both hard to believe that we have the freedom to create values, and hard to believe that the power to do so would be a good thing:

> If that is the true nature of morality, then it would mean each of us is free, morally speaking, to choose whichever moral point of view we find most appealing. The choice of whether to be a Mother Teresa or an Adolf Hitler would be roughly the same choice as whether to become a saxophone player or an organ player. You simply choose the one you find most appealing and worthwhile.[54]

In his slim but seminal book *The Abolition of Man*, C.S. Lewis gave a sustained treatment of what follows from the conception of values as something that we are free to create. Lewis' argument goes like this:

What we call man's power is in fact power possessed by some men (in the generic sense) which they may or may not allow others to profit by. Hence, each new power won by man is also a power over man. Now, the ultimate stage in man's conquest of nature will come when man has obtained the power to control himself, by means of genetic and psychological manipulation. Imagine what would happen if this power were used. R.M. Hare noted that 'the suggestion, that the function of moral judgements was to persuade, led to a difficulty in distinguishing their function from that of propaganda'.[55] Lewis points out that in the older system of education the kind of man that teachers wanted to produce, and their motives for wanting to produce him, were both prescribed by an objective moral standard which transcended pupil and teacher alike. Lewis predicts that this will change if man comes to believe that values are merely natural phenomena. Judgements of value could be produced in the pupil as part of the state's educational conditioning programme. Hence, the moral law will be the product, not the motive, of education. The teachers, or conditioners, will choose what moral law they will to produce in the human race. They

will be the motivators of humanity; but how will they be motivated themselves?

> For a time, perhaps, by survivals, within their own minds, of the old
> [moral law]. Thus at first they may look upon themselves as servants
> and guardians of humanity and conceive that they have a 'duty' to
> do 'good'. But it is only by confusion that they can remain in this
> state. They recognise the concept of duty as the result of certain pro-
> cesses which they can now control . . . One of the things they now
> have to decide is whether they will, or will not, so condition the rest
> of us that we can go on having the old idea of duty and the old reac-
> tion to it. How can duty help them to decide that? Duty itself is up
> for trial: it cannot also be the judge. And 'good' fares no better. They
> know quite well how to produce a dozen different conceptions of
> good in us. The question is which, if any, they should produce . . .
> that is the [moral law] which they may decide to impose in us, but
> which cannot be valid for them. If they accept it, then they are no
> longer the makers of conscience but still its subjects.[56]

It is not that the teachers are bad men, says Lewis, for they are
not men at all:

> Stepping outside the [moral law], they have stepped into the void.
> Nor are their subjects necessarily unhappy men. They are not men
> at all: they are artefacts. Man's final conquest has proved to be the
> abolition of Man . . . Yet the conditioners will act . . . All motives
> that claim any validity other than that of their felt emotional weight
> at a given moment have failed them . . . but what never claimed
> objectivity cannot be destroyed by subjectivism . . . the
> Conditioners, therefore, must come to be motivated simply by their
> own pleasures [or fears] . . . those who stand outside all judgements
> of value cannot have any ground for preferring one of their impulses
> to another except the emotional strength of that impulse.[57]

Therefore, at the moment of man's conquest of nature, we may
find the human race in general subjected to some individuals,
and those individuals subjected 'to that in themselves which is

purely "natural"—to their irrational impulses'.[58] As Kai Nielson has said, 'once you're outside of morality, the only thing you can give is a kind of prudential answer'.[59] Nature rules the conditioners, and through them, humanity:

> Man's conquest of Nature turns out, in the moment of its consummation, to be Nature's conquest of Man . . . . Either we are . . . obliged for ever to obey the absolute value . . . or else we are mere nature to be kneaded and cut into new shapes for the pleasures of masters who must, by hypothesis, have no motive but their own 'natural' impulses. Only the [objective Moral Law] provides a common human law of action which can over-arch rulers and ruled alike. A dogmatic belief in objective values is necessary to the very idea of a rule which is not tyranny or an obedience which is not slavery.[60]

Lewis's argument can easily be applied to the individual who demands that they be 'free' to create their own moral values.

If the moral relativist still wants to argue in this manner, we should reply that we have decided to adopt a new value which says that we win the argument in favour of moral objectivism because we are shorter/taller than they are. To object to this move the Relativist must abandon their assertion that we are free to invent our own values.

Many people fear that God is some sort of moral busy-body out to make sure that no one has any fun, and that everyone feels 'as guilty as sin' if they do. This is a misconception. If, as Christianity says, God is all-good, then all His commands must be for the best. If God's commands are for the best, then it would be silly to disobey if we too desire 'the good'. Again, we should obey God, not out of fear of punishment or the hope of reward, but just because we love God as the source and standard of all goodness, beauty and truth. We do not object to the loss of autonomy when we give ourselves to a loved one. Neither should we object to the loss of autonomy when we give ourselves to the God who is love. When we see the cost of

God's love for us we are released from the misconception of God as tyrant.

6. Moral values are not objective because science, the senses or mathematical reasoning cannot discover them.

Science, the senses, or mathematical reasoning cannot discover many things in life. For example, the assertion that 'only things which are discoverable by science, the senses or mathematical reasoning are objective', cannot be discovered by science, the senses, or by mathematical reasoning! Like the verification principle we met in the Introduction, this criterion of objectivity is self-refuting, because by its own assertion it cannot be objectively true.

7. 'Morality is a biological adaptation no less than are hands and teeth . . . Considered as a rationally justifiable set of claims about an objective something, ethics is illusion.'[61]

Suppose we made contact with sentient beings from another planet. Would rape be 'wrong' for them? A naturalistic evolutionary theory gives us little ground for the assumption that extraterrestrials' morality would resemble our own: 'It all depends on how their particular evolutionary process went.'[62] Suppose the aliens could mate with humans, and that they began to do so, by force. When we complained, mightn't they reply: 'Your moral ideas are only a product of your evolutionary process. They are only like your other adaptations. Any other meaning is an illusion. It doesn't affect us.'[63] If morality were purely the result of evolution, they would be correct. Michael Ruse, a philosopher who advocates an evolutionary explanation of ethics, considers this very example of alien morality. He concludes that, although the immorality of rape is a human constant, we cannot assume that it would be a constant for other beings.[64] As Paul Chamberlain explains:

> if morality is only an evolutionary product, then raping . . . is not really wrong . . . We just have a conviction, the feeling, that they are wrong. But in that case extraterrestrials would be fully justified in ignoring our moral sentiments if they so chose. [65]

The important question that arises if we adopt this view is 'Why shouldn't we rape or do anything else that catches our fancy?' We have a feeling that to do certain things is wrong. The feeling may be very strong, but on this view it is only a biological adaptation. This adaptation may aid our survival, but the feeling that our survival is a good thing is itself only a feeling. The question is, can we live as though apparently terrible acts such as rape are not really wrong in any objective sense, but merely seem so?

We cannot escape the question: when you rescue someone from being raped, are you obeying an objective moral prescription (which you may know about through an intended evolutionary process), or a chance piece of evolutionary programming which reflects no objective moral values whatsoever?

If our moral feelings are merely the products of naturalistic evolution, they are a very powerful illusion indeed: 'when confronted with real moral evil—the horrors of genocide and child abuse, for example—it is hard to believe that moral judgements are just a biologically grounded illusion'.[66] Given that evolution produces such a powerful illusion, it seems strange that anyone has transcended millennia of biological programming to doubt the (supposedly illusory) 'objective truth' of moral values.

'Natural selection' does not seem to have done a very good job. There is no evidence that humans have become more moral. For every sign of hope we can see some cause for despair.

A naturalistic evolutionary picture cannot adequately ground the moral judgement a human being is more valuable than an amoeba:

> On an evolutionary secular scenario . . . Human beings are nothing special . . . the same [blind] process that coughed up human beings coughed up amoebas . . . The view that being human is special is

guilty of speciesism, an unjustifiable bias towards one's own species.[67]

Kai Nielsen testifies that 'morality has developed in such a way that reflective moral agents . . . have also come to an acknowledgement . . . of the necessity of affirming an inherent dignity and the intrinsic worth of all human beings'.[68] The theistic hypothesis gives an adequate ground for believing that humans are more valuable than amoebas by saying that humans are made 'in the image of God': 'I have intrinsic value or worth as I reflect the intrinsic value of God and His worth'.[69]

The atheist lacks any justification for this moral intuition, and must admit that only selfishness causes us to value our own existence over that of a snail. Secular humanists would point to certain qualities of humans (such as reason and creativity) to justify our special worth; but suppose we ask why they select these qualities as meriting special consideration: what makes those qualities so special?

> Why not choose powers of sense perception like sight, smell, hearing? In possession of these qualities, many animals are superior to humans . . . One could almost say: how convenient. You have chosen just those qualities that include your species and exclude others. This looks like the ultimate in arbitrary, preferential treatment. It goes beyond racism and sexism. It's what some call speciesism.[70]

Peter Singer, a philosopher involved in issues of animal rights, uses 'speciesism' to condemn the giving of preferential treatment to members of our own species, because, as a non-theist, he can find no reason to treat humans as being of more value than any other animal. Only a theistic world-view, in which the value of persons is grounded in the value of a creator God in whose image they are made, can justify the intuition that humans are more valuable than amoebas.

If evolutionary forces determine morality, why is it that humans remain free to disregard their morals by disobeying their conscience? The naturalistic explanation of morality might seem to deny that free will, and so human creativity and dignity, exists; but it was these qualities that the argument wanted to defend! If 'being good' comes to us by nature it would seem to make a nonsense of moral accountability.

The argument from evolution reduces morality to an evolutionary determined instinct. However, we don't experience morality as an instinct, but as an 'inner voice' telling us which instinct to follow in which situations. No instinct is always morally right, but the moral law is always right. Therefore, morality is not an instinct.

The argument attempts to derive an 'ought' from an 'is', which is the 'naturalistic fallacy':

> The premise or ground or source of morality for the instinctualist is simply 'this is an instinct,' and the conclusion 'therefore this ought to be done'. But this [argument] is invalid unless you add the second premise 'all instincts ought to be followed'. That premise is obviously false and impossible, since our instincts often contradict each other.[71]

This argument also commits the 'genetic fallacy' of 'faulting the rational justification of something because of where it comes from'.[72] As Robin Le Poidevin writes, 'We can make room for God in the atheist's account by assigning God the job of so constructing us that we respond emotionally in the way we do to certain natural properties of acts.'[73]

I am not arguing against the theory of evolution. I am arguing against the 'explaining away' of moral values as merely the chance product of an unintended natural process.

8. If we have been brought up from our earliest years in obedience to a principle, the thought of not obeying it becomes abhorrent to

us . . . These feelings are reinforced by all those factors which psychologists have listed; and the total result is what is generally called a feeling of obligation. It is a fact that we have this feeling of obligation . . . [but] it is important to point out a fact which has been singularly ignored by some moralists, that to say of someone that he has a feeling of obligation is not the same as to say that he has an obligation.[74]

That someone feels they are obligated does not mean that they are obligated (with this the objectivist may agree), but neither does it mean that they are not obligated! We may be 'conditioned' by society, but we are not determined by society. People can and do question the values society teaches them. To say that we are taught values by society does not necessitate the conclusion that values are relative to society. We are taught many things by society that are not relative, such as mathematics.

9. We all need help at times; and if we aren't willing to help others, then they are less likely to be willing to help us. We are all better off if we agree to certain rules of conduct. It is in my own best interest to obey the rules of morality. As Kai Nielson writes, 'Life in a world without reasonably functioning moral institutions would in Hobbe's famous phrase be nasty, brutish and short. In living we all need moral institutions.'[75]

That self-interest should be the foundation of morality is a contradiction in itself. It reduces and relativises right and wrong to the individual's pragmatic 'useful' or 'un-useful'. It bases morality on self-interest, and therefore amounts to saying that: 'I will adopt the moral point of view except in those cases when it's not in my best interest to do so.'[76]

Atheist Kurt Baier held that morality is based on self-interest without reference to religion.[77] Morality obviously can work in our own self-interest, and there's nothing wrong with that if it is motivated by the unselfish desire to do the right thing. It would be odd if God had created a universe in which being moral was ultimately bad for us! However, what does Baier mean by 'morality', or by things being 'good' or 'bad' for us? On such a pragmatic scheme he must mean something like, 'Morality is rules which it is in everyone's best interests to obey, and everyone's best interest is the maximisation of their own happiness.' Following what most people consider to be a moral path in life can often cut against a person's own 'best interests' defined in this way: 'There is such a thing as being "too good for this world", and the bad man often triumphs where a better man, who was bad only by halves, would fail.'[78] Unless being moral is part of a context wider than a pragmatic here and now, a context in which morality invariably contributes to our true 'best interests' (whatever they are), then there is little pragmatic reason to be moral here and now when morality doesn't serve our worldly 'best interests'. However:

> Baier excludes that kind of self-interest. He restricts self-interest to earthly values. If I respect other people's property, they will respect mine. If I don't harm people, they won't harm me. In that sense, he says, it is in my interest for everyone to act in the right way.[79]

If the ethical egoist attempts to allow for this defect by suggesting the existence of a wider context than the here and now, in which moral behaviour always contributes to our own best interests, this amounts to the admittance of a supernatural realm—and the egoist's underlying naturalism is thereby capitulated:

> It is rational for each man to seek his own happiness. It is also rational for each man to seek the general happiness. In the natural course of events, the actions most fitted to promote the agent's own happiness will not always coincide with those most fitted to promote the general happiness. For perfect coincidence, therefore, we must postulate . . . something like a God who will adequately reward the performance of duty and adequately punish its violation.[80]

Suppose I am about to be put in prison for some crime. It may be in the interest of the majority if the police do not accept the bribe I offer them to let me go free; but it would surely be in my 'best interest' if the police turned a blind eye (and in the police's 'best interest' so long as they don't get caught). Social theorists call this the 'free-rider' problem. Supposing it is true that as a society we would all be better off if everyone acted morally, it does not follow that individuals within society will best serve their interests by being moral: 'I might be better off if everyone acts morally and I, on selective occasions when I am not likely to be caught, disregard morality and simply do what I wish or what I think will benefit me.'[81]

Post-modern pragmatist Richard Rorty has said that, 'All you can say to persuade people is that in a liberal society people would be happier.'[82] Kai Nielsen has highlighted the problem with this approach:

> [A] rational amoralist will be an adroit free-rider. He will have an interest in other people being moral, since other people's immorality . . . will . . . adversely affect his own life . . . He will, if he is thoroughly rational and reflective, want others to restrict their exclusive pursuit of their self-interest. But what he reflectively wants for himself is another matter.[83]

Christianity provides a way to escape from the paradox of morality based on selfishness. Christianity calls upon us to value each person as an end in themselves made in God's image. We are to promote our own good, not out of selfishness, but because we should value ourselves as beings made by God. To disrespect ourselves is to disrespect God. As J.P. Moreland says: 'rewards from God are recognitions of my dignity. So I am justified in seeking them because in obtaining them, I affirm that I am a creature of value who is worthy of such rewards.'[84]

10. If there were objective values, then they would be entities or qualities or relations of a very strange sort, utterly different

from anything else in the universe. Correspondingly, if we were aware of them, it would have to be by some special faculty of moral perception or intuition, utterly different from our ordinary ways of knowing everything else.[85]

If Mackie's argument were simply that objective moral values, and our knowledge of them, would be unlike any other thing or mode of knowledge, then we might simply shrug our shoulders along with J.P. Moreland and point out that there just are things in existence unlike other things:

> If morals do exist, why would anyone expect them to be like other kinds of things? Mackie appears to be faulting moral values for not behaving like physical objects. But this is an absurd example of fault-finding. If moral values are not physical objects, then why should we expect them to be like physical objects?[86]

However, this is not all that is going on in this argument; an argument that J.L. Mackie called, 'The argument from queerness.'

The argument from queerness, given by Mackie, falls into two parts. The first part is about what exists (metaphysics), the second part is about our knowledge of what exists (epistemology). Both parts seem to be a simple application of Occam's famous metaphysical 'razor', a principle of inductive reason which asks us never to multiply the number or complexity of ideas beyond that which is necessary to giving an adequate account of the phenomena in question.

Metaphysically, objective moral values are, says Mackie, different from any other 'entities or qualities or relations'.[87] If we can dispense with them by extending our background knowledge (truths which can be brought to bear upon the likelihood of some explanation), this would be a good thing.

Epistemologically, knowledge of objective moral values would likewise, so Mackie argues, differ from our mode of knowledge in all other cases, and therefore should be razed to the ground by Occam's principle in the interests of a simplicity.

I agree with Mackie that a world where moral values are purely relative and can be 'explained away' as the consequence of evolutionary or social forces is simpler than a world with objective moral values and beings with a distinct mode of moral knowledge. However, I am not inclined to agree that the simpler hypothesis provided by an elimination of objective moral values, and a distinct knowledge of such, is an adequate explanation of the world. Nor am I sure that I want to grant that our mode of knowledge in relation to objective moral values is different from our mode of knowledge in all other cases. My reasons for doubt have been set out in my replies to those preceding arguments that sought to extend our 'background-knowledge' so as to render the existence of objective moral values unnecessary.

Mackie says the following about the epistemological extravagance of moral objectivity:

> When we ask the awkward question, how we can be aware of this authoritative prescriptivity . . . none of our ordinary accounts of sensory perception or introspection or the framing and confirming of explanatory hypotheses or inference or logical construction or conceptual analysis, or any combination of these, will provide a satisfactory answer; 'a special sort of intuition' is a lame answer.[88]

I disagree that 'a special sort of intuition' is 'a lame answer' to the question, 'How do you know that child abuse is wrong?' Mackie allows that 'moral sense' or 'intuition' is 'an initially more plausible description of what supplies many of our basic moral judgements than "reason"'.[89] Certainly, 'a special sort of intuition' is not a metaphysically precise answer, but not everything can be explained in metaphysically precise terms; especially where 'foundations' are concerned. For example, how do we know that the 'laws of reason' are valid? As I argued in the

Introduction, it is impossible to give reasons for this belief. We can only answer that, while we cannot, by the very nature of the subject in question, prove that the laws of reason are valid, yet we know that they are so. And what do we mean by this 'know' but that we believe that the belief, 'the laws of reason are valid', is a true belief? And what is this belief but an unshakeable gut instinct, or, to use another form of words, 'a special kind of intuition'? 'Intuition' is simply a knowing of something without proof.

If Mackie wants to insist on believing nothing for which he can only appeal to 'a special kind of intuition', then he will be in a great deal of trouble; for all reasoning rests upon just such an intuitive, innate act of belief. We cannot deny the validity of intuition simply because it is an intuition in one case, and not do so in all others, without contradicting our intuition that self-contradiction is a bad thing.

We explain things with reference to wider explanatory contexts. To avoid infinite regress we must acknowledge the existence of some explanatory context beyond which we cannot progress—a context that has no context. It is unreasonable to demand an explanation of a thing when we know that this thing is foundational in this way. If God is defined as the un-caused creator of all things except Himself, it is unreasonable to ask for an explanation of God's existence. God, if He exists, is the last word in 'brute facts'. It is unreasonable to request a defence of the validity of the laws of reason, because this request provokes anyone who takes up the challenge into assuming what they set out to prove. 'How do you know that something is wrong or right?' is not the same question as 'Why is something wrong or right?' The non-theistic objectivist might answer the 'Why?' question, 'Just because', while the theistic objectivist might answer, 'Because that thing is either in-line or out-of-line with God's character.' If asked why God's character is good, the theist would be well within their rights to reply, 'Just because', since this is a foundational issue.

God is the uncaused foundation, the widest explanatory context there is. Asking for reasons why God is good, or why 'X is not both X and not X', simply reveals a failure to grasp the foundational nature of these claims. The 'How is it. . ?' question can be plausibly answered by replying that humans are made 'in the image of God' who is 'good', and that we therefore share His concept of right and wrong (although, obviously, imperfectly). On this view, our moral judgements would be correct in so far as they corresponded with God's moral judgements. Our knowledge of objective moral values would then be a piece of 'introspection', a mode of knowledge rejected in this context by Mackie. As Descartes wrote in his Third Meditation:

> it is not to be thought strange that God, in creating me, should have put in me this idea to serve . . . as the mark that the workman imprints on his work; nor is it necessary that this mark should be something different from the work itself. But, from the mere fact that God created me, it is highly credible that he in some way produced me in his own image and likeness, and that I perceive this likeness, in which the idea of God is contained, by means of the same faculty by which I apprehend myself.[90]

Mackie considers the objection to his argument that:

> the best move for the moral objectivist is not to evade this issue, but to look for companions in guilt . . . If the understanding . . . is also the source of new simple ideas of so many other sorts [ideas of essence, number, identity, diversity, solidity, inertia, substance], may it not also be a power of immediately perceiving right and wrong?[91]

He admits that, 'This is an important counter to the argument from queerness'[92], and that, 'The only adequate reply to it would be to show how, on empiricist foundations, we can construct an account of the ideas and beliefs and knowledge that we have of all these matters.'[93]

If the human mind can know truths beyond those discoverable

by empirical methods (seeing, hearing etc., and combination of and abstraction from such knowledge), then we must admit the possibility of our knowing objective moral values even though these are not things which we see, hear, touch, taste or smell.

The offered advantage of the relativist picture of moral values is that moral values can be accounted for as natural reactions to sense data, eliminating the need for a special mode of knowledge whereby we access some 'Platonic realm' of objective values, cutting back from the philosophical undergrowth in one swipe of Occam's razor both a distinct class of things and a distinct mode of knowledge. (Of course, the objectivist may grant that our knowledge of moral values comes by empirical means). However, it is by no means clear that all human knowledge can be accounted for by 'an empiricism as those of Locke and Hume'. (For example, the gaining of knowledge by empirical means presupposes the existence of ability to distinguish X from not X.) Mackie seems to admit this when he writes that 'I can only state my belief that satisfactory accounts of most of these [things known] can be given in empirical terms.'[94] If only most things that we know can be accounted for on empiricist grounds, then there are some things which cannot be thus accounted for, and room remains for the operation of some form of innatism and/or intuitivism.

Mackie attempts to paper over this crack in the argument by suggesting that supposed metaphysical essences that resist such an empirical treatment, 'should be included, along with objective values, among the targets of the argument from queerness'.[95] This amounts to the setting up of an empiricist criterion of philosophically allowable entities; a criterion that I doubt would pass its own examination.

The argument from queerness objects that objective moral values are a distinct type of thing, and that our knowledge of them is of a similarly distinct mode, and that if we can eliminate them from our understanding of reality, then we should. We counter that our knowledge of objective moral values is not a distinct mode of knowledge, and that although a world-view devoid of objective moral values is simpler than one which includes them, such a conception of reality is inadequate.

The objectivist may accept Mackie's insistence upon empiricist origins of moral feelings and counter the relativist's sentence of 'death by Occam's razor' by appealing to the court of reasons to believe that objective moral values exist. It is therefore time that we move on to consider some reasons to beware of non-objectivism, and some reasons to accept objectivism.

Criticisms of moral relativism

1. Moral relativism is unlivable

A philosophy tutor once assigned his ethics class a paper to write, but they were free to choose their own topic. One brilliant student chose to defend his belief that there are no moral absolutes, that moral values are relative. After reading the well-written, well-documented essay, the tutor marked it 'fail'. Having received the disappointing grade, the student marched into the tutor's office and demanded to know what was wrong with his essay. 'There was nothing wrong with your paper,' replied the tutor, 'I just didn't like the folder it came in.' 'That's not fair!' protested the student, 'You should have graded me on the content of my paper, not on the colour of the folder!' Then the tutor asked, 'Didn't your paper argue that moral views are a matter of taste, like some people liking chocolate ice-cream, and other people preferring vanilla?' 'Yes,' agreed the student. 'Well,' said the tutor, 'I don't like the colour of this folder, so you get a fail.' Suddenly, the student realised what was going on—he had been caught by his own words. His expectation to be treated fairly revealed a belief in moral absolutes that he had been previously unwilling to acknowledge.[96]

While unlivability does not directly prove moral relativism false, it surely raises a question mark over the theory. Relativism might seem appealing in abstract, but it is a different matter as soon as we begin to apply it to ourselves in specific cases.

Relativism just does not fit with life as we experience or live it; 'we simply must affirm objective moral values in order to make sense of our lives'.[97] The undesirable results of moral relativism do not disprove it. That something is uncomfortable does not entail it is untrue. However, the results of moral relativism do tug strongly against something within us. We cannot believe that Belsen was merely unpleasant to our sensibilities. We surely want to say that such indiscriminate slaughter is wrong in a sense that goes beyond our feelings or the feelings of our culture. As Richard Swinburne says, 'One is inclined to say that the man who says that there was nothing morally wrong in Hitler's exterminating the Jews is saying something false.'[98]

2. Moral relativism makes the advocacy of progress in morality impossible

Progress is movement towards a goal. Only if morality is objective can one type of society be objectively better than another. If there is no such thing as an objectively better society, then any social alteration is mere change and never progress. If you think that a society which outlaws slavery is really and truly better than a society built upon slave labour, then you think that moral values are objective:

> No one . . . today would argue that a society that discriminates, abuses and kills people purely on the basis of their race or skin colour is morally equivalent to one that does not. What is more, there is such a thing as moral progress or deterioration over time . . . Even if we don't know how we know it, the fact is we know it, and we know that we know it.[99]

If the majority rules, the greatest number being right by definition, the minority are necessarily wrong, and are open to any exploitation and abuse to which the majority agrees:

If moral judgements are defined in terms of that society's central values, no critic of these central values can use moral arguments against them. In a society in which the dominant view is that women shouldn't be allowed to vote, anyone advocating enfranchisement for women would be suggesting something immoral relative to the values of that society.[100]

3. If moral relativism were true, moral debate across cultural boundaries would be impossible

The only way of altering the moral views of other cultures would be by force. This is the reverse of what normative moral relativists seek in emphasising tolerance. Moral objectivism leaves open the possibility of moral debate and change for the better through discussion: 'unless there is an objective moral law, there is no standpoint from which we can critique the moral behaviour or ideologies of others.'[101]

A moral relativist cannot both be consistent and hold that toleration is objectively better than intolerance. A moral relativist can have no argument against those who see no value in tolerance, because they cannot say that tolerance is better than intolerance. Nor can they say that toleration is less valuable than intolerance. A moral relativist must assert that tolerance and intolerance are equally valid moral values. This amounts to holding that there is no distinction between good and evil; ending lives is as 'good' for the Nazi camp commander as saving lives is for the doctor. Saying that contradictory assertions are equally valid also involves the moral relativist in a relativism about knowledge unless they revise what they mean by such assertions.

Arguments for moral objectivism

1. Moral utterances look like straightforward propositional expressions, and so probably have a truth-value

While having a truth-value is not a sufficient condition of having an objective truth-value, it is a necessary condition, and so this argument is a useful one to the moral objectivist: Take a typical moral utterance, 'P', such as, 'You should love your enemies.' 'P' can be put together with a range of modifiers, such as 'it is true that', 'it is a fact that', 'it is the case that', and 'it is false that', which standardly apply to propositions but not to commands or exclamations. Moreover, 'P' can be used perfectly naturally in standard statements such as: 'I believe that', 'I know that', and 'I wonder if.'

Assertions such as 'P' can be used in straightforward arguments such as: '(1) I should love my enemies. (2) X is my enemy. (3) Therefore I should love X.' In this way 'P' combines in argument with utterances which are uncontroversially propositional, factual and non-evaluative, in a way which is hard to understand if 'P' is not propositional. To take the above example, '(1) I should love my enemies (moral). (2) X is my enemy (factual). (3) I should love X (moral).'

Given that moral utterances look and behave like other uncontroversially propositional, factual utterances, it is reasonable to infer that moral utterances are propositional and factual, and that moral utterances therefore have truth conditions.[102] Given that moral utterances have truth conditions, the question becomes whether these truth conditions are subjective or objective.

2. Moral objectivism explains the sense of duty we associate with morality

Moral relativism is simply collective moral subjectivism, and both boil down to the assertion that we ought to follow the dictates of our conscience, whether that conscience is individual or collective. No one advocates doing what you think you ought not to do, however that 'ought' is understood or explained away; and everyone agrees that it is sensible to do whatever one thinks one should do. The only reason a relativist could advance for following the collective conscience of 'society' would depend upon the judgement of their own individual conscience (which they would probably explain as determined by society and, ultimately, by evolutionary forces). However, relativism cannot provide a coherent account of this moral 'ought'.

Even if different people's consciences tell them to do or avoid doing different things everyone accepts the moral absolute, 'Never disobey your conscience.' But where does conscience get such authority? There are only four possible answers: 1) from something less than the individual, 2) from the individual, 3) from society, 4) from something greater than the individual or society. However, individuals cannot be obligated by something less than the individual (such as animal instincts). Nor can we obligate ourselves absolutely, for we are not absolute and do not have the right to demand obedience from anyone. If we bind ourselves, we can let ourselves go free, and so no self-binding can be absolute. Nor can society obligate the individual absolutely, for quantity does not make quality and society is not 'God'. The only possible source of absolute moral obligation is something greater than either the individual or society: 'This binds my will, with rightful demands for complete obedience.'[103]

Bertrand Russell, a moral subjectivist, admitted that his subjectivism didn't account for his moral feelings. Russell took as an example the fact that he would oppose any suggestion that bull-fighting should be introduced in Britain:

> In opposing the proposal, I should feel, not only that I was expressing my desires, but that my desires in the matter are right, whatever that may mean. As a matter of argument, I can, I think, show that I am not guilty of any logical inconsistency in holding to the [prescriptive] interpretation of ethics and at the same time expressing strong ethical preferences. But in feeling I am not satisfied . . . I can only say that, while my own opinions as to ethics do not satisfy me, other people's satisfy me still less.[104]

I suggest that Russell's beliefs about ethics failed to match up with what his heart told him because his heart was right and his philosophy was wrong. Russell fears being 'guilty' of logical inconsistency. The language of moral objectivity slips through from his 'heart' into his intellectual defence of his moral subjectivism.

3. Belief that moral values are objective is common to almost all people of every era

A.E. Taylor was surely right when he wrote that 'it is an undeniable fact that men . . . hold that there is a difference between right and wrong; there are things which they ought to do and other things which they ought not to do'.[105] That there has been some disagreement about which values are objective is beside the point, for there is an almost universal agreement that morality is objective. As J.L. Mackie admitted, 'the main tradition of European moral philosophy includes the . . . claim, that there are objective moral values.'[106]

I have already dealt with the objection to objectivism that people have different moral values. First, there is in fact wide moral agreement. Second, some differences in action do not arise from different moral beliefs, but can be traced to different non-moral beliefs. Third, that people disagree about something is an indication of assumed objectivity, not assumed subjectivity. Either the vast majority of humankind has been wrong about this most fundamental aspect of their lives, or they have been right. It is more plausible to believe that they have been right than that they have been wrong. Therefore it is most plausible to believe that morality is objective.

It might be objected that people can be mistaken, and that we now know people to have been mistaken, for example, in believing the world to be flat. However, if the witness of twenty people contradicted the witness of one person, whose testimony (all other things being equal) would you be inclined to believe? Similarly, if every preceding century gives testimony in a matter where there has been no advance in methods of proof or discovery, and this testimony contradicts the beliefs of our own century, which should we choose to believe? I suggest that to choose our own age over all others is to judge the truth of a proposition by the calendar. The examples of believing the earth to be flat and believing morality to be objective are not comparable. The relativity of moral opinions is an empirical matter that could in principle be disproved by increasing knowledge. The objectivity of moral law is a philosophical matter where the available information remains constant.

4. Moral relativism makes a nonsense out of the laws of reason

If there are no objective moral values then it cannot be objectively true that I ought to be rational and self-consistent, or that I ought to value truth over falsehood and knowledge over delusion. What is wrong with holding false beliefs if there is no such thing as objective right and wrong? 'Why should you,' Nietzsche asked, 'pay attention to the truth?'[107] We certainly could not answer that we objectively ought not to hold false beliefs; but then why shouldn't we believe that objective moral values exist, even if they do not? For the relativist there can be no objective 'shouldn't' about it. The relativist must surely agree that there could be nothing objectively wrong in believing in the existence of objective moral values. There could be something factually wrong in such a belief. But why desire factually accurate, true beliefs? The desire for truth cannot be rationally justified without begging the question. Nor can the relativist say that truth objectively ought to be believed in preference to falsehood, or that we objectively ought to be rational and play by the rules of logic (even if, as a matter of fact, we cannot do otherwise), for they admit that without God there is no objective ought. If the existence of objective moral values depends upon the existence of God, and God does not exist, then the desire to be rational and to believe truly rather than falsely, is merely a rationally and morally indefensible component of our 'passional nature' (to use William James' phrase).

5. Moral objectivism makes much better sense of our common-sense use of language

Consider what happens when two people have a moral disagreement. They say things like, 'That's not fair: you promised,' or 'How would you like it if someone did that to you?', or, 'Leave her alone, she isn't hurting you.' We've all said such things. In saying such things we do not merely mean that we do not like what the other person is doing. Our dislike of their actions is included in our comments, but there is more to what we say under such circumstances than that. We are appealing to a standard of conduct that we claim the other person has violated. Our accusation 'You're not being fair!' might be parcelled out thus: 'There is such a thing as being fair. You ought to be fair. You aren't being fair. Therefore you are in the wrong.' We expect the other person to know about the standard to which we implicitly refer; we never feel the need to ask, 'Have you heard of fairness?' Now, the person you have accused of cheating does not gawp at you in amazement that you should appeal to a standard. Nor, generally speaking, do they say, 'Who cares about being fair?' What usually happens is that they try to show that their conduct actually conforms to the standard to which you have appealed, and that you have made a mistaken value judgement. The existence and validity of the standard is generally unquestioned, and this assumption is so basic to our thinking that it is hard to imagine thinking without it.

There are objective moral values

None of the arguments in favour of moral non-objectivism which I have considered withstood examination. I have advanced several criticisms of moral non-objectivism which bolster the objectivist case by default. I have also advanced several positive arguments for moral objectivism, from existential and explanatory adequacy, to arguments from authority and common consent. I take it that the first premise of the moral argument for the existence of God, that there exist objective moral values, is vindicated. I turn now to some common objections to the second premise.

Objections to the second premise

I will consider two challenges to the second premise of the moral argument which try to show some difficulty in holding that objective moral values depend upon God.

1. Bertrand Russell criticised the view that right and wrong depends upon God as follows:

> if you are quite sure there is a difference between right and wrong, you are then in this situation: is that difference due to God's fiat or is it not? If it is due to God's fiat, then for God himself there is no difference between right and wrong, and it is no longer a significant statement to say that God is good. If you are going to say, as theologians do, that God is good, you must then say that right and wrong have some meaning which is independent of God's fiat, because God's fiats are good and not bad independently of the mere fact that He made them. If you are going to say that, you will then have to say that it is not only through God that right and wrong came into being, but that they are in their essence logically anterior to God.[108]

Russell's dilemma is a false one. The theist may claim that the moral law is neither outside and superior to God, nor arbitrary and unworthy of God. Rather than flowing from God's will, the moral law may be rooted in God's unchangeable nature. If morality is based on God's nature and not on God's will, then the apparent dilemma is resolved. There is no ultimate beyond God to which He is subject; He is subject only to the ultimacy of the good within himself. God cannot be less than absolutely good; His nature demands that he be absolutely good. And it cannot be said that God is arbitrary, for He cannot will contrary to His nature. God cannot decide to be unloving, nor can He desire that cruelty and injustice be performed for their own sake. God's will must perform in accordance with His unchangeably good nature.

Right and wrong are not measured against something beyond God. Nor are they defined by God's will, as if God were some despot who could arbitrarily decide that rape was going to be a good thing next week for a change. Right and wrong are measured against God's essential, unchanging character; a character that will not admit of 'arbitrary' contradictions. Rape can never be a good thing; and although one may be able to imagine situations in which rape might be the lesser of two evils, it remains an evil. 'Right' and 'Wrong' are not little removable labels attached by God's 'fiat' to events which would otherwise have no moral status, and which God can swap around at will. Things like rape, or child abuse, are intrinsically wrong; and this intrinsicness (to coin a word) is grounded in God's unalterable character:

> God's commands could not be arbitrary and capricious in the way the critic envisions. God, for instance, could not command us to kill innocent children 'just for the fun of it', since this would be inconsistent with God's nature . . . Thus, the criticism in question simply fails to apply, and, accordingly, it remains perfectly reasonable to maintain that God's nature is the ultimate origin of the ethical principles we believe to be true.[109]

2. Kai Nielsen has advanced an argument which runs as follows:

> we can claim that God is good . . . only if we already have in mind a standard of goodness by which [God] can be judged. But if this is true . . . then it can, of course, no longer be claimed that the ethical principles that originate in God provide the ultimate ethical standard. Rather, our own ethical intuitions must be acknowledged to be the ultimate standard.[110]

'to oversimplify, instead of morality requiring religion, the very possibility of even understanding the concept of God and in making a religious response presupposes some minimal moral understanding.'[111]

If we cannot call God 'good' then the second premise of the argument from morality is in serious trouble. The answer to this apparently common-sense realisation is that, while we assess God's goodness with reference to the moral law that we find within ourselves, this law got there from God.

Suppose someone inherits a copy of the key to a certain lock. Suppose they then discover the original key, and that by comparing their key with the original they concluded that this other key fits the same lock as does their key. Suppose they argue that, since they judged the key they found with reference to the key they already had, the key they already had must be the original! Wouldn't that be silly? But isn't that like Nielsen arguing that, if we judge God by an ethical standard we find within ourselves, then it is this standard that must be the original, and that God therefore has no role to play in morality? 'Believers need not grant . . . that they judge God by an ethical standard that is separate from, and more ultimate than, God. They can claim, rather, that they judge God by a standard that God has brought it about that they possess.'[112]

Nielsen has, without realising it, given a good statement of the paucity of his own argument:

> in order to understand that something is worthy of worship, you have to have at least some elementary criteria or understanding of what worthiness is [so far I agree, but there follows an unjustifiable assertion that he will recant next sentence], and that is not itself derived from God. Or to put the point more accurately, though rather pedantically [and contradicting his assertion of a moment before], though it may be derived in a causal sense—since everything comes from God—it is not derived in a justificatory or logical sense from God or a belief in God. Our understanding of these things is quite logically prior to any religious response.[113]

I agree that 'Our understanding of these things is quite logically prior to any religious response', and my argument does not require that this be so. I do not know what Nielsen means by saying that, even if our understanding of 'good' derives 'in a causal sense' from God, it does not do so 'in a justificatory or logical sense' (from 'a belief in God' I am happy to allow since atheists are clearly able to tell right from wrong). Our knowledge of 'good' does not require an explicit knowledge of the criteria, only an implicit (we might say innate) knowledge—a true belief about what good is. J.P. Moreland's response to Nielsen's argument is spot on:

> I might have to look at a road map of Chicago before I can know where Chicago is, so the road map might be first in the order of epistemology, but Chicago had to exist prior to the fact of the road map. Similarly, God's goodness would exist prior to the fact of finite, derived goodness, though conceptually or epistemologically, I might have to understand what 'goodness' means before I would be able to make a judgement that God is good.[114]

To say that 'God is good' is to say that God is the origin and standard of our ethical judgements, and is Himself consistent with those judgements.

Arguments for God's goodness

There are at least two purely philosophical arguments for holding God to be good. The first is C.S. Lewis' argument that, unless we trust the goodness of the ultimate reality upon which we depend, then we have no basis upon which to affirm any moral judgements. Yet we do affirm moral judgements. In doing so we assume that the source and standard of those judgements is itself good.

The second argument is that: a) being a rational agent, God couldn't do anything unless He thought it were a good thing to do; b) being all-knowing, God couldn't be mistaken about the morality of any possible action; and c) being unconstrained by outside forces, God is able to carry out any action that He wants, which, given a) and b), will be only good actions. [115] God is ready, willing and able to do all morally obligatory actions, no morally bad actions, and only morally good actions.

Having defended the existence of objective moral values, and the possibility of objective moral values depending upon God, it is time to recapitulate the expanded version of the argument with which we began:

The argument from the existence of objective morality restated

Premise 1) There are objective moral values.

This premise has already been established. The distinction between good and evil is an objective distinction. We objectively ought to do good and to avoid evil.

Premise 2) Objective moral values either require the existence of 'a personal ground', or not.

These options are exhaustive. The moral law either is, or is not, ultimately grounded in a personal ground beyond the actual or possible mental states of finite individuals or any collection of finite individuals.

2i) If objective moral values do not require the existence of a personal ground, then they must be explicable in non-personal terms.

Again, these options are exhaustive. A moral law grounded in finite individuals would be a subjective law, and we are looking for the ground of an objective moral law. If there is nothing personal behind the moral law, then that law must be explained without reference to something impersonal. The only alternative to an explanation that posits a transcendent personal ground of objective moral values, is an explanation that posits a non-personal explanation.

2ii) Objective moral values are not explicable in non-personal terms.

W. David Beck writes that, 'This point is not especially controversial. Most naturalists concede it.'[116] The paucity of non-personal explanations of moral values has already been demonstrated. We have considered, and rejected, several naturalistic accounts of morality which seek to ground values in the decisions or feelings of finite personal beings. None of the theories considered were able to accommodate objective moral values.

Any hypothesis that seeks to ground objective moral values in the existence of finite personal beings thrown up by an impersonal, purposeless process of chance, is doomed. An a-moral, non-personal and purposeless natural process can no more account for the existence of objective moral values than nothing can produce something.

There are three arguments that show why objective moral values cannot be explained in non-personal terms:

The first argument is based upon the observation that in the moral law we meet objective prescriptions. Only persons can make prescriptions (when did you last hear a banana demand anything?). Therefore, there must be a moral law prescriber beyond individual or collective humanity: 'All legislation has a legislator. There can't be an absolute moral law without an absolute moral law Giver, and that's God.'[117] Pointing out that a computer, which is not a personal being, could make a demand doesn't weaken this argument, since computers must be built and programmed by personal beings who can and do make demands.

In her influential paper 'Modern Moral Philosophy', G.E.M. Anscombe argued that the notions of moral obligation and duty only made sense within a theistic framework. She argued that since secularism has left the theistic framework behind, philosophy needed to recognise the redundancy of traditional morality and ditch the notions of moral right and wrong:

> concepts of obligation, and duty—*moral* obligation and *moral* duty, that is to say—and of what is *morally* right and wrong, and of the *moral* sense of 'ought', ought to be jettisoned if this is psychologically possible; because they are survivals, or derivatives from survivals, from an earlier conception of ethics which no longer generally survives, and are only harmful without it.[118]

Anscombe asserted that the emotive effect of moral language is 'the survival of a concept outside the framework of thought which made it a really intelligible one'.[119] Of the idea of an objective moral law Anscombe said, 'Naturally it is not possible to have such a conception unless you believe in God as a lawgiver; like Jews, Stoics, and Christians.'[120] Therefore, if there is an objective moral law, telling and obliging us to do good and avoid evil, then there must be a divine 'law-giver'.

The second argument starts with the fact of moral obligation. In the case of things that I ought or ought not to do, I have a duty to do or to refrain from doing something. But how could something impersonal morally obligate me? The law of gravity is an impersonal force in that it operates on me such that without any opposing force, I fall down. When I trip up, falling to the ground is something I am caused to do (so long as the law of gravity holds); but is it something I ought to do? Moral laws, on the other hand, prescribe things I objectively ought (or ought not) to do, but which I am not forced to do against my will. In matters of the moral law, I have a freedom that I lack in matters of physical law. A moral law, unlike a physical law, is not something which simply is the case, but something which ought to be the case.

To attempt to get from what has to be to what ought to be is to commit the naturalistic fallacy:

> If all there is is matter and what it does [the non-personal], then all there is is [what has to be]. There can be no 'ought'. How can these actions actually be right or wrong? Only if there is a difference between is and ought. But how can there be a difference between is and ought in a world that just is?[121]

Since I cannot be morally obligated to something non-personal, I must be obligated to something personal. After all, I cannot break a promise made to a fish-bowl, because one cannot make promises to fish-bowls, only to other personal beings: 'Responsibility is possible if there is a person to be responsible to. We are all bound by the "law of gravity", but we are not responsible to it.'[122] However, although I can be obligated to other people, an objective moral obligation cannot be grounded in either other people or myself. As Richard Taylor put it, the idea of a moral obligation more important and binding than those imposed upon us by other individuals or by the state is only intelligible if we make reference 'to some lawmaker higher . . . than those of the state'.[123] Such obligations 'can . . . be understood as those that are imposed by God . . . But what if this higher-than-human lawgiver is no longer taken into account? . . . the concept of moral obligation [is] unintelligible apart from the idea of God.'[124]

Therefore, objective moral obligation must be grounded in a transcendent personal reality to whom we are objectively obligated. Our obligations to other people must be derivative of our obligation to a transcendent personal reality to whom our primary obligation is owed.

The third argument is that, since objective moral value judgements require an objective moral standard, and as no moral standard could exist in matter, and no objective moral standard could exist in finite minds, there must be an objective moral standard in an infinite mind. Hastings Rashdall used this argument:

> Only if we believe in the existence of a Mind . . . which is the source of whatever is true in our own moral judgements, can we rationally think of the moral ideal as no less real than the world itself . . . A moral ideal can exist no-where and no-how but in a mind; an absolute moral ideal can exist only in a Mind from which all reality is derived. Our moral ideal can only claim objective validity in so far as it can rationally be regarded as the revelation of a moral ideal eternally existing in the mind of God.[125]

2iii) Objective moral values therefore require explanation in terms of 'a personal ground'.

Given that 1) the objective moral law must be explained either as the result of non-personal forces, or in terms of a transcendent personal ground (whether or not that agent operates through intermediary impersonal causes); and that 2) the action of non-personal forces (alone) cannot explain either the existence of objective moral obligation, or the existence of an objective moral standard; it follows that 3) the transcendent personal explanation, being the only explanation left, must be correct. As W. David Beck argues:

> Only persons can be a source of values, yet no finite and socially conditioned person is in a position to determine authoritatively the values appropriate for other persons. So, if there really are objective values, there must be some 'ultimate' person who has the moral authority to set the standards of right and wrong.[126]

A.E. Taylor agrees:

> there could be no law for the right direction of the will if there were no wills to direct. But were there no will in existence except the wills

of human beings, who are so often ignorant of the law of right and so often defy it, it is not apparent what the validity of the law could mean. Recognition of the validity of the law thus seems to carry with it a reference to an intelligence which has not, like our own, to make acquaintance with it piecemeal, slowly and with difficulty, but has always been in full and clear possession of it, and a will which does not, like our own, often set it at nought, but is guided by it in all its operations.[127]

2iv) This personal ground of objective moral values must be the independent creator who has always existed and is ultimate goodness personified.

Since something non-personal cannot morally obligate us, or make moral prescriptions, the moral law must be based in something personal. 'Personality,' as Dr James W. Sire writes, 'is a necessary aspect of any foundation for morality.'[128] Personhood implies rationality: 'Personality requires two basic characteristics: (1) self-reflection and (2) self-determination.'[129] Self-reflection requires thought, and thinking involves reasoning. Self-determination requires the possession of goals and formulated ways of achieving those goals; which requires reason. This personal origin of objective values must Himself be good. Indeed, He must be goodness personified. In order to say it was not good, we would have to make a judgement by reference to a personal source of moral obligation that was good:

> You must trust the universe in one respect even in order to condemn it in every other . . . unless we allow ultimate reality to be moral, we cannot morally condemn it . . . condemnation of reality carries in its heart an unconscious act of allegiance to the same reality as the source of our moral standards.[130]

The moral law is not something that could have been 'invented' out of thin air. We cannot just 'make up' objective moral values. Upon what would we base our judgement? If we had no reason for our choice of what is right and wrong, then there would be no reason to believe that the things we said were 'right' were right, or that the things we said were 'wrong' were wrong. Morality would be relative. On the other hand, if our judgement of what things are good and bad is a rational one, there must be some standard of right and wrong that exists before we use it in making our judgement, else we would be begging-the-question. The moral law (like the laws of reason) is not something that can come into being, it must be something that has always existed, which has never not existed. Since the moral law depends upon its source, that source must always have existed.

2v) Such a being can appropriately be called 'God'.

An independent source of moral standards who has always existed, and who is goodness personified, can surely be appropriately called 'God'. The attributes of the being who lies at the conclusion of the argument from objective morality are obviously consistent with things traditionally taught about the nature of God. God is personal: 'God our Father, who loved us' (2 Thessalonians 2:16); rational, 'In the beginning was the Word [Logos], and the Word was with God, and the Word was God' (John 1:1); and totally-good, 'Good and upright is the Lord' (Psalm 25:8).

Conclusion. Therefore God exists.

Epilogue: God and evil revisited

If there is no objective standard of right and wrong, a standard that is 'out there' and independent of us, then we cannot judge between our condemnation of the Holocaust and Hitler's approval. At Auschwitz the words of Hitler are clearly stated: 'I freed Germany from the stupid and degrading fallacies of conscience and morality . . . we will train young people before whom the world will tremble. I want young people capable of violence—imperious, relentless and cruel.'[131]

Would you sign your name under these terrible words? Surely not. Yet I suggest that you cannot oppose Hitler's sentiments, if you have no ground upon which to stand and say, 'It is not conscience and morality that are degrading fallacies, but your philosophy of "might makes right,"' then you validate Hitler by default. If there is no privileged opinion about what is right and what is wrong, then all opinions are equally valid, and hence equally invalid. Nietzsche was right when he wrote that,

> When one gives up the Christian faith, one pulls the right to Christian morality out from under one's feet. This morality is by no means self-evident. Christianity is a system, a whole view of things thought out together. By breaking one main concept out of it, the faith in God, one breaks the whole. It stands or falls with faith in God.[132]

To make objective moral judgements we must recognise the existence of an objective moral standard: 'All injustice presupposes a standard of justice by which it is judged to be not-just.'[133] There is, on the subjective view, no logical contradiction involved in saying, 'Torture is good,' because, as Bertrand Russell said, 'There is no outside standard to show that our valuation is wrong.'[134] Such a statement is factually correct or incorrect depending upon the feelings of the majority—feelings that can be manipulated by the minority. Only on the belief that there exists an independent standard can saying, 'Torture is good,' be logically contradictory. As F.C. Copleston said in his debate with Russell: 'the possibility of criticising the accepted moral code presupposes that there is an objective standard.'

Kai Nielsen has written, 'Take something like "It is wrong to torture people." . . . I can't realistically conceive of that ever dropping out [of our moral "reflective equilibrium"]. But in theory you could allow for the logical possibility of its dropping out. But that is not worrisome. It is logically possible that I might start to shrink right before you as well.'[135] However, in many cases torture has dropped out of society's 'reflective equilibrium'. If it is not contradictory to deny that torture is wrong, then torture is not necessarily wrong. I find that worrying.

If we admit no standard by which to make objective moral judgements—reducing every moral ought and ought not to a 'personally I like/don't like'—then we cannot use the argument against the existence of God from the existence of evil. The argument from evil presupposes the existence of objective moral values in the light of which some things are not merely 'wrong for me/my culture', but wrong for everyone, everywhere, and at all times. The admission that the Holocaust was objectively wrong leads to the admission that there must be some standard beyond ourselves in the light of which we know this to be so. The attempt to use the argument from evil to disprove the existence of God comes up against the moral argument for the existence of God.

From dusk till dawn

An excellent illustration of how the recognition of evil, far from disproving the existence of God, actually leads us to recognise God's existence, is the film *From Dusk Till Dawn*. Actor George Cloony plays a bank robber sprung out of jail by his psychotic brother, played by Quentin Tarantino. They embark upon a bloody crime spree as they flee the law, heading for a rendezvous with some gangsters across the Mexican border. They take a minister and his two children hostage in order to smuggle themselves through the border post. This minister is suffering a crisis of faith because his wife was killed in a car crash.

Making it across the border they come to the truckers' stop where they have arranged to have their meeting. After a brief fight with an obnoxious bouncer, they enter the truckers' stop, order some drinks, and sit down to watch the dancing girls. The bouncer who was trounced earlier returns with some of his mates, and a fight ensues in which Cloony and Tarantino kill one of the bouncers, and Tarantino has a knife stuck through his hand. At the sight of blood, the bouncers, bar-staff, band and dancing girls all turn into vampires, and kill Tarantino! At this point the film switches from crime-spree road movie to horror. Only once the director has made his point do we realise that there is a common theme linking these two disparate sections of the film. Lots of bloody mayhem with a touch of black humour ensues as our two anti-heroes and their hostages join forces to fight the common foe.

During lulls in the action George Cloony's character makes the following observations: 'I can hardly believe my eyes, but here we have an embodiment of evil. If such evil exists, then surely there must be an ultimate power of good in the universe as well.' I paraphrase, but you get the point. All this is quite ironic, given that our two criminals are themselves rather nasty pieces of work. However, evil as they are, they pale into insignificance next to the vampire brood. George Cloony's character discovers his common humanity by fighting alongside his former hostages. He uses what amounts to the moral argument for the existence of God to reignite the faith of the minister, who is thereby enabled to bless water ('holy water' being deadly to vampires) and wield a rather effective crucifix. By the time dawn arrives, killing all the vampires when the sun's rays fall upon a rotating disco glitter-globe, only George Cloony and the minister's daughter are left alive to go their separate ways.

The film points to the existence of objective evil (first murder, rape, and lust—then to ultimate evil as symbolised by the vampires), and asks how we can recognise these things as evil without also acknowledging an objective standard of good. The film turns around the argument against the existence of God from the existence of evil (the minister loses his faith because his wife is killed) into the argument for the existence of God (the minister regaining his faith when he is forced to take seriously the implications of the existence of evil). Within that aspect of existence which most shakes our faith in the existence of a good God lies one of the strongest foundations for such faith. As philosopher William Lane Craig has said, the existence of evil 'actually demonstrates God's existence because without God there wouldn't be any foundation for calling anything evil'.[136] The alternative to recognising the existence of God is shown in the dispassionate amorality embodied by George Cloony's character before his meeting with an evil greater than himself—first in his psychotic brother, and then in the vampires.

Conclusion

The form of the moral argument is plainly valid: there either are or are not objective moral values. If there are objective moral values, their existence either depends, or does not depend, upon the existence of something beyond individual or collective humanity. If it depends upon a transcendent cause, that cause is either personal, or not. If impersonal explanations do not suffice, then the personal explanation must be true. It is a simple matter to prove that this 'person' must be all-good, eternal, and connected in some way with our existence. If the name 'God' is an acceptable term for this being (and it surely is), then we may say that 'God' exists.

None of the arguments against the first premise of moral objectivism survived examination. Moral relativism leads to an implausible and unliveable account of moral language, of moral obligation, and contradicts the judgement of philosophical orthodoxy, and the majority of people. Moral objectivism, on the other hand, provides a coherent account of moral language, of moral obligation, and conforms to the judgement of the vast majority of humanity throughout history.

Neither argument advanced against the second premise, that objective moral values are grounded in the existence of God, withstood examination. The supposed dilemma that moral values are either arbitrary (if based on God's will), or independent of God (if not based on His will), is broken by seeing moral value as inherent within God's character. That we must recognise goodness before being able to say that God is good is no more disturbing to the grounding of moral value in God than is the fact that we must be able to read a map to find our destination. The map, although 'before' our destination in 'the order of knowing', is still 'after' our destination in 'the order of being', as it is dependent upon the geography it models.

The most plausible explanation of the existence of objective moral values, and our knowledge (however imperfect) of these values (most fundamentally of the objective distinction between right and wrong) is that there exists an all-good, personal, rational and eternal being who has made humans in His image. Being made in God's image means that introspection provides a familiar and unproblematic mode of knowledge by which we know right from wrong. It would therefore seem reasonable, for the sake of economy, to hold that God created everything other than himself, and is in all likelihood the all-powerful creator. I conclude that the moral argument for the existence of God, as given here, is a valid deductive argument from true premises, which therefore proves its conclusion. Which conclusion is harder to swallow: that morality is subjective, or that God exists?

Recommended reading

W. David Beck, 'God's Existence' in *In Defence of Miracles, A Comprehensive Case For God's Action In History*, R. Douglas Geivett and Gary R. Habermas, eds. (Apollos, 1997). (2)

Paul Chamberlain, *Can We Be Good Without God?* (IVP, 1996). (2)

William Lane Craig, 'The Indispensability of Theological Meta-Ethical Foundations for morality', *http://www.leaderu. com/offices/billcraig/docs/meta-eth.html* (1)

Roger Crisp and Michael Slote eds, *Virtue Ethics*, (Oxford, 1997). (4)

Stephen C. Evans, *Why Believe?* (IVP 1996). (1)

Norman L. Geisler and Paul D. Feinberg, *Introduction to Philosophy—A Christian Perspective*, (Baker, 1997), part five. (1)

Gilbert Harman and Judith Thompson, *Moral Relativism and Moral Objectivity* (Blackwells, 1996). (4)

Arthur F. Holmes, *Fact, Value and God* (Apollos, 1997). (3)

Peter Kreeft, *The Best Things In Life* (IVP, 1984). (1)

Peter Kreeft, *C.S. Lewis for the third Millennium* (Ignatius, 1994).

Peter Kreeft, *The Journey* (IVP, 1996). (1)

Peter Kreeft and Ronald Tacelli, *Handbook of Christian Apologetics* (Monarch, 1995). (1)

C.S. Lewis, *Mere Christianity* (Fount, 1986). (1)

C.S. Lewis, *The Abolition of Man* (Fount, 1978). (3)

C.S. Lewis, 'The Poison of Subjectivism' in *Christian Reflections* (Fount, 1981). (2)

J.L. Mackie, *Ethics—Inventing Right and Wrong* (Penguin, 1990). (4)

Josh McDowell and Norman L. Geisler, *Love Is Always Right* (Word 1996). (1)

J.P. Moreland, *Scaling the Secular City* (Baker, 1987). (3)

J.P. Moreland and Kai Nielsen, *Does God Exist? The Debate between Theists and Atheists* (Prometheus, 1993). (3) The two essays on morality are of particular interest.

Kai Nielsen, 'Why Should I be Moral? Revisited' in *American Philosophical Quarterly*, 21. (3)

Michael Peterson *et al*, *Reason and Religious Belief* (Oxford, 1991). (3)

James Rachels, ed., *Ethical Theory 1—The Question of Objectivity* (Oxford, 1998). (4)

James W. Sire, *The Universe Next Door*, third edition (IVP, 1997). (2)

James W. Sire, *Why Should Anyone Believe Anything At All?* (IVP, 1994). (2)

Keith Ward, *The Battle For The Soul* (Hodder and Stoughton, 1985). (3)

Ravi Zacharias, *Can Man Live Without God?* (Word, 1995). (1)

Films to see

From Dusk Till Dawn (Dir. Robert Rodriguez).

Notes

1. For C.S. Lewis' exposition of the moral argument, see book one of *Mere Christianity* (Fount, 1986); *The Abolition of Man* (Fount, 1978); and 'The Poison of Subjectivism' in *Christian Reflections* (Fount, 1980). Other philosophers who have defended similar arguments include: W. David Beck, F.C. Copleston, Paul Chamberlain, William Lane Craig, Norman L. Geilser, Peter Kreeft, H.P. Owen, Hastings Rashdall, W.R. Sorley and A.E. Taylor.

2. W. David Beck, 'God's Existence' in *In Defence of Miracles*, Douglas Geivett and Gary R. Habermas, eds (Apollos, 1997), pp.160–161.

3. R.M. Hare, *The Language of Morals* (1960), p.1

4. C.S. Lewis, 'The Poison of Subjectivism' in *Christian Reflections* (Fount, 1981).

5. Richard Swinburne, *Responsibility and Atonement* (Oxford, 1989), pp.9, 17–18.

6. C.L. Stevenson, 'The Nature of Ethical Disagreement' in *Ethical Theory 1—The Question of Objectivity*, James Rachels ed., (Oxford, 1998), p.43.

7. *Ibid.*, p.44.

8. *Ibid.*, p.45.

9. *Ibid.*

10. *Ibid.*
11. *Ibid.*, p.47.
12. *Ibid.*
13. *Ibid.*
14. *Ibid.*
15. *Ibid.*, p.49.
16. Robin Le Poidevin, *Arguing for Atheism* (Routledge, 1996).
17. A.J. Ayer, *Language, Truth and Logic*, second edition.
18. Bernard Williams, *Morality* (1993), p.16.
19. A.J. Ayer, *op. cit.*
20. R.M. Hare, *op. cit.*
21. Bernard Williams, *op. cit.*, p.28.
22. Hastings Rashdall, *The Theory of Good and Evil.*
23. Quoted by Paul Strathern, *Nietzche in 90 minutes.*
24. Richard Rorty, *The Times Higher*, 6 June 1997.
25. J.L. Mackie, *Ethics—Inventing Right and Wrong* (Penguin, 1990), p.15.
26. Paul Kurtz, *Forbidden Fruit* (Prometheus Books, 1988), p.73.
27. Nigel Warburton, *Philosophy: the Basics*, p.60.
28. J.L. Mackie, *op. cit.*, p.106.
29. Paul Chamberlain, *Can We Be Good Without God?* (IVP, 1996), p.55.
30. A.E. Taylor, *Does God Exist?* 1947.
31. Jean Paul Sartre, 'The Humanism of Existentialism'.
32. J.L. Mackie, *op. cit.*, p.48.
33. A.E. Taylor, *op. cit.*, p.84.
34. Peter Kreeft and Ronald Tacelli, *Handbook of Christian Apologetics* (Monarch, 1995).
35. Peter Kreeft, *The Best Things in Life* (IVP, 1984).
36. F.C. Copleston, 'The Existence of God' in Bertrand Russell, *Why I Am Not A Christian, and other essays* (Routledge, 1996), p.149.
37. C.S. Lewis, *Mere Christianity* (Fount, 1986).

38. *Ibid.*
39. *Ibid.*
40. *Ibid.*
41. Peter Kreeft, *The Journey* (IVP, 1996).
42. J.L. Mackie, *op. cit.*, p.36.
43. *Ibid.*, p.36.
44. *Ibid.*
45. *Ibid.*, p.37.
46. A.E. Taylor, *op. cit.*
47. Peter Kreeft and Ronald Tacelli, *op. cit.*
48. Michael Peterson *et al*, *Reason and Religious Belief* (Oxford, 1991), p.85.
49. W. David Beck, *op. cit.*, p.161.
50. Peter Kreeft and Ronald Tacelli, *op. cit.*
51. *Ibid.*
52. Josh McDowell and Norman L. Geisler, *Love Is Always Right* (Word, 1996), pp.159–160, 176.
53. Kai Nielsen, *Does God Exist? The Debate Between Theists and Atheists* (Prometheus, 1993), p.104.
54. Paul Chamberlain, *op. cit.*, p.46.
55. R.M. Hare, *op. cit.*, p.14.
56. C.S. Lewis, *The Abolition of Man* (Fount, 1978).
57. *Ibid.*
58. *Ibid.*
59. Kai Nielsen, *Does God Exist? The Debate Between Theists and Atheists* (Prometheus, 1993).
60. C.S. Lewis, *op. cit.*, pp.34–44.
61. Michael Ruse, 'Evolutionary Theory and Christian Ethics' in *The Darwinian Paradigm* (Routledge, 1989), pp.262, 268–269.
62. Paul Chamberlain, *op. cit.*, p.159.
63. *Ibid.*
64. See 'Is Rape Wrong on Andromeda?' in E. Regis, ed. *Extraterrestrials*, (Cambridge, 1985).
65. Paul Chamberlain, *op. cit.*

66. C. Stephen Evans, *Why Believe?* (IVP, 1996), p.44.
67. J.P. Moreland, *Does God Exist? The Debate Between Theists and Atheists* (Prometheus, 1993), p.112.
68. Kai Nielson, 'Why Should I Be Moral? Revisited' in *American Philosophical Quarterly*, Volume 21, Number 1, January 1984.
69. J.P. Moreland, *op.. cit.*, p.119.
70. Paul Chamberlain, *op. cit.*, p.121.
71. Peter Kreeft and Ronald Tacelli, *op. cit.*
72. J.P. Moreland, *op. cit.*, p.11.
73. Robin Le Poidevin, *op. cit.*, pp.81–82.
74. R.M. Hare, *op. cit.*, pp.165–166.
75. Kai Nielson, 'Why Should I be Moral? Revisited' in *American Philosophical Quarterly*, 21.
76. J.P. Moreland, *op. cit.*, p.119.
77. Kurt Baier, *The Moral Point of View* (Ithica, 1958).
78. A.E. Taylor, *op. cit.*, p.95.
79. John Wijngaards, *How to Make Sense of God*, p.169.
80. J.L. Mackie, *op. cit.*, p.88.
81. C. Stephen Evans, *op. cit.*, p.45.
82. *The Times Higher*, 6 June 1997.
83. Kai Nielson, 'Why Should I Be Moral? Revisited' in *American Philosophical Quarterly*, 21.
84. J.P. Moreland, *Scaling The Secular City* (Baker, 1987), p.131.
85. J.L. Mackie, *op. cit.*, p.38.
86. J.P. Moreland, *op. cit.*, p.113.
87. J.L. Mackie, *op. cit.*
88. *Ibid.*, pp.38–39.
89. *Ibid.*, p.38.
90. René Descartes, F.E. Sutcliffe, trans. *Discourse on Method and the Meditations* (Penguin, 1968), 'Third Meditation'.
91. J.L. Mackie, *op. cit.*, p.39.
92. *Ibid.*, p.39.
93. *Ibid.*, p.39.

94. *Ibid.*, p.39.
95. *Ibid.*, p.39.
96. Josh McDowell and Norman L. Geisler, *op. cit.*, pp.38–39.
97. W. David Beck, *op. cit.*, p.160.
98. Richard Swinburne, *The Existence of God* (Oxford, 1991), p.97.
99. Paul Chamberlain, *op. cit.*, p.57.
100. Nigel Warburton, *op. cit.*, p.61.
101. Michael Peterson *et al*, *op. cit.*, p.85.
102. This paragraph is based upon some proposals made by Mr Nicholas Everitt of UEA, although the views expressed are not necessarily to be equated with his own opinions on this matter.
103. Peter Kreeft and Ronald Tacelli, *op. cit.*
104. Quoted by J.L. Mackie, *op. cit.*, pp.34–35.
105. A.E. Taylor, *op. cit.*, p.83.
106. J.L. Mackie, *op. cit.*, p.30.
107. Quoted by Kai Nielsen, 'Ethics without God' in *Does God Exist? The Debate between Theists and Atheists.*
108. Bertrand Russell, *Why I Am Not A Christian* (Routledge, 1996).
109. Michael Peterson *et al*, *op. cit.*, p.238.
110. *Ibid.*
111. Kai Nielson, 'Ethics Without God' in *Does God Exist? The Debate between Theists and Atheists*, p.99.
112. Michael Peterson *et al*, *op. cit.*, p.240.
113. Kai Nielson, *Does God Exist? The Debate between Theists and Atheists*, p.100, my italics.
114. J.P. Moreland, *Does God Exist? The Debate between Theists and Atheists*, p.131.
115. Richard Swinburne, *The Existence of God* (Oxford, 1979), pp.98–101.
116. W. David Beck, *op. cit.*
117. Norman L. Geisler and Josh McDowell, *op. cit.*, p.27.
118. G.E.M. Anscombe, 'Modern Moral Philosophy' in Roger

Crisp and Michael Slote, eds, *Virtue Ethics* (Oxford, 1997), pp.26, 31.

119. *Ibid.*, p.31.
120. *Ibid.*, p.27.
121. James W. Sire, *Why Should Anyone Believe Anything At All?* (IVP, 1994).
122. *Ibid.*
123. Richard Taylor, *Ethics, Faith and Reason*, (Prentice-Hall: Englewood Cliffs, N.J., 1985), pp.83–84.
124. *Ibid.*
125. Hastings Rashdall, *The Theory of Good and Evil.*
126. W. David Beck, *op. cit.*, p.161.
127. A.E. Taylor, *op. cit*, p.93.
128. James W. Sire, *op. cit.*
129. James W. Sire, *The Universe Next Door*, second edition (IVP, 1988).
130. C.S. Lewis, '*De Futilitate*' in *Christian Reflections* (Fount, 1981).
131. Quoted by Ravi Zacharias, *Can Man Live Without God?* (Word, 1995), p.69.
132. Quoted by Ravi Zacharias, *A Shattered Visage—The Real Face of Atheism* (Baker, 1990), p.49.
133. Norman L. Geisler, *Christian Apologetics* (Baker, 1995), chapter 12.
134. Bertrand Russell, 'What I Believe' in *Why I Am Not A Christian.*
135. Kai Nielson, *op. cit.*, p.107.
136. William Lane Craig, quoted by L.Strobel, *What Jesus Would Say.*

CHAPTER THREE

COSMOLOGICAL ARGUMENTS

In the beginning, God created the heavens and the earth. (Genesis 1:1)

Moving on from arguments about good and evil, we come now to arguments that seek to prove that the universe requires a cause that only God can provide. I will consider two cosmological arguments, the 'Kalam' argument, and the 'dependency' argument. I will seek to show that the 'Kalam' argument is invalid, but nevertheless gives rise to a fruitful train of thought. I will support the argument from dependency as a sound argument, but one that needs to be considered together with other theistic arguments to have its full effect.

'Cosmological' comes from the Greek words *cosmos* and *logos*. *Cosmos* means 'ordered beauty', hence cosmetics. *Logos* means 'reason', hence logic. Design arguments would be most appropriately called 'cosmological'. However, history has obviously given design arguments their own label. (I'll come on to design arguments in the following two chapters.) The term 'cosmological' has been reserved for causal arguments for the existence of God.

Cosmological arguments are almost as old as philosophy itself, and can be traced back to Plato and Aristotle.[1] Cosmological arguments for the existence of God have been championed by many philosophers over thousands of years.[2] A successful criticism of one may not apply to another. It is, therefore, well worth looking at a variety of cosmological arguments. In this chapter I will look at two sorts of cosmological argument: the 'Kalam' argument, and the 'argument from dependency'.

The Kalam argument

The 'Kalam' cosmological argument comes from the Islamic tradition of 'Kalam' philosophy. *Kalam* is Arabic for 'speech'.

Although the technical name for this argument may be unfamiliar, it is commonly used at the popular level. For example, anyone who asks a non-theist, 'What caused the Big Bang?' is using a Kalam argument. However, the Kalam argument is not only a staple of popular apologetics. In recent years it has been a matter of intense debate in the highest philosophical circles. Much of the current interest is due to the efforts made by William Lane Craig in the argument's defence.[3] Another notable defender is J.P. Moreland.[4] The basic argument, as defended by Craig, is this:

> Premise 1) Everything that begins to exist has a cause of its existence.
> Premise 2) The universe began to exist.
> Conclusion. Therefore, the universe has a cause of its existence.[5]

Craig says that the first premise 'is so intuitively obvious that I think scarcely anyone could sincerely believe it to be false'.[6] Therefore, he concentrates on defending the second premise. Craig's first line of defence consists in arguments against the possibility of an actually infinite number of things (as opposed to a potentially infinite number of things) existing. If, as Craig argues, an actually infinite number of things is an impossibility, then an actually infinite past cannot exist, and the universe must have a beginning. Most of the current controversy has focused on arguments for and against the possibility of actual infinities existing.[7] However, Craig and his followers have a second line of defence for the second premise; a defence based on the scientific theories of thermodynamics and of the Big Bang.

Thermodynamics is the science of heat and work (from the Greek words *thermos* and *dunamis*, which mean 'heat' and 'power' respectively, as in thermos-flask and dynamo). The second law of thermodynamics states that the amount of energy available for work in a closed system always decreases. A decrease in available energy is called an increase in entropy. In a closed system as a whole, entropy always increases as the amount of available energy decreases. If you came into my room and found a mug of warm coffee you could tell that it had not been there all that long. The second law of thermodynamics says that the coffee will cool down as the temperature of the room, and everything in it, moves towards a state of uniform temperature; the coffee will get cold and the room will get a little bit warmer. As J.P. Moreland explains, 'the second law tells us that the universe is wearing down irreversibly . . . But since a state of maximum entropy has not yet been reached, the universe has not been here for ever. If the universe had already undergone an infinite past, it would have reached that state by now.'[8] If the universe were infinitely old, there would be no available useful energy left, but there is, so the universe can't be infinitely old.

The Big Bang theory draws upon several pieces of converging evidence which all point to the universe having an origin some 10 to 15 billion years ago. That's a long time; but it isn't an infinite amount of time:

> Everything in the universe is expanding outward. The staggering implication of this is that at some point in the past the entire known universe was contracted down to a single mathematical point, from which it has been expanding ever since . . . This initial event has come to be known as 'The Big Bang'.[9]

I refer readers who wish to follow up these arguments for themselves to the recommended reading list at the close of this chapter. I am happy to accept that the universe has a finite past, for the reasons ably presented by Craig, Moreland and company, as well as a myriad of science books written by theists and atheists alike. However, I do not think that the Kalam argument is a good argument. The argument seems very neat and straightforward, but I believe this apparent simplicity is deceptive.

An assessment of the Kalam argument

In my opinion, the Kalam argument falls to pieces over the ambiguous meaning of the words 'begins' and 'began'. There are at least two senses in which something can have a beginning. One sense is that something came to be within a time-stream so that within that time-stream there was a time before it existed. An example of something beginning in this sense of the word is the beginning of a film. First there is a time when the film is not showing, and then the film begins to show. There was a 'before' and a 'beginning' within one and the same time-stream. Another sense is that, while the thing in question did not begin in the first sense, it has nevertheless only existed for a finite length of time. If one were to travel back through the time-stream in which the thing in question has existed, one would reach a limit beyond which one cannot go, at least without transferring into some other time-stream. I think one example of this type of 'beginning' is the universe itself.

We might say that before the existence of our time-stream there was God's time (or the time of another universe), and that at some point in that time our time-stream began. There could then be 'a time before the universe existed', but not in the universe's time! If there was 'a time before the universe', then that time must belong to the existence of something other than the universe. However, there clearly was none of our universe's time before our universe's time began!

In what sense did our time-stream 'begin'? The clearest way to explain the meaning of 'beginning' as it applies to our time-stream is to say that it has a finite past. Either there was no time before our time-stream, or there was the time of some other time-stream. What we can rule out is our time existing before it existed, or coming to be within itself. Even if we accept all the arguments advanced by defenders of the Kalam argument for its second premise, all we are required to admit is that our universe has a finite past. There was, as it were, a first second, a first minute, and so on. The second premise would therefore be more accurately expressed as, 'The universe has a finite past.'

What sense of 'begins' is used in the first premise of the Kalam argument? Is it 'begins' in the sense of something 'coming to be' such that there is a time before it exists and then a time when it does exist within one and the same 'time-stream'? Or is it 'begins' merely in the sense of having a finite past? If it is 'begins' in the first sense, then there is an ambiguity between the meaning of 'begins' in the first premise and 'began' in the second premise which invalidates the argument.

I can see that if something comes into being it must be caused to do so by something—for 'out of nothing nothing comes'. I can see that nothing could cause itself to come into being, since what does not exist can't very well cause anything. I can see, therefore, that if something comes into being it must be caused to do so by something other than itself. However, if this is the meaning of 'begins' in the first premise, it is not the meaning of 'began' in the second premise, and the argument consequently fails.

What if 'begins' in the first premise were meant in the same sense as 'began' is meant in the second premise? That would at least remove the ambiguity; but note what happens to the argument if we use the same sense of begins in both premises. If we retain the use of 'begins' to mean 'coming to be' in both premises the argument looks like this: 'Whatever comes to be is caused by another, the universe came to be, therefore the universe was caused by another.' The first premise is surely correct, but what of the second? We have already seen that the universe could not have 'come to be' in this first sense of 'begins'. The universe could not, and did not, come to be in the sense of there being a time before it existed in one and the same time-stream.

The last hope for the Kalam argument therefore lies in the identical use of 'begins' in the second sense of the word in both premises. If this is done, the argument goes like this: 'Whatever has a finite past is caused by another, the universe has a finite past, therefore the universe is caused by another.' Now I agree with the second premise, but not the first. I agree with Craig and Moreland the ancient Islamic philosophers and the majority of modern cosmologists that the universe has a finite past. However, why should we believe that 'whatever has a finite past is caused by another'? Indeed, I think it is fairly simple to prove that this is one thing we should not believe.

There obviously can be no 'time before time'. Nothing comes from nothing. If once there was nothing, then there would be nothing now, because there would be nothing to cause anything to come to be, and nothing that existed uncaused. Therefore, something has always existed. If the arguments convince us that the past is finite (either because it couldn't be otherwise, or because it just happens to be so) then we *must* say that something has always existed. We must say that the past is finite, and that something exists which is not caused to exist either by itself (which would be impossible), or by anything else (since there either cannot be, or is not, an infinite regress of things being caused by other things).

A bare appeal to the need to explain the Big Bang makes too many assumptions, and is not a good argument for the existence of God.

Is the Kalam argument a total kalamity? (It's a pun)

Is the Kalam argument a total loss for the theist? I don't think so. Theists have always held two beliefs about the universe that, although logically distinct one from another, nevertheless go together historically. These two beliefs are that the universe is totally dependent upon God for its existence, and that the universe has a finite past. The first of these two beliefs is the more important and fundamental, but that doesn't mean that the second belief is unimportant. The philosophical and scientific arguments offered to support the Kalam argument's insistence on a cosmic beginning validate the traditional theological belief that, 'In the beginning, God created the heavens and the earth' (Genesis 1:1).

Having shown that the universe had a beginning, in the sense of a finite past, we are faced with a choice, 'between looking for a cause of the beginning of the universe or settling for no cause at all'.[10] Now, all explanation must end somewhere, but the question is, where should our explanation of the universe end? Somewhere along the line we are bound to meet with a 'brute fact' of one sort or another, but we should seek the best 'brute fact' we can find. A good brute fact is one that accounts for as many other facts as possible in the simplest way adequate for the task. The best 'brute fact' explanation will therefore be one that explains more, or explains an equal amount with greater simplicity and/or adequacy, than other explanations. The question that emerges from the Kalam argument is whether or not we should take the physical universe, and in particular the beginning of the physical universe, as a 'brute fact'.

The universe may have always existed, and the past may be finite, but does the universe exist uncaused? The universe couldn't have been caused to come to be within its own time-stream, but it might have been caused to come to be from the perspective of some other time-stream. Perhaps God has always existed, without cause and for a finite length of time, causing the universe to begin at some point within his time-stream with its own finite time-stream. The universe would then have a finite past, and there would be no space-time before space-time (only God-time), but the universe would be caused and God uncaused. Alternatively, God might be said to exist timelessly, and to timelessly cause the existence of a temporally finite, caused universe.[11]

Richard Swinburne argues that if the universe can be shown to have a beginning, that beginning obviously cannot have a scientific explanation in terms of a previous state of the universe. This being so, we are faced with two alternatives: either the first state of the universe had no cause, or it had a personal cause: 'If the universe is to be explained, personal explanation must be brought in, and an explanation given in terms of a person who is not part of the universe acting from without.'[12]

Swinburne points out that there are actually three possible ultimate explanations: natural (everything can be explained scientifically), personal (everything can be explained with reference to a supernatural agent), and dualistic (both natural and personal explanations are required, and neither can be explained by the other).[13] Clearly, a dualistic world-view is less simple than either a natural or a personal ultimate explanation:

> If scientific explanations can themselves be explained by wider scientific explanations, and personal explanations by wider personal explanations, surely the seeker after truth should consider whether perhaps all personal explanations are in the end themselves susceptible of a complete scientific explanation, or whether perhaps all scientific explanations are in the end susceptible of a complete personal explanation.[14]

So, our first choice is between a natural or a personal explanation of the universe. Only if neither explanation is workable would we be pushed into a more complex dualist explanation. The natural explanation will clearly be simpler than the personal explanation. The final choice of one explanation over the other must therefore lie in their comparative adequacy.

At this stage in the argument I refer readers back to the moral argument, since I believe that this argument shows that a materialistic ultimate explanation is inadequate to the task of accounting for the existence of objective moral values.

I suggest that a material ultimate explanation is inherently implausible. It does not seem implausible to suppose that a rational, personal, all-good God could create the universe, causing it to produce rational, moral, personal beings such as ourselves. However, it does seem implausible to suppose that a non-intelligent, a-moral, impersonal physical brute fact could account for intelligent, moral and personal beings. As Professor Clark H. Pinnock writes:

A stream does not rise higher than its source. It is not reasonable to believe that there are effects such as personality, morality, freedom and intelligence in the world which were not present in the cause of it. It simply does not make full sense to suppose that matter, mindless, amoral and impersonal, is the sole originating cause of things.[15]

In my opinion then, an ultimate personal explanation is more adequate than an ultimate natural explanation. Since adequacy is more important than simplicity, we should prefer the personal explanation. The simplest personal explanation would be that the universe is explicable in terms of a single personal agent. While this conclusion doesn't take us quite as far as theism (being quite compatible with pantheism), it does support theism and contradict atheism.

Two sorts of causation

Being caused by something that exists before you do isn't the only sort of causal relationship going. More fundamental even than such temporal causality is the causality of dependency. If I place a book on a table-top, the table-top causes the book to stay above the floor, but the table-top's causing of the book to stay above the floor is simultaneous with the book's staying above the floor. The book's position depends upon the table. Given this type of causation there is in fact nothing incompatible between the belief that the universe has an infinite past, and that the universe depends for its existence upon God. It is here that our consideration of the Kalam argument leads us to consider the argument from dependency.

The argument from dependency

The argument from dependency that I will defend goes like this:

Premise 1) If something exists it must be either dependent or independent.

Premise 2) It is impossible for everything to be dependent.
Premise 3) Therefore, if something exists, there must exist an independent thing.
Premise 4) Something exists.
Conclusion. Therefore there exists an independent thing.

This argument has two parts of three steps each: the first part (steps 1–3) seeks to establish that if anything exists, then there must exist an independent thing. The second part (step 3 to the conclusion), seeks to establish that an independent thing actually exists, via the fact that something exists. It is at this point that Aquinas, in his famous versions of the cosmological argument, ventured that 'everyone understands this to be God'. I will have something to say about this later.

Defence of the argument from dependency

1. If something exists it must be either dependent or independent

There are only two ways in which anything could exist: dependent upon something (or some things) beyond itself, or not. If something exists without depending upon something (or some things) beyond itself, it must be an independent thing. An independent thing is simply a thing that exists without depending upon something (or some things) beyond itself. There is no third option available between a thing existing with or without being dependent upon one or more other things.

No thing could exist that was both dependent and independent (although a part of an independent whole may depend for its existence upon the rest of the independent whole of which it is a part). To exist in one way is automatically not to exist in the other. If something (or some part of a thing) does not exist in dependence upon one or more things beyond itself, and it does not exist independently of the existence or non-existence of things beyond itself, then it does not exist.

Nothing can depend upon itself for existence (although a part of an independent whole can exist in dependence upon the rest of that whole). If something does not exist, then it cannot depend upon anything, nor be depended upon by anything (including itself), because there is no 'it' to do any depending, or being depended upon.

That which does not exist, but which could exist, is a potential thing. That which is depended upon must be an actual thing. A 'self-dependent' thing 'would be both in a state of potentiality and actuality with regard to being, which is impossible'.[16] A depended-upon thing must exist before anything that depends upon it can exist (where 'before' may not mean 'before in time', but 'logically before', as in the case of the table-top keeping the book off the floor).

A depended-upon thing is, at the very least, *a* cause of whatever exists in dependence upon it. A depended-upon thing is *the* cause of whatever depends upon it if it is the only thing depended upon by that which depends upon it. The cause of a dependent thing's existence is the sum total of things upon which its existence depends. A depended-upon thing must exist prior to that which depends upon it. For example, my parents were involved in causing my existence, but they could not have been involved if they did not exist before I came into existence (before my existence moved from being potential to being actual). Likewise, my existence right now depends upon a series of causes and effects which is not ordered in time, but in logical sequence. I would not be alive if I was not breathing, I could not breathe if there were no oxygen to breathe, and there would be no oxygen to breathe if there were no atoms in existence able to form oxygen molecules. The existence of the laws of physics concerning the holding together of atoms in molecules does not depend upon my existence! On the other hand, if the atoms 'lost it', then so would I.

So, if a thing exists, it must be either a dependent thing, or an independent thing. A dependent thing depends upon other things (the things which are individually its causes and jointly its cause) for its existence. An independent thing does not depend upon other things for its existence. Its existence is independent of, and therefore unconditioned by, the existence or non-existence of anything else. Something must be either temporally or logically 'before' a dependent thing. Nothing can be either temporally or logically 'before' an independent thing.

2. It is impossible for everything to be dependent

If everything had to depend on something else for its existence, nothing could exist. There must be at least one thing which does not stand in need of something to depend upon: 'If each being is a [dependent] being . . . then adding up all these effects does not provide a cause for these effects.'[17]

If a dependent thing exists there must exist either a finite number of things that it depends upon, or an infinite number of things that it depends upon. Saying that each and every thing must depend upon something else leads to an actually infinite regress of dependent things depending on other dependent things, and to all sorts of logical difficulties. An infinite number of dependent things cannot account for the existence of any dependent thing for the following reasons:

An infinite set of causes cannot add up to the cause for any effect, since there is always another cause [depended-upon thing] to take into account. An actually infinite set of depended-upon things can never add up to the cause for the existence of anything. If a potential thing, requiring a cause for its existence, does not receive a cause for its existence, then it will lack a cause for its existence. Lacking a cause for its existence, a potential thing remains a potential thing, and will not become an actual thing. As Bruce R. Reichenbach has argued, for an effect to be produced, there must be present the totality of conditions sufficient to cause that effect. However, in an infinite series, such a totality is never present. The causal explanation is constantly deferred because there is always another condition to take into account: 'Hence, an infinite series of . . . conditions, where at least one more . . . condition is always required to produce an effect, will never yield a sufficient reason for the existence of any [dependent] being.'[18]

Saying 'X depends upon an infinite regress of dependent things', as if that accounted for the existence of X, is like saying that 'no one passed me on the road' and thinking that you had referred to someone called 'no one', when all you have referred to is the lack of anyone. An actual infinity of things that are depended-upon can never add up to the totality of conditions sufficient to produce an effect, for:

> When the existence of each member of a collection is explained by reference to some other member of that very same collection then it does not follow that the collection itself has an explanation. For it is one thing for there to be an explanation of the existence of each dependent being and quite another for there to be an explanation of why there are dependent beings at all.[19]

As F.C. Copleston said in his debate with Bertrand Russell, if you add up chocolates you get chocolates and not a sheep, and even if you could add up chocolates to infinity, you'd still get (an infinite number of) chocolates. Likewise, even if you could add up dependent things to infinity, you'd still get (an infinite number of) dependent things, not an independent thing; and 'An infinite series of [Dependent] beings will be . . . as unable to cause itself as one [Dependent] being.'[20]

If you are like me, talk of one thing causing another thing brings before your mind's eye the picture of a series of boxes, one before the other. Here is one box, but this box can only exist if this other box exists, and so on into the horizon of your imagination. The important thing is not to get led astray by such an illustration. The temptation is to imagine one box as existing and then to imagine, as existing, the previous box upon which the first depends, and so on. Having already given several boxes such a mental existence, one might be led to imagine that the existence of boxes is not made problematical by the fact that there are boxes stretching back into an infinity wherein no box exists without there being a preceding box. Surely, you might think, each box is caused by the previous box, and for every box there is a previous box, so what's the problem? The problem is that none of these imaginary boxes should be imagined to exist at all. A far better mental image with which to work would be a series of empty boxes that need to be filled. Each box must be filled with water taken from the previous box. An empty box represents something that would exist if only sufficient cause were provided for its existence. A full box represents the existence of something that has received a sufficient cause for its existence. Now, imagine your first empty box preceded by an empty box. Can you fill the first box? Of course not. Imagine a great number of empty boxes. Has the situation improved? No? Imagine that an actually infinite number of empty boxes exists. Are you any closer to filling even one box? Saying that an infinite regress of dependent things accounts for the existence of even one dependent thing is just like saying that an infinite regress of empty boxes accounts for the existence of even one full box.

Furthermore, there is reason to believe that the existence of an actual infinity is impossible. David Hilbert, one of the greatest mathematicians of the twentieth century, testified that 'The infinite is nowhere to be found in reality. It neither exists in nature, nor provides a legitimate basis for rational thought . . . The role that remains for the infinite to play is solely that of an idea.'[21]

Strange paradoxes arise when we imagine that an actual infinity exists in the real world: 'Although in mathematics we can speak about an actual infinite, mathematical actual infinities concern only the ideal world of mathematics. If they are applied to the real world, absurdities result.'[22] This being so, it is doubtful that everything is dependent, and reasonable to believe that there must be at least something that is independent.

For example, imagine that your local library has an actually infinite number of books. Suppose that there is an infinite number of red books, and also an infinite number of black books. Does it really make sense to say that if all the red books were out on loan, the total number of books in the library would be the same as if none of the books were out on loan? Furthermore:

> if we had an infinite number of books, this would include all the books beginning with the letter A. Suppose that we also have an infinite number of books that begin with A. Then, though the first set contains the second set and more, both sets have the same number of books. But one would expect that if one set is the subset of the other, the subset would be less than the set.[23]

Then again, suppose that each book in the library has an infinite number of pages. The first book in the library would contain as many pages as the entire collection, and someone who read only one book from that collection would have read as many pages as someone who read each and every book! This is surely a situation so odd that it is a *reductio ad absurdum* of the hypothesis that an actually infinite set of things can exist. A *reductio ad absurdum* is a disproof of a hypothesis by the demonstration that unacceptable paradoxes result from its acceptance.

But surely, you might be thinking, if a book has an infinite number of pages, one could never finish reading it, there would always be more to read. Quite so; and this leads us to the third problem with the hypothesis that everything which exists (if anything exists) is a dependent thing.

If every step in the time-ordered series of 'things depending upon other things' depended upon a previous thing, then there would be no first thing, nothing that was not preceded by something else upon which it depended for its existence. But with no first thing there couldn't possibly be a second thing, or a third thing, and so on. With no beginning, reaching the present would be like counting from negative infinity to zero. This is like trying to leap out of a well with no bottom. The same problem would apply to the logically ordered series of things depending upon other things (such as my existence now depending upon my body chemistry, which depends upon my molecules, and so on).

If everything that exists (granted the existence of something) is a dependent thing, this implies the existence of an actually infinite number of dependent things, which, besides being a rather extravagant picture of existence, is impossible for the reasons just explained. We can therefore exclude the hypothesis that there could exist an infinite number of dependent things, and only an infinite number of dependent things.

What then of the alternative hypothesis that there could exist only dependent things, but a finite number of dependent things? This suggestion is also unsupportable, for, if everything that exists were dependent and finite in number, then everything would depend upon nothing, which is impossible. There is nothing outside everything to depend upon. 'Nothing' isn't a thing; 'nothing' is the total lack of anything. No thing can depend upon nothing, so everything can't depend upon nothing. Only actual things can be depended upon, but there is nothing beyond everything to depend upon, and so everything cannot be a dependent thing:

> Are all things caused to exist by other things right now? Suppose they are. That is, suppose there is no Uncaused Being . . . Then nothing could exist right now. For remember, on the no [Independent thing] hypothesis, all things need a present cause outside of themselves in order to exist. So right now, all things, including all those things which are causing other things to be, need a cause . . . Everything that exists, therefore, on this hypothesis, stands in need of being caused to exist. But caused by what? Beyond everything there is, there can only be nothing. But that is absurd: all of reality dependent—but dependent upon nothing![24]

Cannot the whole be more than the sum of its parts? Might not everything be 'the set of dependent things' and yet neither include the existence of an independent part, nor imply the existence of a transcendent independent cause, by being the set of dependent things which is itself independent?

The whole can, under the right circumstances, be more than the sum of its parts. But the whole cannot be more than the sum of its parts in the sense required by the claim that the whole universe, though composed of dependent things (whether finite or infinite in extent) is itself independent. One water molecule is not wet, but many water molecules together give rise to wetness. Wetness is an 'emergent property' of water molecules, which depends upon the union of constituent parts. Similarly, team spirit depends upon the team, not the other way around. In the same way, independence cannot depend upon a conglomeration of dependent parts! Put lots of little bricks together and, admittedly, you get a big brick wall. However, put little bricks together and you get a brick wall, not a marsh-mallow. Similarly, put dependent things together and you get a dependent thing, not an independent thing.

If 'the universe' is a set of dependent things, whether that set is finite or infinite in extent, then the universe is a dependent thing which cannot exist without there existing an independent cause upon which it depends. However many dependent things there are, there must exist an independent thing which is not an emergent property of dependent things, but the 'foundation' which provides for the existence of dependent things in the first place. Of course, this independent thing may itself have parts; all the argument from dependency demands is that the independent thing be an independent whole.

Whether finite or infinite in number, dependent things require the existence of an independent thing upon which to depend. This independent thing must be separate from that which depends upon it. Independence cannot be the 'emergent property' of a set of dependent things, for emergent properties depend upon those things which lead to their emergence, and in the case of dependent things, without a prior independent cause there would be nothing to lead to the emergence of any property.

3. Therefore, if something exists, there must exist an independent thing

It could not be the case that everything that exists is dependent, whether that 'everything' be a finite number of dependent things (from one to as large a number as you care to mention) or an infinite number of dependent beings. Hence it must be the case that if anything exists, there must exist at least one independent thing. Taking this conclusion as the first premise in the second part of the argument, we move on to prove that:

4. Something exists

Few people, besides particularly awkward philosophy students, would attempt to deny that they exist, and hence that something exists. In order to deny that anything at all exists, you, at least, must exist. Whatever cannot be denied without self-contradiction is true. Just as self-contradiction is the basic proof of falsity, so undeniableness is the basic proof of truth. This is because the opposite of what is true is false. You cannot deny your own existence without self-contradiction. As Descartes famously put it, 'I exist, therefore I am.'[25] Or as Augustine put it a thousand years before, 'If I err, I exist.'[26] If I said, 'I do not exist,' I would be wrong; and so when I say, 'I exist,' I must be right. Therefore, something exists.

5. Therefore, there exists an independent thing

'And this everyone calls God.' This last claim is the most important step in any cosmological argument. Perhaps an atheist will agree with the argument as presented above, but as its conclusion stands, this acceptance would not contradict atheism. All that we have proved is the existence of an independent thing.

Now, theists have always believed that God is an independent personal 'thing', so at the very least the argument from dependency shows that the idea of God being independent is eminently sensible. Nevertheless, the argument does not prove that God exists; only that there exists at least one independent thing. Occam's 'razor' compels us to say that there exists only one independent thing, upon which any and all dependent things depend.

What would an independent thing be like?

What is the nature of this independent thing, in addition to its independent existence? The independent thing must be all-powerful. Since anything that depends upon it depends upon it for any power that it has, there is no question of there being anything more powerful than the independent thing. In respect to anything dependent upon it, the independent thing may be called the sustaining creator.

An independent thing (let us call it 'X' for now) is limited only by its own essential qualities. Essential qualities are those qualities that a thing cannot exist without; they are essential to its being what it is. X does not depend upon anything for what it is, and so nothing external to itself can limit it, unless X allows this to be so, in which case this 'limitation' is really a self-limitation, and the label 'all-powerful' may still be applied. The only limitation upon X is that of being what it is rather than what it isn't (because to exist is to be a thing of a particular sort). Whatever qualities X has, it therefore has without any external limitations.

It would seem impossible for an independent thing to come into existence, or to pass out of existence. There is no sufficient condition which must be fulfilled in order to move X from being a potential thing (a thing whose existence is possible but not actual) to being an actual being. X simply exists uncaused. If X cannot come into existence, it would seem difficult to conceive of X as passing out of existence. We may therefore say that X is eternal.

We cannot morally judge anything, including X, without assuming that the standard of right and wrong by which I make such a judgement, is itself good; and we cannot do that without assuming that X is good. This is because, as the sustaining creator, X is the ultimate basis of that standard, and unless X were good, we would have no reason to trust the standards which depend upon it. If we can pass moral judgement upon X, we must therefore judge it to be good (and in the light of the above, good without limit).

Since we are intelligent, rational and personal beings, it would seem reasonable to suppose that X is also rational and personal. To do otherwise would be to believe that the greater came from the lesser. If X is rational, it must also be personal, because non-personal things cannot reason. If X is rational and personal, it must know things. Being externally unlimited, X must know things without external limitation. This is not to say that X must be all-knowing, but it is to say that X might be all-knowing.

An independent, all-powerful, eternal, rational, personal, knowing (possibly all-knowing), all-good being upon whom objective moral judgements depend, can appropriately be called 'God'.

God or the universe?

The atheist might accept the conclusion that there exists an independent thing and yet insist that the universe itself is that independent thing. In doing so, the atheist would deny that X is personal, rational or knowing; and would probably deny the existence of objective moral values.

Even granted that dependent things exist, I have admitted that an independent thing may contain dependent parts. It seems certain to me (due to the above arguments) that there exists at least one independent thing, and for the sake of Occam's razor we should say that there is only one such thing unless further evidence prompts us to revise this estimate. The crucial issue is whether this independent thing is 'God' in any meaningful sense, or merely 'the universe itself' as an atheist might say.

After all, there is nothing beyond 'the universe' if we define 'the universe' as 'everything'. If the universe so defined does not include the existence of God, then the universe is still independent and all-powerful. Considered as a whole, one could argue that space-time is also eternal in the sense of being atemporal (without time), since time itself is not in time. The universe is also, ultimately, the source of our (subjective) moral standards. So the atheist might argue.

If we agree that the universe (by which we mean 'everything') is independent, we must choose between saying that the universe includes an independent part upon which the rest of the whole depends, or that the universe is an independent whole. If we say that the universe is an independent whole, we must either conclude that it contains no parts, or is composed only of dependent parts. The atheist is probably best off holding that the universe is an independent whole composed only of dependent parts.

The distinction between theism and atheism is not to be found in disagreement about the *existence* of an independent thing, but in disagreement about its *nature*. The atheist unconvinced by the argument from dependency is likely to stick with the assertion that the universe (defined as 'everything' and excluding the existence of God) consists of an actually infinite number of dependent things. Such an assertion nevertheless requires the existence of an independent thing, namely the universe itself.[27] Theists say that the independent thing is a transcendent personal reality (God) upon which a dependent universe of dependent things depends. Atheists say that the independent thing is a collection of dependent things (probably an actually infinite collection) which cannot as a whole be identified with 'God'. Pantheists agree with atheists that the cosmos lacks a transcendent personal independent cause, but disagree with atheists by holding that the whole of reality is 'God'. In other words, we must choose between theism, pantheism, and atheism.[28]

I suggest that atheism implausibly explains the greater by the lesser. I also suggest that theism scores over atheism in that the personal ground of theism can account for the existence of objective moral values, whereas the impersonal nature of atheism cannot. The moral argument also counts against pantheism because 'there is neither ground for absolute Good nor an ultimate distinction between good and evil in a pantheistic universe'.[29] The moral argument concludes with the existence of an all-good personal being, so unless you are prepared to deny that the universe contains Wrong, the universe cannot be equated with God (assuming the validity of the moral argument that is). Of the options, theism would seem to be the best bet.

Conclusion

If something exists it must be either a dependent thing or an independent thing. If a dependent thing exists, then there must also exist an independent thing. Something undeniably exists, and so there must exist at least one independent thing. This independent thing must be all-powerful and eternal. Furthermore, as the foundation of our moral sense, we cannot morally condemn it in anything but a subjective way. Occam's razor leads us to acknowledge the existence of one such independent thing. Other considerations lead us to attribute personality, rationality and knowledge to this independent being. Some of these attributes have been given a stronger justification than others, but all in all it seems to me that this being can appropriately be called 'God', and that God therefore exists.

Taken together, the moral and cosmological arguments

present us with an ultimate explanation in terms of an independent, eternal, all-powerful, all-good, personal agent who creates and sustains the cosmos. While less simple than the atheist's alternative, this explanation appears to be far more adequate.

Recommended reading

The Kalam argument

William Lane Craig, *Reasonable Faith*, second edition (Crossway, 1996). (3)

William Lane Craig, *The Kalam Cosmological Argument* (Macmillan, 1979). (4)

William Lane Craig, *The Virtual Office of William Lane Craig*: *http://www.leaderu.com/offices/billcraig/menus/index.html*

Brian Davies, *An Introduction to the Philosophy of Religion*, new edition (Oxford, 1982). (2)

Stephen T. Davies, *God, Reason and Theistic Proofs* (Edinburgh, 1997). (3)

Peter Kreeft and Ronald Tacelli, *Handbook of Christian Apologetics* (Word, 1995). (1)

J.P. Moreland, *Scaling the Secular City* (Baker, 1987). (3)

J.P. Moreland and Kai Nielson, *Does God Exist? The Debate Between Theists and Atheists* (Prometheus Books, 1993). Cosmologically, this debate centres on the Kalam argument, but Dallas Willard presents a sort of hybrid Kalam/dependency argument. (2)

God and the Big Bang

William Lane Craig and Quentin Smith, *Theism, Atheism and Big Bang Cosmology* (Oxford, 1993). (4)

W. Mark Richardson and Wesley J. Wildman eds, *Religion and Science—History, Method, Dialogue* (Routledge, 1996), case study one—Cosmology and Creation. (4)

Russell Stannard, *Doing Away with God? Creation and the Big Bang* (Marshall Pickering, 1993). (1)

Keith Ward, *God, Chance and Necessity* (OneWorld, 1996). (3)

David Wilkinson, *God, The Big Bang and Stephen Hawking* (Monarch). (1)

Other cosmological arguments

W. David Beck, 'God's Existence' in R. Douglas Geivett and Gary R. Habermas eds, *In Defence of Miracles* (Apollos, 1997). (2)

Samuel Clarke, *A Demonstration of the Being and Attributes of God—And Other Writings* (Cambridge, 1998). (4)

F.C. Copleston, *Aquinas* (Pelican Books, 1957), chapter three. (2)

Brian Davies, *An Introduction to the Philosophy of Religion*, new edition (Oxford, 1982). (2)

Stephen T. Davies, *God, Reason and Theistic Proofs* (Edinburgh, 1997). (3)

Norman L. Geisler and Paul Feinberg, *Introduction to Philosophy—A Christian Perspective* (Baker, 1987). (2)

J.J. Haldane and J.J.C. Smart, *Atheism and Theism* (Blackwells, 1996). (4)

John Hick, ed., *The Existence of God* (Macmillan, 1964). (1)

John Hick, *Arguments for the Existence of God* (New York: Herder, 1971). (2)

Peter Kreeft and Ronald Tacelli, *Handbook of Christian Apologetics* (Word, 1995). (1)

Michael Peterson *et al*, *Reason and Religious Belief*, (Oxford, 1991). (2)

Bruce R. Reichenbach, *The Cosmological Argument, A Reassessment*, (Springfield, Ill.: Charles C. Thomas Publishers, 1972). (4)

William L. Rowe, *The Cosmological Argument* (Princeton University Press, 1975). Rowe concentrates on Samuel Clarke's cosmological argument. (4)

Richard Swinburne, *The Existence of God*, revised edition (Oxford, 1991). (4)

Richard Taylor, *Metaphysics*, fourth edition (Prentice Hall). (2)

Notes

1. See Donald R. Burrill, ed., *The Cosmological Arguments— A Spectrum of Opinion* (Anchor Books/Doubleday, 1967).

2. Among whom we might mention: Aquinas, F.C. Copleston, William Lane Craig, Samuel Clarke, Norman L. Geisler, J.J. Haldane, Peter Kreeft, Leibnitz, J.P. Moreland, Bruce R. Reichenbach, Richard Swinburne, Richard Taylor and Dallas Willard.

3. See: William Lane Craig, *The Kalam Cosmological Argument* (Macmillan, 1979); Craig's debate with Quentin Smith, *Theism, Atheism and Big Bang Cosmology* (Oxford, 1993); and Craig's, *Reasonable Faith*, revised edition (Crossway, 1996).

4. See J.P .Moreland, *Scaling the Secular City* (Baker, 1987) and in *Does God Exist? The Debate between Theists and Atheists*, (Prometheus, 1993).

5. William Lane Craig, 'The Finitude of the Past and the Existence of God' in *Theism, Atheism and Big Bang Cosmology* (Oxford, 1993), p.4.

6. William Lane Craig, *Reasonable Faith*, revised edition (Crossway, 1994), p.92.

7. For example, see: Nicholas Everitt, 'Interpretations of God's eternity', *Religious Studies* 34, pp.25–32, 1998; and William Lane Craig and Quentin Smith, *Theism, Atheism and Big Bang Cosmology* (Oxford, 1993).

8. J.P. Moreland, *Scaling the Secular City* (Baker, 1987), p.35.

9. William Lane Craig, *Reasonable Faith*, revised edition (Crossway, 1994), p.101.

10. R. Douglas Geivett, 'Is Jesus the Only Way?' in Michael J. Wilkins and J.P. Moreland, eds, *Jesus Under Fire* (Paternoster Press, 1996), p.191.

11. On God's relation to time see: William Lane Craig, 'God, Time And Eternity' @ http://www.leaderu.com/offices/bill-craig/docs/eternity.html; Brian Davies, *An Introduction to the Philosophy of Religion*, new edition (Oxford, 1993); Michael Peterson *et al* eds, *Philosophy of Religion, Selected Readings* (Oxford, 1996); Richard Swinburne, *The Christian God* (Oxford, 1994); and Keith Ward, *Religion and Creation* (Oxford, 1996).

12. Richard Swinburne, *The Existence of God*, revised edition (Oxford, 1991), pp.121, 126.

13. *Explaining* everything with reference to a personal or non-personal ultimate does not necessitate *reducing* everything to that ultimate. Dualism here does not equate with Cartesian dualism of mind and body, but to a view of reality where natural and supernatural are equally basic constituents of reality.

14. Richard Swinburne, *op. cit.*, p.104.

15. Clark H. Pinnock, *Reason Enough* (Paternoster Press, 1980), p.68.

16. Norman L. Geisler, *Christian Apologetics* (Baker, 1976).

17. *Ibid.*

18. Bruce R. Reichenbach, *The Cosmological Argument* (Charles C. Thomas Publishers: Springfield, Ill., 1972).

19. William L. Rowe, *The Cosmological Argument* (Princeton University Press, 1975).

20. F.C. Copleston, 'The Existence Of God' in John Hick, ed., *The Existence of God* (Macmillan, 1964).

21. David Hilbert, 'On the Infinite', in Paul Benacerraf and Hillary Putnam eds, *Philosophy of Mathematics* (Prentice Hall: Englewood Cliffs, NJ, 1964), pp.139, 141.

22. Michael Peterson *et al*, *Reason and Religious Belief* (Oxford, 1991).

23. *Ibid.*
24. Peter Kreeft and Ronald Tacelli, *Handbook of Christian Apologetics* (Monarch, 1995), p.51.
25. René Descartes, F.E. Sutcliffe trans, *Discourse on Method and The Meditations* (Penguin, 1968), p.53.
26. Augustine, *City Of God* (Penguin), p.461.
27. My thanks to Mr David Bacon (BA, MSci, Jesus College, Cambridge) for a useful conversation on cosmological arguments in which this point was brought home to me.
28. I am using 'pantheism' as a convenient label for the option that the universe lacks a transcendent independent personal cause, but is itself, in its ultimate reality, personal rather than impersonal as in secular atheism. Pantheism is the belief that 'God is the one, infinite-impersonal, ultimate reality . . . God is all that exists; nothing exists that is not God. If anything that is not God appears to exist, it is *maya*, illusion, and does not truly exist.' (James W. Sire, *The Universe Next Door*, third edition [IVP, 1997.]) In most forms of pantheism however, personality is viewed as an ultimately illusory lower manifestation of an impersonal ultimate beyond description. The sort of pantheism considered in the main text is therefore closer to the Westernised New-Age variant of Eastern pantheism which emphasises the central reality of the divine individual (see James W. Sire, *op. cit.*) Aside from problems caused by the impossibility of making objective moral judgements in a pantheistic world, pantheism requires the pantheist to affirm that 'God' is, but that they, as an individual, ultimately are not. Of course, the pantheist must exist in order to make this affirmation, and so the view is self-defeating. Moreover, belief in an 'ultimate reality' that is 'beyond description' is self-contradictory. A close relative of pantheism is panentheism, a sort of half-way house between pantheism and theism. Panentheists say with theists that there is a transcendent personal reality, but go on to say that all non-transcendent

reality has a personal dimension because God is in the world as the human mind is in a body (as against pantheism which says that the cosmos *is* God, although a God that is ultimately beyond categories such as 'personhood'). Panentheism is basically the belief that 'God is to World as soul is to body'. (Norman L. Geisler, *Christian Apologetics*, p.193). Unlike the God of theism, the God of panentheism is 'intimately and internally related with the space-time world' in such a way that God is not 'distinct from and independent of the world' (*ibid*, p.206). For a critique of pantheism and panentheism see Norman L. Geisler, *Christian Apologetics*, (Baker, 1976).

29. Norman L. Geisler, *op. cit.*, p.189.

CHAPTER FOUR

DESIGN ARGUMENTS

The heavens declare the glory of God;
the skies proclaim the work of his hands.
Day after day they pour forth speech;
night after night they display knowledge.
There is no speech or language where their voice is not heard.
(Psalm 19:1–3)

After a long history, design arguments for God's existence fell out of favour in the twentieth century due to the mistaken view that evolution by natural selection did away with the need to explain biology with reference to intelligent design. However, design arguments have made a come-back. Far from doing away with the design hypothesis, modern scientific knowledge actually provides strong evidence of design. The existence of reliable, elegant and beautiful natural laws discoverable by the human mind which emerges from the evolution of organisms containing information and irreducible complexity supports the conclusion that the cosmos is indeed the product of design.

Had I been present at the creation, I would have given some useful hints for the better ordering of the universe.

(Alfonso the Wise—after studying Ptolemy's theory of the universe)

Design arguments have been popular for thousands of years. Plato referred to all things being 'under the dominion of the mind which ordered the universe'.[1] Another early assertion of design was Cicero's *De Natura Deorum*, where a character called Lucilius asks, 'What could be more clear or obvious when we look up to the sky and contemplate the heavens, than that there is some divinity of superior intelligence?'[2]

Design arguments fell out of favour in the twentieth century, due mainly to the impression that evolution by natural selection falsified the appearance of design in nature. However, design arguments have made a come-back; so much so that I will devote two chapters to them. In this chapter I will look at a broad range of arguments, paying particular attention to our current understanding of biology and evolution. In the following chapter I will consider just one argument in greater detail, based on the 'fine-tuned' nature of the laws which permit and encourage the existence of intelligent life.

Design arguments sometimes draw analogies between things

made by humans on the one hand and the world on the other hand, to argue that a supernatural creator made the world. Analogical arguments do not prove their conclusions, but they do provide rational support for them, and such support is not to be sniffed at.

Mathematics, human understanding and the mind of God

Paul Davies, like many other thinkers, is impressed by our ability to understand fundamental aspects of the universe through mathematics:

> It may be no surprise that human minds can deduce the laws of falling objects, because the brain has evolved to devise strategies for dodging them. But do we have any right to expect extensions of such reasoning to work when it comes to nuclear physics, or astrophysics, for example? The fact that it does work, and works 'unreasonably' well, is one of the great mysteries of the universe.[3]

Davies points out that evolution by natural selection has trouble accounting for this astounding ability. As the Oxford Mathematician Roger Penrose writes:

> It is hard for me to believe . . . that such SUPERB theories could have arisen merely by some random natural selection of ideas leaving only the good ones as survivors. The good ones are simply much too good to be the survivors of ideas that have arisen in a random way. There must, instead, be some deep underlying reason for the accord between mathematics and physics.[4]

This deep match suggests that our ability to do abstract mathematics 'is no mere accident, no trivial detail, no insignificant byproduct of evolution that is piggybacking on some other mundane property'.[5] Rather, it points to 'the existence of a really deep relationship between minds that can do mathematics and the underlying laws of nature that produce them'.[6] This leads us to wonder why the laws of nature lead to the emergence of minds capable of mathematics, who can encode the very laws which produced them: 'It's almost uncanny,' writes Davies, 'it seems like a conspiracy.'[7]

It is reasonable to suppose that the process of evolution will have given humanity an intellectual capacity proportionate to the needs of survival. However, astoundingly, we possess an intellectual capacity which far outstrips the requirements of survival. Mathematician Eugene Wigner talked about the 'unreasonable effectiveness of mathematics' in uncovering the physical structure of reality. Why should beautiful equations be the clue to understanding nature? Why should our minds be able to access the depths of cosmic order? As John Polkinghorne suggests, 'Our surplus intellectual capacity, enabling us to comprehend the microworld of quarks and gluons and the macroworld of big bang cosmology, is on such a scale that it beggers belief that this is simply a fortunate by-product of the struggle for life.'[8]

A far better explanation of our intellectual ability would be that it is the intended result of some unevolved intellect behind the universe. Then it would be no surprise that the human mind has the capacity for understanding nature that it has, for the human mind would be a reflection of the mind behind nature.

The beauty of nature

Everywhere we look, from the rings of Saturn, to the subatomic world, nature is infused with beauty. Nature, at least figuratively speaking, is a work of art. Such beauty could be seen as the work of a supreme artist. We all know the experience of perceiving the beauty of art. This beauty is not the product of chance, but is introduced into a medium by an artist. Even when an artist splashes a canvas with paint 'at random', they choose the colours, the size of canvas, the method of 'random' application to be used, and so on. When we encounter the physical universe (or mathematical descriptions of its underlying regularities) we have an experience similar to appreciating a painting, or listening to music: 'Here too we are impressed with the world as a work of art and feel drawn to express gratitude to the unseen artist.'[9]

Beauty is a familiar indication of truth in science. The great mathematical physicist Paul Dirac famously wrote that,

> It is more important to have beauty in one's equations than to have them fit experiment . . . because the discrepancy may be due to minor features which are not properly taken into account and which will get cleared up with further developments of the theory . . . It seems that if one is working from the point of view of getting beauty into one's equations, and if one has a really sound instinct, one is on a sure line of success.[10]

Even if we say that evolution has picked up on beauty as a sign of truth, and that this explains our capacity to spot beauty, we still have not explained why beauty is a sign of truth in the first place. Isn't our appreciation of nature's beauty better explained as a reflection of God's appreciation of creation in minds created in his image?

The teleological elegance of nature

The Greek word for 'end' or 'goal' is *telos*. For this reason, design arguments are often called 'teleological' arguments. In the thirteenth century, Thomas Aquinas offered the view that natural bodies act as if they were guided towards an end, 'so as to obtain the best result'.[11] As J.P. Moreland writes, 'nature usually takes the simplest, most efficient means to achieve an end'.[12] The fitting of means to ends implies, argued Aquinas, an underlying intention. However, natural bodies lack consciousness, and so have no intentions of their own. Besides, how would all these natural bodies co-ordinate their actions in the way that we observe? Therefore some intelligent being exists who directs all natural things to their end:

> An orderliness of actions to an end is observed in all bodies obeying natural laws, even when they lack awareness. For their behaviour hardly ever varies, and will practically always turn out well; which shows that they truly tend to a goal, and do not merely hit it by accident. Nothing however that lacks awareness tends to a goal, except under the direction of someone with awareness and with understanding . . . Everything in nature, therefore is directed to its goal by someone with understanding and this we call 'God'.[13]

Science reveals a universe that works according to simple, mathematically elegant rules. As John Polkinghorne puts it, 'We live in a world whose physical fabric is endowed with transparent rational beauty.'[14] The beauty of the equations that express the regularities of nature (and the fact that these equations can be discovered and understood by humans) implies the existence of a mind behind the cosmos.

Why should nature work in such an elegant way? Either we seek an explanation of this state of affairs or we don't. Not to do so would be to shrug our shoulders and accept nature's economy and elegance as a brute fact. If we do seek an explanation, it must be in terms of the creative will of a powerful immaterial agent with a sense of elegance.

The laws of nature and nature's law giver

The existence of scientific laws is inexplicable unless we move beyond science into the realm of metaphysics, postulating the existence of a powerful personal agent who intends those laws for a reason.

It is a presupposition of science that 'the regularities and processes discovered on a limited scale hold throughout the universe'.[15] Here we meet the problem of induction. Just because we have always observed things to work in one way doesn't prove that things always do or always will work in that way. Consider a turkey who reasons on the basis of experience that, since every morning so far the farmer has fed it, the farmer will feed it every morning. One morning the turkey will get its neck wrung for Christmas! We are in much the same position with the laws of science. Paul Davies writes that,

> Just because the sun has risen every day of your life, there is no guarantee that it will rise tomorrow. The belief that it will—that there are indeed dependable regularities of nature—is an act of faith, but one which is indispensable to the progress of science.[16]

Science makes generalisations from our very small experience of a very large reality. Just because cannon balls have always fallen when dropped off the leaning tower of Pisa, this is no proof that the next cannon ball won't simply hang in mid-air. Of course, if the law of gravity continues to apply then the ball will fall; but what reason is there to believe that the law of gravity must hold true in all places at all times?

The laws produced by such generalisations are assumed to apply universally. This assumption is what makes the law useful in giving a scientific explanation or prediction. Assuming that Newton's law of gravity will hold I can accurately predict what will happen when an elephant sits on me. I'll be squashed. Newton's law predicts that the elephant will squash me, but Newton's law does not explain my being squashed. The law of gravity can hardly explain why there is gravity in the first place! Nor can it explain why gravity applies in any particular instance (why didn't the elephant float off into the sky like a pink balloon?). The law of gravity doesn't explain why I am squashed when an elephant sits on me. To explain why I am squashed we have to add that gravity applied to the elephant, and why. This is a question that cannot be given a scientific explanation:

There is a mystery about the fact that the material stuff of the universe obeys general laws. If the whole thing was really random, a matter of pure chance, one would expect that the regularities which the laws of physics describe would change or simply cease to exist after a time.[17]

Science moves from generalised experience to formulate theories that best explain those generalisations. The ultimate goal of science is to explain all the 'low level' generalisations in terms of a single 'high level' theory of everything, or TOE as scientists like to call it: 'Science . . . explains particular phenomena and low-level laws in terms partly of high-level laws. But from the very nature of science it cannot explain the highest-level laws of all; for they are that by which it explains all other phenomena.'[18] Even if scientists arrive at a TOE, this theory will not explain itself; nor will it provide any reason to believe that the universe won't radically alter tomorrow in a manner that is not predictable from the TOE and is describable only by a whole new TOE.

If the universe really is the product of purposeless chance, then why should nature obey elegant mathematical laws? If you think the universe has its origins in chance, doesn't it make sense to think that its existence and form of existence will be equally chancy? Atheistic scientists work on the assumption that the universe is rationally understandable because it runs on rational principles, but they have no justification for this belief.

The Revd Garth Barber, Anglican Chaplain at the University of East Anglia, is a member of the Society of Ordained Scientists. He recently wrote a letter to *New Scientist* magazine that read:

If a complete explanation for the origin of the Universe in terms of natural laws and mathematical equations is ever found then the question could still be raised: 'Who is the author and guarantor of those laws?' Or as Stephen Hawking himself vividly asks: 'What breathed fire into the equations?'[19]

Our trust in the continued existence and applicability of the laws of nature can be likened to trust in a person. We are generally correct to assume that those who love us will give their time and attention to us. The belief that someone loves us justifies us in such an assumption. If we take the laws of nature as expressing the will of a consistent supernatural personal agent, we will have a justification for assuming that those laws will apply in any given case.

Although our assumption of natural consistency would be rendered rational by such a move, we could not rule out the creator having good reason to do things differently now and again. Someone's love for us does not guarantee that they will give us time when we want it. They may have good reasons for being unable to talk with us on any given occasion. Similarly, it may be good that the law of gravity applies in most situations, and so the creator would have reason to cause things to behave in the manner described by Newton's law in most situations. But there might be situations in which it would be good that the law of gravity did not apply; and so God would have reason to cause things to behave in a manner not describable by that law. As C.S. Lewis put it, 'The philosophy which forbids you to make uniformity absolute is also the philosophy which offers you solid grounds for believing it to be general.'[20] This view was held by Sir Isaac Newton, who saw the laws of nature as existing within God's mind, and believed that God ensured physical particles obeyed the laws. Because God could change the laws at any time given a good reason to do so, Newton accepted the occurrence of miracles. This view is endorsed by modern-day theologian Keith Ward:

> The continuing conformity of physical particles to precise mathematical relationships is something that is much more likely to exist if there is an ordering cosmic mathematician who sets up the correlation in the requisite way. The existence of laws of physics . . . strongly implies that there is a God who formulates such laws and ensures that the physical realm conforms to them.[21]

Stephen Hawking says that 'one could always say that the laws of science are the expression of the will of God'.[22] Indeed, it was just such a belief that underpinned the growth of the scientific project in the West. Belief in a single, rational creator meant that nature was a true cosmos, a structure of ordered beauty. Human beings made in the image of God could hope to gain a measure of intellectual insight into the order of an artefact made by a mind greater than, but still similar to, their own. Since nature was not divine, but the creation of the divine, experimenting upon it was not sacrilege. In fact, experimenting with nature could fuel respect for the great architect of being.

Viewing of the laws of nature as a reflection of intentions within the mind of a divine natural-law-giver is reinforced by a consideration of the status of those laws. The elegant mathematical equations that describe the normal workings of nature do just and only that; they describe. A law of physics never has caused, and never can cause, anything whatsoever:

> The laws are the pattern to which events conform: the source of events must be sought elsewhere. This may be put in the form that the laws of nature explain everything except the source of events . . . Science, when it becomes perfect, will have explained the connection between each link in the chain [of events] and the link before it. But the actual existence of the chain will remain wholly unaccountable.[23]

A law of nature can predict (within various parameters of accuracy) what will happen given that things continue to behave in the normal way; and it can explain (within various parameters of accuracy) how some state of affairs has come about given that things behaved as they normally do. And that's all.

It is inviting to see the mathematical laws discovered by physicists as describing intended means to ends within the mind of God. Stephen Hawking was perhaps closer to the mark than he might have imagined when he wrote that:

If we discover a complete theory, it should in time be understandable in broad principle by everyone, not just a few scientists. Then we shall all, philosophers, scientists, and just ordinary people, be able to take part in the discussion of why it is that we and the universe exist. If we find the answer to that, it would be the ultimate triumph of human reason—for then we would know the mind of God.[24]

William Paley and the argument from analogy

Look at a watch, suggested the eighteenth-century theologian William Paley, and observe, 'that its several parts are framed and put together for a purpose'.[25] According to Paley, even if we had never seen a watch before, an inspection would lead us to conclude that it was designed and made for a purpose. Observe the universe and its objects and we see once again an intricate interplay of parts and physical laws arranged together and achieving a collective end (the evolution of intelligent life forms). The universe is analogous to the watch. The watch had a designer, so it is reasonable to think that the universe had a designer. Modern knowledge has only increased the strength of this analogy:

> Solar-powered machines capture the energy of photons and store it in chemicals. Electrical machines allow current to flow through nerves. Manufacturing machines build other molecular machines, as well as themselves. Cells swim using machines, copy themselves with machinery, ingest food with machinery. In short, highly sophisticated molecular machines control every cellular process.[26]

Does evolution exclude design?

People tend to bring up the subject of evolution as if this cuts the above analogy to shreds. 'We need not refer to a designer to account, for example, for the eye,' they say: 'Such organs are the result of a natural process.' Robin Le Poidevin makes just this criticism of the argument:

Evolution through natural selection is the non-teleological account of what, prior to Darwin, seemed an extraordinary fact requiring the hypothesis of a benevolent creator to explain it . . . What undermines the analogy is the discovery of a natural, non-teleological explanation for phenomena like the eye, such as the theory of natural selection.[27]

Evolution may account for the existence of complex arrangements of matter such as eye-balls; but evolution is itself a complicated process involving raw material being worked upon by the laws of natural selection (the mutation of genes, survival of the fittest, and so on). Evolution does not destroy the analogical design argument, it merely pushes it back a step, from the objects that make up the world, to the substances and processes that make the objects that make up the world! Evolution cannot account for ultimate origins or the existence of order, because its operation requires the existence of entities with certain possible behaviours in an environment that works upon those entities in an ordered way:

> *any sort of evolution of order of any kind will always presuppose pre-existing order and pre-existing entities governed by it.* It follows as a simple matter of logic that not all order evolved. Given the physical world—however much of evolution it may or may not contain— there is or was some order *in it* which did not evolve . . . We come here upon a logically insurpassable *limit* to what evolution, however it may be understood, can accomplish.[28]

The universe certainly seems to have an inbuilt drive towards complexity and the production of life. Life may be the product of evolution, but that just makes it look suspiciously like the universe is a 'life-producing factory':

> evolution can only have taken place, given certain natural laws . . . Nature . . . is a machine-making machine . . . men make not only machines, but machine-making machines [for example, we make

robotic production lines that churn out cars]. They may therefore naturally infer from nature which produces animals and plants, to a creator of nature similar to men who make machine-making machines.[29]

Science and personal explanations

The objection that evolution by natural selection excludes design exemplifies a common way that science is misused in order to attack religion. Some people think that science explains everything so well in its own terms that there is no need for explanation in any other terms. God is 'a hypothesis we can do without'.

This view is attractive because it is simple, and because some people have mistakenly used God to explain gaps in scientific theories that then get filled in scientifically making it look as if God is out of a job. However, this view is too simple. Just because you can explain something in scientific terms does not and cannot mean that it has no explanation in any other terms. Science ignores what Richard Swinburne calls 'personal explanation'. Why is the water in the kettle boiling? A scientific answer will include lots of chemistry and physics, talk of thermodynamics and so on. What it will not mention is that the water is boiling because I want a cup of tea. This is a 'teleological' explanation in terms of an end, goal, intention or purpose. Only minds can intend things, and this is why Swinburne calls teleological explanations involving intent 'personal' explanations.

An 'end' that doesn't involve an intention simply means the natural stopping point of a process. For example, the end of fire is burning itself out having burnt up all the available fuel. This doesn't mean that fire intends its end (fire isn't an agent), but nor does it mean that the fire's end wasn't intended by an agent, such as an arsonist. This terminology of ends comes to us from the Greek philosopher Aristotle who distinguished between material, formal, efficient and final causes. The classic illustration of these four causes is provided by the house. What causes a house to exist? There is a material cause: the bricks and other stuff of which the house is made. There is a formal cause: the form that these materials are arranged in. There is an efficient cause: the means whereby the material comes to be in the form that makes a house (in this cause the physical work of builders). Last there is the final cause: the purpose of the house.

A football passes between two posts. Why? Because the sun's atomic energy became the chemical energy in a bowl of corn flakes, which became the chemical energy stored in my body, which became the kinetic energy of my foot impacting on the ball. To use Aristotle's terminology this is an explanation in terms of the efficient cause. The material cause is the stuff involved (reducible to quarks and so on). The formal cause is that these quarks and so on formed a football and not a hedgehog, goalposts and not banana trees; and that the relation of the football and the goal posts took on the form 'passing between' rather than 'bouncing off the corner-post'. The scientific explanation could be given in more detail, but you get the gist.

However, the ball was kicked between the posts because I wanted to score a goal. This is the final cause. If I hadn't wanted to score a goal I wouldn't have kicked the ball between the goalposts! Both explanations are true, and we need both of them if we are to understand what's happening.

Of course, there needn't be a final cause for why the ball passes between the goalposts. I might produce the effect accidentally, or a violent gust of wind might blow it through. Still, science cannot rule out the existence of a final cause. It is logically possible that God intended my apparently accidental stumbling, or that gust of wind that caused the ball to move.

Science might be able to tell us how the football ended up where it did, or how the universe began, but it can never tell us if there is a reason for the universe existing or the football moving as it does. Nor can science tell us, if there is a reason, what that reason is. If I asked a scientist why anything exists at all, could she give me a scientific answer? No. She might say that 'there is no reason', but that wouldn't be a scientific answer. That would be her metaphysical interpretation upon the existence of the universe: that it lacks a teleological, personal explanation. Science can't rule out the opposite interpretation, because science is a discipline that works by excluding personal explanations in the first place. As John Polkinghorne explains, 'The fact is that science has purchased its success by the modesty of its exploratory and explanatory ambitions. It limits itself to an impersonal encounter with the world, deliberately bracketing out those personal experiences that give human life its greatest satisfaction.'[30]

A window is very good at letting in light without letting in the wind. Windows were invented to maximise light and warmth inside houses. Science is very good at explaining physical phenomena in terms of law-like regularities, uncovering increasingly fundamental levels of material reality. Science was invented by the Greeks to explain physical events without mentioning the gods (because intellectual Greeks became fed up with the crude pantheon of gods and goddesses of popular Greek religion), without appealing to personal explanations. But to make science and scientific explanations the arbiter of what is real is like using a window to argue that the wind does not exist. 'Look,' says the atheist, 'science explains everything without mentioning anything supernatural; God doesn't exist.' 'Look,' says the glazier, 'light is coming through this window, but no wind. Wind doesn't exist.' Well, of course no wind is coming through the window, that's the whole point! That's what the window is for, and that's why it does its job of keeping the house bright and warm so well. Of course science doesn't explain anything with reference to God, that's the whole point! That's what science is for, discovering the physical explanations behind physical things; and that's why science does its job of explaining nature in physical terms so well. Evolution cannot exclude divine design.

Christian theism and evolution

There are three senses of evolution. First, it can mean a theory about what happened and when in the history of life. More complex species appeared on earth over time (as shown by the fossil record). Second, it can mean a theory about how this happened, by 'natural selection'. Third, it can mean the absence of divine design, as distinct from God intending natural selection. This third sense is not scientific at all, but an interpretation of scientific theory. Some Christians accept evolution in sense one but not two or three, while others accept it in senses one and two, but not three. Evolution in sense three clearly contradicts Christian belief, but evolution in this sense is not scientific. Richard Dawkins explains the distinction between the first two senses of 'evolution':

> Natural selection is Darwin's particular theory for the *mechanism* of evolution. Evolution itself means that species are descended from other species that are different from themselves . . . Natural selection, which is the main mechanism of evolution, is the nonrandom survival of randomly varying hereditary characteristics.[31]

Evolution in the first sense is not a new idea. Aristotle taught that humans were developed from fish. And guess who made the following assertion: 'In the beginning were created only germs or causes of the forms of life which were afterwards to be developed in gradual course.' It wasn't Charles Darwin, or Richard Dawkins. It was St Augustine, according to whom the world was created like an expectant mother, pregnant with the causes of things yet to be. Augustine held that the Genesis reference to six days of creation was symbolic. He was not alone in this view:

Though it is true that the doctrine of God as creator, together with other beliefs (such as those concerning the nature of the man-woman relationship and the status of man in the animal kingdom), were all derived from Genesis, that is not to say the early church held to a literal interpretation of those writings. The lack of literal intention was in fact asserted by many of the early church [leaders]—not only by Augustine.[32]

As philosopher Peter van Inwagen writes, 'A lot of people seem to think that all Christians were literalists before the geological discoveries of the early nineteenth century . . . This is historically false.'[33] I hope that we may all agree with Darwin, who wrote in *On the Origin of Species*, 'I see no good reason why the views given in this volume should shock the religious feelings of anyone.'

What Darwin proposed was a theory about how evolution works. He suggested that variations within animals and plants might lead, in the right circumstances, to some varieties having a greater chance at survival and reproduction than others. This process Darwin called 'natural selection'. Those life forms which reproduced most successfully in their environment would pass on their characteristics to their children. Some of these children might happen to be even better adapted than their parents, and so would out-survive their contemporaries to pass on their advantages to the next generation, and so on.

Environmental conditions would mould the evolution of creatures from one generation to the next by pruning out those which were unfit for their surroundings in favour of those with advantages of form. Small changes in creatures would enable them to exploit different environmental niches and, given enough time, these alterations would accumulate to such a degree that one variation on an original theme would be so different from another that two species would exist when once there was one. This leads to the theory of common ancestry. Contrary to popular belief, Darwinian evolution does not suggest that humans evolved from apes (still less from monkeys), but rather from a common ancestor which diversified through natural selection and led to the existence of both humans and apes.

Arguments against natural selection as a mechanism of evolution do not directly detract from evolution itself; although the lack of any plausible mechanism for evolution would count against it. Biological evolution, by whatever mechanism, happens within the wider context of cosmic evolution from the Big Bang. 'Evolution' as applied to the universe as a whole simply means 'historical development', from small to big, young to old. The possibility of biological evolution is wrapped up in the finely tuned laws that describe cosmic evolution. For example, as carbon-based life forms, we depend upon carbon made in stars which exploded millions of years ago.

This is evolution, the cosmic development from the simple to the complex, including biological evolution from stardust to people. The evidence for evolution comes from several sources, including: cosmology, the fossil record which exhibits a progression from simple to complex forms, similar structures in the anatomy of different species, the modification of plants and animals by breeders, vestigial organs like the 'tail' of the human embryo, biological changes due to geographical distribution and the construction of an evolutionary tree through molecular biology. This evidence forms an elegant picture of development according to simple laws which is highly suggestive of divine design:

> The exactness of our universe argues for the anthropic principle, which basically states that the existence and sustenance of man is not brought about by a random universe but is dependent on a universe with a very particular character in its basic laws and circumstances. It is like an acute Copernican revolution, not restoring earth to the centre of the cosmos, but linking the nature of the universe with its potential for the existence of man.[34]

However, evolution has its critics (many, but by no means all, of whom are 'fundamentalist' Christians who take the Genesis creation story literally). As Professor Donald M. Mackay wrote, 'Doubtless the God of truth will expect us to judge this theory, like others, on its own scientific merits; and it is well to remember that, however widely accepted today, it is still a speculation on trial, and liable itself to evolve as time goes on!'[35]

I agree with creationist Dr David Rosevear that 'The evolutionary worldview of blind chance producing the watch, as with Dawkin's The Blind Watchmaker, is very unsatisfactory, because it leaves no room for meaning and purpose in life.'[36] But we need not be pushed into the false alternative of miraculous divine creation without any chance element. The Christian theist may not want to get rid of evolution as an account of species development, but they may want to reject it as a complete explanation. God can 'have his cake and eat it' by working through 'chance'. God can intend the operation of chance elements within evolution just as the creator of Monopoly intended the chance elements involved in throwing the dice and picking cards from the randomly shuffled 'community chest'. The random element within biological evolution doesn't ruin the purpose of life any more than the random elements within Monopoly ruin the point of playing the game! The crucial point is not what mechanism underlies life, but whether or not that mechanism is intended. So long as the 'chance' element in evolution does not outweigh the 'unfolding' of the anthropically precise laws of nature, we can join with those Christian scientists and theologians who see the 'chance' element of evolution as integral to what God is doing in creation. As Keith Ward says:

> If there is an element of randomness, it lets in some freedom, some openness, some creativity. But it's not going to be so big as to cancel out God's ability to say where the universe is going, and God's ability to ensure that it gets there. So I'm all in favour of a bit of randomness.[37]

John Polkinghorne explains that a scientific way to refer to the 'orderly openness of cosmic history'[38] is to refer to the interplay of 'chance' and 'necessity'. 'Chance' represents a shifting exploration of nature's inherent possibilities. 'Necessity' here means the orderliness of the physical world: 'The relatively reliable transmission of genetic information from one generation to the next permits the preservation of new forms of life. These new forms flourish if they prove advantageously adapted to their lawful environment. Thus regularity sifts the offerings of happenstance.'[39] Chance provides novelty in an evolutionary world while necessity selects the fruitful. A world of pure chance would be chaotic and unfruitful. A world of mechanical necessity would be rigid and unfruitful. Only the combination of the two can produce the fruitfulness of our universe:

> The recognition of a degree of historical contingency in the details of what is happening does not negate the claim that a creatorly purpose is nevertheless being fulfilled within an evolutionary universe ... that the world has proved capable of evolving selfconscious worshipping beings seems to have been built into its physical fabric from the start.[40]

Accounting for DNA

One of the toughest challenges facing the theory of evolution is the existence of DNA. DNA is a crucial component of evolutionary theory. It both passes the form of creatures from one generation to the next, and provides the variation necessary for natural selection when this copying is imperfect. The science journal *Scientific American* (February 1991) summed up the conundrum of DNA in the following manner: 'Proteins cannot form without DNA, but neither can DNA form without proteins. To those pondering the origin of life, it is a classic chicken-and-egg problem. Which came first, proteins or DNA?'

What the problem comes down to is the question of how,

from the material present before life, there arose the complex, information-bearing and transmitting system which is a prerequisite of evolution by natural selection. Evolution works upon systems that pass on information from one generation to the next, so the first such system could not have evolved:

> cumulative selection presupposes some form of replication possessed by the original and intervening living entities. They need to have some mechanism of reproduction . . . These powers cannot themselves be the product of cumulative selection. . somehow non-replicating entities just turned into reproducing species.[41]

Natural selection cannot account for the origin of life.

Cells contain molecules, essentially proteins and the nucleic acids DNA and RNA. Proteins are like chains of beads (amino acids) strung together in a very particular order. This is not the repetitive order of a snowflake but what biologists Lane Lester and Raymond G. Bohlin call 'design as information'. The genes that determine our form, passing on characteristics from our parents, are found in the chromosomes of the nucleus of every cell in our bodies. Genes are made of DNA, another chain molecule with four types of 'beads' called nucleotides. 'The arrangement of these nucleotides can be copied into another long molecule, messenger RNA, and then used by the protein-making machinery of the cell to produce the exact sequence of amino acid beads in each protein.'[42] DNA contains the 'genetic code', a message written in a four-letter alphabet along the DNA chain: 'the problem of the origin of life comes down to the problem of arranging a DNA or perhaps RNA necklace of say, 10,000 beads in the correct order. In such a case there would be $10^{8,000}$ possible arrangements, a vast number!'[43]

How are we to account for the coming together of nucleotides and amino acids in the precise arrangement of proteins, DNA and RNA? Sir Fred Hoyle notoriously argued that the emergence of life from the random shuffling of molecules is 'as ridiculous and improbable as the proposition that a tornado blowing through a junk yard may assemble a Boeing 747'. Hoyle calculated the likelihood of life beginning through the 'chance' combination of twenty component amino acids into two thousand enzyme molecules at one in ten to the power of forty thousand ($10^{40,000}$). This calculation has been criticised by biologist R.J. Berry:

> The relevant chance is some far simpler self-replicating system, capable of development by natural selection, being formed at any place on earth, and at any time within a period of 100 million years. We cannot calculate this probability, since we know neither the nature of the hypothetical self-replicating system, nor the composition of the 'primeval soup' in which it arose. The origin of life was obviously a rare event, but there is no reason to think that it is as extraordinary or unlikely as Hoyle calculated.[44]

What Berry is really saying is that, although life might have had a simpler beginning than that for which Hoyle calculates the odds, we have no idea about what biological system does stand at the starting line of evolution, or how that system came into being: 'The admission is unblushing. Science just does not have knowledge of the beginnings in the genuine sense of the term. It cannot answer the how, much less the why.'[45]

The sketchy nature of our knowledge in this area makes any calculation of the chances of life coming from non-life by the random shuffling of molecules a matter of educated guesswork. As Robert Shapiro says: 'We don't know the key recipe—the set of special ingredients and forms of energy that could lead chemical systems up the ladder of organization on the first steps of life. These circumstances may be quite rare and difficult or, once you have grasped the trick, as simple as brewing beer.'[46]

Advocates of the 'chance formation' theory take some comfort from the famous experiment devised by Stanley Miller and Harold Urey in 1953, which showed that certain amino acids could be easily formed when electrical energy was passed through a simple mixture of gases: 'These amino acids are building blocks of proteins, one of life's key components . . . Unfortunately, life is vastly more organized than the "prebiotic" chemical mixtures formed in Miller-Urey-type experiments.'[47] The formation of amino acids is an important step in the right direction from non-life to life, but it is a small step. Besides which, the conditions of this experiment, a guess at conditions on the early earth, are a matter of controversy.

Perhaps Hoyle's calculation is an exaggeration. Perhaps David Wilkinson's lowest estimate of one in 10^{30}, or Tim Hawthorne's figure of one in $10^{8,000}$, is closer to the mark. But whether the chances of life forming through chance are one in $10^{40,000}$ or 10^{30}, the odds do not look good. As J.J. Haldane said in a written debate with the atheist Jack Smart: 'The emergence of life and the start of speciation call for explanations and what reductionism has to offer fails to provide these, giving at best a blank cheque to chance, which is to say offering no intelligible explanation at all.'[48]

In reply, Smart asked why self-replicating molecules couldn't come about 'through the coming together of a number of non-replicating molecules?'[49] Admitting that such an occurrence would be rare, he simply reminded Haldane that 'the universe is immensely large and was in existence for a long time before the beginning of life. Of course such small proto-replicators would have to evolve by natural selection into the DNA molecules of present-day life. But I see no implausibility in this.'[50] This is, as Haldane noted, in effect a 'why not?' reply:

> Standard evolutionary explanations posit replication as spontaneously arising some three or four billion years ago in a form more primitive than DNA. Needless to say there is no direct evidence of this . . . So the task is to show how DNA could have arisen from more primitive replication, say RNA, and how that could have resulted from non-replicating systems.[51]

Does taking into consideration the size and age of the universe increase the likelihood of life emerging from non-life somewhere in space-time more likely, as Smart suggests?

> If we assume that planets form when stars themselves form, then there are only between 10^{19} and 10^{24} planets in the universe. Comparing this with the chances of life appearing spontaneously, it is clear that life should only exist on one planet within the observable universe, this is the earth![52]

Faced with odds of $10^{40,000}$ to one, multiplying the trial rate by 10^{19} has little effect on the outcome. (The odds of one in 10^{30} in a universe with 10^{24} planets is, however, approaching the realms of likelihood.) If the emergence of life was a 'freak of nature', an event that happened by chance against all the odds, this would seem to cut against the view that the universe was set up by God for the purpose of producing people. This is just the sort of argument atheists like Dawkins seize upon; but in doing so they ignore or discount all the evidence for the existence of God, including the anthropic teleological argument from the laws of nature which strongly indicates that one of God's purposes in creation was the creation of people. It looks very much as if the universe was set up as a suitable home for people. The universe is a place where people can evolve and have evolved. Why would God go to all the trouble of creating and sustaining just the sort of one-in-a-billion universe where this is possible, and not even ensure that its emergence is probable?

The popular scientific explanation by 'chance' is hardly an explanation at all. The 'chance' theory says that the existence of life is very unlikely—and yet life exists. It would not normally be considered the mark of a good theory to make the occurrence of what has occurred so very unlikely! We should prefer any theory that makes the emergence of life from non-life more probable than does the 'random shuffling' theory. Paul Davies lays out the options:

The main reason why the origin of life is a puzzle is because the spontaneous appearance of such elaborate and organized complexity seems so improbable . . . if I shuffle a pack of cards and then deal them to four players and find that each player has received an exact suit in correct numerical sequence, am I to suppose a miracle has occurred to interfere with the physical process of shuffling? It is certainly *possible* that ordinary 'natural' shuffling will produce an exactly ordered sequence of cards, but because the odds are so small, the occurrence of such an event would arouse deep suspicion that something had happened to interfere with the randomness of the process.

There are two ways in which such interference could arise. One is the actual violation of a law of physics. For example . . . a molecule could suddenly reverse direction for no reason of physics in order that it might combine with another nearby molecule as part of an essential step in the life-creating process . . . The second is the purposeful manipulation of matter within the laws of physics. We know that matter can be so manipulated because human beings do it all the time. We can contrive to produce highly non-random processes (such as unusual card sequences) without violating any laws of physics, so presumably a purposeful Deity could also do this.[53]

We could say that the crucial step from chemistry to biochemistry was the result of a miracle.[54] However, as Professor C.A. Coulson says, 'When we come to the scientifically unknown, our correct policy is not to rejoice because we have found God; it is to become better scientists.' Invoking a miracle to fill in a gap in present scientific knowledge smacks of the 'God of the gaps'. Before we assert that the origin of life was a miracle— God working in an extraordinary manner—we should search for an explanation that is consistent with what we know of God's ordinary mode of operations (as described by the laws of science).

A recent article in *New Scientist* reported arguments that life evolved independently on two occasions on the Earth.[55] Professor of Geology, Mark McMenamin, believes that a group of creatures called Ediacarans were *a parallel evolutionary thread* cut short by our own: 'Complex life evolved twice and only one form made it to the present day.' Ediacarans were protoplasmic blobs that popped up about 600 million years ago among the mats of algae and mould that were the main inhabitants of the earth at the time. Some scientists believe that Ediacarans were a class of life-form all of their own, others think they were lichen. McMenamin is convinced that they were multi-cellular organisms. Ediacarans colonised most of the earth, including the ocean floor. Theirs was a world without predators, a world playfully called 'The garden of Ediacara' by McMenamin, and so these creatures had no defensive capabilities.

Over tens of millions of years the Ediacarans developed into several varieties and shapes, including some with antenna and even the first sign of primitive eyes. McMenamin even thinks that a variety of Ediacara called Spriggina were evolving crude 'brains': 'They were developing ways to pick up environmental clues and process that information in ways that would allow them to adapt better and leave more progeny.' Says McMenamin, 'Edicarans represent the first evidence of anything like intelligence on earth.'

Just as Ediacarans were beginning to exploit their potential, they disappeared in the 'Cambrian explosion', a geological blink of the eye when animal evolution accelerated to warp speeds. Some palaeontologists think that geological upheavals clouded the oceans and cut the Ediacarans off from their energy source, the sun. McMenamin thinks that new predators ate them out of existence.

If McMenamin is right, we have proof of an inbuilt drive towards complexity and intelligence within the laws of nature. As McMenamin says, 'the forces and structures of the Universe evoke life, which evokes complex life, which evokes intelligence.' Other scientists, such as Rudolf Raff, a biologist from the University of Indiana, think that the evolution of complex life-forms is not inevitable, but that if and when they arise it creates a positive feed-back loop, 'Once a nervous system evolves, it becomes a driver for natural selection—to outcompete the other guys with nervous systems or just to avoid being eaten by them.' This is a weaker indication of an inbuilt natural drive towards complexity and intelligence than suggested by McMenamin's views, but it is still an indication.

If our estimate of the likelihood of life occurring is increased by the fact that it has occurred, and if intelligent life may well have begun to evolve twice (once successfully and once not so successfully), then it is likely that the origin of intelligent life is not such an iffy event as is suggested by the 'random shuffling' theory.

There is plenty of evidence to suggest that there must be more to the origin of life than the chance combination of amino acids formed from the primeval soup. The universe was fine-tuned to produce conditions suitable for life. Elements appearing from the initial conditions of the Big Bang formed amino acids necessary to the construction of proteins and DNA. Natural selection weeds out life forms ill adapted to their environment. Sentient beings evolve on at least one planet (that's us folks!). There are even signs that Ediacarans were developing in the direction of intelligence before they were wiped out. We have reason to believe that the universe is created by a god, and we have good reason to think that he is interested in the emergence of sentient beings such as ourselves. The universe, and the god behind it, seem to have gone to so much trouble that I find it hard to believe that the origin of life was a fluke—a cosmic mistake. We should be looking for a view that is consistent with what we know about cosmic evolution and God.

Atheists like Bertrand Russell and Richard Dawkins are happy to say that life is a cosmic mistake—but this cuts against the existence of meaning and purpose in life. As J.J. Haldane rightly says, whatever other function it might serve, 'practical reasoning is for successful action, and philosophical speculation is for the sake of attaining and understanding truth.' [56] Therefore, 'Descriptions and explanations in terms of purposes cannot be ignored. They can only be rejected in favour of [reductionistic] mechanism or attributed to the agency of a designer.'[57]

When we look at the fossil record, and compare it with the age of the earth, we find that life began pretty much just as soon as it possibly could: 'Within a few 100 million years of the earliest possible time that life could have evolved on Earth, it did. This is very encouraging . . . these results indicate that intelligent life can evolve in a rather short interval on the cosmic scale—a billion years or so.'[58] Professor of Physics and Astronomy, Lawrence M. Krauss, stresses how significant it is that life exists: 'The important fact to recognize is that life did form in the galaxy at least once. I cannot overemphasize how important this is. Based on all our experience in science, nature rarely produces a phenomenon just once.'[59] Again, the evidence points to the emergence of life being more fundamental to the existence of this universe than can be accounted for by the 'chance' hypothesis.

Paul Davies is notable for the consideration he gives to the interface between science and religion. He is not a Christian. Nor is he a theist in the full sense of the word. However, he does seem to hold some sort of deism, which makes him more sympathetic towards theism than out-and-out atheists. Consideration of the anthropic principle forces Davies to 'put his money on design'. Davies thinks that there is an 'optimistic arrow of time' working within the limitations of the second law of thermodynamics which means that the emergence of life from non-life is no accident, but something integral to the 'fine tuning' of the universe apparent from the anthropic principle:

> In recent years it has become clear that many physical and chemical systems can, in certain circumstances, leap spontaneously to states of greater organizational complexity . . . the laws of physics and

chemistry are such as to channel matter towards states of even greater complexity, amplifying the probability that complex biochemical molecules will be synthesized . . .

[Biochemist Stuart] Kauffman claims the innate tendencies of complex systems to exhibit order spontaneously provide nature with the 'raw materials' on which selection can act. Natural selection, he claims, moulds an already existing biological order. There are thus two forces for change rather than one, with self-organization the more powerful and sometimes proceeding despite selection. As these forces tangle and vie in co-evolving populations, so selection tends to drive the system towards the edge of chaos, where change and adaption are most efficient . . .

Kauffman believes that, given the laws of physics, life will automatically emerge from an inert chemical soup under the right conditions. No miracles, no stupendously improbable molecular accidents need be involved. Chemical self-organization can do the trick: 'Life is an expected, collectively self-organized property of catalytic polymers . . . if this is true, then the routes to life are many and its origin is profound yet simple.'[60]

This 'optimistic' view is not widely accepted by biologists, although as long ago as 1913 the distinguished Harvard biochemist, Henderson, wrote that, 'The properties of matter and the course of cosmic evolution are now seen to be intimately related to the structure of the living being and to its activities . . . the biologist may now rightly regard the universe in its very essence as biocentric.' Henderson considered the 'fitness of the environment' for life too great to be accidental, and asked what manner of law was able to explain the match. Perhaps we are only beginning to answer his question:

Kauffman's ideas about self-organization effectively introduce into biology a sort of 'law of increasing complexity' . . . While biologists hate this, non-biologists find it unremarkable . . . the universe began in a state of featureless simplicity and has evolved over time, in a long and complicated sequence of self-organizing processes . . . Biological evolution is . . . just one more example of this law-like progressive trend that pervades the cosmos . . . the general trend from simple to complex . . . seems to me to be built into the laws of nature in a basic way.[61]

This theory is hotly debated. This might be because it indicates the existence of a biological 'anthropic principle' which lends itself to theistic interpretation. However, this new biological teleology does have some heavyweight apologists. Stanley Millar has declared that the primeval soup of life-forming molecules could have produced living cells within 10,000 years. Millar believes, on the basis of his experiments, that given the right mix of chemicals and environment life would form on any planet. According to Frank Drake, 'Where life could appear, it would appear.'[62] Nobel Prize-winning chemist Melvin Calvin and Carl Sagan agree, believing that life is more likely to form than not on a suitable planet. Carl Sagan has written that, 'The available evidence strongly suggests that the origin of life should occur given the initial conditions and a billion years of evolutionary time. The origin of life on suitable planets seems built into the chemistry of the universe.'[63] Secular biologist Michael J. Denton's studies convinced him that the laws of nature are uniquely and intentionally fit for the evolution of life like our own. He recently published his findings as *Nature's Destiny—How the Laws of Biology reveal Purpose in the Universe* (Free Press, 1998).

There is other evidence that sentient life is written into the 'Cosmic Blueprint', as Davies puts it. Biological convergence, where nature arrives at similar solutions to a problem from different starting points, 'smacks of a law-like trend'.[64] For example, the eye has been 'invented' independently several times during the Earth's history. Moreover:

> To say that consciousness is merely an accident sounds like the ultimate Just So story. It's awfully ad hoc . . . In fact, it's just as much a cop-out as saying: 'It's a miracle! Life was busily evolving . . . and then a miracle occurred and consciousness appeared!' So I say: no miracles and no stupendously unlikely accidents. If we really want to under-

stand consciousness, we've got to fit it into the general picture of nature, into the laws of physics, in a manner that is fundamental and integral, and not appeal to some special accident along the way . . .

I conclude [that] consciousness, far from being a trivial accident, is a fundamental feature of the universe, a natural product of the outworkings of the laws of nature to which they are connected in a deep and still mysterious way . . . One of the depressing things about the last three hundred years of science is the way it has tended to marginalize, even trivialize, human beings and thus alienate them from the universe in which they live. I think we do have a place in the universe—not a central place but a significant place nevertheless.

No words better encapsulate this sentiment than those of Freeman Dyson: 'I do not feel like an alien in this universe. The more I examine the universe and study the details of its architecture the more evidence I find that the universe in some sense must have known we were coming.'[65]

As David Wilkinson writes:

It is interesting to observe that this 'innate tendency in the laws of nature to bring forth life' has parallels within religious thought . . . certainly, if it were shown that such a tendency was present in the laws of nature, it would raise the question of why should this be so? Quite a natural answer would be that God has created a Universe which has the inevitable consequence of Life. Perhaps Davies' 'conspiracy' is divine creativity.[66]

The veiled hand of God

I want to turn now to the suggestions of another eminent thinker, Keith Ward, who is Regius Professor of Divinity at Oxford University. In *God, Chance and Necessity* (OneWorld, 1996), he does a masterful job of showing how the atheistic arguments of scientists like Stephen Hawking, Peter Atkins and Richard Dawkins are flawed. The book caused quite a stir at the time of its publication, with an exchange of views between Ward, Atkins and Dawkins in *The Times*.

Ward begins by saying that it is no harder to suppose that God brought life into existence through a long process of evolution than to think that creation happened over a short period of time. Indeed, the evolutionary path might be seen as the more impressive. According to Ward, there is every reason to regard the evolutionary account and belief in God as mutually reinforcing, for 'evolution from a state where no values are apprehended to states in which values can be both created and enjoyed gives an overwhelming impression of purpose or design'.[67]

Ward goes on to note, as we have, the inadequacy of current biological orthodoxy when it comes to the question of origins. Complex molecule chains have appeared with the amazing ability to make copies of themselves. According to the orthodoxy of biologists like Richard Dawkins, the existence of self-replicating life forms is highly improbable; yet they exist. Like Paul Davies, Ward sees the long odds against the formation of self-replicating systems, not as evidence for naturalism, but as a sign of the paucity of the naturalist's account which therefore lends credence to the alternative offered by design. He admits that theists can't deny that DNA could have come about by chance, but argues that if this is the best explanation the naturalistic hypothesis can provide, it is inferior to any hypothesis that makes the occurrence of self-replicators more probable. One hypothesis that makes the existence of self-replicators more probable is that God exists and exerts an influence upon the outworkings of the natural systems in question.

Ward goes along with Davies in arguing that God selects the laws of nature with a view to the emergence of sentient beings. He goes a step beyond Davies by introducing the concept of 'top-down' causation—whereby God influences the course of nature within the framework of the laws he established. This takes up Davies' suggestion that God could actively manipulate matter within the laws of physics towards the fulfilment of the divine will. Davies leaves this suggestion on the shelf (along with the possibility of God acting in a manner contrary to the laws of nature) in favour of God setting up the laws in such a way as to guarantee life. All three explanations are possibilities. By arguing that a combination of these options is a better explanation than picking one alone, Ward reminds us that these possibilities do not exclude each other.

The theory of natural selection, says Ward, asserts that random mutations occur, 'in such a way that some mutated organisms will be more efficient at reproducing and will thus tend to survive',[68] passing on their genes to the next generation. After generations of mutation and natural selection, the resulting life-forms will by definition be the best survivors and reproducers. How does this explain the emergence of such complex, conscious beings as ourselves? There are so many things that might go wrong with the process. The mutations might be too large, or too small. Environmental catastrophes might wipe out whole life forms. In Ward's opinion, natural selection does not make the development of sentient life inevitable: 'there is nothing in the principle to guarantee that the "right" type of progressive mutations will ever occur, that the environment will favour them, or that in a struggle for life, the more complex organisms will be favoured.'[69]

All the theory can predict, according to Ward's analysis, is that organisms with a certain degree of complexity are likely to be selected 'if all the relevant causal and environmental conditions are right',[70] which means 'the 'right' mutations occurring in the 'right' environment'.[71] This, in turn, 'is a necessary condition of the existence of consciousness, which is likely to be selected if it ever occurs'.[72] Hence, even in Ward's pessimistic assessment of evolution by natural selection, we meet a weak indication of a 'conspiracy' favouring the evolution of sentience. Perhaps the remaining credibility gap is closed by the existence of those 10^{24} other planets. Ward thinks not.

In Ward's judgement then, the same problem which attends the supposed 'chance' coming together of chemicals to form the first self-replicating system upon which natural selection could work, also applies to the mechanism natural selection itself. In both cases that problem is the gargantuan odds against the process in question having such fruitful results as were in fact achieved. While some might see the apparent 'chanciness' of our existence as counting against God's existence, Ward turns the tables by pointing out that making the occurrence of what actually happens improbable is rather an odd thing for a scientific theory to do. It is precisely because (as he believes) the theory of natural selection does not make the appearance of sentient life probable that Ward thinks we should favour the theistic explanation.

Ward admits that it is possible for the theist to argue that the laws of nature make the development of sentient life forms probable. We would then see natural selection as the way God works, without interfering in the laws of nature, to realise his purpose in creation. But Ward does not take this view himself. He believes that God is more intimately involved in the evolutionary process. The idea of 'top-down' causation, developed by priest and former biochemist Arthur Peacocke, provides Ward with a way to view this involvement. 'Top-down' causation happens when the nature of a complex whole affects the behaviour of its parts. For the theist, 'the ultimate complex whole consists of the universe and God'.[73] God sustains the universe at every moment of its existence, making every moment a moment of creation wherein God's transcendent being may have an immanent effect not excluded by the preceding state of the universe. This is the contrast between the naturalist's view of the universe as a closed system of cause and effect, and the theist's view of the universe as an open system amenable to God's transcendent 'out-side' influence.[74]

Ward's suggestion is that a full-blooded concept of a personal God means that he not only transcendently initiates and sustains natural laws with certain ends in mind, but exerts an imminent influence upon the outworking of those laws. This divine causal influence is not a constant breaking of his own laws (although this is possible). Rather, it preserves God's 'hidden-ness', from all but the eyes of trusting or seeking faith, by working within the self-imposed 'limitations' of those laws. The possibility of such divine influence requires that a wholly deterministic account of physical causation is impossible to give; but as Ward says, 'Such an account cannot be given anyway.'[75]

We cannot specify initial conditions in physical systems with absolute precision because we run up against Heisenberg's famous Uncertainty Principle, which says that we cannot have simultaneous knowledge of all the relevant physical variables. If we know a particle's velocity we can't know its exact position, and vice versa. This uncertainty has a knock-on effect in the large-scale world in 'chaotic' regimes where small changes at the 'micro-level' can lead to large changes at the 'macroscopic' level. This is the so-called 'butterfly effect', because a good illustration of the theory is that a little butterfly flapping its wings can theoretically begin a cascade of efficient causes that result in a big storm. It is this sort of consideration that limits the accuracy of long-range weather-forecasting. As far as physics is concerned, God can influence events in the large-scale physical world (within certain limits) by altering the events in the small-scale world in ways we could never detect.

Christianity can not only accommodate evolution by natural selection, it can assimilate it into a richer explanatory context which provides a far better explanation of the facts than can be offered by any purely scientific account. As Ward says elsewhere:

> This is a universe which generates out of itself its own creatively emergent future . . . the direction is built into the structure of things from the first; and, for the theist, things are drawn towards new creative actualisations by the attraction of the ideal, the supreme perfection of God. To use an old analogy, God is like the sun, drawing out plants from the earth to flower and blossom in its light.[76]

God desires the creation of finite personal beings capable of entering into freely chosen relationships with Him and each other. This means our existence is meaningful, because it has a purpose. The universe exists as a necessary condition for the existence of certain values, primarily the value of chosen love. In this sense, love really does 'make the world go round'. To this end, God sustains a universe in a manner normally described by the laws of science. God can exert His influence by working within the self-imposed 'limits' of the laws of nature. In so doing He veils His activity—retaining maximum natural consistency, and preserving our freedom to ignore Him if we wish—under our inability to specify initial conditions with absolute precision. As John Polkinghorne writes, God's 'immanent action . . . will always lie hidden in those complexities whose precarious balance makes them unsusceptible to prediction'.[77]

It remains a possibility that God may act in a way contrary to that described by scientific laws, providing that He has sufficient reason so to act. If the origin and evolution of life towards sentient beings can be adequately explained in (theistically interpreted) scientific terms, and if God is unlikely to over-rule His 'laws' for nature if 'lawful' means will suffice, we need not appeal to a 'miracle' in order to account for the facts. Whether the evolution of sentient beings is guaranteed by the laws of nature (as Paul Davies believes) or not (as Keith Ward thinks), a theistic interpretation of the process improves upon the naturalistic account, and the theory of evolution therefore supports belief in the existence of God.

DNA, information and analogy

Far from destroying the argument from design then, our greater knowledge of biology has led to several new design arguments. One of the most interesting of these new arguments takes as its starting point DNA: 'The crucial thing about DNA is that it has to exist before there are intelligent creatures, and yet it has the character of encoded information which can only be produced by an intelligence.'[78]

We can distinguish several types of design. One is 'design as order'. Such design involves the repetition of a simple structural unit, as found in crystals and snowflakes. These structures have high order but little 'information content'. They are like the repetition of NONONO. Structures with order like this can be explained as the result of the internal properties of their component parts. For example, the order in an ice crystal is due to the properties of hydrogen and oxygen.

In contrast to 'design as order' is 'design as information'. The information content of a structure is defined as 'the minimum number of instructions needed to specify it'.[79] For example, snowflakes and wrapping paper with 'Merry Christmas' written all over it are highly ordered, but have little information content. Both patterns can be specified with only a few instructions, ie: '1) Write "M-e-r-r-y C-h-r-i-s-t-m-a-s" and 2) Do it again.'[80] Structures with a high information content, on the other hand, take a lot of instructions to specify. If you wanted a computer to reproduce the text of the Bible, you'd have to feed it a long programme specifying each letter and punctuation mark in turn: 'This is the kind of order we find in DNA. It would be impossible to produce a simple set of instructions telling a chemist how to synthesize the DNA of even the simplest bacterium. You would have to specify each "letter," one by one.'[81]

DNA information 'must be described by making quite literal use of the linguistic terms, *code, transcribe,* and *translate*'.[82] The genetic code in DNA is transcribed into RNA and RNA is translated into proteins. The genetic code has 'letters' (nucleotides), 'words' (codons or triplets), 'sentences' (genes), 'paragraphs' (operons), 'chapters' (chromosomes), and 'books' (organisms): 'Such talk is not anthropomorphic, it is literal. Living organisms do not contain only order but information as well. By contrast to the simple repetition of ME, the genetic code is like the *Encyclopaedia Britannica*.'[83] Indeed, a single cell of the human body contains as much information as all thirty volumes of the *Encyclopaedia Britannica*—three or four times over! Richard Dawkins describes DNA in *The Blind Watchmaker*:

> It is raining DNA outside. On the bank of the Oxford canal at the bottom of my garden is a large willow tree, and it is pumping downy seeds into the air . . . Not just any DNA, but DNA whose coded characters spell out specific instructions for building willow trees that will shed a new generation of downy seeds. Those fluffy specks are, literally, spreading instructions for making themselves. They are there because their ancestors succeeded in doing the same. It is raining instructions out there; it's raining programs; it's raining tree-growing, fluff-spreading algorithms. That is not a metaphor, it is the plain truth. It couldn't be plainer if it were raining floppy discs.[84]

If it was raining floppy disks, and those floppy disks, like DNA, carried a programme (for making other floppy disks), wouldn't everyone agree that this information must have originated in some mind or minds? Following Dawkins' usage, both the floppy disk and the willow seed are physical packets carrying complex encoded information. At the very least then there is a strong analogy to be drawn between DNA and a computer programme on a floppy disk. We know that computer programmes come from minds; should we not also conclude that the information encoded by DNA comes from a mind?

The point here isn't how the information in DNA is currently produced (by natural processes), but how the information encoded in DNA arose in the first place. Our floppy disk encoded programme may have been copied from one self-building robot to another, passing through the generations like human DNA (we can even imagine the necessity for a combination of information from 'male' and 'female' robots). Still, the question remains, how did the programme come to be in the first place, and how did it come to be encoded in a physical structure? In the case of a computer programme we would say that it was the invention in the mind of a designer, who encoded it in a physical system designed for the job. Why should we not conclude that the information encoded in present DNA is the adapted ancestor of information originally formulated within the mind of a designer, and that DNA is a physical encoding system invented to carry (and, in conjunction with other factors, adapt) that information?

We can also argue by analogy with the search for ET-life via the scanning of radio signals. How would we recognise signs of alien life? Scientists look for coded messages by scanning the sky at different radio frequencies in an attempt to pick up alien signals. If we came across a signal with a non-random sequence that carried information then we would recognise it as the product of intelligent life. Yet we look at the simplest cell here on earth (the 468 gene M. genitalium), with its incredibly miniaturised design and information, and wonder if it could have arisen by chance! Accepting the implications of this analogy requires a theistic interpretation of evolution, not a rejection of evolution.

DNA and scientific explanation

So far I've argued on the basis of a strong analogy between DNA and physically encoded computer programmes on a floppy disk. But the argument from DNA can be pushed to another level when we point out that there are no known natural phenomena that can account for the arrangement of physical components into an information-bearing structure. Physical forces have two characteristic effects. The first is the creation of random patterns, like a pile of leaves in the gutter or the debris of an explosion. The second characteristic effect is ordered, repetitive structures like crystals or ripples on a pond. However, 'information theory teaches us that neither random nor repetitive structures carry high levels of information'.[85]

The complexity and information-loaded order of DNA has led some scientists to abandon 'chance' theories of life's origin in favour of some sort of 'spontaneous self-organization'. So far, the best theories draw an analogy between DNA and spontaneous ordering in non-living structures like crystals. Chemist Graham Cairns-Smith has proposed that DNA came about by sticking to crystals in certain clays, with the crystals acting as a template for life's building blocks. However, 'If the forces that produced DNA were analogous to those that produce a crystal, then DNA would consist of a single or at most a few patterns repeating again and again.'[86] DNA would resemble Christmas wrapping paper, not the *Encyclopaedia Britannica*: 'DNA exhibits too much "design work" . . . to be the product of mere chance, yet . . . no known physical laws . . . produce the right kind of ordered structure: one with high information content.'[87]

This second stage argument from DNA may suggest that DNA (or some simpler but nevertheless complex information-bearing and self-replicating ancestor of DNA) had a supernatural origin. Since no known natural force can account for 'design work' seen in DNA, it can only be accounted for by a miracle. This argument might be said to repeat the old mistake of the 'God of the gaps'. At the present time, the appeal to some as yet unknown physical process which will account for DNA is just as much an act of faith as the suggestion that 'God did it'. The fact that science has sometimes managed to explain things that once seemed scientifically inexplicable does not mean that everything must be scientifically explicable. Perhaps the origin of DNA really is scientifically inexplicable. At the very least, it is presently scientifically unexplained. Nevertheless, I am inclined to look for a theistically interpreted scientific explanation whenever possible.

It is important to remember that scientific explanations cannot exclude personal explanations. If the origin of DNA is one day to be given a scientific explanation, that explanation will say nothing about whether or not God exists as the intender of the laws which produce DNA. The question of God's existence is not scientific, but metaphysical. Nevertheless, science requires metaphysical interpretation, and the theist may argue that the existence of God provides the best metaphysical interpretation of science.

Suppose that science discovers some physical mechanism which produces 'design as information'. What would follow? What accounts for the existence of a physical mechanism that produces encoded information? My computer is a physical system that encodes information. It was designed and built by sentient beings. Why then should we not conclude that DNA was designed and built by at least one sentient being (a being who, as the creator of biological life, must be non-biological)? The discovery of a physical mechanism that produced encoded information would only add to the design argument.

Even more perplexing for the atheist is the question, 'What accounts for the information encoded in this supposed mechanism?', for 'Encoded messages are independent of the physical medium used to store and transmit them . . . There is nothing intrinsic in the chemicals themselves that explains why particular sequences carry a particular message.'[88] Information is non-physical. The physical marks on this page are not information, they *exhibit* and *encode* information. This information was previously exhibited and encoded by a different physical medium (a computer hard-drive), and translated into this form by a physical system capable of 'reading' that code (a printer). However, the information that was physically encoded, exhibited and translated in this way did not originate in my computer, but in my mind. We know from our everyday experience that information comes from minds. The physical parts of DNA can be explained scientifically (and the theist says that God explains the laws that explain those parts). What has *not yet* been explained scientifically is the arrangement of those parts into the information-bearing DNA code. What *cannot* be explained scientifically is the origin of the information encoded in DNA.

We may draw an analogy between the information in this chapter transmitted through my computer's memory and resulting in a print out, and the information in DNA transmitted through DNA and resulting in an organism. The information in this chapter originated in my mind (and in the minds of those I have read and quoted). The computer hardware involved is made of parts that can be explained scientifically (atoms, molecules, and so on). The arrangement of these parts can only be explained with reference to the intentions of a person or persons. The result is a structure with order and a high information content (my computer's hard drive carrying this chapter in encoded form). Likewise, the information in DNA cannot be explained without reference to at least one originating mind.

Suggesting that the information in DNA could be the result of chance, like the drawing of a sentence out of a bag of scrabble pieces, doesn't help the atheist much. For a start, such a result indicates that the supposedly chance process which produced it mightn't be so chancy after all. The result may well be 'fixed' in some way. Then again, the 'chance' scrabble sentence wouldn't encode information at all unless minds had already produced information and a system for encoding it. Even if a chance process throws up an information-bearing result, that does not and cannot explain the existence of information to be encoded in the first place.

The 'primeval soup' is like a bag of randomly shuffled scrabble pieces (nucleotides). To spell out words (codons or triplets), sentences (genes), paragraphs (operons), chapters (chromosomes) and books (living organisms), they must not merely be 'drawn from the bag' in a repetitive order (NONONO), but in an order which encodes information (AN ELEPHANT NEVER FORGETS); and this requires the existence of information which can be encoded. Information, although it can be encoded in matter, can only originate within a mind that has some connection with the system of 'symbols' which encodes it. The computer programme 'tells' the computer what to do, but only because it is the encoding of the programmer's intentions according to a system established by the computer's designer.

The physical and chemical hardware involved in DNA can be

explained scientifically, but the arrangement of parts involved can be likened to the arrangements of scrabble pieces or of magnetic fields on a computer disc to encode information, and the original information involved must come from mind. Experience tells us that objects with high information content, such as books and musical scores, are products of intelligence. It is reasonable to conclude by analogy that DNA is also the product of intelligence.

This conclusion does not require us to assign a miraculous origin to DNA (although this is a possibility). All it demands is that we assign a supernatural origin to the physical processes which resulted in the arrangement of material parts to form DNA, and to the original information encoded in the first DNA molecule.

Thermodynamics and directed energy

Dr David Rosevear presents an argument from thermodynamics which reinforces the conclusion that DNA requires a supernatural source of information. Rosevear notes that every day in open systems where directed energy is applied we see a temporary increase in local order. He gives the example of a building site, where energy is expended by builders following an architect's plans. While a building has more order than its constituent parts, the process of organisation is not spontaneous by any stretch of the imagination. Both energy and information are invested in the materials. In Aristotle's terminology, both efficient and formal causes are invested in the building's material cause. Likewise, an acorn grows into an oak with a temporary increase in local organisation. Nutrients, water and sunlight all contribute to an open system in which the genetic information in the seed directs these to increase order.

Having given these examples, Rosevear notes that the third law of thermodynamics says that order is at a maximum at absolute zero, so that adding undirected raw energy (by raising the temperature) reduces order. A bull in a china factory will not produce tea-pots!:

> Our examples above, of the building site and the acorn, both show that what is needed is directed energy . . . primeval soup contains no information, so the third law rules it out as the precursor of life . . . In order to increase organization, an open system requires an input, not simply of energy, but of directed energy; energy plus information. Creation involves an input of directed energy.[89]

Rosevear says that 'primeval soup contains no information', so that, according to the third law, merely adding an input of raw energy would be about as constructive as putting a bull in a china factory. However, while 'primeval soup' contains no information, the laws of physics may well do just that, if (as I have argued they indeed are) those 'laws' are our description of the way God normally causes His creation to behave. This argument provides further reason to think of the universe as the creation of a god; but it does not require us to reject evolution in either the first or second sense of the term. This argument merely says that evolution cannot happen without an input of directed information.

Irreducible complexity

It seems to me that the Christian can happily accept evolution. I am unimpressed by most of the creationist literature I have read, impressed by much of the evolutionist literature I have read, and convinced that nothing in the Bible requires a literal interpretation of the Genesis creation story.[90] The theist cannot accept the naturalistic world-view that accompanies the evolutionary views of some scientists, but science itself places no such requirement upon us.

Despite this happy state of affairs it is nevertheless true to say that there are problems with evolutionary theory. These problems are more worrying for the atheist than the theist, because while the atheist has no alternative explanation unless they admit God, the theist has already admitted God. Some of these problems can be accommodated within a theistic evolutionary view such as that of Keith Ward. Indeed, that theistic evolution copes with these problems better than atheistic evolution is an argument for the existence of God.

The problems with evolution do not support the views of full-blown 'creation science'. Nevertheless, they make the view that a transcendent miracle is required to account for life unworthy of ridicule. By a 'transcendent' miracle I mean an act of God that transcends the laws of nature, as opposed to an 'immanent' miracle that God works within those laws. The transcendent miracle hypothesis can accept the Big Bang, a universe billions of years old, microevolution (changes within a species), and perhaps even macroevolution (one species changing into another). What such a view rejects is that life can be explained without divine intervention of a transcendent nature. I am currently doubtful of this scenario, although I remain open to the possibility.

A sophisticated argument that dramatically elevates the plausibility of such a view (making it, at the very least, a view worth serious consideration) has recently been produced by the Professor of Biochemistry at Lehigh University, Michael J. Behe. Behe caused quite a stir when he published *Darwin's Black Box—The Biochemical Challenge to Evolution*. He argues that the biochemical machinery of life cannot have evolved in a Darwinian manner, that no known physical process can explain the biochemical machinery of life, and that this machinery must therefore have been designed—either by God or some other higher non-biological intelligence.

Behe's argument deserves serious consideration for several reasons. First, even his atheistic opponents 'readily admit that Behe is clearly a reputable scientist from a reputable institution. . . . '[91] Second, Behe testifies that 'I was taught that the best scientific answer, so far, for how God made life was Darwinian evolution.'[92] In other words, Behe had no theological motives for supporting divine intervention in the creation of life: 'I didn't have any a priori theological objections for . . . life being produced by a completely natural process.'[93] Rather, his own studies led him to conclude that Darwinian evolution is not the whole story, and that the hypothesis of design needs to be brought into the scientific explanation of life's origins.

Behe points out that when Darwin proposed his theory of natural selection, the cell was a mysterious 'black box':

> a black box is a machine or device or system that does something, but you don't know how it works . . . because you can't see inside or because you just can't comprehend it. To Darwin and to his 19th Century contemporaries the cell was a black box . . . the science of the day had no tools to investigate it; microscopes of the time were still rather crude and people could only see the outline of a cell. So, many scientists thought the cell was rather simple, like a blob of microscopic jelly.[94]

Now biochemistry has opened the black box of the cell to reveal a world of staggering complexity. The cellular world is full of tiny molecular machines made primarily of proteins. This discovery has added to Paley's design argument from the analogy between the world and man-made artefacts: 'Design is evident when a number of separate, interacting components are ordered in such a way as to accomplish a function beyond the individual components. The greater the specificity of the interacting components required to produce the function, the greater is our confidence of design.'[95] As Behe said in a recent interview, 'Whenever we see such systems in . . . the macroscopic world of our everyday life, we find that they are, in fact, designed. Nobody comes across a mousetrap and wonders whether it was designed or not.'[96] By implication, when we come across molecular machines in the cell, we should embrace the idea of intelligent design. However, this is not the focus of Behe's argument. Rather, he points to the particular type of complexity discovered within the cell by biochemistry.

In *The Origin of Species*, Darwin stated that, 'If it could be demonstrated that any complex organ existed, which could not possibly have been formed by numerous, successive, slight modifications, my theory would absolutely break down. But I can find no such case.'[97] Behe argues that the reason Darwin couldn't find a counter-example to his theory was that the cell was a 'black box' at the time. The cell is no longer a black box, but has been opened to reveal a host of counterexamples. The type of complexity exhibited by these counterexamples is 'irreducible complexity'. As Behe explains, something is irreducibly complex 'if it's composed of several parts and each part is absolutely necessary for the structure to function'.[98] The implication of irreducible complexity is that the molecular machines which exhibit it 'cannot be built by natural selection because in natural selection, each component must be useful to the organism as the molecular machine is built'.[99]

Behe uses the example of a mousetrap. Any mousetrap, by the very nature of the task it performs, requires a minimum number of working parts: a base to hold all the other parts together in the right way, a hammer to kill the mouse, a spring to give the hammer power, a holding bar to keep the energised hammer in position and a catch mechanism that trips the holding bar, releasing the hammer when there is a mouse to be caught. Any mousetrap that lacked even one of these components would not function at all. If we try to imagine a mouse trap 'evolving' through several generations, starting with a base perhaps, and then gaining a spring, then a hammer, then a holding bar, and then a catch, we soon run up against an insurmountable problem. A mousetrap with just a base is useless. The addition of this or that component doesn't help in the slightest. Only the precise combination of mutually tailored parts can perform the mousetrap task. Likewise, it is impossible to imagine an irreducibly complex molecular machine evolving by additional steps. To be of any advantage to the wholes of which these machines are parts, every necessary component must be in place simultaneously. An irreducibly complex molecular machine with half its bits missing would be useless. Indeed, the production of such machines would be a drain on the resources of the cell, and would impose an evolutionary disadvantage upon any cell that produced such a half-finished piece of work. Therefore, any cell containing irreducibly complex molecular machinery (and that means every cell) cannot have evolved in a step-by-step fashion through natural selection. Rather, everything must have been in place from the word go.

Consider just one of the irreducibly complex molecular machines Behe mentions in his book, the cilium. Cilia are tiny hair-like structures on the outside of cells that help to move fluids over stationary cells (for example, in your lungs), or are used by the cell to swim (as in the single-celled paramecium). Without going into details, cilia are molecular paddling units. Any system that swims needs a paddle to make contact with the liquid, a motor or energy source to power the paddle, and something to transfer energy from the motor to the paddle. This complexity is inherent to the task of swimming, and no system that lacked one of these components could swim. The cilium is a swimming machine with microtubuals for paddles, dynein arms for motors and nexin arms for connectors:

> The complexity of the cilium and other swimming systems is inherent in the task itself. It does not depend on how large or small the system is, whether it has to move a cell or a ship: in order to paddle, several components are required. The question is, how did the cilium arise?[100]

The cilium could not have arisen by the evolutionary accoutrement of small steps, since none of the steps before the completion of such an irreducibly complex system would have had any evolutionary advantage. What use is a motor with nothing to do? What good is a connector with nothing to connect? What help is a paddle that can't paddle? Indeed, as Dr Ray Bohlin says, 'nature would select against the continued production of the miscellaneous parts if they are not producing an immediate benefit to the organism.' So, the cilium must have arrived on the scene as a package deal. How, asks Behe, do we explain that?

> To say that Darwinian evolution cannot explain everything in nature is not to say that evolution, random mutation, and natural selection do not occur; they have been observed (at least in the case of micro-evolution) many different times . . . I believe the evidence strongly supports common descent. But the root question remains unanswered; what has caused complex systems to form?[101]

The chances against random mutations producing every necessary component at the same time are unimaginably large, and that's without taking into account the requirement that each and every necessary component be linked together into a cohesive whole. (To get a grasp on the complexities involved I can't do better than refer the reader to Behe's book.) The cell would not produce cilia unless it was specifically instructed to do so by its DNA. As Behe says about another irreducibly complex system, the flagellum, 'The only way a cell could make a flagellum [or any irreducibly complex system] is if the structure were already coded for in its DNA.'[102] This means that either DNA arrived on the scene complete with instructions for building irreducibly complex molecular machinery never before seen, or cells arrived on the scene complete with irreducibly complex molecular machines. Neither possibility can be accounted for by Darwinian evolution.

There is no other scientific explanation available. As Behe demonstrates, 'If you search the scientific literature on evolution, and if you focus your search on the question of how molecular machines—the basis of life—developed, you find an eerie and complete silence.'[103] For example, The *Journal of Molecular Evolution* was established in 1971, and is dedicated to explaining how life came to be at the molecular level. None of the papers published in JME has ever proposed a possible route for a single complex biochemical system to arise in a gradual, step-by-step Darwinian process. The nature of these systems precludes the possibility of a Darwinian explanation. Behe concludes that, 'The laboratory work of graduate students piecing together bits of genes in a deliberate effort to make something new is analogous to the work that was done to cause the first cilium.'[104]

What response has Behe had to his book? The general criticisms levelled against Behe seem to be based on an inadequate engagement with his central argument, combined with an expression of faith in the eventual discovery of a naturalistic explanation for the origin of complex biomolecular systems. This expression of faith is no doubt motivated in many cases by the fear of the theistic implications of Behe's 'intelligent design' hypothesis:

> The critics of my book have uniformly agreed that the biochemical systems I describe are enormously complex and currently unexplained, but they differ in their prescriptions. Some of them say, 'Well, Darwinism will eventually explain this.' Other people say, 'Well, we don't know how it will be explained, but we'll come up with something in the near future.' My reply is that the something that we can come up with in the near future is intelligent design theory.[105]

Behe says that while the hypothesis of intelligent design may have religious implications, 'it's a clear scientific theory based soley on observations of biochemical systems that we should embrace and build on'.[106]

Francis Crick, one of the Nobel Prize-winning co-discoverers of DNA, has written several times about the problems of an undirected origin of life on Earth. Crick thinks the problems with a purely naturalistic explanation are so great we should consider the hypothesis that aliens seeded the earth with spores to begin life. Behe responds:

> Well, that's an unusual idea, but you can see that Crick's idea fits with intelligent design theory also; he's invoking an outside cause to get life started. If Francis Crick claimed intelligent aliens not only seeded life but actually designed life that is on the earth, I could not point to a biochemical system and argue against him. I might think it was a little far-fetched, but I would have to go to philosophical or theological or historical argument to rebut that. [107]

One way to rebut Crick's suggestion would be to point out that any alien containing irreducibly complex structures would pose just as much of a problem to Darwinian evolution as life on earth. It would seem hard to conceive any alien life-form complex enough to seed the earth that didn't depend upon any irreducibly complex structures. Therefore, it is hard to see what help Crick's suggestion is in explaining life on earth. The aliens proposal 'still leaves open the question of who designed the designer—how did life originally originate?'[108] However, as Behe admits, 'The question of the design of the designer can be put off in several ways . . . perhaps the original life is totally unlike ourselves, consisting of fluctuating electrical fields or gasses; perhaps it does not require irreducibly complex structures to sustain it.'[109]

Indeed, to avoid an infinite regress of designed designers, we must assume the existence of an un-designed designer, a designer who does not depend upon any irreducibly complex physical systems. Such a being would be non-biological, and probably immaterial. That makes 'God', or 'the gods', a good answer to the question posed by the existence of designed life forms such as, so Behe argues, the first cellular life forms.

We would do well to remember that the God hypothesis has

a lot of other evidence in its favour, such as the moral, cosmo-logical, and other design arguments that we have already con-sidered. The hypothesis of a single God who designed the original physical life in the cosmos (however He brought it into being) is a more adequate explanation than the 'gods' sugges-tion. As J.P. Moreland says, 'One God is a simpler explanation than the polytheistic one and it makes more intelligible the fact that we live in a *uni*verse and not a plurality of universes.'[110]

So, to recap, either 1) DNA arrived on the scene complete with instructions for building irreducibly complex systems, or 2) cells arrived on the scene complete with irreducibly complex systems. Neither possibility can be accounted for by Darwinian evolution. If DNA arrived on the scene complete with instruc-tions for making useful and as yet non-existent things, that rather looks like forward planning. Only intelligent beings think ahead. If irreducibly complex machines arrived on the scene without being produced by cells which 'knew' how to make them in the scientifically describable way in which present-day cells carry on, then how did they get here? The only possibility would seem to be the design of some powerful and intelligent being or beings whose existence is independent of any irredu-cibly complex systems. This second possibility sounds very much like transcendent miraculous intervention on a grand scale. The first possibility also suggests divine involvement in the existence of biological life, but seems compatible with a sce-nario like that envisaged by Keith Ward where God is imma-nently involved in evolution. For reasons primarily of explanatory elegance, I prefer the immanent option.

Design and proper function

The respected American philosopher, Alvin Plantinga, has recently produced a powerful re-casting of the analogical argu-ment from design. Take any human artefact, such as a watch, and it will have what Plantinga calls a 'design plan'. A 'design plan' is the way in which an artefact's designer intends it to work. The designer of a watch wants it to tell the time; so the 'design plan' of a watch is, if you will, a 'blue-print' in the watchmaker's mind according to which he makes the watch with the intended result that the watch tells the time. If the watchmaker is good at his job he conceives and implements a good watch 'design plan', and so long as the watch works according to its design plan, the design plan will cause the watch to tell the time.

When an artefact works as its designer intends (in line with the 'design plan'), then that artefact is said to be functioning properly. When a watch tells the time, then it is functioning properly; because this is what its designer intended it to do. Plantinga summarises his argument using these concepts like so:

> suppose you believe that there really is such a thing as proper function . . . for any natural organs or systems, and suppose you further believe . . . that there is no naturalistic account, reduction, or analysis of the notion of proper function: then you have the materials for a powerful argument against metaphysical naturalism.[111]

Metaphysical naturalism is the belief that everything is ultimately explicable by reference to material nature. If everything cannot be explained in this way, then we must posit some spiritual ultimate reality, and this would clearly support theism over atheism.

Having introduced the concepts of 'design', 'design plan' and 'proper function', Plantinga notes that these concepts are most at home in talk about things designed and made by personal agents. However, as well as using terms like 'proper function' to speak of human artefacts, we also use them to speak about things that obviously were not designed by humans. It seems quite natural to talk about a heart 'working properly'. We think that the 'purpose' of the heart is to pump blood at a certain rate around our bodies, and we think that a heart that pumps only a few times a minute is not 'functioning properly'. We assume that there is something wrong with it, just as we would assume that a watch which said the date was 31 February was malfunctioning.

The crunch point is this: if notions such as proper function (notions which—as applied to human artefacts—entail the existence of intelligent and purposeful design) apply to things (like hearts) which we know have no human designer, this entails the existence of intelligent, purposeful non-human design.

I am inclined to agree with Plantinga that atheists commonly say that this or that organ has a function, and that theists and atheists alike, 'naturally and inevitably think this way'.[112] I am also inclined to agree that if the analogy between such talk as used of a watch and as used of a heart holds good, then it is reasonable to conclude that the heart, like the watch, was designed.

We needn't say that the heart was designed in exactly the same way that the watch was designed. We could take evolution into consideration. We would have to say that the process of evolution was designed to evolve organisms, and that in so far as an organ contributes to the existence of an organism, then it is fulfilling a role in that grander design of which it is a part. An evolved organ can have a function; that of contributing to the existence of an organism which has evolved according to the design plan of evolution itself (where this process is aimed at some goal, such as the production of sentient life forms). An evolved organ couldn't have a function if it is merely part of an unintended process, as evolution must be unless it is itself an artefact. Plantinga's argument is only an argument against a naturalistic view of evolution, 'unguided and unorchestrated by God or anyone else'.[113]

The real question is whether or not a satisfactory naturalistic explanation of the notion of proper function can be given. Giving a plausible naturalistic explanation of function is not easy. Let us pursue this question by reviewing some attempted naturalistic explanations.

Some attempted naturalistic explanations of 'proper function'

John Pollock admits there is no difficulty in saying what it is for a human artefact to function properly: 'The obvious way to interpret such [talk] about machines is by appeal to the intentions of the designers. They work properly when they work as they were designed to work.'[114] This sort of explanation is unavailable to the atheist in considering natural organisms. With what can this straightforward sort of account be replaced? Pollock suggests that 'what is important . . . is that the disruptive happenings [such as the heart beating too slowly] are unusual'.[115] So, according to Pollock, the functional generalisation 'hearts are for circulating blood' is true given the existence of a structure hearts generally have, and that this structure circulates blood. However, it really will not do to equate a thing's functioning properly with its functioning the way in which most things of its sort function, because you can obviously function properly even if you don't do it in the way most of your contemporaries do: 'Most 60-year-old carpenters have lost a finger or thumb; it is not the case that those who have not [lost a finger or thumb] have hands that are not normal and not capable of proper manual function; and the same would hold even if we were all carpenters.'[116]

Ruth Millikan has proposed that 'the functions of a thing are those of its powers or properties which account for its survival and proliferation . . . Hearts proliferated because they pump blood, so pumping blood is the heart's function.'[117] But surely it is obvious that a thing need not have ancestors to have a proper function? 'Whether or not God did create Adam and Eve instantaneously out of the dust of the earth, he could have; and if he had, wouldn't Adam's heart have had a function?'[118]

Then again, suppose an evil dictator introduced a mutation into the population whereby those born with the mutation are blind.[119] The dictator arranges for everyone born without the mutation to be exterminated. The mutation therefore prolife-rates until the majority of the world population is blind. If you like, this situation can be said to prevail for so long that the majority of all humankind past and present are blind. Consider some future generation human being, Oedipus, who is blind. Oedipus is a member of a reproductively established family, and has a certain reproductively established characteristic; namely, blindness. He has ancestors, among whom there is a causal con-nection between their being blind and their surviving to pass on this characteristic to their offspring. Despite the fact that Oedipus' blindness is a characteristic of his which accounts for its own 'survival and proliferation', wouldn't it seem odd to say that his eyes are functioning properly? If so, there must be some-thing wrong with Millikan's account, and we have yet to find a plausible naturalistic account of proper function.

John Bigelow and Robert Pargetter propose a similar, but more sophisticated account whereby 'an organ . . . has a func-tion if and only if it has a property . . . that confers a survival-enhancing propensity . . . upon its owner in the latter's natural habitat.'[120] This gets around the problem of Oedipus' blindness by saying that a world in which an evil dictator introduces a mutation and causes that mutation to be beneficial to survival is not Oedipus' natural environment. The problem is that Bigelow and Pargetter's analysis of function is circular. Their account depends upon the idea of an organ's natural habitat, but in defining what an organ's natural habitat is, Bigelow and Pargetter use concepts that involve the notion of proper func-tion. They say that the natural habitat of an organ is a function-ing, interconnected system usual for the species in question. However, as Plantinga says, 'A functioning system of organs, one supposes, is a properly functioning system.'[121]

Bigelow and Pargetter's account also overlooks those systems or organs whose proper function is damage control; for the natural habitat of such systems is an environment which is *not* functioning properly.[122]

Proper function as useful fiction

None of the above proposed naturalistic explanations of function work. The only alternative to giving such an analysis is to say that talk of hearts having a proper function is merely 'as if' talk; that the notion doesn't *really* apply. This move would mean giving up any literal ascription of function to natural entities. Proper function must instead be viewed as a 'useful fiction'.

To take the 'as if' get-out involves going against the clear preference of the majority of humanity for taking talk of proper function as literal across the board, whether the object of such talk is a watch or a heart. Moreover: 'The functionalist stance is awkward: to accept it you are to think that George's heart isn't really malfunctioning . . . but you are to treat it and think about it, somehow, as if it were malfunctioning.'[123]

Taking the 'as if' escape hatch also complicates the meaning of the terms used. In other words, Occam's razor should encourage us to accept the simplest adequate analysis of any term, including 'proper function'. The simplest analysis of the meaning of a term is one which keeps the meaning of that term as similar as possible across a range of applications. The use of 'proper function' which entails the existence of a designer is clearly necessary when the term is applied to human artefacts, and so the simplest use of the term as applied to natural entities is a use which similarly entails the existence of a designer. Such an explanation of 'proper function' is surely adequate; and so the literal use of the term across the board is the simplest adequate analysis.

Consider a parallel example from science. 'Anti-realists' suggest that scientific models don't really tell us anything even approximately true about the world; they are just 'useful fictions'. However, 'realists' reply that the fact that a scientific model successfully predicts events we can observe is evidence that the model corresponds, at least in an approximate way, to the world beyond observation. A similar line of reasoning should encourage us to take a realist view of the language of proper function.

Proper function and the argument against naturalism

Taking these conclusions, Plantinga advances the following argument. Suppose that we are convinced that there is no naturalistic way to make sense of the notion of proper function and that we are unwilling to resort to the language of 'as if'. If we are also sure that naturalism is true, then we must give up the notion of proper function in cases other than human artefacts. On the other hand, suppose we are convinced (along with the majority) that for natural organisms there really are such things as proper function, and so on. In that case we have a strong argument against naturalism: 'Given the plausible alternatives, what you have, more specifically, is a powerful theistic argument.'[124]

This concludes the first stage of Plantinga's design argument; but Plantinga presses the concept of proper function further into the heart of naturalism by applying it to our own thinking, or 'cognitive', apparatus.

Darwin's doubt

Most people, says Plantinga, think that a function of our cognitive faculties 'is to provide us with true beliefs'.[125] Indeed, most of us think that our cognitive faculties do provide us with true beliefs. However, doesn't this present the naturalist, who believes that our cognitive abilities arrived on the scene through a blind process of natural selection, with a problem? 'If our cognitive faculties have originated as [the naturalist] thinks, then their ultimate purpose or function (if they have a purpose or function) will be something like survival . . . but then it seems initially doubtful that among their functions . . . would be the production of true beliefs'.[126]

The nub of the problem is summed up somewhat colourfully by naturalist Patricia Churchland who writes that:

> Boiled down to essentials, a nervous system enables the organism to succeed in the four Fs: feeding, fleeing, fighting and reproducing. The principle chore of nervous systems is to get the body parts where they should be in order that the organism may survive . . . Truth, whatever that is, definitely takes the hindmost.[127]

The trouble with Churchland's statement is that if truth 'takes the hindmost' in the priorities of evolution, then we have cause to doubt the conclusion that this is the case, since this conclusion (on naturalistic assumptions) is based upon the workings of just such a purposelessly evolved natural system. Plantinga dubs this sort of self-defeating assertion 'Darwin's doubt', as it can be traced back to Charles Darwin. 'With me,' wrote Darwin, 'the horrid doubt always arises whether the convictions of man's mind, which has been developed from the mind of the lower animals, are of any value or at all trustworthy.'[128] Plantinga interprets 'Darwin's doubt' as questioning the probability of human cognitive faculties being reliable truth-finding apparatus given the assumption that they have been produced by an unintended evolutionary process.

The issue is the value of the conditional probability that our cognitive faculties are reliable given that they arose through a naturalistic evolutionary process. Patricia Churchland seems to think that this probability is fairly low. This conclusion undermines the platform on which it is built; but when the reliability of our cognitive faculties is in question we cannot use this fact against a low estimation of reliability without begging the question. Here we reach the rock-bottom fact that we cannot argue in favour of the reasonableness of the laws of reason without assuming what we set out to prove. As Plantinga notes: 'Once I come to doubt the reliability of my cognitive faculties, I can't properly try to allay that doubt by producing an argument; for in so doing I rely on the very faculties I am doubting.'[129]

Still, digging ourselves into a pit of despair about the trustworthiness of our minds isn't going to get us very far. So, assuming that our cognitive faculties are generally reliable, we have something to weigh in the balance against naturalism (and in favour of theism), since it was naturalism that provided us with grounds to doubt the reliability of the natural systems upon which we rely when arriving at any picture of the world, including naturalism itself:

> suppose you concur in Darwin's Doubt . . . But suppose you also think, as most of us do, that in fact our cognitive faculties are reliable . . . Then you have a straight forward probabilistic argument against naturalism—and for traditional theism, if you think these two the significant alternatives.[130]

The belief that our cognitive faculties are reliable gives us reason to reject naturalism. The person who believes in naturalistic evolution has reason to doubt any belief he or she holds, including belief in naturalistic evolution. This really is a case of 'heads I win, tails you lose'. If you think that naturalistic evolution gives you cause to doubt the reliability of human cognitive faculties, but you think those faculties are reliable, then you have reason to reject naturalism. If you think naturalistic evolution gives you cause to doubt the reliability of human cognitive faculties, and you agree that the reliability of these faculties is suspect, then you have reason to doubt your conclusion that naturalism (or anything else for that matter) is true. Either way, naturalism doesn't look too healthy.

Naturalistic evolution and cognitive reliability

The central question here is clearly the probability of our cognitive faculties being reliable given the truth of naturalistic evolution. Evolutionary theory in its present state, considered apart from the existence of God, certainly cannot offer sufficient reason to judge the probability of our cognitive faculties being reliable as high: 'if Darwinian selection guarantees anything, it is only that the organism's behaviour is adaptive: there isn't anything in particular it needs to believe.'[131] As Richard Purtill writes, 'the natural selection process is simply one of adaption to the existing environment, not a process of improvement or progress in any general sense.'[132] The ability to know the true from the false is not necessary to survival. All survival requires is that an organism interacts with its environment consistently. For example: 'if an organism always saw blue things as though they were red and vice versa, or large things as small and vice versa, that organism and its offspring would adapt to its environment.'[133] We would hardly say that an amoeba understands the world, but it interacts consistently with it: 'It will react to heat in a consistent way regardless of whether or not it grasps the essence of heat.'[134] Moreover, 'The mind grasps abstract truths which do not seem to have anything to do with the survival value they impart to the organism.'[135]

This is really a version of the old 'brain-in-a-vat' question: How do you know that you are not a brain-in-a-vat being fed false sensory information by an evil scientist? How do you know that appearances are not deceptive? No one seriously thinks that appearances are deceptive (at least, not that deceptive), but neither can anyone logically exclude the bare possibility that they are such a brain-in-a-vat. Any experiment you think of to determine the truth can have an outcome that could be determined by the aforementioned evil scientist! We could have all sorts of beliefs which are not true but which pass the evolutionary test of survival; at least on the standard naturalistic picture of evolution. As Richard Purtill says:

While practical cunning evidently has survival value, it is not so clear that theoretical reasoning of the kind used in philosophy or science

246 THE CASE FOR GOD

has such value, especially in the primitive conditions in which the
natural selection process has immediate and direct application . . .
If our question is 'Can human intelligence give us a trustworthy
picture of the universe?' we do not answer *that* question by showing
(if we can show) that intelligence has a survival value at a particular
stage of the development of species.[136]

There are several solutions one might propose to avoid this
problem. One is to say that although evolution does not guarantee the reliability of our cognitive faculties, we just happen to
be exceedingly lucky in that evolution, purely by chance, has
given us reliable faculties.

Perhaps it might be said that there are many other evolving
eco-systems on far distant planets, or in alternative universes,
which have not produced reliable cognitive faculties; but that
there was bound to be one such system that produced reliable
faculties eventually. This is an application of the 'monkeys at
typewriters eventually producing Shakespeare's plays' idea.
Several responses can be made. First, isn't this just what some of
those poor, cognitively challenged creatures in far-distant galax-
ies might be saying to themselves in the face of the odds?
Moreover, it simply isn't true that enough monkeys at enough
typewriters given enough time are *bound* to reproduce
Shakespeare. The longer they go on typing the more likely it is
that they will have done so, but there is no logical compulsion
about the matter. They might reproduce 'The cat sat on the mat'
for all eternity! Likewise, if evolution really does work merely by
blind chance, then there is no necessity that compels it to
produce different results every time. Whether or not you take this
route also depends upon your estimation of the likelihood of
there being other evolving systems in this or any other universe.

Another solution is to say that God somehow worked within
the evolution of our species to guarantee the general reliability
that evolution alone could not guarantee. There are several
problems with this option. First, it seems a little too much like

the 'God of the gaps'. The advance of scientific understanding is likely, on past experience, to fill in the gap and make God appear redundant. One might also question why God couldn't make the artefact of evolution more efficient so that such intervention was unnecessary. But perhaps there is some reason why it is impossible to construct such a 'hands-off' system, or greater value in creating a 'hands-on' system.

A third option is to say that the current understanding of evolution is incomplete, and that there must be a closer link between the evolution of sentient beings with reliable cognitive faculties and the laws of the universe. This option does not exclude God. Indeed, as has already been argued, the analogy of proper function should lead us to posit the existence of a designer whose artefact evolution itself is. Indeed, if there is a closer link than the current evolutionary picture posits between properly functioning, generally reliable cognitive faculties in creatures and the scientific laws that have given them birth, then the question faces us as to why the universal laws are so 'finely tuned' as to achieve this result.

It is interesting to read the secular philosopher Thomas Nagel grappling with this question. Nagel writes that 'If we can reason, it is because our thoughts can obey the order of the logical relations amongst propositions—so here again we depend on a Platonic harmony [between our thoughts and the cosmos].'[137] Nagel feels that this insight is alarming:

> it is hard to know what world picture to associate it with, and difficult to avoid the suspicion that the picture will be religious, or quasi religious . . . Even without God, the idea of a natural sympathy between the deepest truths of nature and the deepest layers of the human mind, which can be exploited to allow gradual development of a truer and truer conception of reality, makes us more *at home* in the universe than is secularly comfortable . . . I believe this is one manifestation of a fear of religion which has large and often pernicious consequences for modern intellectual life.[138]

Nagel considers several possible explanations for this harmony between thought and reality:

> Probably the most popular . . . answer nowadays [to the question of why our thinking apparatus is generally reliable] is an evolutionary naturalism: We can reason in these ways because it is the consequence of a more primitive capacity of belief formation that had survival value during the period when the human brain was evolving. This explanation has always seemed to me laughably inadequate.[139]

He sees the attraction of what he calls the 'religious' answer to this conundrum:

> The universe is intelligible to us because it and our minds were made for each other . . . While I think such arguments are unjustly neglected in contemporary secular philosophy, I have never been able to understand the idea of God well enough to see such a theory as truly explanatory . . . But perhaps this is due to my inadequate understanding of religious concepts.[140]

While Nagel does not take either the 'evolutionary' or 'religious' view, his only alternative amounts to a 'why not?' shrug of the shoulders: 'Perhaps there is something wrong with the hope of arriving at a complete understanding of the world that includes an understanding of ourselves as beings within it possessing the capacity for that very understanding.'[141]

I think that the idea of God is understandable enough that we can explain things with reference to His existence and actions. If naturalistic evolutionism is inadequate for explaining our ability to know the history of evolution and the laws of quantum mechanics, then theistic evolution offers a serious alternative. Here we have moved beyond argument from design (by analogy), into argument for design (argument to the best explanation), a theme I will continue in the following chapter. The best explanation of the form, intelligibility and beauty of the cosmos is that it was designed and made by some powerful immaterial intelligence. It is my conclusion that design arguments give worthy support to belief in the existence of God.

Recommended reading

Michael J. Behe, *Darwin's Black Box—The Biochemical Challenge to Evolution* (The Free Press, 1996). (3)

Stephen R.L. Clark, *God, Religion and Reality* (SPCK, 1998). (3)

Charles Darwin, *The Origin of Species* (Penguin, 1968). (3)

Brian Davies, *An Introduction to the Philosophy of Religion* (Oxford, 1993). (2)

Paul Davies, *The Mind of God* (Penguin, 1993). (2)

Paul Davies, *Are We Alone?* (Penguin, 1995). (1)

Paul Davies, *The Fifth Miracle—The Search for the Origin of Life* (Allen Lane, Penguin Press, 1998). (2)

Stephen T. Davies, *God, Reason and Theistic Proof* (Edinburgh, 1997). (3)

Richard Dawkins, *The Blind Watchmaker* (Norton: New York, 1986). (3)

Michael Denton, *Evolution: A Theory in Crisis* (Burnett Books: London, 1985). (3)

Michael Denton, *Natures Destiny—How the Laws of Biology reveal Purpose in the Universe* (Free Press, 1998). (3)

Kitty Ferguson, *The Fire in the Equations* (Bantam Books, 1995). (2)

R. Douglas Geivett and Gary R. Habermas eds, *In Defence of Miracles* (Apollos, 1997), esp.: Richard Purtill, 'Defining Miracles'; Norman L. Geisler, 'Miracles and the Modern Mind'; Ronald H. Nash, 'Miracles and Conceptual Systems'; and W. David Beck, 'God's Existence'. (2/3)

Tim Hawthorne, *Windows on Science and Faith* (IVP, 1986). (1)

John Hick, ed., *The Existence of God* (Macmillan, 1964). (1)

David L. Hull and Michael Ruse, *The Philosophy of Biology*

(Oxford, 1998). Of particular relevance are Part IV: Function, and Part X: Creationism. (4)

Phillip Johnson, *Darwin on Trial* (Regnery Gateway: Washington, 1991). (1)

Phillip Johnson, *Testing Darwinism* (IVP, 1997), especially chapter five 'Intelligent Design'. (1)

Peter Kreeft and Ronald Tacelli, *Handbook of Christian Apologetics* (Monarch, 1995). (1)

C.S. Lewis, *Miracles* (Fount, 1974), chapter three. (2)

J.P. Moreland, *Scaling the Secular City* (Baker 1987). (3)

J.P. Moreland and Kai Nielson, *Does God Exist? The Debate between Theists and Atheists* (Prometheus, 1993). (2)

Thomas Nagel, *The Last Word* (Oxford, 1997). (3)

Michael Peterson *et al*: *Reason and Religious Belief—An Introduction to the Philosophy of Religion* (Oxford, 1991). (2)

Clark H. Pinnock, *Reason Enough—A Case for the Christian Faith* (Paternoster Press, 1990), chapter three. (1)

John Polkinghorne, *Belief in God in an Age of Science* (Yale University Press, 1998). (2)

Alvin Plantinga, *Warrant and Proper Function* (Oxford, 1993). (4)

W.S. Rhodes, *The Christian God* (SPCK, 1998). (1)

J.J.C. Smart and J.J. Haldane: *Atheism and Theism*, (Blackwells, 1996). (4)

Richard Swinburne, *Is There a God?* (Oxford). (3)

Richard Swinburne, *The Existence of God* (Oxford, 1991). (4)

F.R.Tennant, *Philosophical Theology*, vol. 2, 'The World, the Soul and God' (Cambridge, 1956), chapter IV: Cosmic Teleology. (4)

Keith Ward, *God, Chance and Necessity*, (OneWorld, 1996). (3)

Keith Ward, *God, Faith and The New Millennium—Christian Belief in an Age of Science* (OneWorld, 1998). (3)

David Wilkinson, *Alone in the Universe?—The X Files, Aliens and God* (Monarch, 1997). (1) A response to Paul Davies' *Are We Alone?*

Notes

1. Plato, *Laws* 12.966e.
2. Cicero, *De Natura Deorum*, quoted by Brian Davies, *An Introduction to the Philosophy of Religion* (Oxford, 1993), p.94.
3. Paul Davies, *The Mind of God* (Penguin, 1993).
4. Roger Penrose, *The Emperor's New Mind* (Vintage, 1991), p.430.
5. Paul Davies, *Are We Alone?* (Penguin, 1995).
6. *Ibid.*
7. *Ibid.*
8. John Polkinghorne, *Belief in God in an Age of Science* (Yale, 1998), pp.3–4.
9. Clark H. Pinnock, *Reason Enough* (Paternoster Press, 1980), p.65.
10. Paul Dirac, 'The Evolution of the Physicist's Conception of Nature', *Scientific American*, May 1963, quoted by Kitty Ferguson, *Fire in the Equations* (Bantam Books, 1995), p.60.
11. Paul Davies, *The Mind of God*, p.200.
12. J.P. Moreland, *Scaling the Secular City* (Baker, 1987), p.47.
13. Thomas Aquinas, *Suma Theolgica*, I.
14. John Polkinghorne, *op. cit.*, p.2.
15. Michael Peterson *et al*, *Reason and Religious Belief* (Oxford, 1991), p.210.
16. Paul Davies, *op. cit.*, p.81.
17. Keith Ward, *God, Chance and Necessity* (OneWorld, 1996).
18. Richard Swinburne, *The Existence of God* (Oxford, 1991).
19. Garth Barber, *New Scientist*, October 1997.
20. C.S. Lewis, *Miracles*, (Fount, 1974), p.106.
21. Keith Ward, *op. cit.*
22. Stephen Hawking, 'Is Everything Determined?' in *Black Holes and Baby Universes* (Bantam Books, 1993).

23. C.S. Lewis, 'The Laws of Nature' in *God in the Dock* (Fount, 1979).

24. Stephen Hawking, *A Brief History of Time* (Bantam Books).

25. William Paley, 'Natural Theology' in John Hick, ed., *The Existence of God* (Macmillan, 1964), p.100.

26. Michael J. Behe, *Darwin's Black Box* (Free Press, 1996), pp.4–5.

27. Robin Le Poidevin, *Arguing for Atheism* (Routledge, 1996), pp.46, 57.

28. Dallas Willard, 'Language, Being, God and the Three stages of Theistic Evidence' in *Does God Exist? The Debate between Theists and Atheists* (Prometheus Books, 1993), pp.208–209.

29. Richard Swinburne, *op. cit.*, pp.135–136.

30. John Polkinghorne, *Scientists as Theologians* (SPCK, 1996), p.3.

31. Richard Dawkins in Russell Stannard, *Science and Wonders* (Faber and Faber, 1996).

32. Russell Stannard, *Science and the Renewal of Belief* (SCM), pp.11–12.

33. Peter van Inwagen, 'Genesis and Evolution' in *God, Knowledge and Mystery* (Cornell University Press, 1995).

34. Ravi Zacharias, *A Shattered Visage—The Real Face of Atheism* (Baker, 1995), p.42.

35. Donald MacKay, *The Clockwork Image* (IVP, 1997), p.52.

36. David Rosevear, *Creation Science* (New Wine Press, 1991), p.18.

37. Keith Ward in Russell Stannard *Science and Wonders* (Faber and Faber, 1996).

38. John Polkinghorne, *op. cit.*

39. *Ibid*.

40. *Ibid*.

41. J.J. Haldane, *Atheism and Theism* (Blackwells, 1996), p.102.

42. Tim Hawthorne, *Windows On Science and Faith* (IVP, 1986), p.57.
43. *Ibid.*, p.57.
44. R.J. Berry, *God and Evolution.*
45. Ravi Zacharias, *op. cit.*, p.37.
46. Robert Shapiro, 'Where Do We Come From?'
47. *Ibid.*
48. J.J. Haldane and J.J.C. Smart, *op. cit.*
49. *Ibid.*
50. *Ibid.*
51. *Ibid.*
52. David Wilkinson, *Alone in the Universe?* (Monarch, 1997).
53. Paul Davies, *Are We Alone?* (Penguin, 1995), pp.18–20.
54. Christian biochemist Professor J.N. Hawthorne says that 'At this point "special creation" seems to leap out at us.' Tim Hawthorne, *Windows On Science and Faith* (IVP).
55. Bennett Davies, 'Cast out of Eden', *New Scientist*, 16 May 1998, No. 2134.
56. J.J. Haldane, *op. cit.*
57. *Ibid.*
58. Lawrence M. Krauss, *The Physics of Star Trek* (Harper Collins, 1996).
59. *Ibid.*
60. Paul Davies, *op. cit.*, pp.52–53.
61. *Ibid.*
62. Frank Drake and Dava Sobel, *Is Anyone Out There?*
63. Michael White, *The Science of The X Files* (Legend, 1996).
64. Paul Davies, *op. cit.*
65. *Ibid.*, p.71.
66. David Wilkinson, *op. cit.*, p.60.
67. Keith Ward, *op. cit.*, pp.62–63.
68. *Ibid.*, p.65–66.
69. *Ibid.*
70. *Ibid.*
71. *Ibid.*

72. *Ibid.*
73. *Ibid.*
74. See: C.S. Lewis, *Miracles* (Fount, 1974). Ronald H. Nash takes up Lewis's anti-naturalism argument in 'Miracles and Conceptual Systems' in R. Douglas Geivett and Gary R. Habermas, eds, *In Defence of Miracles* (Apollos, 1997).
75. Keith Ward, *op. cit.*
76. Keith Ward, *Holding Fast To God* (SPCK, 1983), p.110.
77. John Polkinghorne, *Science and Providence* (SPCK,), p.32.
78. W. David Beck, 'God's Existence' in R. Douglas Geivett and Gary R. Habermas, eds, *op. cit.*, pp.157–158.
79. Nancy R. Pearcey, 'DNA: The Message in the Message', First Things, *http://www.leaderu.com/ftissues/ft9606/pearcy.html*
80. *Ibid.*
81. *Ibid.*
82. J.P. Moreland, *Scaling the Secular City*, p.51.
83. *Ibid.*
84. Richard Dawkins, *The Blind Watchmaker* (Norton: New York, 1986), p.111. Ian G. Barbour describes DNA in *Religion in an Age of Science* (SCM, 1990): 'DNA embodies effective information, that is, a set of instructions.' (p.163.)
85. Nancy R. Pearcey, *op. cit.*
86. *Ibid.*
87. *Ibid.*
88. *Ibid.*
89. David Rosevear, *op. cit.*, p.26–28.
90. On Genesis see Keith Ward, *God, Faith and The New Millennium* (OneWorld, 1998).
91. Dr Ray Bohlin in his review of 'Darwin's Black Box' for Probe Ministries, *http://www.leaderu.com/orgs/probe/docs/darwinbx.html*
92. Michael Behe, interview, 'The Evolution of a Skeptic', 10 January 1997, *http://www.leaderu.com/real/ri9602/behe.html*

93. *Ibid.*
94. *Ibid.*
95. Michael Behe, *Darwin's Black Box* (Free Press, 1996), p.194.
96. Michael Behe, 'The Evolution of a Skeptic', *op. cit.*
97. Quoted by Dr Ray Bohlin in his review of *Darwin's Black Box*, *op. cit.*
98. Michael Behe, 'The Evolution of a Skeptic', *op. cit.*
99. *Ibid.*
100. Michael Behe, *Darwin's Black Box*, p.65.
101. *Ibid.*, pp.175–176.
102. *Ibid.*, p.192.
103. *Ibid.*, p.5.
104. *Ibid.*, p.205.
105. Michael Behe, 'The Evolution of a Skeptic', *op. cit.*
106. *Ibid.*
107. *Ibid.*
108. Michael Behe, *Darwin's Black Box*, p.249.
109. *Ibid.*, p.249.
110. J.P. Moreland, *op. cit.*, p.65.
111. Alvin Plantinga, *Warrant and Proper Function* (Oxford, 1993), p.216. Plantinga notes that his argument is similar to arguments presented by C.S. Lewis (*Miracles*, chapter three) and Richard Taylor (*Metaphysics*, chapter ten). See also Karl Popper and John Eccles, *The Self and its Brain* (Springer International, 1977), esp. pp.74–81.
112. *Ibid.*, p.189.
113. *Ibid.*, p.229.
114. John Pollock, *How to Build a Person*, p.148.
115. *Ibid.*
116. Alvin Plantinga, *op. cit.*, p.201.
117. Peter-Godfrey Smith's review of Millikan's 'Language, Thought and Other Biological Categories'.
118. Alvin Plantinga, *op. cit.*, p.203.
119. This argument follows one suggested by Plantinga, *Warrant and Proper Function*, p.204.

120. Alvin Plantinga's summary, *Warrant and Proper Function*, p.205.
121. Alvin Plantinga, *Ibid.*, pp.192, 206.
122. *Ibid.*, p.207.
123. *Ibid.*, p.214.
124. *Ibid.*, p.214.
125. *Ibid.*, pp.216–218.
126. *Ibid.*
127. Patricia Churchland, *Journal of Philosophy*, 84, October 1987, p.548.
128. Letter to William Graham, 3 July, 1881, *The Life and Letters of Charles Darwin Including an Autobiographical Chapter*, Francis Darwin, ed.
129. Alvin Plantinga, *op. cit.*, pp.234, 237.
130. *Ibid.*, pp.228, 231.
131. *Ibid.*, p.232.
132. Richard Purtill, *Thinking About Religion* (Prentice-Hall: Englewood Cliffs, NJ, 1978), pp.10–11.
133. J.P. Moreland, *op. cit.*, p.50.
134. *Ibid.*, p.50.
135. *Ibid.*
136. Richard Purtill, *op. cit.*, pp.10–11.
137. Thomas Nagel, *The Last Word* (Oxford, 1997), p.129.
138. *Ibid.*, pp.129–130.
139. *Ibid.*, p.75.
140. *Ibid.*, p.75–76.
141. *Ibid.*, p.76.

CHAPTER FIVE

THE ANTHROPIC TELEOLOGICAL ARGUMENT

Now the earth was formless and empty, darkness was over the face of the deep, and the Spirit of God was hovering over the waters. And God said, 'Let there be light,' and there was light. God saw that the light was good, and he separated the light from the darkness.

(Genesis 1:2–3).

Continuing with the theme of design, this chapter takes a closer look at the argument for God's existence from the finely tuned nature of the scientific laws that allowed and even encouraged the evolution of intelligent life from the Big Bang on.

Recent scientific discoveries have led to the formulation of a new design argument, the 'anthropic teleological argument'. 'Anthropic' is from the Greek for 'person' (hence anthropology—the study of people). 'Teleological' is from the Greek *telos* meaning 'end' and *logos* meaning 'reason'. The 'anthropic teleological argument' argues for the existence of God as the best explanation for the existence of a universe that produces people. This argument does not work by analogy, but by inference from scientific data to the best explanation for that data. In common with analogical design arguments, the anthropic teleological argument cannot offer conclusive proof. However, it is a stronger form of argument because an inference to the best explanation involves more stringent criteria than argument by analogy.

Outline of the argument

Premise 1) In order for life to exist, the universe had to have a very unlikely set of physical laws.

Premise 2) If something that is unlikely to occur happens, we should look for an explanation.

Premise 3) Two explanations for universal 'fine-tuning' are

advanced: Either there are a great many universes, all with different laws, or there's only one universe, which has this unlikely set of laws because it was set up that way for a reason by a powerful and intelligent creative mind, ie God.

Premise 4) The best explanation of the unlikely nature of our universe is in terms of the creative purpose of God.

Conclusion. And so God probably exists.

Defence of the argument

1) In order for life to exist, the universe had to have a very unlikely set of physical laws.

The 'fine tuning' of the laws which allows life to exist is called 'the anthropic principle'. This says that if you were to select a set of values for physical laws at random from all the possible variations, the likelihood of making a selection which would result in anything as complex as life, is extremely small: 'Don N. Page of the institute for Advanced Study in Princeton, N.J., recently calculated the odds against the formulation of our universe, and the figure was . . . one in $10,000,000,000^{124}$, a number so large that to call it "astronomical" would be to engage in a wild understatement.'[1] Let me give you some more examples of this fine-tuning:

- 'In the formation of the universe, the balance of matter to antimatter had to be accurate to one part in ten billion for the universe to arise.'[2]
- 'If nuclei were bound together slightly more weakly, or slightly more strongly, the universe would lack a chemistry . . . If the electric force were slightly stronger than it is, evolution would not reach organisms before the sun went out. If it were only slightly less, stars would not have planets, and life would be unknown.'[3]
- 'Entropy has been increasing ever since the Big Bang, which means that the early moments of the universe must have been a time of extremely low entropy when the state of the universe was

extremely highly ordered. The Oxford mathematics professor Roger Penrose has considered the entropy of the early universe and just how special it had to be. He estimates that of all the possible early universes, it had to be special to the tune of one part in $10 (10^{123})$.'[4] This is a number so large that it is 'too big to write down in full even if every proton in the entire universe were used to write a digit on!'[5]

(More examples can be found in the books listed for recommended reading.) As Paul Davies puts it: 'Suffice to say that, if we could play God, and select values for these quantities at whim by twiddling a set of knobs, we would find that almost all knob settings would render the universe uninhabitable.'[6]

2) If something that is unlikely to occur happens, we should look for an explanation.

The universe could so easily have been one in which nothing much at all could have happened. Some explanation of its fruitfulness is called for. Of course, you could just shrug your shoulders and say, 'How lucky for us that the universe just happens to have the scientific laws which enable us to exist. Of course the universe has those laws; if it didn't, we wouldn't be here to ask why the universe has just those laws! Why should I ask why the universe has those laws?', but that would be akin to intellectual suicide: 'It is a truism that we can only observe a universe that is consistent with our existence . . . On the other hand, the fact that even slight changes to the way things are might render the universe unobservable is surely a fact of deep significance.'[7]

Richard Swinburne tells a story that illustrates why it is rational to look for an explanation of the way the world is. Suppose, he says, that a lunatic kidnaps someone and locks them in a room with a card-shuffling machine. This machine shuffles ten packs of cards, draws one card from each pack, and then exhibits all ten cards. The kidnapper tells his victim that the machine will soon go to work and make a draw. Unless the draw consists of an ace of hearts from every pack, the machine will simultaneously explode, killing the victim. As a result of this explosion the victim will not see which cards the machine drew, unless they are all the ace of hearts. The kidnapper leaves and the machine makes its draw. To the victim's relief, it draws ten ace of hearts cards, and doesn't explode. The victim naturally believes that there must be some explanation for his amazing good luck. Perhaps the machine was rigged to pick the cards it did and this has all been some fantastic practical joke. However, the kidnapper returns and pours cold-water on this suggestion. He says that it is not at all surprising that the machine drew the only safe selection of cards, for the victim would not be alive to see any other draw. That draw is a precondition of the victim seeing any draw at all. However, the kidnapper is clearly wrong:

> There is indeed something extraordinary in need of explanation in ten aces of hearts being drawn. The fact that this peculiar order is a necessary condition of the draw being perceived at all makes what is perceived no less extraordinary and in need of explanation. The theist's starting-point is not that we perceive order rather than disorder, but that order rather than disorder is there.[8]

If something happens which is unlikely to have happened, then we are justified in seeking out an explanation. If I rolled 10 (10^{123}) sixes in a row it would be reasonable of you to suspect me of using loaded die! It is extremely unlikely that the universe should work according to such a finely tuned set of laws as those necessary for the existence of anything even remotely interesting. Therefore, we should look for an explanation. The fact that, if the universe didn't have those laws then we wouldn't be around to look for an explanation, is neither here nor there.

3) Two explanations for universal 'fine-tuning' are advanced: Either there are a great many universes, all with different laws,

or there's only one universe, which has this unlikely set of laws because it was set up that way for a reason by a super-powerful and intelligent creative mind, ie God.

Either there are so many universes with different laws that it's hardly surprising one of them has produced a great deal of complexity; or there is one universe, and it's hardly surprising that it has just those physical laws which lead to complex things like us, because it was created with this outcome in mind. In whose mind? Obviously in the mind of someone very powerful, intelligent and creative; in the mind of God:

> if there is a single fly on a big brick wall, its being hit by a bullet surely calls for some sort of explanation. Either a marksman has been at work or many shots were fired, one of which by chance hit this isolated target.[9]

You might suggest that the fly was hit by a single fluke shot, but only if you had disproved both the 'marksman' and the 'many bullets' explanations.

4) The best explanation of the unlikely nature of our universe is in terms of the creative purpose of God.

How should we choose between these two explanations of the 'anthropic principle'? We can apply Occam's razor. This tool for deciding between competing explanations is named after William of Occam (whose name, due to the vagaries of medieval spelling, can also be spelt 'Ockham'). The 'razor' asks us not to multiply entities beyond necessity. That is, we should always explain things as simply as possible. The razor cuts out all excess. We can choose between two hypotheses that both explain the observed data by choosing the simpler hypothesis.

If you are trying to explain something by inferring the existence of something else that explains it, then there's no point in that something else being any more complicated than it has to be to do the job: 'Experience has shown that nature does share our sense of economy, efficiency, beauty, and mathematical subtlety, and this approach to research can often pay dividends.'[10]

Take this book. How did all that ink come to be arranged in words in a meaningful order on sheets of paper bound together in sequence between covers? Here are two possible explanations: 1) An author wrote the book and a publisher had a printing press mass-produce it for sale; 2) A terrorist caused an explosion in a printing press, and this explosion caused ink and paper to fly about the place, and the ink just happened to fall on the paper in the form of words, and the paper just happened to flutter down together in an order that made sense of the words, and the sequenced sheets of paper landed in an appropriate cover and glue was fortuitously in the right place at the right time to stick the sheets into the covers. Which explanation would you choose? Both are logically possible. There is nothing self-contradictory or incoherent about either explanation. I'm sure you would choose the first explanation. Why? Because the first explanation is much simpler than the second explanation. It accounts for all the known facts with greater economy than the 'explosion in a printing-works' hypothesis. That's Occam's razor in action. It's a tool of thought we use every day to make inferences to the best, most likely explanation.

You could explain the existence of a particular book with reference to a person who wrote it and a publisher who published it. Alternatively, you could try to explain it by arguing that there exist billions upon billions of books, and so it is hardly unlikely that this particular book, this particular arrangement of ink on paper, should exist. The existence of a billion randomly cobbled together books (typed, no doubt, by those famous monkeys on their typewriters) certainly increases the likelihood of a particular randomly generated volume existing. However, it gives no explanation of why there should exist any books in the first place! Not only is an explanation in terms of an author far simpler than the monkeys on their typewriters/explosion in a printing press explanation, but it is also a far more adequate explanation.

Now, on the one hand we have an explanation requiring us to believe that there exist a more than astronomically huge number of universes, all with slightly different physical laws. On the other hand, we have an explanation that requires us to believe in the existence of the only universe we experience, and in one other entity, God. Which, according to Occam's razor, should we choose? It looks plausible to say the second one. As Richard Swinburne writes, 'To postulate a trillion other universes, rather than one God in order to explain the orderliness of our universe, seems the height of irrationality.'[11] For 'The postulation of God is the postulation of one entity of a simple kind . . . The postulation of the actual existence of an infinite number of worlds, between them exhausting all the logical possibilities . . . is to postulate complexities beyond rational belief.'[12]

According to Swinburne, it's not just that God is one thing whereas the 'many-universes' explanation posits the existence of a lot, or even an infinite number, of things (although that is part of the reason why the God hypothesis is simpler). It is also the fact that God is a single being of a simple kind. The simplest ultimate explanation is one that postulates a single ultimate cause. Theism postulates as a single ultimate cause a person with infinite degrees of the qualities essential to being a person. A person with absolutely no power, knowledge, goodness or freedom is an impossibility. To imagine an arbitrary finite limit to these qualities is more complicated than to imagine no limit: 'Hence theism provides the simplest kind of personal explanation of the universe.'[13]

It might be asked why we should explain the universe as the work of just one being, why not a whole committee of gods? Well, in the absence of any evidence in support of such a 'many gods' explanation, I needn't spell out the results of applying Occam's razor to these two competing theories.

Also, if there existed more than one divine being, they would infringe upon each other's freedom of action unless a) their power and freedom to act was less than infinite, or b) they all co-operated perfectly, sharing the same infinite power, knowledge and so on. The first possibility is clearly less simple than the second. The second possibility is really the postulation of one personal divine nature shared equally between more than one divine 'persons'. This possibility allows for the Christian belief that God is Trinity. This belief might be less simple than the belief that God contains only one 'centre of personhood', but if there were reason to think that God is composed of more than one divine 'person', then the simpler hypothesis would not do justice to the available data. In all inferences to the best expla-nation we must balance simplicity with adequacy. The data con-sidered by the anthropic teleological argument obviously only requires the existence of a single-personed deity, and any indi-vidualisation within God would have to be justified at a later date by the need to adequately account for further data.[14]

5) And so God probably exists.

Paul Davies concludes that 'Ockham's razor compels me to put my money on design.'[15] Using scientific data, and standard sci-entific methodology to choose between hypotheses, it seems apparent that the most reasonable explanation for the existence of our universe is that it originates in the mind and creative action of an infinitely powerful and intelligent personal being: God. As Swinburne says:

> I do not deny that science explains, but I postulate God to explain why science explains. The very success of science in showing us how deeply ordered the natural world is provides strong grounds for believing that there is an even deeper cause of that order.[16]

However, all that can be said has not yet been said.

Further moves

You might read the above and think, 'OK, the existence of God would be the best explanation of the universe given the data you've included in your argument, but the 'many universes' answer is still a possible solution, and I've got other data which forces me to choose it, rather than the existence of God, to explain the facts. After all, Occam's razor says that we should pick the simplest possible explanation that accounts for all the known facts.'

If I were to ask what facts you had in mind that I hadn't mentioned, you might reply (as you might reply to any of my arguments) that you had reason to believe that God doesn't exist, and so that no argument I gave could possibly work. You might also say, with reference to the argument for design, that you had reason (besides the desire to avoid the conclusion that God exists!) to think that there are other universes.

How can I reply to these two moves? You can hardly expect particular arguments for the existence of God to include refutations of every conceivable argument for the non-existence of God before making its point. I admit that if you think you have a compelling disproof of the existence of God, then it would be reasonable for you to say that the argument for design (and indeed, any argument for the existence of God) cannot prove its point, since you can't prove what isn't so. I know of no argument for the non-existence of God which has seemed to me to work (obviously, or I wouldn't still believe in God!). In other words, if you want to make this move, our intellectual and spiritual journey shouldn't grind to a halt, but should move on to different ground. Just because I believe there are good arguments for the existence of God, and that none of the arguments I have seen against God's existence work, does not excuse me from defending these beliefs against criticism. Likewise, even if you think you have strong reasons for believing that God doesn't exist, you should consider and attempt to refute both my arguments and my criticisms of your arguments, if only in the hope of showing me the error of my ways! At the very least, we will come to understand each other better.

However strongly convinced we are by the truth of our own beliefs, we are not all-knowing, infallible beings incapable of being deluded into false beliefs. Therefore, if we really do care about truth, we ought never to adopt an attitude of blind faith. 'Blind faith' is a contradiction in terms. Faith involves trust. It involves belief in the truth of some idea about how reality really is, and such trust is not scared to question itself. If you really believe that a rope will hold your weight, you will be prepared to trust your life to its strength. If you claimed to believe that a rope would support you, but, when faced with a situation where you would have to 'put your life where your mouth is', refused to act in accordance with your professed belief, I would have reason to doubt you ever actually believed in your rope's ability to support you.

Belief or disbelief in God is just such a life or death situation. I believe in God, I have faith in Him, and this presupposes the belief that He actually exists! Having this faith, I am prepared to put my belief to the test. Since I've trusted my life to God, it's no skin off my nose to put my belief to the test of anyone's anti-God arguments. If this wasn't so, you'd rightly conclude that my professed belief was not what it claimed to be. It would be unnecessarily gauche of me to spell out the application of this principle to the atheist's position; I'm sure you can do that for yourself.

Many universes?

What about the claim that there are reasons (besides the wish to avoid believing in the existence of God) for accepting the existence of many universes; reasons which make the postulation of God's existence unnecessary to account for the existence of our universe?

There is one interpretation of quantum mechanics (called the 'many worlds' interpretation) which says that our universe is constantly dividing into an ever-increasing myriad of parallel worlds: 'This supposes that the different outcomes of quantum measurement all actually occur, but in disjoint worlds into which physical reality splits at each such act of measurement.'[17] This view of quantum mechanics is contentious, but, 'even if it were true the result would be the generation of worlds with different histories but not universes with different laws of nature.'[18] Our particular universe with its particular laws of physics would have to exist before it could start dividing into different worlds. So, even if the 'many worlds' theory were true, it would provide absolutely no support to the 'many universes' alternative to the existence of God.

Rolling a die several times increases the chances of throwing a six, but doesn't explain why there should be a six on one face of the die. Similarly, a universe that 'splits' at every alternative may well give more 'rolls of the die' in the atheist's game-of-chance picture of evolution. But the number of chances provided for the operation of physical laws likely (or even certain) to produce living creatures has nothing to do with the question of why the die of fate should have a face labelled 'life' on it at all. In all the many-universe theories that come from actual physics, the laws of nature are the same in every universe. Many-universe theories provide a spread of alternative universe states, not a spread of different physical laws. The 'many-universes' option proposes the existence of a large or infinite number of dice in the attempt to up the likelihood of a six being thrown (the emergence of life), but it has nothing to say about the more fundamental issue of why the finely-tuned laws necessary for life exist in this or any other universe.

Another reply to the suggestion that there is evidence in support of the existence of many universes would be that there is also other evidence for the existence of God. The other arguments for the existence of God constitute good reason to explain the existence of our universe as something intended by God rather than as the blind outcome of the existence of myriad distinct and different universes.

The existence of many other universes is totally compatible with the existence of God—so long as it is, all things considered, a good thing that whatever universes exist do exist. Nevertheless, assuming that God exists, the lack of evidence for the existence of other universes means that it remains a simpler explanation of our universe to say that God created it and that there are no other universes, than to say that God created many different universes, including our own.

One universe, different regions?

'Perhaps,' you might say, 'there is only one universe after all, but one which is a patch-work of huge regions with distinct physical laws, and where we naturally happen to inhabit a region where life is possible.' Such a picture of the universe is provided by the scientific theory of 'spontaneous symmetry breaking', whereby it might be the case that, 'There could be different cosmic domains in which . . . the effective forces of nature would be different.'[19] These different areas are imagined as having formed as the early universe expanded and cooled.

This proposal is certainly better than the 'many-universes' suggestion. It does at least concern itself with the existence of different physical laws. However, what is the difference between 'a universe which is divided into regions with different laws of physics', and 'lots of separate universes with different laws of physics'? If such a 'multi-verse' is to be considered as different from separate 'parallel' universes, surely there must be some unifying factor which makes it reasonable to group these different 'regions' together under a single concept? But what could provide such a unifying reason apart from laws of physics that are at the very least similar enough to allow interaction between regions? Yet, if the so-called 'different regions' are similar enough to interact with each other, can we be justified in thinking of them as disjoint areas of reality? I think not.

Even if such a view of the universe were true, it wouldn't be of help to the atheist, for 'there would still be significant anthropic conditions to be satisfied by the universe as a whole'.[20] The laws that governed how the universe developed into such a multi-verse of different areas would have to be such that at least one region able to evolve life would itself evolve from the universe as a whole. The 'multi-verse' hypothesis simply pushes the anthropic question back a stage; it does not, and cannot, get rid of the question.

Metaphysics, not science

Over and above the preceding considerations I'd like to point out with John Polkinghorne that any 'many-universes explanation of anthropic fine tuning is metaphysical in character, depending upon an appeal to the existence of worlds of whose being we can have no direct, scientifically motivated, knowledge. It is a metaphysical guess that they might be there'.[21] No 'many-universes' theory can claim the support of scientific data, for such theories are metaphysical interpretations of the scientific data. We only have direct scientific knowledge of one universe, and it seems to be simpler to accept metaphysical interpretations of the scientific data which need only to mention the one universe with which we are aquainted. It seems that no 'many universes' explanation of how we came to exist can be as metaphysically simple, elegant and satisfying as the hypothesis that God exists and wills whatever else exists to be, for some divine reason.

Simplicity v. adequacy

I recently came across a criticism of the anthropic teleological argument that I had not considered before, and which seems to me to be a more persuasive criticism than those so far mentioned. This criticism is one made by the atheist J.J.C. Smart in response to the anthropic argument defended by J.J. Haldane in their published debate *Atheism and Theism* (Blackwells, 1996.) Smart argues that, in positing a designer, we are positing the existence of a mind containing a sort of 'blueprint' for the universe, a blueprint that is probably as complicated as the universe it describes. God is traditionally thought to be omniscient, that is, all-knowing. The problem this point raises is this—we can either explain our universe as one unintended universe among a very large number of different unintended universes, or as the single intended product of a single divine mind (or as one universe among many intended by God). The God and one universe hypothesis seems simpler until we notice that a divine mind is an all-knowing mind which contains the 'blueprints' for every possible universe. To say that our universe is the creation of a divinity is therefore to posit the existence of the 'blueprints' of every possible universe *and* of the divine mind itself. This means that the God hypothesis is actually less simple than the many unintended universes explanation:

> the designer's mind would have to have within it a structure at least as complex as the conjunction of fundamental laws and initial conditions . . . Thus, even if it were supposed that the designer determines only the laws of nature (with non-arbitrary constants in them) and a suitable set of initial conditions, then considerations of simplicity and of Ockham's razor suggest that the supposition was an unnecessary one which should be rejected.[22]

Smart's criticism, if successful, doesn't completely destroy the anthropic teleological argument. It seems to imply that the existence of a god who is not omniscient would make for a simpler adequate explanation of cosmic fine-tuning than the 'many-universes' gambit. However, theists believe that God is in some sense all-knowing, and so while this point may bring the atheist some discomfort, it will not in itself give much comfort to the theist.

What can we say in response to Smart? J.J. Haldane replies that the 'many universes' hypothesis, 'appears as entirely *ad hoc*, introduced only to avoid what for the naturalist is an unpalatable conclusion, [in this case], that the general regularities and particular fine tuning are due to the agency of a designer.'[23] Haldane may well be right about this, but he does seem to be objecting to the atheists rather than their argument.

Doesn't Smart's criticism contradict Richard Swinburne's argument that theism provides 'the simplest kind of personal explanation of the universe there could be'? Well, it may be true that God is the simplest type of personal being, and that no personal explanation, however simple, is simpler than a non-personal explanation. Persons, of whatever sort, are pretty complex things.

Is Smart right to say that an omniscient mind must contain the blueprints of every possible universe? Perhaps not; but any such rebuttal feels rather like a 'grasping at straws' to me. I will therefore assume that Smart's criticism is valid, and that the God hypothesis is less simple than the 'many-universes' alternative. What follows?

Even if, after all I have said, you want to plump for the idea that, by the existence of many universes our existence was only to be expected, you will have no answer to the question why the universe bothers to exist. But that takes us back to the cosmological argument.

Occam's razor appeals to two criteria: simplicity and adequacy. Adequacy is more important than simplicity. Supposing that the 'many universes' hypothesis is simpler than the God hypothesis, we can still ask if one is more adequate than the other. Both are adequate answers to the 'why this cosmic fine-tuning?' question in that both answers make the existence of the observed fine-tuning more likely than on the 'brute fact'

THE ANTHROPIC TELEOLOGICAL ARGUMENT 273

explanation. The crux of the issue is therefore whether or not the God explanation is more adequate than the 'many-universes' alternative.

The weakness of the anthropic teleological argument comes from the narrow range of data it considers. If all we are doing is looking for the best explanation of anthropic fine-tuning, the theistic explanation is adequate, but too complex. The 'many-universes' explanation wins on grounds of simplicity. However, if we widen our argument in search of the best explanation for the universe, then the theistic explanation, though complex, triumphs because of its greater adequacy. The no-God hypothesis seems unable to ground objective moral values, or to give an adequate foundation for the existence of purpose. Perhaps this is partly a temperamental judgement on my part, an inability or a refusal to see amoral and purposeless nature as an adequate foundation for the existence of moral and personal qualities which I cannot bring myself to 'explain away' as atheists do.

While it's easy for the personal explanation to include the existence of the non-personal, it is, at the very least, far harder for the non-personal explanation to account for the existence of the personal. An ultimately personal explanation is simpler than a world-view in which neither personal or non-personal reality is ultimately explicable in terms of the other, and more adequate than a world-view which attempts to reduce the personal to the non-personal, and is therefore to be preferred. This world-view is theism.

The basic point is this: if you hold that everything is explicable in terms of 'nature' it is possible to give a more ultimate explanation by saying that 'nature' is intended by an infinite personal being; whereas, if you hold that everything is ultimately explicable with reference to an infinite personal being, the attempt to go beyond this by explaining the personal by the non-personal is less adequate than stopping with the personal explanation:

all explanation is reducible to personal explanation, in the sense that the operation of causal [laws] cited in scientific explanation is always explicable by the action of a person [God]. A personal explanation of a scientific explanation states which persons with which intentions, beliefs, and capacities bring about the existence of the initial conditions . . . and the operation of laws of nature . . . for the theist, explanation stops at what, intuitively, is the most natural kind of stopping-place for explanation—the choice of an agent.[24]

However, it would be nice to make a reply to Smart from within the remit of the argument he is attacking.

It doesn't really help to say that given enough time, or enough different universes, or both, the evolution of life was bound to happen, and that this therefore explains why we exist. It doesn't help because it isn't true. It is wrong to think that, given enough chances, every possible world must exist or come into existence eventually. Of course it is possible, but it isn't logically necessary by any stretch of the imagination:

Even if there were an infinity of universes it would not be inevitable that this or any other one should be among them. All one can say is that as the number of universes proceeds towards infinity the probability of a difference between the actual distribution and the probable one diminishes to zero . . . Infinitely many orderings may never yield the significant ordering.[25]

Think of it like this: if you shuffle pages numbered 1 to 1000 over and over infinitely many times, then the chances of not getting the pages into the order 1 to 1000 falls. However, there is no *guarantee* that the pages will ever appear in the order 1 to 1000.

We can easily imagine that only one or two possible universes ever get actualised, that is, become actualities rather than remaining possibilities. Postulating even an infinite number of cosmic 'throws' does nothing to explain why a universe likely to produce beings such as ourselves would *have* to become actual, rather than remaining a mere possibility. Nothing that is, except God.

And what is it that defines what is and what is not a possible world? Only something which is itself actual. But nothing physical can explain why the die of physics has a face labelled 'life'. Only something non-physical can explain that, and God fits the bill rather well.

If many or all possible universes exist, and if there is a possible universe which is created by God, then, far from doing away with God, the hypothesis that many or all possible universes exist opens up at least the possibility, and perhaps the certainty, that God exists! Unless the very concept of 'God', or of 'A universe created by God' is incoherent, it is a logical possibility that a universe created by God exists. The only remaining question is then whether this possibility is also an actuality. The more universes the atheist introduces to explain the fine-tuning of our own universe, the more likely it is that one of these universes is a universe created by God. Now, part of the definition of 'God' is 'an independent being'. Granted the existence of an independent being, Occam's razor would compel us to anchor all dependent existence in the independent reality of God. The 'many universes' hypothesis therefore rebounds upon the atheist and suggests that this universe, together with any other universes, exist in dependence upon God. But in this case, we may as well cut down the number of proposed universes to a very adequate single universe: this one. The atheist might object that by 'universe' they mean 'a universe not created by God', but such a response seems to be *ad hoc*, and to beg the question against God's existence.

Even if Smart's criticism is correct, the anthropic teleological argument is not a total loss. There is a lack of evidence in favour of the many-universes hypothesis (beyond its simplicity) in explaining the anthropic fine-tuning of our universe, and there exists what I take to be good, independent evidence for the existence of God. This being so, the theistic interpretation of the anthropic principle becomes compelling, and the anthropic teleological design argument can add significantly to our reasons for believing that God is an intelligent, rational, knowing and powerful personal being somewhat analogous to a human, but of far greater capacities, who has created our universe for the purpose of bringing about the existence of free, sentient beings such as ourselves. The anthropic argument may not be a good argument for the existence of God, but placed within a theistic framework it provides significant support for the traditional beliefs about the nature of God: 'So, if one asks what caused the universe, or why it is as it is, the theistic answer is that God brought the universe into being in order to realise a set of great and distinctive values.'[26]

Conclusion

The anthropic teleological argument is what the American philosopher C.S. Peirce called an 'abductive inference', an argument that takes the following form: '[some] surprising fact B, is observed. But if A were true, B would be a matter of course. Therefore, there is reason to suspect that A is true.'[27] Two alternative explanations for 'B', the fine-tuning of our universe, are proposed. The first is that God created our universe. The second is that there exist many different universes. Both explanations would render B 'a matter of course' rather than a 'brute fact'. Cosmic 'fine-tuning' is evidence in favour of both hypotheses. Both explanations are adequate. However, it seems that the 'many universes' explanation is simpler than the 'creation' explanation. This judgement is not the outcome of an exact science. Nevertheless, the weight of argument seems to me to indicate that the theistic hypothesis, while compatible with the data, loses out to the 'many-universes' hypothesis on grounds of simplicity.

On the other hand, the creation hypothesis seems to be *more adequate* than the 'many-universes' alternative. The 'many-universes' hypothesis does not guarantee the existence of our universe, and so the existence of our universe remains an unexplained brute fact. Nor does the 'many-universes' hypothesis explain why *different* universes exist. The atheist must leave the existence of different universes as a brute fact. While we do not know enough to say that the God hypothesis guarantees the existence of this universe (or of any universe), it does at least provide an explanation for the existence of our universe.

If we widen the data considered in the quest for the best world-view, the theistic hypothesis seems more adequate than any materialist alternative, because it is more natural to explain the impersonal in terms of the personal than it is to explain the personal in terms of the impersonal. The first type of explanation leads to theism, while the second leads to reductionistic naturalism. As J.J.C. Smart writes, 'At any rate this purposive explanation of the happy values of the constants of nature and of the forms of the fundamental laws could strengthen belief in a deity whose existence was made probable by some other argument.'[28]

Given the utility of other theistic arguments then, the theistic explanation of cosmic fine-tuning becomes compelling, and the anthropic teleological argument shows itself to be an important piece of natural theology with much to say about the nature of 'God' as the architect of an inherently fruitful universe.

Recommended reading

L. Stafford Betty and Bruce Cordell, 'The Anthropic Teleological Argument', M. Peterson *et al*, eds, in *Philosophy of Religion, Selected Readings* (Oxford, 1996). (3)

Paul Davies, *The Mind of God* (Penguin, 1993). (2)

Stephen T. Davies, *God, Reason and Theistic Proofs* (Edinburgh University Press, 1997). (3)

J.J.C. Smart and J.J. Haldane, *Atheism and Theism* (Blackwells, 1996). (4)

John Leslie, *Universes* (Routledge: New York, 1989). (4)

J.P. Moreland, *Scaling the Secular City* (Baker, 1987). (3)

J.P. Moreland and Kai Nielson, *Does God Exist? The Debate between Theists and Atheists* (Prometheus Books, 1993). (3)

John Polkinghorne, *Beyond Science* (Cambridge, 1996). (1)

John Polkinghorne, *quarks, chaos and christianity* (Triangle, 1994). (1)

John Polkinghorne, *Belief in God in an Age of Science* (Yale University Press, 1998). (2)

Richard Swinburne, *Is There a God?* (Oxford, 1996). (3)

Richard Swinburne, *The Existence of God*, revised edition (Oxford, 1991). (4)

F.R. Tennant, *Philosophical Theology*, vol. 2, 'The World, the soul, and God', (Cambridge, 1956). (3)

Keith Ward, *God, Chance and Necessity*, (OneWorld, 1996). (3)

Notes

1. L. Stafford Betty and Bruce Cordell, 'The Anthropic Teleological Argument' in Michael Peterson *et al*, eds, *Philosophy of Religion—Selected Readings* (Oxford, 1995).
2. J.P. Moreland, *Scaling the Secular City* (Baker, 1987).
3. Peter Atkins, *Creation Revisited*.
4. John Houghton, *The Search for God—Can Science Help?* (Lion, 1995), p.36.
5. Roger Penrose, *The Emperor's New Mind* (Vintage, 1991), p.445.
6. Paul Davies, *The Mind Of God* (Penguin, 1993).
7. *Ibid.*, p.200.
8. Richard Swinburne, *Is There a God?* (Oxford, 1995), pp.66–67.
9. John Polkinghorne, *Beyond Science* (Cambridge, 1996).
10. Paul Davies, *op. cit.*, pp.209–210.
11. Richard Swinburne, *op. cit.*, p.68.

12. Richard Swinburne, 'Argument from the Fine-Tuning of the Universe' in *Physical Cosmology and Philosophy*, J.Leslie, ed. p.172.
13. Richard Swinburne, *op. cit.*
14. See: Alister McGrath, *Understanding The Trinity* (Kingsway, 1987) (1); John Polkinghorne, *Science and Christian Belief* (SPCK, 1994) (4); H.P. Owen, *Christian Theism* (TT Clark, 1984) (3); and Richard Swinburne, *The Christian God* (Oxford, 1994) (4).
15. Paul Davies, *op. cit.*
16. Richard Swinburne, *op. cit.*, p.68.
17. *Ibid.*
18. *Ibid.*
19. John Polkinghorne, *op. cit.*
20. *Ibid.*
21. *Ibid.*
22. J.J.C. Smart, *Atheism and Theism* (Blackwells, 1996), pp.25–26.
23. J.J. Haldane, *Ibid.*, p.127.
24. Richard Swinburne, *The Existence of God*, revised edition (Oxford, 1991).
25. J.J. Haldane, *op. cit.*, p.125.
26. Keith Ward, *God, Chance and Necessity*, (OneWorld, 1996), p.59.
27. Quoted by Hugo A. Meynell, *The Intelligible Universe.*
28. J.J.C. Smart, *op. cit.*, p.26.

CHAPTER SIX

ARGUMENTS FROM COMMON CONSENT, AUTHORITY AND RELIGIOUS EXPERIENCE

Taste and see that the Lord is good;
blessed is the man who takes refuge in him.
(Psalm 34:8)

I argue that the best explanation for the fact that so many people, including many great intellectuals, believe in God and feel themselves to be in relationship with Him, is that God exists. If God does not exist, a great many otherwise sane individuals are not merely mistaken about the validity of their religious experience, but deluded. Despite the implausibility of such a state of affairs, this is precisely the position adopted by atheists like Sigmund Freud who see belief in God as the product of wish-fulfilment and psychological projection. However, one can plausibly argue that the atheist's disbelief is more likely than the theist's belief to be the product of wish-fulfilment and other psychological factors. On the premise that we should take our experience at face value unless and until we have reason not to do so, I conclude that the religious experience of so many people in so many different historical and cultural circumstances is best explained by the existence of God.

In this chapter I will present some reasons for believing in the existence of God based upon the beliefs and feelings of people, categorised by numbers or intellectual quality. Arguments from common consent and authority are the weakest form of argument. However, they are serious arguments which must be taken into account. I believe that the arguments for God's existence from common consent and authority are strong examples of their sort. I believe that these arguments, together with the argument from religious experience, make a useful addition to the overall case for theism.

In my discussion of religious experience I will pay particular attention to Christian religious experience. No denigration of the religious experiences of non-Christians is intended. As a Christian theist, I interpret my religious experience within the framework of Christian beliefs about the divinity of Jesus and the trinitarian nature of God as Father, Son and Holy Spirit. I will take Christianity, which is the largest faith movement, as an exemplary test case of theistic religious experience in general. It is my hope that some readers will be inspired to investigate the person of Jesus for themselves; and to this end I have included a selection of relevant material in my list of recommended reading at the close of the chapter.

Christian apologists, perhaps understandably, tend to paint a rather rosy picture of Christian religious experience. The fact is that being a Christian can be tough. I therefore preface the following discussion by taking some words of C.S. Lewis as my own: 'The truth is, I haven't any language weak enough to depict the weakness of my spiritual life.'[1] These words, from the greatest and best-loved Christian writer of the twentieth century, have been a great source of solace to me in contemplating the frequent shallowness of my response to what I perceive of God in my life. I can only hope and pray that, paradoxically, the fact that I notice the weakness of my emotional response to God indicates that at some other level I must be on the right track.

There are Christians who appear to live lives of joy-filled religious vigour; and I wish them well. Their enthusiasm often provides a much-needed spiritual tonic. The fact that these bubbly people can sometimes make those of us with a more 'hum-drum' spiritual life feel ill at ease is probably more our fault than theirs. I think the stereotypical 'charismatic' v. 'church pew' dichotomy has quite as much to do with different personalities as it does with different traditions and theologies. Professor Clark H. Pinnock admits, 'I certainly go through periods in my life when God seems distant from me or I from him, and I don't think this is always due to failure on my part.'[2] Rather, he says, 'it relates to the sovereign freedom of God in giving himself to be known . . . Although there are steps toward spiritual preparation, they are not infallibly productive as if we could bend God to do our will.'[3]

Every Christian is unique, and God relates to individuals individually, as well as to communities of individuals. It would be odd to expect every son and daughter in a family to relate to their parents in exactly the same way. Likewise, it would be odd to expect every Christian to experience God in the same way. One should expect both similarities and differences. Still, however thin my spiritual life may seem, I know from the inside out what the Christian experience of God is like.

Outline of the argument from common consent

1) Most people believe in God.
2) Either this believing majority has been wrong about this profound element in their lives, or not.
3) Of these alternatives, it is more plausible to believe that they have been right.
4) Therefore, God probably exists.

Defence of the argument

Why is it plausible to believe that the majority has been right rather than wrong in the matter of God's existence? First of all, I'd better establish that I'm right to claim that the majority believes in God.

The current world population is about 5,716 million. The number of Christians in the world at present is about 1,928 million. Add to this Muslims (1,099 million) and Jews (12.8 million), and the numbers total up to 3,039.8 million people, or 65% of the world population, believing that God exists! In some regions the percentage is much higher: '98% of the United States Population say they believe in God.'[4] Now, not all the people counted as Jews, Christians or Muslims actively believe in God (for example, 20% of American Jews are secular[5]), but polls of non-believers indicate that these figures for theists are in the right ballpark.

Atheist Michael Martin reports that about 21% of the world population consists of non-believers. Of these, 210 million are atheists and 805 million are agnostic.[6] That means that 5% of the world population are atheists, while 15% are agnostic. These figures do not include members of religions such as Jainism that involve no belief in God. Neither, however, do they include religions besides Judaism, Christianity and Islam which involve belief in a god, such as certain forms of animism. Other polls indicate that around 30% of people are either atheists or agnostics. If we take into account current percentages for Hindus and Buddhists we can make the following educated guess at the distribution of belief: theists (Christians, Muslims, Jews and others) 60%, agnostics 15%, Hindus 13%, Buddhists 6%, secular atheists 5%, and others 1%. It looks very much as if theism is the majority belief-system in the world today.

So, only about 40% of people profess not to believe in the existence of God. Many of these people are agnostic. They do not claim to know that there is no God, but merely that they do not know that there is or isn't a God. For all they know God might exist—they do not rule God's existence 'out of court'. This leaves us with an even smaller minority of atheists, people who believe that there is no God (25%).

Even this minority may be smaller than it seems: 'It may be true in one sense that many people profess not to believe in God, but . . . given the right circumstances, a much wider group will betray a deep, latent, almost built-in belief in God.'[7] What are the first words out of an atheist's mouth when they go through a horrifying experience or narrowly escape death? Isn't it something like: 'Oh my God!'? What does almost every person do when someone they love is suffering from some terrible illness? They pray. To whom? To God. Although we might be able to explain away these responses as the result of social conditioning (being on a par with the unpremeditated use of swear-words), experience teaches us that something deeper than this is going on, at least in some cases. It is responses like this which give rise to the saying, 'There are no atheists in fox-holes.' As Paul Chamberlain puts it:

The professing atheist is not living consistently with his atheism if he responds to crisis by uttering a prayer . . . Our reactions in a crisis may show our most gut-level beliefs. All I'm saying is that if we were to take people who had called on God or thanked God or gotten angry with God in the midst of a crisis and ask them if they believed in God at those times, the number of professing atheists would be very low.[8]

C.S. Lewis likened such latent belief to rats in a closet. If you approach the closet with a lot of noise, giving the rats plenty of time to hide, when you open the door, you won't see them. But if you creep up on them and suddenly fling open the door, you'll see the rats running for cover. Similarly, if you give an atheist time to think about their beliefs and responses, you will find no belief in God. But if you catch them unawares, in a moment of fear or grief perhaps, then you often find that they reveal a latent belief in God. A sudden, unexpected crisis can reveal this belief, just as the sudden entry to the closet reveals the rats. (I do not recommend going about frightening atheists in order to unearth latent religious belief! However, many people do find God during or after times of acute crisis, and the rats-in-the-closet analogy may explain why this is so.)

Belief throughout history

The above figures concern belief today. However, belief in God has been around for as long as humans:

> anthropological research has indicated that among the farthest and most remote primitive peoples today, there is a universal belief in God. And in the earliest histories and legends of peoples all around the world the original concept was of one God, who was the creator. An original high God seems once to have been in their consciousness even in those societies which are today polytheistic.[9]

For most of history, theism has been humanity's world-view of choice. Belief in God is one of the oldest beliefs around. It has stood the test of time. It has outlasted the polytheism of the ancient Egyptians, Greeks, Vikings and Romans. Lions in the arena, communist prisons and labour camps, torture and brain-washing—all have tried and failed to destroy belief in God. All have been outlived by the faith they threatened. Nietzsche declared, 'God is dead.' 'God' out-lived him.

Flat-Earth syndrome?

You may be tempted to reply to the argument from 'common consent' that people can be mistaken. For example, we now know people to have been mistaken in believing that the world is flat. The majority surely once held belief in a flat world, but they were wrong, so it is possible that the majority who believe God exists are wrong. I agree that it is possible for the majority to be wrong. However, all I need to defend for the purposes of the common consent argument is that the majority is unlikely to be wrong in this case. 'One million Frenchmen' can be wrong, but it is less likely than one hundred Frenchmen being wrong. If the witness of seven people contradicted the witness of three people, whom would you believe, all other things being equal? Similarly, if every preceding century gives overwhelming testimony in a matter where there has been little or no advance in relevant methods of discovery and proof, but this testimony contradicts a minority view in your own century, which testimony are you going to believe? I suggest that to choose the contemporary view could only be chronological snobbery, the narrow-minded determination to believe something simply because it is 'modern'.

The example of believing the earth to be flat is not comparable with belief in the existence of God. The flatness of the Earth was made susceptible to being proved wrong through developments in technology. Once you can sail back to where you started without turning round it's pretty obvious that the world has no edge! The existence of God isn't the sort of belief that can be disproved if only you possess enough technological sophistication, which could only be believed by people who lacked modern scientific knowledge. A modern scientist is more likely to be right in scientific matters than a medieval 'natural-philosopher' (as scientists used to be called), but not more likely to be right with regards to God's existence.

The fact that so many people believe and have believed in God over such a long period of time and in so many different circumstances is evidence in favour of God's existence. As Aristotle said, 'No word on many people's lips is wholly lost.'[10]

Outline of the argument from authority

Premise 1) Many of the greatest minds believe in God.
Premise 2) Whatever many of the greatest minds believe is likely to be true.
Conclusion. Therefore it is likely that God exists.

Defence of the argument from authority

Some people think that listening to the voice of authority means abandoning reason. Not so. We all rely on authority for a great deal of what we believe without being at all irrational. Any knowledge that we gain from trusting the word of other people (such as our teachers at school, our parents, or a journalist's newspaper article) is based upon authority. There are illegitimate appeals to authority, but there are legitimate appeals as well. We should choose our authorities with care. There are rational criteria to which we can appeal in legitimising an appeal to authority. We can say that someone is an 'authority' if they are recognised as having an above average amount of knowledge or experience in a given field of expertise. People with degrees in a subject can be wrong, but they are less likely to be wrong *about that subject* than people without degrees in that subject.

Appeals to authority can be strong or weak, legitimate or illegitimate. The best sort of argument from authority would be one where a great number of recognised authorities all agreed, with few other obvious connections between them besides their agreement on the subject in question. This would exclude the existence of social or political factors which might influence agreement. The appeal to authority on behalf of theistic belief is just such an appeal. It would be hard to find an issue upon which so many great philosophers, both past and present, agreed besides the existence of God. René Descartes was a 'rationalist', John Locke an 'empiricist', George Berkeley an 'idealist', but they all agreed that God exists.

Peter Atkins is recognised as an expert in the scientific field of chemistry. If you and I were having a debate about some aspect of chemistry, and you could quote Atkins in your support, that would be a strong and legitimate appeal to authority. As an expert on the matter in hand, Atkins' opinion carries a certain weight which must be given due respect. If I responded by quoting Chaucer in my defence that would not be a good appeal to authority! Chaucer is not recognised as an authority on chemistry. On the subject of chemistry, Atkins trumps Chaucer.

However, suppose you and I were having a debate on the relationship between science and belief in God. You quote Atkins (an atheist) in support of the belief that scientific knowledge makes belief in God redundant. That would be an illegitimate appeal to authority, because Atkins is not a recognised authority on theism or the relationship between theism and science (although he is an intelligent person who has written about the topic and whose views therefore deserve a measure of respect). Moreover, I could quote John Polkinghorne in defence of the belief that science and theism can go hand in hand. As a scientist and a minister who has written several well-received books on the subject in hand, Polkinghorne is a legitimate authority on the relationship between science and God. On the subject of science and theism, Polkinghorne trumps Atkins. If you could produce a recognised authority on science and religion who disagreed with Polkinghorne, then we would have to make judgements about the relative qualifications and stature of our opposing authorities.[11]

Many recognised authorities have believed in God. Anselm, Aquinas, Augustine, Boethius, F.C. Copleston, Kant, Kierkegaard, Leibniz, C.S. Lewis, Pascal and A.E. Taylor are but a few of the experts I could mention.

Christianity has a rich intellectual heritage; but it is not 'resting on its laurels'. Belief in God is no dead historical relic. The heritage of academically rigorous Christian belief will be carried into the third millennium after the birth of Jesus by the likes of William P. Alston, William Lane Craig, C. Stephen Evans, Stephen T. Davies, Peter Kreeft, Alvin Plantinga, Richard Swinburne and Keith Ward.

There are bright minds on both sides. You can read the debate between atheist Kai Nielsen and Christian J.P. Moreland; with contributions from the likes of atheist Antony Flew, and theist Dallas Willard.[12] You can read the debate between the Christian philosopher J.J. Haldane and atheist J.J.C. Smart.[13] We see the atheism of scientists like Richard Dawkins and Peter Atkins, and the Christian beliefs of R.J. Berry and John Polkinghorne.

Belief in God can't be dismissed as belonging only to the ill-educated. Of course, I'd also have to admit that disbelief in God has nothing to do with a lack of intelligence. Belief or disbelief in God depends more upon how you use what intelligence you have than on how much intelligence you have. You don't need a degree or a PhD to believe in God, but plenty of highly qualified people do believe.

Convinced sceptics

Many sceptical non-believers have become convinced believers in God, and in Jesus as God incarnate. C.S. Lewis, who studied philosophy at Oxford, 'gave in, and admitted that God was God'[14] as a Fellow and Tutor of Magdalen College at Oxford University in 1929. Dr C.E.M. Joad was head of the philosophy department at the University of London. He believed that Jesus was only a man and that there was no such thing as sin. Given a little time, he thought, humankind would have heaven on earth. In 1948, the magazine section of the *Los Angeles Times* carried a picture of this scholar, and with it a statement about a dramatic change in his life. He related how he had been antagonistic towards Christianity for many years. Now he had come to believe that sin was a reality and that the only explanation for sin was found in the Bible, and the only solution in the cross of Jesus.[15]

The American philosopher Mortimer J. Adler spent much of his time thinking about God and religious topics. In his 1976 Autobiography, *Philosopher at Large*, he wrote that religious commitment 'would require a radical change in my way of life', and that 'The simple truth of the matter is that I did not wish to live up to being a genuinely religious person.'[16] In 1980 he published a book called *How to Think about God: A Guide for the 20th Century Pagan*, in which he strongly argued for God's existence but still drew back from any personal commitment. Adler says that the thinking he did in writing this book 'was influential in my becoming a Christian in 1984'.[17]

Two Oxford professors, Gilbert West and Lord Lyttleton, were determined to destroy the basis of Christianity. West was to demonstrate the fallacy of the resurrection and Lyttleton was to prove that Saul of Tarsus [St Paul] had never converted to Christianity. Both men came to the opposite conclusion and became followers of Jesus. Lord Lyttleton wrote: 'The conversion and apostleship of Saint Paul alone, duly considered, was of itself a demonstration sufficient to prove Christianity to be a Divine Revelation.'[18]

English journalist Frank Morison (an expert in putting together information to form a picture of events) had a similar experience. Morison set out to prove that the story of Christ's resurrection was nothing but a myth, but he ended up believing it. He went on to write a famous book on his findings called *Who moved the stone?* 'The opportunity came to study the life of Christ as I had long wanted to study it, to investigate the origins of its literature, to sift some of the evidence at first hand, and to form my own judgement . . . I will only say that it affected a revolution in my thought. Things emerged from that old-world story which previously I should have thought impossible.'[19]

American apologist Josh McDowell was a university student when he was challenged to investigate the historical evidence about Jesus (see the end-of-chapter appendix). He writes:

> My new friends challenged me intellectually to examine the claims that Jesus Christ is God's Son . . . I thought this was a farce . . . Finally, I accepted their challenge, but I did it out of pride, to refute them. But I didn't know . . . there was evidence a person could evaluate. Finally, my mind came to the conclusion that Jesus Christ must have been who he claimed to be. In fact, the background to my first two books was my setting out to refute Christianity. When I couldn't, I ended up becoming a Christian.[20]

The fact that such a great number of recognised authorities both past and present believe in the existence of God, together with the fact that many of these authorities have been converted from a position of scepticism, is good reason to believe that God does in fact exist. The argument from authority in defence of theism is a strong and legitimate appeal to authority. At the very least, these facts are enough to justify a believing attitude on the part of anyone who lacks the intellectual capacity to reason through the arguments for and against God's existence for themselves.

Outline of the argument from religious experience

Premise 1) Many people genuinely claim to experience God.
Premise 2) Whatever many people genuinely claim to experience is most likely real.
Conclusion. Therefore, God is most likely real.

Defence of the argument

Experience may be defined as the conscious awareness of the individual. An experience is 'the awareness of a subject but not necessarily a mere subjective awareness'.[21] While all experience has a subjective aspect, in that it is something subjects have, not all experience is wholly subjective, in that at least some experiences have objective referents. Experience is therefore 'the state of consciousness of an individual who is aware of something as other whether or not it really is other'. [22]

No one doubts the existence of religious experience. The Religious Experience Research Centre at Oxford has found that 'a large number of people even today possess a deep awareness of a benevolent non-physical power which appears to be partly or wholly beyond, and far greater than, the individual self'.[23] Non-believers must explain away religious experience as a delusion of one sort or another. They may argue that religious experience is purely subjective, or has an objective referent that is not God. The argument from religious experience attempts to establish that at least some religious experience has an objective referent, and that this referent is God.

It is notoriously difficult to define either religion or religious experience. Both are best known from the inside out. However, most definitions of religion include as a common element an awareness of 'transcendence'. Religious experience can involve transcendence in at least two senses. The first is self-transcendence, 'the process of overcoming the conditions of one's finitude or frustrations'.[24] The second is the experience of the transcendent as the object of religious experience. Something is transcendent if it goes beyond one's immediate consciousness of it. In this sense the human subconscious is transcendent in that although we are aware of its existence, it surpasses our immediate conscious awareness. To be perceived as transcendent in a religious sense something must be believed to be ultimate. The subconscious is not transcendent in the religious sense except for a few New Age believers who worship themselves: 'The Transcendent is the object of a total commitment—that for which one would make even the supreme sacrifice . . . that More in view of which one sees no need of more.'[25]

There are close links between moral, aesthetic and religious experiences. As I argued in Chapter Two, the recognition of an objective moral law leads us to recognise the existence of an objective moral lawgiver. Hence, as theologian Paul Tillich writes, 'morality is intrinsically religious, as religion is intrinsically ethical.'[26] While ethics responds to the moral law, religion responds to the moral lawgiver. If we are objectively obligated by the moral law, we must believe ourselves objectively obligated by and to the moral lawgiver, who we must therefore believe to be all-good. The moral argument shows how our moral experience should draw us to acknowledge a morally ultimate giver of moral value and obligation. This being is clearly transcendent in that he surpasses what we perceive of him, and in that, as the source of moral value, he demands total commitment. A consideration of morality would quickly tell us that we should only give our total commitment to something worthy of such commitment. Nothing sub-personal can deserve such devotion, and nothing equal to ourselves can ground the felt objectivity of the moral law. Therefore, if anything deserves our total commitment, it must be something both personal and greater than ourselves. In other words, the religious thirst of humanity can only be quenched in the worship of a transcendent, all-good, personal being.

The appreciation of beauty, especially in the natural world, often produces in us feelings of touching some sublime transcendent reality beyond nature. If, as theism says, the universe is the creation of a transcendent divinity, this feeling is quite to be expected. When we look at a great painting, or listen to a great symphony, we often feel that we understand something of the artist who produced these artworks. Similarly, beauty touches us with the feeling that in aesthetic pleasure we understand something deeply meaningful about reality, something mysterious, ultimate, and clearly transcendent. The only question then is whether we trust this feeling or dismiss it as purely subjective.

Morality, beauty and religion all involve the notion of transcendence. Theism combines these areas of experience by explaining moral and aesthetic transcendence in terms of religious transcendence. The element that binds together the theistic view of transcendence is total commitment to an ultimate personal reality. Theism 'involves not only an awareness of the transcendent but an awareness of it as ultimate and as demanding an ultimate commitment'.[27] Belief in God gathers these similar but distinct experiences together in a coherent way that produces an elegant explanatory view of reality. Beauty and goodness are both grounded in the nature of God. This is a point in favour of theism as a world-view.

C.S. Lewis describes several strands of theistic religious experience in the introduction to *The Problem of Pain*. The first strand is experience of the 'numinous', a term coined by one Professor Otto. Lewis introduces the concept of the numinous through the following example. If someone told you that there was a tiger in the next room (and you believed them), you would probably feel frightened because you would know you were in danger. If you were told that there was a ghost in the next room (and believed it), you would feel a different kind of fear, 'for no one is primarily afraid of what a ghost may do to him, but of the mere fact that it is a ghost'. [28] A ghost is more uncanny than dangerous, and excites a special kind of fear called dread. With the uncanny, says Lewis, we have reached the fringes of the numinous:

> Now suppose that you were told simply, 'There is a mighty spirit in the room', and believed it. Your feelings would then be even less like the mere fear of danger: but the disturbance would be profound . . . this feeling may be described as awe, and the object which excites it as the Numinous.'[29]

This awe cannot be 'explained away' as 'fear of the dead' as some have attempted to do, for this explanation does not explain why the dead should be found awe-ful. Lewis draws attention to the alternative views we might take of numinous experience:

Either it is a mere twist in the human mind, corresponding to nothing objective and serving no biological function, yet showing no tendency to disappear from the mind at its fullest development in poet, philosopher, or saint; or else it is a direct experience of the really supernatural.[30]

The second common element mentioned by Lewis is the moral sense. Throughout human history people have acknowledged some kind of moral law; feeling about some actions the experiences expressed by phrases like 'I ought' and 'I ought not'. If the moral law were a human invention, it surely would not be as demanding as it is.

The numinous and moral experiences of humanity have not always and invariably been linked together: 'In many forms of Paganism the worship of the gods and the ethical discussions of the philosophers have very little to do with each other.'[31] However, the association is an economic one; and it was that made first by the Jewish people from whom modern belief in one God sprung. Again, this identification is either a most unnatural thing, or a supernatural revelation. Lewis asserts that while we can rebel against our numinous and moral experience, the price of doing so is high. It means that we must part company with many great poets and prophets, saints and sages, as well as the common mass of humanity.

The final element given by Lewis is a historical event which contributes to the formation of the Christian world-view, and hence influences the Christian interpretation of religious experience. For Christianity, the central historical event is the incarnation of God-the-Son in Jesus, who claimed to be one with the numinous presence behind nature identified by the Jewish people as the giver of the moral law:

The claim is so shocking—a paradox, and even a horror, which we may easily be lulled into taking too lightly—that only two views of this man are possible. He was a raving lunatic of an unusually abominable type, or else he was, and is, precisely what He said . . . If the records make the first hypothesis unacceptable, you must submit to the second.[32]

If we submit to the second conclusion, Lewis argues, everything else Christianity proclaims becomes credible; that Jesus died and rose from the dead, and that His death and resurrection hold the key to a positive change in our relationship with God.

The Christian experience of being accepted and forgiven by the moral lawgiver whose law we both know and break is intimately connected to belief in the divinity, death and resurrection of Jesus. Christians believe that it is in these events that we find God's heart for humanity; a heart of love willing to absorb the pain of the creation of people who often reject their maker; a heart that offers a transforming eternal life which begins in the gritty here-and-now and will flourish in heaven.

In the gospels Jesus says, 'Ask and it will be given to you; seek and you will find; knock and the door will be opened to you' (Matthew 7:7 and Luke 11:9). The Bible also reports Jesus as saying, 'Here I am! I stand at the door and knock. If anyone hears my voice and opens the door, I will come in and eat with him, and he with me' (Revelation 3:20). The experience of feeling God 'knocking' on the door of one's life as one considers Jesus in the pages of the Bible or the words of a preacher, and opening that door to positive results, therefore constitutes an experiential verification of the Christian world-view, and hence of the existence of God.

The life-changing nature of religious experience

Think of the changes brought about in the lives of people through faith in God and Jesus. For example, before he became a Christian, St Paul was an active opponent of the Church, involved in murdering Christians. He even thought that he was doing the will of God:

I too was convinced that I ought to do all that was possible to oppose the name of Jesus of Nazareth. And that is just what I did in Jerusalem. On the authority of the chief priests I put many of the saints in prison, and when they were put to death, I cast my vote against them. Many a time I went from one synagogue to another to have them punished, and I tried to force them to blaspheme. In my obsession against them, I even went to foreign cities to persecute them (Acts 26:9–11).

Then he had an experience of God (as revealed in the risen Jesus), and he realised he hadn't been following God, but opposing the real God by following his own 'wish-fulfilment' of what he wanted God to be:

As he neared Damascus on his journey, suddenly a light from heaven flashed around him. He fell to the ground and heard a voice say to him, 'Saul, Saul, why do you persecute me?' 'Who are you, Lord?' Saul asked. 'I am Jesus, whom you are persecuting,' he replied. 'Now get up and go into the city, and you will be told what you must do.' (Acts 9:3–6)

His life turned inside out: 'At once he began to preach in the synagogues that Jesus is the Son of God' (Acts 9:20). Talk about U-turns! Nor was this the result of hours of soul-searching; one minute he was a convinced sceptic, the next minute he was a believer. Whatever you believe about Jesus, this is certainly the subjective experience that Paul had (see 1 Corinthians 9:1), and it transformed his character, and his message. Millions of people have had similar life-changing experiences of God. Furthermore, millions attribute their changed lives to the same objective source, to Jesus.

The appendix to this chapter draws together a handful of Christians as they describe their religious experience in their own words.

The correlation of religious experiences

Doesn't the power and similarity of these subjective experiences make you suspect that they have an objective source? For the Christian, behind his or her subjective experience is an objective reality to which they can point: Jesus. Suppose someone came into the room and said, 'Guys, I have stewed apple in my shoes. This stewed apple has changed my life. It has given me peace and joy, helped me give up drugs, and I can now run the hundred metres in eleven seconds.' It would be hard to argue with such a person, especially if their life backed up their claims. But there are some tests we can apply to such a testimony. First: what is the objective reality claimed to underlie the subjective experience? Second: How many other people have had substantially the same subjective experiences from being related to the same objective reality? Let's apply these two tests to our friend with stewed apple in his trainers. To the first question he would reply, 'Stewed apple in my trainers.' Then the second question would be, 'How many people have experienced peace and joy, the ability to give up drugs, and increased track speed as a result of having stewed apple in their trainers?' Not many. But apply these questions to Christian religious experience. What is the objective reality claimed to underlie Christian experience? God, or more specifically, Jesus, an undeniably real character of history. How many other people have had significantly similar subjective experiences from being related to the same objective reality, Jesus? A lot!

Wishful thinking?

Is it really likely that such changes of both heart and mind have been brought about by 'wishful thinking'? As Oxford philosopher Richard Swinburne notes, 'humans are creatures of limited intelligence and notoriously liable to hide from themselves conclusions which seem to stare them in the face when those conclusions are unwelcome.'[33] Think of Paul: yes he believed that God existed, but when he had an experience of God meeting with him, it wasn't at all what he expected! Instead it changed his deepest convictions and led him to endure great hardship and the persecution he had once meted out to others:

> I have worked much harder, been in prison more frequently, been flogged more severely, and been exposed to death again and again. Five times I received from the Jews the forty lashes minus one. Three times I was beaten with rods, once I was stoned, three times I was shipwrecked, I spent a night and a day in the open sea. I have been constantly on the move. I have been in danger from rivers, in danger from bandits, in danger from my own countrymen, in danger from Gentiles; in danger in the city, in danger in the country, in danger at sea; and in danger from false brothers. I have laboured and toiled and have often gone without sleep; I have known hunger and thirst and have often gone without food; I have been cold and naked (2 Corinthians 11:23–27).

All this for 'wish-fulfilment'?!

There are a number of other things to be said in response to the charge that religious experience is 'merely wishful thinking' or a matter of 'wish-fulfilment'. The first thing to note is that such a charge presumes that God does not exist. Freud, who popularised this view, thought that there were no good reasons to believe that God exists. This is an assumption challenged by arguments like those that I have presented in this book. What is more, the charge that 'People believe in God because they want God to exist' can just as well cut the other way. Perhaps atheists don't believe in God because they don't want Him to exist. Psychologist Paul Vitz has investigated the psychology of atheism. After listing several psychological factors (such as personal convenience) which may contribute to a rejection of belief in God, Vitz argues that 'in the Freudian framework, atheism is an illusion caused by the Oedipal desire to kill the father and replace him with oneself'.[34] Noting that many prominent atheists had poor opinions of their fathers, Vitz proposes a 'Theory of Defective Father', whereby a defective father may contribute to a person's rejection of God the 'heavenly Father'.

Defective fathers may be 'weak, cowardly, and unworthy of respect', 'physically, sexually or psychologically abusive', or 'absent through death or by abandoning or leaving the family'.[35] If an earthly father is absent, or perceived as weak, or untrustworthy, these concepts tend to carry over into our view of God. For example, Freud lacked respect for his father who failed to stand up for himself against anti-Semitic abuse. Karl Marx did not respect his father, who converted to Christianity out of a desire to make life easier for himself, and was the first in his family not to become a rabbi. When Feuerbach was thirteen, his father abandoned the family to live with another woman. One of America's best known atheists today is Madalyn Murray O'Hear. For some as yet unknown reason, she reportedly attempted to murder her father with a ten–inch butcher's knife. She failed but screamed, 'I'll see you dead. I'll get you yet. I'll walk on your grave!'[36]

Vitz writes that 'Many children . . . interpret the death of their father as a kind of betrayal or an act of desertion. In this respect it is remarkable that the pattern of a dead father is so common in the lives of many prominent atheists.'[37] Bertrand Russell's father died when Russell was four years old. Nietzsche was the same age when his father died. Camus lost his father as a one year old. Sartre lost his father before he was born.

I don't doubt that some people do create gods in their own image. The gods of ancient Greece, for example, are just the sort of gods you'd expect people to invent: immortal, powerful, larger-than-life, and immoral! Modern men and women make gods out of everything from sex to science. The holy and demanding God of Christian belief, on the other hand, isn't at all the sort of 'god' you'd expect people to 'invent'. As J.P. Moreland says,

If one is going to give an account of religious belief or antibelief in terms of some theory of projection, then it would seem that atheism is a more likely candidate for projection than theism . . . If one were going to project a god to meet one's needs, a being much tamer, much more human, much more manageable would be a better candidate.[38]

Many people wish that God did not exist. Consider the frank admission of American philosopher Thomas Nagel:

I want atheism to be true and am made uneasy by the fact that some of the most intelligent and well-informed people I know are religious believers. It isn't just that I don't believe in God and, naturally, hope that I'm right in my belief. It's that I hope there is no God! I don't want there to be a God; I don't want the universe to be like that.[39]

I don't think that 'wish-fulfilment' or 'psychological projection' are adequate explanations for people's experiences of God. Josh McDowell relates how a drunkard with vivid memories of past struggles and new hope in Christ responded to the charge that his faith was a delusion:

He said: 'Thank God for the delusion; it has put clothes on my children and shoes on their feet and bread in their mouths. It has made a man of me and it has put joy and peace in my home, which had been a hell. If this is a delusion, may God send it to the slaves of drink everywhere, for their slavery is an awful reality.'[40]

Could all that really be the result of 'positive thinking'?

All of this aside, it's a mistake to confuse the origin of an idea with its truth. I grew up in a Christian home, and this must have 'rubbed off on me' because I can't remember a time when God's existence didn't seem totally natural and very real. I'd be the first to admit that believing in God because your parents did is not a good reason for believing in Him; but it was where my belief originally came from. However, that doesn't mean that my belief must be wrong any more that it means my belief must be right! I don't believe in God because my parents do, but because I think He really does exist and I can provide what seem to me to be good reasons for this belief. So, even if every case of belief in God could be explained in terms of 'psychological projection' (which I have argued seems unlikely), that would not exclude a positive answer to the question 'Does God exist?'

Of course it's true that nothing outside of our own thoughts exist just because we want them to, but it would be daft to argue that something doesn't exist because we want it to exist! If I'm thirsty and want a milk-shake, that doesn't mean milk-shakes don't exist! Likewise, if I feel a desire for God, that doesn't mean He doesn't exist! In fact, just as it would be very odd if I were thirsty in a universe without liquid, wouldn't it be strange if I felt a need for God in a universe without a God? (I will re-examine this argument in Chapter Seven). Those who argue that man has created God in his own image should be open to the possibility that man is made in God's image, and be willing to examine the evidence.

When was the last time you heard of an atheist who said that their life had been turned around for the better when they took up that faith? When did you last see a change for the better in someone's life when they decided that they didn't believe in God? On the other hand, do you know anyone whose life changed for the better when they took up faith in God and became a Christian?

The late Harry Ironside was preaching some years ago when a heckler shouted 'Atheism has done more for the world than Christianity!' 'Very well,' said Ironside, 'tomorrow night you bring a hundred men whose lives have been changed for the better by atheism, and I'll bring a hundred who have been transformed by Christ.' Needless to say, his heckler friend did not appear the next night.[41]

With Christianity, thousands from every nation testify to personal transformation through faith in Jesus.

Experiencing God

The existence of theistic religious experience clearly does count as evidence for the existence of God. As William P. Alston writes:

> if I could not find any confirmation of the Christian message in my own experience, I would be less justified in accepting that message than I am in fact . . . suppose that no one had ever experienced communion with God, had ever heard God speaking to him or her, had ever felt the strengthening influence of the Holy Spirit in a difficult situation. In that case Christian belief would be a less rational stance than it is in fact.[42]

Perhaps you've never had an experience of God, but that doesn't mean He isn't there:

> If three witnesses in a law court claim (independently) to have seen the suspect in some street at a certain time, and three witnesses who were in the street at that time claim not to have seen him, then . . . the court will surely normally take the view that the suspect was there, and that the latter three witnesses simply didn't notice him.[43]

In order to even 'balance out' the witness of the first three people in the above thought experiment, the other three witnesses would have to have carefully looked everywhere in the street, at the right time, and have found no trace of the suspect. (Even then, mightn't the suspect have simply kept on moving his hiding place when the witnesses weren't looking?) If the court didn't have conclusive evidence against the first three witnesses' testimony, then surely the court should accept the testimony of the first witnesses.

The point is that a lack of evidence in favour of something

being true isn't necessarily the same as positive evidence against its truth. The sort of evidence that would count for or against a belief depends on what sort of thing is being believed. If I claimed that there was an elephant in my room, and you had a look and saw no elephant, you'd have good reason to think I was having you on. If I claimed to have seen a mouse in my room, you could take a look for yourself, but if you didn't see it, you wouldn't have evidence that I was either lying or mistaken, because you wouldn't really expect to see anything. All that your non-mouse experience would show is that you hadn't ruled out the logical possibilities that I was either lying or mistaken, as would have been the case had you seen the mouse.

An elephant in my room isn't going to disappear without the presence of a magician or a pretty big hole in the wall. A mouse, on the other hand, could be hiding under any number of objects, or it could be keeping behind you, or it could have moved next-door, or the cat could have eaten it . . . The point is that before you can say, 'I haven't experienced God, therefore he doesn't exist,' you must ask yourself, 'How likely is it that I should have experienced God by now?' (you might experience him any minute of course), and 'If I were to experience God, what sort of experience would it be?' An elephant is hard to miss, but even then you must look in the right places! Someone who knew nothing about elephants might see one without knowing what they had seen, so it's important to find out what sort of experience you should be expecting. In the case of elephants I could say to look out for large, grey, four-legged mammals with tusks, a trunk and big ears. In the case of God I could say something like, 'Watch out for the feeling that a person of great power and love and who you can't see, is making His presence known to you.'

It is said, for example, that an experience of God is accompanied by a unique sense of humility, of creatureliness, of fear and awe mingled with a strong sense of passivity and dependence. The object of the experience is usually said to be holy, awe-inspiring, loving, and so on.[44]

In a letter to a friend, C.S. Lewis, who was for many years an atheist, described his growing feeling of God's presence like this: 'Terrible things are happening to me. The "Spirit" or "Real I" is showing an alarming tendency to become much more personal and is taking the offensive, and behaving just like God. You'd better come on Monday at the latest or I may have entered a monastery.'[45]

The initial experience of God can feel quite disturbing, even 'alarming'! (Surely not the sort of thing produced by 'wishful-thinking'?) The 'lost sheep' might well shy away from the shepherd's arms before realising that they are held out in love rather than hunger.

The principle of credulity

If you have had an experience which seems to you to have been an experience of God, and if you don't have any reasons of at least equal strength which give you cause to doubt your original impression, then you should trust your 'intuition'. Richard Swinburne calls this principle the 'principle of credulity': 'we ought to believe that things are as they seem to be . . . unless and until we have evidence that we are mistaken.'[46] He points out that if we decided never to trust appearances until they were proved to be reliable, we would never have any beliefs, 'For what would show that appearances are reliable, except more appearances?'[47] Swinburne therefore concludes that, just as we are right to trust our five ordinary senses, 'so it is equally rational to trust your religious sense'.[48]

The sort of thing that might reasonably cause you to doubt your experience would be: a) you know you couldn't possibly have experienced God because you know he doesn't, or can't, exist; b) You're often given to imagining strange things under the influence of alcohol or other drugs, and you've been indulging recently. (In other words, just the same sort of thing that would make you doubt any of your other senses.)

Swinburne also argues that the believability of such experiences of God is increased by the fact that they are just what we would expect if there is a God. If a theory leads us to make a prediction, and the prediction matches with what we observe, then that's evidence in favour of the theory. This is surely true since, if a theory leads to a testable prediction that turned out to be wrong, we would quite rightly take this as an indication that there was something wrong with the theory. Swinburne argues that, if God existed, we would expect Him to desire communication with His creatures, and so expect there to be religious experiences 'in the sense of experiences apparently of God'.[49] The fact that millions have had experiences that seem to them to be experiences of God, is therefore evidence in favour of the theory that God exists.

If you haven't had such an experience of God, perhaps you just haven't been looking. As Pascal wrote, 'There is enough light for those whose only desire is to see, and enough darkness for those of the opposite disposition.'[50] Besides, you still have the testimony of billions of witnesses, many of whom were originally sceptical: 'We trust the reports of others on what they see unless we have reason to suppose that they are lying, or deceiving themselves . . . We ought to do the same with their reports of religious experience.'[51]

Swinburne points out two reasons for not believing someone's testimony: 1) We have reason to believe they are lying, and 2) We have reason to believe they are deceiving themselves. Let's apply these tests to the examples I gave earlier of sceptics who had a change of heart. Could they be lying? I don't think so. Why would St Paul endure such hardship and persecution for a lie? Paul was eventually martyred for his belief in Jesus as God, and as Josh McDowell says, 'Nobody knowingly and willingly dies for a lie.'[52] Were they deceiving themselves? Was their faith a matter of 'psychological projection' hastened and eased by 'wish-fulfilment'? We've already seen that if anyone is projecting, it's at least as likely, if not more likely, to be the atheist. Do you really think Paul had a subconscious desire to suffer hardship, persecution and martyrdom?! Mortimer J. Adler's decision to become a Christian wasn't what you might call a spur-of-the-moment thing. Nor did it sound as if C.S. Lewis really wanted God to exist. If he did, why did he describe himself in his autobiography, *Surprised by Joy*, as 'perhaps the most dejected and reluctant convert in all England'?

If God doesn't exist, then the worship of millions of people has never once had a real object. It may be possible to believe with Freud that so many people in such varied circumstances have been mistaken in their belief that they have a relationship with God; but is it plausible? Is such a widespread and enduring belief likely to be a delusion?

Naturally, if we think that it is unlikely that God exists, then we will be sceptical about people's claims to have experienced Him. However, religious experience is evidence to be accounted for. Given a background of openness to the possibility as to God's existence (a background hopefully provided by my previous arguments), then the straightforward 'face value' interpretation becomes an appealing proposition that adds to the accumulation of evidence in favour of God's existence. Surely the burden of proof rests with the non-believer to give a better explanation for all of this than the obvious one, that God exists.

Appendix: more witnesses

Philosopher—William P. Alston

I was raised as a Methodist and then I went through the usual adolescent revolt. Later, when I began teaching philosophy at the University of Michigan, I found myself drawn to the Episcopal Church. I was fairly active for about ten years. But then things seemed to go sour, and I jumped ship again and was completely out of it for years. It was about ten years ago that I came back to the Church. I hope and trust that the third time is the charm; at least it seems to have taken this time . . . I'm a Christian not because I have been convinced by some impressive arguments: arguments from natural theology for the existence of God, historical arguments concerning the authenticity of the Scriptures or the reliability of the Apostles . . . My coming back was less like seeing that certain premises implied a conclusion than it was like coming to hear some things in music that I hadn't heard before, or having my eyes opened to the significance of things that are going on around me. G.K. Chesterton once wrote: 'In the last analysis, the reason why I am a Christian is that the Church is a living and not a dead teacher.' That pretty much sums it up for me. I'm a Christian because it was in the Christian Church that I came to discover the presence and activity of God in my life . . . because it was in the Christian Church that I was enabled to begin to participate in the joint effort of God and His people . . . I have discovered, and entered into effective contact with, the vertical through being absorbed into a stretch of the horizontal that is already open to the vertical. (William P. Alston, 'Why I am a Christian', *Truth Journal*, @ http://leaderu.com/truth/1truth23.html)

Theologian—Alister McGrath

I grew up in Northern Ireland, noted for its religious tensions, back in the 1960s . . . I became a Marxist while at high school, and turned my back on the Christian faith. I was told that it was just the 'narcotic of the people'. I knew little about Christianity, despite attending a very religious high school. All I knew was that, whatever it was, I didn't want it. It was an irrelevance. And so I rejected something I did not know or understand, on the basis of what other people said about it—other people, it turned out, who knew as little about it as I did.

Then I went to Oxford University as a student. I began to hear people explaining what Christianity was for the first time. I began to realise what it was all about. It bore virtually no relation to the dull and tedious stereotype which I had uncritically absorbed. I thought Christianity was about believing certain things to be true, and having a really boring life as a result. Nobody had told me about the joy and delight of knowing a risen Saviour and Lord, and being given the hope of eternal life! I realised that I had rejected a caricature, and missed out on the reality. I soon put that one right![53]

Philosopher—Stephen T. Davies

I enjoy discussing theistic proofs, consider the enterprise valuable, and even consider that there do exist successful theistic proofs. Nevertheless, the reason I am a theist has almost nothing to do with theistic proofs. It has a great deal to do with experiences I have had that I interpret in terms of the presence of God—experiences I find myself interpreting in terms of divine forgiveness, divine protection, divine guidance. That is why I would be extremely suspicious of any apparently successful atheistic proof. That is why I claim to know that God exists.[54]

Drug addict—Dave

Shortly before getting sentenced to five years [for attempted armed robbery], I became a Christian . . . It was about eighteen months later when I finally, after many mistakes and falling back into drugs, stopped using them. I haven't touched even cannabis now for six months . . . Why do I think I don't want the comfortably numb life of a junkie any more? Because I can rely on God to give me the love and happiness and joy I and every junkie needs. If I didn't believe in God, why bother to stop using drugs? . . . When people used to tell me I was slowly killing myself, I wasn't bothered, because life without meaning isn't a life at all. It's just existence. I don't need the meaning of drugs any more, which is hedonism, because I have got a mystery which is much more fun.[55]

Recommended reading

Mortimer J. Adler, *A Second Look in the Rear View Mirror* (1992). Adler's second autobiography which gives an account of his final conversion to Christianity. (1)

William P. Alston, *Perceiving God: The Epistemology of Religious Experience* (Cornell University Press, 1991). (4)

Augustine, *Confessions*, Henry Chadwick, Trans. (Oxford, 1992). (1)

G.K. Chesterton, *The Everlasting Man* (Hodder and Stoughton, 1927). (2)

Kelly James Clark, *Philosophers who Believe* (IVP, 1993). (2)

Brian Davies, *An Introduction to the Philosophy of Religion*, second edition (Oxford). (2)

Stephen T. Davies, *God, Reason and Theistic Proofs* (Edinburgh, 1997). (3)

Norman L. Geisler and Winfried Corduan, *Philosophy of Religion*, second edition (Baker, 1988). (3)

Norman L. Geisler and Paul D. Feinberg, *Introduction to Philosophy—A Christian Perspective* (Baker, 1987). (1)

Peter Kreeft and Ronald Tacelli, *Handbook of Christian Apologetics* (Monarch, 1995). (1)

C.S. Lewis, *Surprised by Joy* (Fount, 1977). (1)

C.S. Lewis, *The Problem of Pain* (Fount, 1977). (1)

C.S. Lewis, *Prayer—Letters to Malcolm* (Fount, 1977). (1)

Josh McDowell, *Evidence that Demands a Verdict*, vol. 1 (Alpha). (1)

J.P. Moreland, *Scaling the Secular City* (Baker, 1987). (3)

J.P. Moreland and Kai Nielsen, *Does God Exist? The Debate between Theists and Atheists* (Prometheus Books, 1993). (2/3)

Michael Peterson *et al*, eds, *Philosophy of Religion—Selected Readings* (Oxford, 1996), Part One. (3)

Clark H. Pinnock, *Reason Enough—A Case for the Christian Faith* (Paternoster Press, 1980). (1)

W.S. Rhodes, *The Christian God* (ISPCK, 1998). (1)

Richard Swinburne, *Is There a God?* (Oxford, 1995). (3)

Richard Swinburne, *The Existence of God* (Oxford, 1991). (4)

A.E. Taylor, 'The Argument from Religious Experience' in John Hick, ed., *Arguments for the Existence of God* (Macmillan, 1964). (2)

Paul C. Vitz, 'The Psychology of Atheism', *Truth Journal*: http://www.leaderu.com/truth/1truth12.html

General introductions to Jesus

The Bible—especially the Gospels of Matthew, Mark, Luke and John.

C. Stephen Evans, *Why Believe?* (IVP, 1996), chapters seven and eight. (1)

Michael Frost, *Jesus the Fool* (Albatross Books, 1994). (1)

Michael Green, *Strange Intelligence/men as trees walking (the gospel of Mark)* (IVP, 1997). (1)

C.S. Lewis, *Mere Christianity* (Fount, 1986). (1)

Alister McGrath, *Jesus—Who He Is and Why He Matters* (IVP, 1994). (1)

James W. Sire, *Why Should Anyone Believe Anything at All?* (IVP, 1994). (1)

Carsten Peter Thiede, *Jesus—Life or Legend?* (Lion, 1997). (1)

Tom Wright, *What Saint Paul Really Said—Was Paul of Tarsus the real founder of Christianity?* (Lion, 1997). (3)

Ravi Zacharias, *Can Man Live Without God?* (Word, 1994). (1)

The reliability of the historical evidence about Jesus

Craig L. Blomberg, 'The Historical reliability of the New Testament' in William Lane Craig, *Reasonable Faith*, revised edition, (Crossway, 1994). (2)

Craig L. Blomberg, *Jesus and the Gospels* (Apollos, 1998). (3)

F.F. Bruce, *The New Testament Documents: Are they reliable?* (IVP, 1972). (1)

Norman L. Geilser, *Christian Apologetics* (Baker, 1995). (2)

Gary R. Habermas, *Ancient Evidence For The Life of Jesus— Historical Records of His Death and Resurrection* (Thomas Nelson, 1984). (2)

J.P. Moreland, *Scaling the Secular City* (Baker, 1987). (2)

J.P. Moreland and Michael J. Wilkinson, eds, *Jesus Under Fire— Modern Scholarship Reinvents the Historical Jesus* (Paternoster Press, 1996). (3)

Carsten Peter Thiede, *Jesus—Life or Legend?* (Lion, 1997). (1)

Jesus' Resurrection

The Bible, esp. Matthew 27–28, Mark 15–16, Luke 23–24, John 19–21, Acts 1 and 1 Corinthians 15.

William Lane Craig, *Reasonable Faith*, revised edition, (Crossway, 1994). (2)

Stephen T. Davies, *Risen Indeed—Making Sense of the Resurrection* (SPCK, 1993). (3)

R. Douglas Geivett and Gary R. Habermas, eds, *In Defence of Miracles* (Apollos, 1996). (2)

Gary R. Habermas, *Ancient Evidence For The Life of Jesus— Historical Records of His Death and Resurrection* (Thomas Nelson, 1984). (2)

Gary Habermas and Antony Flew, *Did Jesus Rise from the Dead?* (Harper and Rowe, 1987). (3)

Peter Kreeft and Ronald Tacelli, *Handbook of Christian Apologetics* (Monarch, 1995). (1)

Josh McDowell, *The Resurrection Factor* (Here's Life, 1981). (1)

J.P. Moreland, *Scaling the Secular City* (Baker, 1987). (2)

J.P. Moreland and Michael J. Wilkinson, eds, *Jesus Under Fire— Modern Scholarship Reinvents the Historical Jesus* (Paternoster Press, 1996). (3)

Frank Morison, *Who Moved the stone?* (Faber and Faber, 1981). (1)

John Wenham, *Easter Enigma—Are the Resurrection accounts in conflict?*, Second edition, (Paternoster Press, 1992). (2)

Jesus' divinity

William Lane Craig, *Reasonable Faith*, revised edition (Crossway Books, 1994). (2)

Norman L. Geilser, *Christian Apologetics* (Baker, 1995). (2)

Peter Kreeft, *Between Heaven and Hell* (IVP, 1982). Written in an engaging dialogue form. (1)

Peter Kreeft and Ronald Tacelli, *Handbook of Christian Apologetics* (Monarch, 1995). (1)

C.S. Lewis, *Mere Christianity* (Fount, 1986). (1)

Josh McDowell and Bart Larson, *Jesus—A Biblical Defence of His Deity* (Campus Crusade for Christ/Here's Life Publishers, 1983). (1)

The meaning of Jesus' death

Alister McGrath, *Making Sense of the Cross* (IVP, 1994). (1)

Richard Swinburne, *Responsibility and Atonement* (Oxford, 1989). (3)

Philosophical issues relating to historical evidence, Jesus' miracles and divinity

William Lane Craig, *Reasonable Faith*, revised edition (Crossway Books, 1994). (3)

Stephen T. Davies, *Risen Indeed—Making Sense of the Resurrection* (SPCK, 1993). (2/4)

Norman L. Geisler, *Christian Apologetics* (Baker, 1995). (2)

R. Douglas Geivett and Gary R. Habermas, eds, *In Defence of Miracles* (Apollos, 1997). (3)

Peter van Inwagen, *God, Knowledge and Mystery* (Cornell University Press, 1995). (4)

C.S. Lewis, *Miracles* (Fount, 1974). (2)

Thomas Morris, 'Jesus Christ Was Fully God And Fully Human' in Michael Peterson *et al*, eds, *Philosophy of Religion—Selected Readings* (Oxford, 1996). (3)

Michael Poole, *Miracles—Science, The Bible and Experience* (Scripture Union, 1992). (1)

Richard Swinburne, *The Christian God* (Oxford, 1994). (4)

Music to listen to

Adrian Snell, *The Passion* (KCD308, Kingsway, 1980). A rock-opera about Jesus' death and resurrection.

Notes

1. C.S. Lewis, *Letters to Malcolm: Chiefly on Prayer* (Fount, 1977), p.113.
2. Clark H. Pinnock, *Reason Enough* (Paternoster Press, 1980), p.44.
3. *Ibid.*
4. *Times Higher Educational Supplement*, 1997.
5. Richard Robinson, 'Judaism and the Jewish People', in Dean C. Halverson, ed., *The Compact Guide to World Religions* (Bethany House, 1996).
6. Michael Martin, *Atheism—a Philosophical Justification* (Temple University Press, 1990), p.3. This estimate is taken from *The World Christian Encyclopaedia* 1982, and is a projected figure for 1985.
7. Paul Chamberlain, *Can We Be Good Without God?* (IVP, 1996).
8. *Ibid.*, p.169.
9. Paul Little, *Know Why You Believe* (IVP), pp.24–25.
10. Aristotle, *Nicomachean Ethics*.
11. I am not saying that only a believing minister, theologian or philosopher who is also a scientist can qualify as an expert on science and religion. Any atheist who took qualifications in science and philosophy of religion would qualify as an expert on the relationship between these two subjects.

12. *Does God Exist? The Debate between Theists and Atheists* (Prometheus Books, 1993).

13. J.J.C. Smart and J.J. Haldane, *Atheism and Theism* (Blackwells, 1996).

14. C.S. Lewis, *Surprised by Joy* (Fount, 1977).

15. Josh McDowell, *Christianity, a ready defence* (Alpha), p.454.

16. Mortimer J. Adler, *Philosopher at Large* (Macmillan, 1976).

17. Mortimer J. Adler, *Adler's Philosophical Dictionary* (Scribner, 1995), p.186.

18. Josh McDowell, *op. cit.*, p.434.

19. Frank Morison, *Who moved the stone?* (Faber and Faber, 1981).

20. Josh McDowell, *Evidence that demands a verdict*, vol. 1, (Alpha).

21. Norman L. Geisler and Winfried Corduan, *Philosophy of Religion*, second edition (Baker, 1988), p.13.

22. *Ibid.*

23. A. Hardy, *The Spiritual Nature of Man* (Oxford, 1979), p.1.

24. *Ibid.*

25. *Ibid.*, p.17.

26. Paul Tillich, *Morality and Beyond* (Harper and Row, 1963), p.15.

27. Norman L. Geisler and Winfried Corduan, *op. cit.*, p.35.

28. C.S. Lewis, *The Problem of Pain* (Fount, 1977).

29. *Ibid.*

30. *Ibid.*, p.17.

31. *Ibid.*, p.18.

32. *Ibid.*

33. Richard Swinburne, *Is There a God?* (Oxford, 1996), p.123.

34. Paul C. Vitz, 'The Psychology of Atheism' in *Truth Journal*. http://www.leaderu.com/truth/1truth12.html

35. *Ibid.*

36. Quoted by Vitz, *Ibid.*

37. Paul C. Vitz, *op. cit.*

38. J.P. Moreland, *Scaling the Secular City* (Baker, 1987).
39. Thomas Nagel, *The Last Word* (Oxford, 1997).
40. Josh McDowell, *op. cit.*, p.434.
41. Paul Little, *op. cit.*, p.160.
42. William P. Alston, 'Christian Experience and Christian Belief' in Alvin Plantinga and Nicholas Wolterstorff, eds, *Faith and Rationality* (University of Notre Dame Press, 1983), p.103.
43. Richard Swinburne, *op. cit.*, p.133.
44. Brian Davies, *An Introduction to the Philosophy of Religion*, new edition (Oxford, 1993), p.127.
45. Josh McDowell, *Evidence that demands a verdict*, vol. 1, (Alpha).
46. Richard Swinburne, *op. cit.*, p.132.
47. *Ibid.*
48. *Ibid.*
49. *Ibid.*
50. Blaise Pascal, Honor Levi, trans. *Pensées and other writings* (Oxford, 1995), *Pensées* 274.
51. Richard Swinburne, *op. cit.*, p.134.
52. Josh McDowell, *More than a Carpenter*.
53. Alister McGrath, *Explaining your Faith* (IVP, 1995).
54. Stephen T. Davies, *God, Reason and Theistic Proofs* (Edinburgh, 1997), p.193.
55. *Response, The Family Magazine*, Winter 1996.

CHAPTER SEVEN

NEEDING GOD—ARGUMENTS FROM DESIRE AND ABSURDITY

'As a deer longs for a stream of cool water, so I long for you, O God.'
(Psalms 42:1, GNB)

An overview of Aristotle's teleological thought as applied to human action leads us to the hypothesis that relationship with God is the human *telos*. The existence of human desires that find no earthly fulfilment points to the existence of human needs that correspond to some supernatural object of satisfaction. Correspondence between the prediction that human existence will be ultimately unfulfilled unless God exists and is known, and observation of human nature with its desires and aspirations, argues for God's existence. Although Kant's moral argument for the existence of God as a necessary hypothesis of practical reason is invalid, further reflection reveals a valid version of Kant's argument. This points out that without God, human existence would be absurd. Given that life is not absurd, it follows that God exists. If we accept the premise that life in a Godless universe would be absurd, our response to the question of life's absurdity or sanity will determine whether our actions are consistent with our world-view.

In this chapter I will advance several 'existential' arguments for the existence of God. These arguments focus upon the needs and meaning of human existence. These arguments do not say that God exists because we need Him, but that we need God because He exists. That is, God's existence is advanced as the best explanation of various aspects of human need.

I will begin by arguing that the needs in question must or probably can be fulfilled, and that God therefore exists, or probably exists. Another way to view these existential arguments is to see them as saying that unless God exists life is absurd, so that if life is not absurd, God must exist. The crux of this form of argument is whether life is or is not absurd. Our response to this question is likely to be coloured at least as much by our emotional state as by any arguments we may consider. The real issue is then one of rational consistency between our world-view and our actions, an issue which has as much to do with ethics as with logic.

Outline of the argument from desire

Premise 1) Every innate natural desire in us points to some corresponding object of fulfilment.

Premise 2) There exists in us innate natural desires which only God could satisfy.

Conclusion. So God must exist.

Defence of the argument

Aristotle applied the concept of teleological causes to human action in his *Ethics* (often called *The Nicomachean Ethics* after Aristotle's son Nicomachus who may have edited his father's work). Aristotle pointed out that humans generally act for a purpose. We normally act in order to achieve an end or *telos* that we have in mind. Behaviours motivated by the hope of achieving an end are a 'means' to that end. Means may be good or bad, depending on their own nature as well as upon the nature of the end to which they are means.

We try to achieve ends because we desire things. We use the word 'good' as a label for things we regard as desirable in a moral sense. As Mortimer J. Adler puts it, 'the good and the desirable—are inseparably connected. As axiomatic as Euclid's "the part is less than the whole" and "the whole is greater than the part" are "the good is desirable" and "the desirable is good."'[1]

The fact that we desire something does not, however, make it desirable in the moral sense of the word. We can be mistaken about what is desirable. While the good is desirable, and the desirable is good, what we desire is not necessarily desirable. Hitler desired the Holocaust, but the Holocaust was not desirable in the sense of being a good goal. Hitler may have desired the Holocaust because he was under the delusion that it was desirable, but it most certainly was not. Aristotle therefore distinguished between 'real' and 'apparent' goods. Apparent goods are ends we call good because we desire them. Real goods are ends that are desirable whether we actually desire them or not; they are ends that we ought to pursue. As Mortimer J. Adler explains:

> We may actually desire what we ought not to desire, or in fact fail to desire what we ought to desire. That which is really good for us is something we ought to desire . . . But that which only appears to be good for us . . . may be something we ought not to desire . . . even though, at the time we want it, it appears to be good because we want it.[2]

Aristotle argued that since human needs are based on common human capacities and requirements, what is really good for one person is, on the whole, really good for all people. For example, everyone needs food to survive, and so food is a real good for all people. The crucial question then becomes, 'What is the good life, and what are the real goods that we should seek in order to live it?' This question was central to ethics for many hundreds of years, but it has been largely ignored in modern times. Traditional ethics dealt with three questions that have been likened to the three things a fleet of ships needs to know. The first is how to avoid hitting each other, which is social ethics. The second is how to stay afloat and avoid sinking, which is personal ethics. The third and most important thing a fleet needs to know is why they are at sea in the first place, what is their destination, their goal? As Peter Kreeft writes: 'I think I know why modern philosophers dare not raise this greatest of questions: because they have no answer to it.'[3]

Aristotle divided ends and means into several classes. Some means are merely means and are never themselves ends in the pursuit of which other means are employed. For example, money is a means and never an end. Money is useful for the ends its possession can bring about, but the possession of money is not itself an end. Even the miser who hoards money does not see the possession of money as an end, but as a means to feeling secure, or powerful.

Some ends are themselves means to other ends. Eating food is an end because we employ various means (such as spending money) to secure the possession of food to be eaten. However, eating food is also a means, a means to satisfying hunger and to staying alive. As Mortimer J. Adler says, 'bodily goods . . . are means to the ultimate end of happiness or good life. But they are also themselves ends for which other goods serve as means. For the sake of our bodily health, vitality, and pleasure, we need food, drink, shelter, clothing, and sleep.'[4]

At least one end, however, must be an end-in-itself. As Adler argues, 'If there were nothing that we desired for its own sake and not for the sake of something else, our practical thinking could not begin.'[5] An end-in-itself is an end that is not the means to any other end. Aristotle calls such an end an ultimate end. The conjunction of all ultimate ends which are real goods is the 'total good' or '*totum bonum*'. The highest good among all the real goods that comprise the *totum bonum* is the '*summum bonum*':

> If therefore among the ends which our actions aim there be one which we wish for its own sake, while we wish the others only for the sake of this, and if we do not choose everything for the sake of something else (which would obviously result in a process ad infinitum, so that all desire would be futile and vain), it is clear that this one ultimate end must be the good; and indeed the supreme good.[6]

The good life is the life directed towards the *totum bonum*, which means primarily a life directed by the pursuit of the *summum bonum*. Aristotle argues that the *totum bonum* of humanity is *eudaimonia*, which is traditionally translated as 'happiness', for 'happiness above all else appears to be absolutely final in this sense, since we always choose it for its own sake and never as a means to something else'.[7] This 'happiness' refers primarily to an objectively blessed state of being 'rather than the feeling of happiness or joy (*delectatio*) which accompanies it'.[8] Many philosophers today therefore prefer to translate *eudaimonia* as 'flourishing'.

Real goods further divide into 'limited' and 'unlimited'

goods. For example, wealth and food are limited goods. You can want more money or food than you need, and more than is good for you. More money or food is not always better. On the other hand, knowledge and love are unlimited goods because more of them is always better.

Furthermore, ends are either 'normative' or 'terminal'. A terminal end is 'one that can be reached and rested in'.[9] If you are going on a journey, your destination is a terminal end. Once you have arrived, you have completed your goal. A normative end, on the other hand, cannot be rested in. A normative end is not a goal you complete before moving on to other ends, but a process you engage in. Love and knowledge are normative ends, because they are ongoing processes.

Terminal ends must be limited goods. Unless an end was one you could complete (like reaching the finish line of a race) you would never be able to have enough of that end complete your terminal goal. But by definition, you cannot have enough of an unlimited good. Therefore, a terminal end has to be a limited good. Normative ends, on the other hand, must be unlimited goods. In the ongoing process of a normative end, one would eventually reach the point of having too much of a good thing unless the good in question was an unlimited good.

Eternal life as *telos*

To call the ultimate end and real good of humanity 'heaven' or 'eternal life' would be out of context with Aristotle's thought; but it would constitute a legitimate interpretation of the ultimate goal of human existence. Indeed, Aristotle's teleological thought was given just such a Christian interpretation by Thomas Aquinas, who quotes from the Bible, 'Now this is eternal life [the *totum bonum* of humanity]: that they may know you, the only true God, and Jesus Christ, whom you have sent' (John 17:3).

The Christian answer to Aristotle's question about the good

life is therefore that 'the good life is one built around a recipro-cal love relationship with God within the community of people who love God because he first loved them'. Love of God is our *summum bonum*, and it directs us towards our *totum bonum*. Both begin in this life, and flourish in the next. This end is *an unlimited and normative real good* because it involves knowing and loving God and neighbour for eternity as God intended from the foundation of the universe. As Ravi Zacharias puts it, 'Man's primary pursuit should be God himself, and all secon-dary and tertiary pursuits fall into place.'[10]

The arguments of this chapter all attempt to show that God, or 'heaven' interpreted as 'eternal life in relationship with God and the community of the faithful', is the human *telos*. The 'argument from desire' says that the best interpretation of human desire is as a longing for 'heaven' that results from a need caused by God making us such that our ultimate end is just such a state. This argument was powerfully presented and popular-ised by C.S. Lewis in the 1940s, but its theological roots stretch back into antiquity. The Old Testament book of Ecclesiastes can be read as an extended treatment of this existential argument, and Aquinas wrote that, 'The natural desire to know cannot be stilled until we know the first cause, not in any sort of way but in its essence. Now, the first cause is God. Therefore, the end of the rational creature is the vision of the divine essence.'[11]

Bonaventure v. Aquinas

The thirteenth-century philosopher Bonaventure Giovanni Fidanza (1221–1274) asserted that human beings have an implicit knowledge of God which can be made explicit through reflection. He argued that since every human naturally desires happiness, and since happiness consists in the possession of the supreme good, which is God, every human naturally desires God (whether they know this explicitly or not). F.C. Copleston comments that:

Aquinas does not deny all force to this line of argument. For he admits that man's natural desire for happiness implies a kind of implicit knowledge of God, in the sense that when we once know that God exists and that possession of Him constitutes human happiness we can interpret the desire for happiness as the desire for God. But this does not show that anyone has a natural innate knowledge of the truth of the proposition that God exists. [12]

Aquinas' reply to Bonaventure's argument ran as follows:

> To know that someone is coming is not to know that Peter is coming, although the person coming is in fact Peter. And many have thought that man's perfect good, which is happiness, consists in riches; others that it consists in pleasure; others that it consists in some other thing. [13]

Bonaventure's argument, discussed by Aquinas, is purely theological. It shows that *if* God exists then people will have a natural desire for Him. Of course, Christian theology also says that people are inherently self-seeking, or 'sinful', and that this shows itself in a demand for an autonomy from God that fights against our natural desire for God. The strength of our desire for autonomy theologically explains the fact that, as Aquinas wrote, 'many have thought that man's perfect good . . . consists in riches . . . in pleasure . . . [or] in some other thing'. [14]

Aquinas rejected Bonaventure's claim that an innate desire *for* God implies an innate knowledge *of* God 'since desire for something presupposes knowledge of that thing'. [15] However, his counter-example of knowing that *someone* is coming but not thereby knowing *who* is coming, does not carry the force he intends. After all, if I know that someone is coming (I can hear footsteps approaching), I surely know some things about what and who is coming. For example, I know that it is a human (with all that entails), has functional legs, and is wearing shoes (bare feet just don't cause that sort of echo). Similarly, from a desire for God we could deduce several facts about the object of our desire, even if we did not know that the object was 'God' when we begin to think through the implications of our desire. For example, we would know that, as the object of an unfulfilled desire, the object of that desire was something or someone we currently lacked. As Boethius wrote, 'Now a man must be lacking something if he misses it, mustn't he?'[16] We would know that certain things (such as riches or pleasure) failed to satisfy our desire, and were therefore not the object we sought. Calling our desire for God 'a desire for happiness', we might search out that which would make us happy, and, I submit, discover that the only object which answers our desire is God, and so that our desire for 'happiness' was in fact a desire for God.

Aquinas, in rejecting the apologetic possibilities of an argument from the desire for God (a desire he admitted existed), missed two crucial observations. The first is that, although there is some confusion about what will satisfy our quest for happiness (some seeking it in riches, others in art, and so on), there is nevertheless a consensus about which objects of desire do not 'deliver the goods'. As C.S. Lewis said, if a man sought out the object of his happiness, rejecting each and every supposed object that failed to meet his expectations, then he would surely be led to some object that did not fail.

If God existed, we would expect to find a desire in man which found no earthly satisfaction. If we find such a desire, then this is reason to believe the assumption which predicts this state of affairs. This is the second point missed by Aquinas. Perhaps a parallel example will make things clearer. A scientific theory makes certain predictions about the universe. If we find a match between the universe as we observe it, and the universe as that theory predicts it will be, this is evidence in favour of that theory. Similarly, the theory that God exists predicts that, as man's highest good, humanity will have a natural desire to know God which will not be answered by any other object. Hunger can be calmed only by food, for hunger is the desire for food. Likewise, only God can meet man's spiritual hunger, for man's spiritual hunger is a hunger for God. That is the hypothesis. If the evidence verifies the existence of a hunger that cannot be met by anything which we know is not God, then, by elimination of the alternatives, this is verification of the hypothesis that God exists.

C.S. Lewis and the argument from desire

All Bonaventure argued for was an innate knowledge of God which has not been given explicit propositional form. What we are envisaging here is the sort of knowledge whereby someone who 'found God' would say, 'Here at last is what I was looking for all along—this is the object which answers to those innate needs which I tried to satiate before with so many false things. I knew all along what I wanted, but only now have I found it, and realised that what I wanted was God.' The search for the object of this desire is a search to discover that which answers to the 'description' given by our desire, that which answers our spiritual hunger. The search for the object of this desire is something C.S. Lewis wrote much about:

> Creatures are not born with desires unless satisfaction for those desires exists. A baby feels hunger: well, there is such a thing as food . . . If I find in myself a desire which no experience in this world can satisfy, the most probable explanation is that I was made for another world.[17]

Lewis argues that if this is not so, the universe 'is a fraud':[18]

> It appeared to me therefore that if a man diligently followed this desire, pursuing the false objects until their falsity appeared and then resolutely abandoning them, he must come at last to the clear knowledge that the human soul was made to enjoy some object that is never fully given—nay, cannot even be imagined as given—in our present mode of subjective and spatio-temporal experience. This desire was, in the soul, as the siege Perilous in Arthur's castle—the

chair in which only one could sit. And if nature makes nothing in vain, the One who can sit in this chair must exist.[19]

To reject this understanding of human desire would force us to take a gloomy view of life as ultimately unfulfilling. It would also force us to make an exception to our understanding of desires as relating to real objects of desire. It would surely be difficult to dismiss the universal human experience that nothing in this world brings final or lasting satisfaction for our deepest desires and longings. As Pascal wrote:

> What does this greed and helplessness proclaim, except that there was once within us true happiness of which all that now remains is the outline and empty trace? Man tries unsuccessfully to fill this void with everything that surrounds him, seeking in absent things the help he cannot find in those that are present, but all are incapable of it. This infinite abyss can be filled only with an infinite, immutable [unchanging] object, that is to say, God himself. He alone is our true good. From the time we have forsaken him, it is a curious thing that nothing in nature has been capable of taking his place.[20]

Isn't it often those who have the most who find life most hollow? As the writer of the Old Testament book Ecclesiastes put it:

> I denied myself nothing my eyes desired;
> I refused my heart no pleasure.
> My heart took delight in all my work,
> and this was the reward for all my labour.
> Yet, when I surveyed all that my hands had done
> and what I had toiled to achieve,
> everything was meaningless, a chasing after the wind;
> nothing was gained under the sun
> (Ecclesiastes 2:10–11).

The phrase 'under the sun' refers to life considered without God. Every other human desire points to the existence of a genuine human need, which in turn points to the existence of something which can fulfil that need. Since we find within ourselves a longing that nothing in the world satisfies, this points to the existence of something beyond this world which is the matching fulfilment of that desire.

What is it that we desire? Love, beauty, goodness, freedom and truth. We desire to be a part of something greater than ourselves, and yet to have our intrinsic value recognised. We desire meaning and purpose. We desire wholeness. Aren't all these things exactly what life with God offers? Christian apologist Dr Ravi Zacharias relates how knowing God can bring fulfilment, and thus wholeness, to every aspect of life:

> The Christian . . . sees himself, endowed with the image of God and an integration of different capacities. This means that his individuality, when lived out within the moral boundaries of a loving relationship with God, brings a total fulfilment through a diversity of expressions, converging in the purpose of creation . . . His conscience responds to the holiness of God; his mind is nurtured and nourished by the truth of God; his imagination is enlarged and purified by the beauty of God; his heart, or impulses, respond to the love of God; his will surrenders to the purpose of God.[21]

The need for self-transcendence

In my consideration of religious experience in the previous chapter, I noted that one sense of the 'transcendent' in religion was the need to transcend the adverse conditions of human existence. As Walter Kaufmann writes, 'Religion is rooted in man's aspiration to transcend himself.'[22] However, it is impossible to transcend oneself without the help of something that transcends oneself. To the theist, the humanist's hope of creating heaven on earth sound as likely as being able to pull oneself up by one's own bootlaces. If we are the problem, we can hardly be the solution. I therefore think that Aquinas was onto something when he wrote that 'Natural reason tells us that because of the inadequacies we perceive in ourselves we need to subject ourselves to some superior source of help and direction; and whatever that source might be, everybody calls it *God*.'[23]

Can't get no satisfaction

The religious desire to transcend the vicissitudes of life obviously comes from dissatisfaction with life. When we stop to think about it, this dissatisfaction is a very odd thing indeed. As Peter Kreeft and Ronald Tacelli note, 'Complaint about anything shows that there must be an alternative, something more and better.'[24] We do not complain about two and two equalling four. We do not complain about squares lacking roundness. In other words, we do not complain about things that cannot be other than they are. We do complain about lacking time, or about evils. This suggests that alternatives are possible. If we complain about life in this world, then there is probably another world that is good enough.

A hope only for hereafter?

Christianity has been accused of offering 'pie in the sky when you die'. Such a weak accusation ignores the important question of whether or not there is any 'pie' to be gained, or lost. However, Christianity doesn't just hold out the hope of being with God after death. Knowing God is a relationship which can begin in the here and now. I have not yet had my fill of divine 'pie'; my relationship with God can't be 'consummated' until I die, but I have tasted the 'pie', and I know it 'reaches the parts other pies cannot reach':

> A man's physical hunger does not prove that man will get any bread; he may die of starvation . . . But surely a man's hunger does prove that he comes of a race which repairs its body by eating and

inhabits a world where eatable substances exist. In the same way, though I do not believe (I wish I did) that my desire for Paradise proves that I shall enjoy it, I think it a pretty good indication that such a thing exists and that some men will.[25]

Experiencing the lack of God or the non-existence of God?

There is no such experience as 'experiencing God's non-existence' any more than there is such an experience as 'experiencing the non-existence of a square circle', or 'experiencing a unicorn's non-existence'. We can of course 'see' that a square circle can't exist, and we can reasonably believe that unicorns don't exist, but experience by itself only gives knowledge of what is. We work out what isn't by experiencing what is. Non-existence isn't a quality of a thing to be experienced. Rather, it is the non-existence of that which is other than that which is. Non-existence is a negative thing and not a positive thing. For example, there is no such thing as 'darkness', only the lack of light. You can't see darkness, you can only fail to see anything. There is, however, the experience of 'missing someone', and there is the experience of missing God. But of course, you can't miss someone who doesn't exist. You might wish for someone that doesn't exist, but you can't miss them, because they never existed in order that you could miss them.

Wishes v. inherent desires

Although I may wish for a milk-shake, I do not have an innate desire for a milk-shake because I do not need milk-shake. I do have a need, and so an innate desire, for drinkable liquid; but a milk-shake is not the only drink that would answer that need and so that desire. My desire for a milk-shake reveals the existence of an inherent desire for drink caused by the existence of an inherent need for drink. It does not reveal an innate desire for milk-shake caused by an innate need for milk-shake! A milk-shake may be something I want or wish for without being something I need. However, the fact that I wish for a milk-shake does point to the existence of an innate desire for something that I do need, namely water.

Someone might wish that there existed an alcoholic drink that drowned their sorrows without adverse side-effects. Such a wish doesn't mean that such a drink must exist, but nor does it mean such a drink doesn't or can't exist. Outside of *Star Trek*'s 'Synthale' no such drink in fact exists. However, isn't the person with such a wish displaying a real innate desire caused by a real need? They are displaying a desire, not for the non-existent object of their wish, but for an object that will satisfy the real need which gave rise to their wish. Wouldn't you agree that such a person was really giving vent to a desire for something that would solve the problems which cause them to want to drown their sorrows, only without the equally undesirable side-effects of alcoholism?

Our would-be drunkard is simply mistaken about what object will fulfil their desire. For them, getting drunk is an apparent good, but it is not a real good. Even if Synthale did exist, it wouldn't be the solution (if you'll excuse the pun) they were looking for. In the same way, someone who wants to kill themselves is mistaken, not about the existence of their need (to have a life worth living, etc.), but about what will truly answer that need. It's pretty obvious that getting drunk doesn't fulfil any real need, and that suicide doesn't solve your problems.

If we apply this to the existence of God, the relevant question isn't, 'Is the desire for God a real desire or only wishful thinking?', because wishful thinking points to real desires and so to real needs. The real question is, 'Is the "wish" for God misplaced or not?' If a proposed object of desire answers the requirements of the need causing the 'wish', then it must be the thing the lack of which causes the need that causes the desire, and so the wish. For example, if 'wholeness' answers the requirements of the need which causes my desire to solve my problems which results in my wish for alcohol, then 'wholeness' is what I need, however much I want a pint. Likewise, if the existence of God would answer the requirements of our need, and nothing else would answer those requirements (or at least, not as successfully), then God must be the object of our innate desire, and must therefore exist.

I think there is enough evidence to conclude that God really is the answer to people's need for meaning, direction, and so on; and that it is the lack of God which therefore causes these desires. The evidence comes from those who say their experience of God meets those deep needs, and from the fact that these needs are just what we should expect people to have if God exists and they are not correctly related to Him. The desire for God is not a misplaced desire, it is the search for the real answer to a real need. It's our endless, out-of-proportion wishing for more money, possessions, popularity, fame, sex, drink and drugs that are the misplaced desires.

Drugs v. eternal life

In my opinion, drug use is a misplaced attempt to satisfy a real need. The real need in question is, I believe, the need for 'eternal life'. Drug-taking is a 'heaven' substitute mistakenly seen as a real good when it is only an apparent good. Christian writer Debbie Goddard has spent many years counselling people with drug and alcohol problems. An ex-drug-user herself, she writes that 'The fact is that drugs are one of the things people may get into when they don't realise who they are and what they're here for.'[26]

Some people find in drugs an almost mystical experience that they feel takes them closer to God. I was recently involved in a debate at the University of East Anglia debating society where the motion was, 'This house would rather be high than holy.' The defender's central argument was that there need be no dichotomy between drug-taking and holiness, if drug-taking is, or can be, a genuinely spiritual activity which brings us closer to God. Aside from attempting to clear up various misconceptions about 'holiness', my response was that even if drug-taking is 'just one more route to knowing God' (I don't believe that it is), then why use drugs when there are other, less harmful routes to the divine? Moreover, Christians believe that God offers Himself to us. We do not need to struggle to find God, because God has already found us. God doesn't need to use drugs to bring us into 'eternal life'!

Drug-taking is a young person's game. Drugs are just one more thing that one in three young people try out. Drugs don't stay the distance. When a couple first fall in love, that love has a particular intensity and quality that fades away with time. The love which does 'stay the distance' is of a different character. Marriages that are founded on the first flush of romance often founder when the tide goes out and the couple realises how thin their love really was. The sort of love that lasts a lifetime doesn't exclude romantic feelings, but nor does it rely upon them. Likewise, new Christians often find that their experience of God is just such a bright and sparkling thing as romantic love; and just like romantic love, the intensity fades and settles down. However, just as a good marriage continues to be a fulfilling relationship once the 'honeymoon period' is over, so a relationship with God continues to be fulfilling even after those first, heady days. It is quite possible to be 'high' on God, just as with any other relationship. The Bible talks about either being a 'slave to sin' or a 'slave to righteousness'; addicted to God, or addicted to self. There is no other path, and we all must choose.

In my experience, the 'high' times are there, just as any couple have their special occasions and candle-lit meals, but often the relationship takes real character-forming struggle and grit. Yet the relationship goes on. It can last the distance. I know people who have been Christians since childhood who are now collecting their old-age pensions. Do you know many, or even any pensioners who have been drug-users since childhood?!

An important factor in the popularity of 'recreational drug-taking' is the feeling of unity which drugs can give. This feeling has been described as a feeling of unity with other people—and as a feeling of unity with something bigger than us—a kind of mystical experience. I believe that this factor in drug use testifies to the fact that humans are missing something in their lives, namely, an existence in union and community with each other, and with something or someone 'bigger' than us. I am also convinced that drugs are a false answer to this desire, just as I am convinced that relationship with God is the true answer to this desire. As a Christian I have certainly never been attracted to taking drugs, and there are many people who testify to finding something better than drugs in Christian religious experience. It is therefore plausible to think that Christian religious experience is at the very least closer to being the innate end to which drugs are a patently false means.

While a drug may produce a *feeling* of unity, does it produce actual, real unity? When you take a drug you may feel universal love and peace—but when the drug wears off, what then? When you take a drug you may *feel* as if you find peace and acceptance within some higher spiritual dimension; but what assurance do you have that this feeling is true? At least the Christian can look to the historical record of Jesus' life, death and resurrection as objective realities upon which their confidence in God's love rests.

Drugs are like a one-night stand. Knowing God is like a marriage. The drug Ecstasy produces a 'high' by causing a serge of Serotonin in the brain. Serotonin is a chemical that is involved in the working of the brain's synapses. A couple of years ago I suffered from depression, and my doctor prescribed some drugs which helped my brain to retain and use the Serotonin it produced. This helped lift my depression. Ecstasy works, not by aiding the up-take of the Serotonin the brain produces, but by causing a massive rush of excess Serotonin. Initially, this has basically the same effect as the anti-depressant I was given by my doctor. However, unlike my anti-depressant, Ecstasy has the effect of desensitising the brain to Serotonin. The result is that the brain requires more than normal amounts of Serotonin to feel normal—so you take more 'E', so you get more desensitised and depressed, so you take more 'E' and so on. Once I was over my depression, caused by the state of my mind, I came off the anti-depressants, and my brain was working normally. You can't do that with Ecstasy. Ecstasy gives a short-term 'high', but produces a long-term 'low'.

As well as depression, some Ecstasy users have developed schizophrenia. Ecstasy use leads to confusion and paranoia. No one knows what the long-term effects of Ecstasy use are, and doctors fear that the next century will reveal many psychological problems among today's drug-users. There have been around thirty deaths from Ecstasy use in the UK so far, and many more people find themselves in hospital. All in all, the pain simply does not seem to be worth the gain.

The question society must face is why young people feel so depressed that they are prepared to take expensive and potentially lethal drugs in the forlorn hope that they will make life worth living. Drugs are just one of the many distractions young people engage in to paper over the cracks in the heart of their personal and social lives. They feel that something is missing, and hope to find the answer, or at least a distraction from the problem, in drugs (or extra-marital sex, or excessive drinking). As Pascal noted, 'take away their distractions and you will see them wither from boredom. They feel their hollowness without understanding it, because it is indeed depressing to be in a state of unbearable sadness as soon as you are reduced to contemplating yourself, and without distraction from doing so.'[27] A growing number of ex-drug-users testify to finding a beneficial and long-term answer to this malady in perceived relationship with God. Remember the testimony of ex-drug-addict Dave:

Why do I think I don't want the comfortably numb life of a junkie any more? Because I can rely on God to give me the love and happiness and joy I and every junkie needs. If I didn't believe in God, why bother to stop using drugs? . . . When people used to tell me I was slowly killing myself, I wasn't bothered, because life without meaning isn't a life at all. It's just existence. I don't need the meaning of drugs any more . . . because I have got a mystery which is much more fun.[28]

(I refer readers to the testimonies in Debbie Goddard's book.) Drug-taking produces limited apparent goods and real evils. Knowing God, if it is possible as Christianity says it is, produces unlimited real goods.

The God-shaped hole—objections and conclusions

So, if we need God, He must exist. Furthermore, we must have some 'acquaintance' with Him that we can experience the lack of Him which causes our felt need, some knowledge of what it would mean to know Him that can produce in us pangs of longing. I would explain this 'acquaintance' with God by the fact that God created us and keeps us in being. There is within us a sort of 'maker's mark' by which we recognise God, a 'God-shaped hole' that only He can fill.

One objection to this line of argument is to suggest that the desires interpreted as a 'God-shaped hole' by the argument from desire exist, but are caused by the subconscious memory of the womb. In the womb each of us experienced a state of existence where all our needs were met, where we were a part of something greater than us and upon which we depended. When this suggestion is first raised, the parallels between womb-life and eternal-life are striking. It then appears reasonable to explain away the proposed 'God-shaped gap' by reducing it to an unfulfillable nostalgia for the womb.

However, on closer examination, the dissimilarities between

womb-life and eternal-life become more apparent. The 'womb memory' objection can, at best, only account for some unfulfilled desires. For example, womb-life centres on receiving not giving. We receive warmth, food and security. We give nothing. While eternal-life certainly includes a fair amount of receiving, it also crucially involves giving; being able to make a valuable contribution to the 'kingdom of God'. It also seems to me that while a hankering to return to the womb may explain a desire for certain basic bodily and spiritual goods, it cannot explain away the more complex goods involved in the notion of eternal life which seem to fit the requirements of our desire so well. Eternal life involves receiving forgiveness, engaging in communal activities, worship and moral struggle; none of which find an easy parallel in womb-life.

We might also reply to this objection by saying that a universe that creates within us needs which cannot be fulfilled (we cannot return to the womb) is an absurd universe. If we do not think that the universe is so absurd, then we should not think that the universe equips us with needs we cannot satisfy, and so we should not think that the desires highlighted by the argument from desire are the product of a need to return to the womb. Certainly, such an interpretation of the facts runs up against the great number of cases where we know that desires correspond to needs grounded in the existence of things that can be obtained by us (food, water, sleep, knowledge, love, etc.). It seems *prima facie* unlikely that the universe should give us an unfulfillable need to return to the conditions provided for by womb-life.

Of course, if the desire for God *can* be explained with reference to a hankering after womb-life, this does not exclude the possibility that God places within us the desire for him through the natural causal mechanism of 'womb-life memory'. Since we cannot return to the womb, we naturally seek some fulfilment for our needs which can be achieved. Intermediate causes are incidental to the question of needs and their corresponding fulfilment.

Another objection to this line of argument might be that religious belief does not reliably or fully satisfy our supposed need for God. When you are hungry, eating enough food stops you being hungry (for a while). Although people feel a desire for God, purported religious experience doesn't seem to satiate that desire. This, it might be held, counts against taking the desire for God as based upon a real need for God. However, this objection is like arguing that since a little food does not satiate people's hunger, hunger is not the result of a need for food!

The analogy with hunger, like all analogies, is misleading if pushed too far, because while food is a limited good, eternal life crucially includes unlimited goods (such as love and knowledge). While we can have enough or even too much of a limited good, we can never have enough or too much of an unlimited good. Eternal life includes goods which form part of an eternal process of increasing value; so pointing out that believers can't get enough of God to satisfy them doesn't count against the argument from desire. The theistic hypothesis is that eternal life (which requires the existence of God) is the human *telos*, without which we would be ultimately unfulfilled. Eternal life is something that can begin here and now, but Christians have never claimed that eternal life can truly flourish until the advent of the 'new heavens and the new earth'. In heaven then, it is claimed, the eternal life which begins here and now can progress to a higher level because the limiting factor of sin will be stripped away. In the meantime, the fact that purported experiences of God meet certain needs within people better than the alternatives is evidence that heaven is the human *telos*, just as the fact that a little food takes the edge off hunger proves that enough food will satiate it.

In a world where we are made by God, for God, and yet with the freedom to choose for or against relationship with Him, a God-shaped gap exists within us as the natural consequence of not choosing to know our maker. As Augustine put it so well,

'You made us for yourself, O Lord, and our hearts are restless till they rest in you.'[29] The person who feels that life is meaningless, suffers from an unfulfilled desire; but their suffering reveals their need and, if they allow it to, this need can lead them to the discovery that God answers their need. In this way suffering can be an integral (and therefore worthwhile) part of a person's path to wholeness.

The other side of the coin

'That God does not exist I cannot deny, but that my whole being cries out for God I cannot forget.' (Jean-Paul Sartre)

If there exists a God who created the universe and everything in it, including us, He must have done so for a reason. Everything would find its origin and its reason for existing in God who is 'the Alpha and the Omega, the Beginning and the End' (Revelation 21:6). If so, then only by acknowledging our origin and purpose as given in God, only by acknowledging our dependence upon Him, could we hope to live in step with God's perfect purpose for us, and so to be all that we are meant to be:

> So why would we think it appropriate to say that human beings have a function? Well, if human beings were made to do something, in the same way as, say, corkscrews were made to open bottles, it would obviously be appropriate to ascribe to them a function. In essence, this is the interpretation of Thomas Aquinas: God made us for a purpose and thereby gave us a function.[30]

Theologian John Calvin was right to say that, if God is our creator, 'knowledge of God and of ourselves are connected'.[31] Not to run our lives with proper reference to God would be like trying to run a car on water rather than fuel; you'd expect problems! As Augustine confessed: 'my sin was this, that I looked for pleasure, beauty, and truth not in him but in myself and his other creatures, and the search led me instead to pain, confusion, and error.'[32]

If God is our creator and we do not recognise this, we should expect to feel a sense of alienation from our origins. If God made us for a reason and we don't bother to find out what that reason is, we should expect to find a lack of purpose and direction in our lives; we should expect the questions 'Why am I here?' and 'What is the meaning of life?' to be live questions.

I have already argued (along with Alvin Plantinga) that (for dependent beings) having a designer is a necessary condition for having an objective purpose. Faced with the question of what the purpose of humanity is, one can only reject the question as meaningless, reply that we have no objective purpose, or refer to the purpose of an independent designer.

Atheists often argue that the lack of an objective purpose to human existence does not matter, because we can still have subjective purposes. We can set our own goals and find pleasure in pursuing and achieving these goals, so why worry about such cosmic purpose? Kai Nielson says that 'there can be purposes *in* life, even if there is no purpose *to* life. You have lots of intentions, interests, aims, goals, things that you care about, that, God or no God, remain perfectly intact.'[33] Of course, if you have no purpose, then your purposes have no purpose. Any interests, aims, goals or things you care about in a universe without God have no objective value. They cannot be things that you *ought* to be interested in, or aim at, or be interested in.

The question of the objective purpose of human existence appears to be a quite straight-forward question that cannot be rejected as meaningless. It can only be answered by the conclusion that our existence has a purpose, or that it does not. Most people feel that their existence ought to have an objective purpose. After all, the common question is not, 'Does life have a meaning?' but 'What is the meaning of life?' And this question presupposes that life has an objective meaning. As Peter Kreeft and Ronald Tacelli write:

We all experience the instinct and absolute demand that human life must have an adequate meaning, purpose, point, goal, good or end—what Aristotle called a 'final cause' or *telos*. Viktor Frankl, in *Man's Search for Meaning*, calls this our primary need. Even pleasure, power, peace and freedom can be, and have been, sacrificed—if only there is a reason, a meaning, an adequate purpose for the sacrifice.[34]

What would constitute an adequate purpose for human existence? An adequate purpose for life must 1) be objective and 2) must be an end worth striving towards for its own sake (ie it must be what Aristotle called an ultimate end, and so must include real, unlimited normative goods). 'The first qualification is obvious,' write Kreeft and Tacelli, for 'Ends less than the self are not adequate for the self to believe in and live for. But invented, subjective ends are less than the self. Therefore such ends are not adequate to live for.'[35] The second qualification is equally obvious. If there is no ultimate end then there is no adequate motivation for employing any means to it, and so no motive for doing anything. This is because all means are means to a motivating end, and with no ultimate end, no subsidiary means or ends have any purpose. The Christian notion of eternal life fits the bill of an objective ultimate end. It is perhaps not the only theistic view that fits the bill, but it does fit. Certainly, some sort of theistic view will answer the demand for objective purpose, and only a theistic view can do so. If there is no designer, then we have no objective purpose.

Predictions and observations

If we don't know God's will for our lives, we should expect to have unanswered questions about how to live, how to deal with life, with our vocation and goals: 'If God has created us to be in an intimate relationship with himself, but we have broken that relationship, it is no wonder that we are obsessed with questions of loneliness, purpose, identity, fear and salvation.'[36]

The theory that God exists predicts things about human experience that we'd expect to be the case: that people would have to choose how they relate to God. That without reference to the God who is the origin and ultimate goal of life, people would lack satisfying answers to important questions like 'Why am I here?' and 'What is the meaning of life?' That they would feel a sense of alienation, and lack any basis for morality. Do these predictions match with what we observe? I think so.

'Man', writes Loren Eisely, 'is the Cosmic Orphan. He is the only creature in the universe who asks, "why?"'[37] Without reference to God, when people ask, 'Why am I here?' they can only answer, 'By pure chance.' Without God the answer to the question, 'What is the meaning of my existence?' must be 'There is no meaning.' Sartre suggested that we create meaning by choosing a course of action. However, the universe does not acquire meaning just because I say it does. A universe without God remains objectively meaningless, no matter how we regard it. Sartre was really suggesting that we *pretend* the universe has meaning; but that is only to lie to ourselves.

This is deeply disturbing. 'Who am I?' humankind asks. 'Why am I here? Where am I going?': 'Since the Enlightenment, when he threw off the shackles of religion, man tried to answer these questions without reference to God. But the answers that came back were not exhilarating, but dark and terrible.'[38] We are the accidental and unintended by-product of time plus matter plus chance. There is no purpose that our existence fulfils and our destiny is the grave. So runs the received wisdom of secular belief. As William Lane Craig writes, 'Modern man thought that when he had gotten rid of God, he had freed himself from all that repressed and stifled him. Instead, he discovered that in killing God, he had also killed himself.'[39]

Such an answer causes us to feel alienated from the rest of reality. The philosopher W.E. Hocking expressed this sense of

alienation thus: 'Human life is mounted upon a subhuman ped-
estal and must shift for itself alone in the heart of a silent and
mindless universe.'[40] Friedrich Nietzsche wrote of Dante and
Spinoza that,

> Of course, their way of thinking, compared to mine, was one which
> made solitude bearable; and in the end, for all those who somehow
> still had a 'God' for company . . . My life now consists in the wish
> that it might be otherwise with all the things that I comprehend, and
> that somebody might make *my* 'truths' appear incredible to me.[41]

Modern-day atheist Peter Atkins says:

> I've always thought that I was insignificant. Getting to know the size
> of the Universe, I see just how insignificant I really am! And I think
> the rest of the human race ought to realise just how insignificant it
> is. I mean, we're just a bit of slime on a planet belonging to one
> sun.[42]

Atkins surely knows he feels different from 'slime'; he knows he
is different from 'slime', but he doesn't know why. There is no
reason in his atheistic world-view; that's just how it is.

Without reference to God, people ask, 'What's the meaning
of life? Why should I go on living?' and can only answer, 'There
is no meaning, no reason.' People who avoid the question, who
only ask, 'Why do I go on living? Where do I find meaning in
life?' tend to answer either in abstract or material terms. But
none of it satisfies. None of it quite hits the spot. Without reference to God people ask, 'What should our goals be?' and can
only answer, 'Anything we like, anything at all, we are free!' But
to the question, 'What *should* our goals be?' there is no answer.
And if nothing *should* be, then it matters very little what is, and
everything is drained of meaning. As Keith Ward says, 'in the
end, such freedom is empty. It leaves you alone in the world, free
to do anything in a world in which nothing is any longer worth
doing.'[43] If nothing should be, then ethics is reduced to 'what I

want' and the resulting moral chaos in a world populated by selfish beings such as us is only to be expected. What use is freedom without meaning? What use is ethics without truth?

Perhaps there are people who don't feel any unease or disquiet without God; people who are quite happy to live out their lives from one experience to the next without ever asking the deep questions. Even if there are such people, the death of a loved one, the birth of a child, can make seemingly contented people suddenly uneasy as they are brought up short, face to face with the raw reality of being alive. Those who do ask the deep questions and stare reality in the eye without reference to God, come to the same conclusion: life has no meaning, the individual is insignificant, we are alienated from reality, with no objective basis for morality, or for explaining why we exist. As Jacques Monad wrote: 'The ancient covenant is in pieces; man at last knows that he is alone in the unfeeling vastness of the universe, out of which he emerged by chance. Neither his destiny nor his duty have been written down.'[44] The world-view of the clear-sighted, self-consistent atheist is well summed up by the atheistic biologist Will Provine: 'No God. No life after death. No free will. No ultimate meaning in life and no ultimate foundation for ethics.'[45]

While some atheists admit that they don't want God to exist, others have expressed the opposite wish. Jean-Paul Satre wrote, 'I needed God . . . I reached out for religion, I longed for it, it was the remedy.'[46]

> The novels and plays of Jean-Paul Sartre portray man's futile attempt to create meaning . . . underlying his pessimism is an outright denial of the existence of God . . . Either God exists and thereby guarantees life's meaning and wholeness, or else God does not exist, religion is irrelevant, and life falls apart.[47]

For Sartre, atheism was 'a cruel and long-range affair'.[48] Other atheists, unable to live with their belief that humanity came to be for no purpose, almost subconsciously begin to ascribe personality and motives to the physical processes of the universe. Halfway through his book *The Origin of the Genetic Code*, Francis Crick begins to spell nature with a capital 'N', and elsewhere he slips into speaking of Nature as being 'clever' and as 'thinking' what to do. A similar tendency can be seen in the work of Carl Sagan. The English astronomer Fred Hoyle attributes to the final stages of the universe itself many of the qualities traditionally ascribed to God. As William Lane Craig suggests, although these men say they don't believe in God, 'they smuggle in a God-substitute through the back door because they cannot bear to live in a universe in which everything is the chance result of impersonal forces'.[49]

Bertrand Russell believed that:

> man is the product of causes that had no prevision of the end they were achieving . . . his origin, his growth, his hopes and fears, his loves, his beliefs, are but the outcome of accidental collocations [placings side by side] of atoms . . . [while] the whole temple of man's achievement must inevitably be buried beneath the debris of a universe in ruins . . . Only within the scaffolding of these truths, only on the firm foundation of unyielding despair, can the soul's habitation, henceforth, be safely built.[50]

Suppose Russell's belief's really were 'the product of causes that had no prevision of the end they were achieving', being 'but the outcome of accidental collocations of atoms'. Surely there could be little reason to think that his beliefs, the accidental products of goalless causes, have the purposeful goal of being about reality?! Russell's atheistic beliefs about reality cannot explain his ability to have atheistic beliefs about reality. And how can Russell's 'scaffolding of . . . unyielding despair' be a 'firm foundation' upon which to build a life? 'This is psychologically impossible and logically contradictory;

despair is not a "firm foundation" but precisely the lack of one.'[51] As Satre wrote, 'hope needs a foundation'. Russell's scaffolding is more likely to lead to a suicidal hanging than to a firm foundation for life! Indeed, Russell said of his own life: 'The centre of me is always and eternally a terrible pain—a curious wild pain—a searching for something beyond what the world contains.'[52] How sad that he had to rail against the God who loved him and longed to erase that pain as only He could.

Summary

The argument from desire is good reason to think that people's unfulfilled desire for meaning is an expression of their lack of relationship with God. In turn, it is also reason to hold that, if God existed, we should expect a match between people's relationship with God, and their satisfaction in matters relating to the great questions of life, and that as this is the match we find, this is evidence in favour of God's existence. The 'argument from desire' explains why people's experience of God, and of the lack of God, takes the form it does. Since the argument gives us a detailed prediction as to the form we'd expect experience of God to take, it allows us to make a more detailed check between the theory that God exists and observed data. Since our observations match with these predictions, this provides a more detailed, and therefore stronger confirmation of the theory that God exists. These two reasonable expectations: that our unfulfilled desires point to God, and that the absence of God in our lives (were there a God), would cause us to feel unfulfilled, are two sides of the same coin. The fact that people feel unfulfilled without God is therefore evidence that God exists; as is the evidence that, with God, people find the fulfilment they once lacked. As Pascal said, 'There is a god-shaped vacuum in the heart of every man, and only God can fill it.'[53]

Kant and the absurdity of morality in a Godless universe

In the nineteenth century, Immanuel Kant proposed a moral argument for the existence of God that went as follows:

> morality must postulate the existence of God, as the necessary condition of the possibility of the *summum bonum* . . . We ought to endeavor to promote the *summum bonum*, which, therefore, must be possible. Accordingly, the existence of a cause of all nature, distinct from nature itself and containing the principle of this connection, namely, of the exact harmony of happiness with morality, is also postulated.[54]

Kant's argument produces the existence of God as an assumption of ethical reasoning; something we should believe if we want to rationally retain certain ethical beliefs: 'It must be remarked here that this moral necessity is subjective, that is, it is a want, and not objective, that is, itself a duty . . . as a principle of explanation, it may be called a hypothesis . . . a pure rational faith.'[55]

However, as it stands, Kant's argument fails. Even granted the existence of a moral obligation to promote the *summum bonum*, it does not follow that it is possible to achieve the *summum bonum*. Kant argues that 'ought' implies 'can', but even so, all that follows from an obligation to promote the highest good is that we can promote the highest good. Whether or not we can attain the highest good is another question. Under certain circumstances, I would be unable to save someone's life without a fire-extinguisher; but this does not guarantee that there will be a fire-extinguisher to hand. Similarly, the fact (if fact it is) that I cannot achieve the highest good unless God exists, does not guarantee that He does.

Nevertheless, it seems to me (as it has seemed to many others) that Kant is on to something with his moral argument. My obligation to save life *if I can* does not guarantee that I can. True.

Still, we can all agree that there being a fire-extinguisher to hand may, in the right conditions, be a necessary condition of my being able to save a life. Likewise, our obligation to pursue the *summum bonum* does not logically guarantee that we can achieve it, only that we can pursue it. True enough. However, if the existence of God is a necessary condition of our achieving the *summum bonum*, just as the existence of a nearby fire-extinguisher may be a necessary condition of my being able to save a life, then we can make several deductions. If God exists, we can achieve the *summum bonum*, and our sense of moral obligation to pursue it seems quite at home in the universe. On the other hand, if God does not exist, then we cannot achieve the *summum bonum*, and our sense of duty with respect to pursuing the greatest good possible suddenly seems to make very little sense.

The underlying thought of Kant's argument seems to be this: unless God exists, human moral life is absurd, because it makes demands that the universe cannot satisfy. If there is no God, humans feel constrained by an obligation to serve an ideal that can never be realised. However, if the universe is not absurd in this manner, then God must exist. This argument, unlike Kant's expression of it, seems to be valid. This leaves us with two vital questions. The first is, 'Is God a necessary condition for the achievement of the *summum bonum*?' The second is, 'Is the universe absurd?'

The absurdity of morality in a world without God

George I. Maverodes, Professor of Philosophy at the University of Michigan, attempts to answer the first of these questions with reference to the atheist's world-view as exemplified in the thought of Bertrand Russell. Readers are by now well aware of Russell's world-view: 1) There is no creator God, 2) such personal phenomena as minds and thoughts are the product of purely impersonal causes, and 3) humanity is doomed to extinction and death is the end of each individual life.

Maverodes calls a world as described by these points a 'Russellian world', and a benefit that can accrue to a person in such a world a 'Russellian benefit'. Going to heaven is not a Russellian benefit, because it cannot happen in a Russellian world. On the other hand, a contented old age, or the thrill of sexual pleasure, are Russellian benefits.

Noting the existence of moral obligations, Maverodes then makes the obvious point that 'in the actual world we have some obligations that, when we fulfill them, will confer on us no net Russellian benefit—in fact, they will result in a Russellian loss'.[56] If the actual world is a Russellian one then Russellian benefits and losses are the only possible benefits and losses. If there exist moral obligations whose fulfilment results in a net loss of Russellian benefits to those who fulfil them in a Russellian world, doesn't that seem odd? 'I suggest,' writes Maverodes, 'that it would be very strange to have such obligations—strange not only in the sense of being unexpected or surprising but in some deeper way . . . Perhaps the best thing to say is that were it a fact that we had such obligations, then the world that included such a fact would be absurd—we would be living in a crazy world.'[57] Therefore, if there do exist moral obligations the fulfilment of which results in a net loss of Russellian benefits, and if the world is not crazy, then our world is not a Russellian world, and God exists.

Maverodes relates his argument to Kant's by suggesting that the underlying insight which unites them is 'the recognition that there cannot be, in any "reasonable" way, a moral demand upon me, unless reality itself is committed to morality in some deep way'.[58] A world that obliges us to pursue the *summum bonum* but does nothing to further this end itself, is absurd. As Kant put it, there is 'an open contradiction' between 'a final end within, that is set before them (man) as a duty, and a nature without, that has no final end, though in it the former end is to be actu-alized'.[59]

Do there exist moral obligations the fulfilment of which result in a net loss of Russellian benefit? We can clearly imagine situations in which it would be our moral duty to risk our own lives in the interest of saving other lives. I may be unable to save someone's life in the absence of a fire-extinguisher; but this pos-sibility does not excuse me from *attempting* to save life, and making the attempt may prove life-threatening to myself. The question then is why should I risk my life in response to a demand from a reality which shows no interest in furthering the cause it demands that I pursue? Such a Russellian universe is incapable of playing fair, so why play its game? The same sort of question can be asked of morally praiseworthy acts that we are not obliged to enact. In a Russellian universe, what would be the point in enacting a risky act of heroism? Would the possible Russellian benefits outweigh the probable Russellian losses?

If God exists, we can be much more confident of everyone getting their 'just deserts' in the long run. Theism would seem to be the only serious contender for a world-view in which this is the case. Indeed, I have already argued that theism is the only world-view that can make sense of the notion of objective moral obligations. The moral demands of a theistic universe would seem less likely to be made against our own long-term good, and are made by an ultimate reality who works towards the guaran-teed achievement of the very end he obliges us to pursue. As Norman L. Geisler and Paul D. Feinberg argue, only God can guarantee the victory of good over evil:

(1) Since God is all-good, he has the *will* to defeat evil.
(2) Since God is all-powerful, he has the *power* to defeat evil.
(3) Evil is not *yet* defeated.
(4) Therefore, evil *will* one day be defeated.[60]

So far so good; but we are still left with one question: 'Is the uni-verse absurd?'

Nihilism—the absurd world-view

The French existentialist philosopher Albert Camus believed that the most pressing philosophical question was, 'Why not suicide?' he wrote, 'There is but one truly serious philosophical problem, and that is suicide. Judging whether life is or is not worth living amounts to answering the fundamental question of philosophy.'[61] For Camus, the answer to the question of suicide is related to whether or not the universe is absurd, and to our response to our answer to this fundamental issue. Camus defines 'the absurd' in *The Myth of Sisyphus*:

> absurdity springs from a comparison . . . between a bare fact and a certain reality, between an action and the world that transcends it. The absurd is essentially a divorce. It lies in neither of the elements compared; it is born of their confrontation. [62]

An absurd universe is one which does not form a coherent whole. If there is a divorce between the demands placed upon humanity by the universe and what humanity can achieve, or between the needs of humanity and what the universe has to offer by way of satisfaction, then life is absurd. As Stephen T. Davies writes:

> Camus's basic assumption was that life is absurd . . . We long for some sort of Meaning in Life, but there is none . . . We want there to exist a kindly, loving God, but no such being exists . . . We hope for life after death, but death is the end of our existence. We long for some sort of grand, over-arching explanation of life and history and human existence, but no such over-arching explanation is available.[63]

The title of Camus' book, *The Myth of Sisyphus*, refers to the Greek myth of Sisyphus who betrays the gods by revealing divine secrets to humanity. As a punishment, the gods force Sisyphus to roll a large stone up to the top of a mountain and watch it roll down again, repeating this exercise for all eternity. In other words, the gods punish Sisyphus by giving him an existence without purpose. Sisyphus will never achieve anything of lasting value. Camus' use of this myth is to suggest that, without God, we are all Sisyphus.

Camus' answer in the face of absurdity is to live absurdly, to 'revolt' against the absurdity of life by abandoning hope for the future and living in the transient now. He quotes the poet Pindar with approval: 'O my soul, do not aspire to immortal life, but exhaust the limits of the possible.' Camus joins with Sartre in asserting that while life has no meaning, we should nevertheless live as if it did. On Camus' own principles the decision to live must be just as absurd as the decision to die; but in advocating the acceptance of life he clearly assumed that life is valuable, saying that 'the sole deficiency to be made good, is constituted by premature death'.[64] Existentialists like Sartre and Camus continue to affirm life while rejecting any objective basis for their affirmation. Pindar's fine sounding rhetoric is likely to appear somewhat pallid when we realise that while we may 'exhaust the limits of the possible', to do so is absurd to the point of being no more meaningful than the decision to commit suicide. This conflict between belief in an absurd and meaningless world and the affirmation of life and personal meaning seems to me to cut fatally into the heart of all such existential philosophies.

Is life absurd? I suspect that our answer to this final question will depend as much upon our emotional character as on any arguments we 'bring to the table'. For myself, I see no reason to believe that life is absurd, and plenty of reasons to think otherwise. Answering this final question in the negative appears to lead to the conclusion that God exists. What is the alternative? To say that the universe is absurd is a form of nihilism: 'Nihilism is more a feeling than a philosophy. Strictly speaking, nihilism ... is a denial of philosophy, a denial of the possibility of knowledge, a denial that anything is valuable ... Everything is gratuitous, de trop, that is, just there.'[65] Nihilism is the result of admitting that a universe without God is absurd while rejecting the existentialist's self-contradictory 'let's pretend' response.

We live in a 'post-modern' age. The Indian writer Ravi Zacharias gives a fascinating example of what 'post-modernism' means:

> the latest arts building opened at Ohio State University, the Wrexner Centre for the Performing Arts [has been] branded . . . 'America's first deconstructionalist building' . . . inside you encounter stairways that go nowhere, pillars that hang from the ceiling without purpose, and angled surfaces configured to create a sense of vertigo. The architect, we are duly informed, designed this building to reflect life itself—senseless and incoherent . . . I had just one question: did he do the same with the foundation?[66]

It is clear that post-modernism is essentially nihilistic in its rejection of transcendent meaning and purpose. During the Enlightenment, God was often thought of as a sort of 'watchmaker' who wound the universal machine up at the start, and then sat back to enjoy the show, without getting involved. Modernism simply left God out of the picture altogether. Post-modernism is the realisation that without God, nothing makes the sense that it used to any more. Life is full of 'stairways that go nowhere'. The atheistic philosopher Nietzsche predicted our post-modern condition in a famous philosophical parable:

> Have you not heard of that madman who lit a lantern in the bright morning hours, ran to the market place and cried incessantly, 'I'm looking for God, I'm looking for God!' As many of those who did not believe in God were standing together there, he excited considerable laughter. 'Why, did he get lost?' said one. 'Did he lose his way like a child?' said another . . . Thus they yelled and laughed . . . 'Where is God?' [cried the madman]. 'I shall tell you. We have killed him—you and I. All of us are his murderers. But how have we done this? . . . Who gave us the sponge to wipe away the horizon? What did we do when we unchained this earth from its sun? Where is it

moving now? Where are we moving now? Away from all suns? Are we not plunging continually backward, sideward, forward, in all directions? Is there any up or down left? Are we not straying through an infinite nothing? Do we not feel the breath of empty space? Has it not become colder? Is not night and more night coming on all the time? Must not lanterns be lit in the morning? Do we hear anything yet of the noise of the grave-diggers who are burying God? Do we not smell anything yet of God's decomposition? Gods, too, decompose. God is dead, and we have killed him. How shall we, the murderers of all murderers comfort ourselves? What was holiest and most powerful of all that the world has yet owned has bled to death under our knives. Who will wipe this blood off us? What water is there for us to clean ourselves? What festivals of atonement . . . shall we have to invent? Is not the greatness of this deed too great for us? Must we not ourselves become gods simply to seem worthy of it?'[67]

Humans have attempted to become 'gods', making everything relative to ourselves. Giving up belief in God has led to giving up belief in any moral authority above our own inventiveness. We do smell the stench of God's decomposition: in the gas chambers of Auschwitz. Auschwitz survivor Viktor Frankl wrote:

The gas chambers of Auschwitz were the ultimate consequence of the theory that man is nothing but the product of hereditary and environment—or, as the Nazis liked to say, 'of blood and soil'. I am absolutely convinced that the gas chambers of Auschwitz . . . were ultimately prepared not in some ministry or other in Berlin, but . . . in lecture halls of nihilistic scientists and philosophers.[68]

If there is no God, to who or what will we appeal to justify our sense of moral outrage at Auschwitz?

Death and futility

The secular atheist believes that death is life's final curtain, and must characterise human life with Martin Heidegger as 'being-unto-death'.[69] At death, the individual ceases to be, and will never be again. In his poem *Ozymandias*, Shelley depicts a ruined monument consisting of 'Two vast and trunkless legs of stone' and 'a shattered visage' lying alone in a desert:

> And on the pedestal these words appear:
> 'My name is Ozymandias, king of kings:
> look on my works, ye Mighty, and despair!'
> Nothing beside remains, Round the decay
> Of that colossal wreck, boundless and bare
> The lone and level sands stretch far away.

For the secular atheist, everything we do, everything we are, will end up like Ozymandias. Indeed, our fate will be worse, for while we can still guess at the glories of this 'king of kings', all will eventually be forgotten in the ruins of a burned-out, lifeless universe. If the universe continues to exist and to function as it does now, entropy will increase to the point where disorder is at a maximum, and all life will cease. As the universe expands everything grows colder and available energy is used up. Eventually, the stars will burn out and matter will collapse into black holes: 'So not only is the life of each individual doomed; the entire human race is doomed.'[70] Doomed that is, unless we can depend upon some outside intervention of precisely the sort envisaged by Christian theism. The Old Testament book of Isaiah claims, with poetical but startlingly scientific accuracy, to record the promise of God:

All the stars of the heavens will be dissolved and the sky rolled up like a scroll; all the starry hosts will fall like withered leaves from the vine, like shrivelled figs from the fig-tree . . . Behold, I will create a new heavens and a new earth. The former things will not be remembered, nor will they come to mind. But be glad and rejoice forever in what I will create, for I will create Jerusalem to be a delight and its people a joy. (Isaiah 34:4; 65:17–18)

In the New Testament, Jesus' follower Peter writes that, 'In keeping with his promise we are looking forward to a new heaven and a new earth, the home of righteousness' (2 Peter 3:13). In the last book of the Bible, John writes a vision of this new cosmic order:

> Then I saw a new heaven and a new earth, for the first heaven and the first earth had passed away, and there was no longer any sea [a symbol of chaos]. I saw the Holy City, the new Jerusalem [the Church], coming down out of heaven from God, prepared as a bride beautifully dressed for her husband. And I heard a loud voice from the throne saying, 'Now the dwelling of God is with man, and he will live with them. They will be his people, and God himself will be with them and be their God. He will wipe away every tear from their eyes. There will be no more death or mourning or crying or pain, for the old order of things has passed away.' (Revelation 21:1–4)

Without getting into the issue of purported divine revelation, it is clear that the existence of an all-good God who has created both the universe and people for a purpose offers a coherent and plausible future hope where atheism offers only doom. Why would God bother to create our universe only to let every good within it perish? Why would God create a universe containing evils but not defeat evil in the long run if this were possible? Given the existence of God and of our universe, it seems that the concept of 'a new heaven and a new earth' into which we can enter follows logically. As Stephen T. Davies affirms: 'If God exists, then it is possible for me confidently to affirm that my existence does not end with my death.'[71] If we believe in God, we can believe in the guaranteed defeat of evil and the eternal value of moral endeavour. If we do not believe in God, we must reconcile ourselves to the contrary consequences.

In his book *Arguing for Atheism*, Robin Le Poidevin devotes a whole chapter to the subject of death, entitled: 'Should the atheist fear death?' He attempts to answer this question by comparing two philosophical concepts of time. Rather than interact with Le Poidevin's metaphysical arguments, I will simply rephrase his question: 'Should the atheist look forward to death?' At best, the atheist might welcome death as the end to a life of pointlessness and suffering. For the Christian theist on the other hand, death is not the end, and it can be the gateway to heaven.

Does atheism describe an absurd universe?

On the assumption that God does not exist:

1) Human existence has no objective purpose.
2) There are no objective moral values.
3) Human beings have no objective or intrinsic worth.
4) We are the accidental by-product of impersonal forces that place within us the mere feeling that objective moral values exist and oblige us to pursue the *summum bonum*.
5) Ultimate reality is impersonal and so does not share in this project.
6) There is no guarantee that 'good' will triumph over 'evil'.
7) Each life ends in death and humanity is doomed along with the universe to extinction.
8) Nothing we do, as individuals or as a species, has anything but a temporary, subjective value.[72]

Is such a universe absurd? Is such an existence worth living? We must each answer these questions for ourselves, but I believe that the universe described by atheism is absurd. There does not seem much worth living for, or even dying for, within such a universe. Sartre was right to point out that suicide is the use of freedom to take away freedom. However, there seems to be little reason not to negate our existence in this most final of ways if the universe is as atheists like Russell or Nielson believe it to be. Is life actually worth living? Again, we must each answer this for ourselves. However, if we think that life *is* worth living, and if we think that a Godless world is *not* worth living in, then we must conclude that our world is not such a Godless reality, and that God therefore exists.

Recommended reading

Mortimer J. Adler, *Aristotle For Everybody* (Macmillan, 1978), part three. (1)

Mortimer J. Adler, *Adler's Philosophical Dictionary* (Scribner, 1995). (1)

Aristotle, *The Nicomachean Ethics* (Wordsworth Classics). (3)

The Bible, 'Ecclesiastes'. (1)

Boethius, V.E. Watts, trans. *The Consolation of Philosophy* (Penguin, 1969). (2)

Albert Camus, Justin O'Brien, trans. *The Myth of Sisyphus* (Penguin, 1975). (4)

F.C. Copleston, *Aquinas* (Pelican Books, 1957). (3)

F.C. Copleston, *History of Philosophy—Volume II, Augustine to Scotus*, chapters XXVI and XXXIX (Burns and Oates, 1966). (3)

Lawrence J. Crabb, *Effective Biblical Counselling* (Marshall Pickering, 1990). Professor Crabb is a clinical psychologist. His book includes an analysis of human needs and a biblical approach to God-centred wholeness. (1)

William Lane Craig, *Reasonable Faith*, revised edition (Crossway Books, 1996). (2)

Stephen T. Davies, *God, Reason and Theistic Proofs* (Edinburgh, 1997). (3)

C. Stephen Evans, *Why Believe?* (IVP, 1996). (1)

C. Stephen Evans, *Subjectivity and Religious Belief* (Eerdmans: Grand Rapids, Mi., 1978). (4)

Norman L. Geisler and Winfried Corduan, *Philosophy of Religion*, second edition (Baker, 1988). (3)

Debbie Goddard, *Undrugged and still dancing* (Scripture

Union, 1997). Includes case histories of several former drug-users turned Christian believers. (1)

Peter Kreeft, *Three Philosophies of Life* (Ignatius, 1989).

Peter Kreeft and Ronald Tacelli, *Handbook of Christian Apologetics* (Monarch, 1995). (1)

C.S. Lewis, 'The Weight of Glory' in *Screwtape proposes a toast—and other essays* (Fount). (1)

C.S. Lewis, *The Pilgrim's Regress* (Fount, 1977). (3)

C.S. Lewis, *Mere Christianity* (Fount, 1986). (1)

C.S. Lewis, *Surprised by Joy* (Fount, 1977). (1)

Timothy McDermott, *Thomas Aquinas, Selected Philosophical Writings* (Oxford, 1993). (3)

Alister McGrath, *Bridge Building* (IVP, 1992). (2)

Alister McGrath, *A Cloud of Witnesses* (IVP, 1992). (1)

J.P .Moreland, *Scaling the Secular City* (Baker, 1987). (3)

Blaise Pascal, Honor Levi, trans. *Pensées and other writings* (Oxford, 1995). (3)

Robin Le Poidevin, *Arguing for Atheism* (Routledge, 1996), chapter ten. (3)

Nick Pollard, *Why do they do that? Understanding teenagers* (Lion, 1998)

Francis Shaeffer, *Trilogy* (IVP). (2)

James W. Sire, *The Universe Next Door*, third edition (IVP, 1997), chapters five and six. (1)

Keith Ward, *The Battle for the Soul* (Hodder and Stoughton, 1985). (3)

Ravi Zacharias, *Can Man Live Without God?* (Word, 1995). (1)

Ravi Zacharias, *A Shattered Visage, The Real Face of Atheism* (Baker, 1995). (1)

Notes

1. Mortimer J. Adler, *Aristotle for Everybody* (Macmillan, 1978), p.83.
2. *Ibid.*, pp.88–89.

3. Peter Kreeft, *Three Philosophies of Life* (Ignatius Press, 1989), p.18.

4. Mortimer J. Adler, *op. cit.*, pp.95–96.

5. *Ibid.*, p.73.

6. Aristotle, *The Nicomachean Ethics* (Wordsworth Classics), p.3.

7. *Ibid.*, p.11.

8. Timothy McDermott, in *Aquinas—Selected Philosophical Writings* (Oxford, 1993), p.315.

9. Mortimer J. Adler, *Adler's Philosophical Dictionary* (Scribner, 1995), p.89.

10. Ravi Zacharias, *A Shattered Visage—The Real Face of Atheism* (Baker, 1995), p.168.

11. Thomas Aquinas, *Compendium Theologiae*, 104, quoted by F.C. Copleston, *Aquinas* (Pelican Books, 1957).

12. *Ibid.*, pp.107–108.

13. Thomas Aquinas, *Summa Theologica*, 1*a*, 2, 1, *ad*1, quoted by F.C. Copleston in *Aquinas*.

14. *Ibid.*

15. *Ibid.*

16. Boethius, V.E.Watts, trans. *The Consolation of Philosophy* (Penguin, 1969), p.83.

17. C.S. Lewis, *Mere Christianity* (Fount, 1977).

18. *Ibid.*

19. C.S. Lewis, *The Pilgrim's Regress* (Fount, 1977).

20. Blaise Pascal, Honor Levi, trans. *Pensées and other writings*, (Oxford, 1995), *Pensées* 181.

21. Ravi Zacharias, *op. cit.*, p.149.

22. Walter Kaufmann, *Critique of Religion and Philosophy* (Doubleday, 1961), p.354.

23. Thomas Aquinas, quoted by Timothy McDermott, in *Aquinas, Selected Philosophical Passages*, Introduction.

24. Peter Kreeft and Ronald Tacelli, *Handbook of Christian Apologetics* (Monarch, 1995), p.250.

25. C.S. Lewis, 'The Weight of Glory' in *Screwtape Proposes a Toast—and other essays* (Fount, 1979).

26. Debbie Goddard, *Undrugged and still dancing* (Scripture Union, 1997), Introduction.

27. Blaise Pascal, *op. cit.*, *Pensées* 70, p.16.

28. *Response, The Family Magazine*, Winter 1996.

29. Augustine, *Confessions*, Henry Chadwick, trans. (Oxford, 1992).

30. Stephen Watt, *The Nichomacean Ethics*, Introduction (Wordsworth Classics).

31. John Calvin, *Institutes*.

32. Augustine, *op. cit.*

33. Kai Nielson, 'Ethics Without God' in *Does God Exist? The Debate between Theists and Atheists* (Prometheus, 1993), p.104.

34. Peter Kreeft and Ronald Tacelli, *op. cit.*, (Monarch, 1995), p.248.

35. *Ibid.*, p.248.

36. David Wilkinson, *Alone In The Universe?* (Monarch, 1997), p.145.

37. William Lane Craig, *Reasonable Faith*, revised edition (Crossway Books, 1994), p.57.

38. *Ibid.*

39. *Ibid.*

40. W.E. Hocking, *Types of Philosophy*.

41. Friedrich Nietzsche, in *The Portable Nietzsche*, Walter Kaufmann, ed. (Doubleday, 1954), p.441.

42. Peter Atkins in Russell Stannard, *Science and Wonders*, (Faber and Faber, 1996). Apart from anything else, Atkin's argument that we are insignificant because we are small is clearly fallacious; otherwise tall people would be more valuable than short people!

43. Keith Ward, *The Battle for the Soul* (Hodder and Stoughton, 1985), p.14.

44. Jacques Monad, *Chance and Necessity.*
45. Will Provine in Russell Stannard, *Science and Wonders.*
46. Jean-Paul Sartre, *The Words*, B. Frenchman, trans. (George Braziller: New York, 1964), p.97, 102.
47. Arthur F. Holmes, *All Truth is God's Truth* (IVP, 1979).
48. Jean Paul Sartre, quoted by Norman L. Geisler and Winfried Corduan, *Philosophy of Religion*, second edition (Baker, 1988), p.72,
49. William Lane Craig, *op. cit.*, p.69.
50. Bertrand Russell, 'A Free Man's Worship' in *Why I Am Not a Christian and Other Essays* (Routledge, 1979).
51. Peter Kreeft and Ronald Tacelli, *op. cit.*
52. Quoted by Philip Yancey, *Disappointment with God*, p.253.
53. Blaise Pascal, *op. cit.*
54. Immanuel Kant, *Critique of Practical Reason*, bk. II chapter II section V, Thomas K. Abbot, trans. *Kant's Theory of Ethics*, fourth edition, 1889.
55. *Ibid.*
56. George I. Maverodes, 'Religion and the Queerness of Morality' in Robert Audi and William J. Wainwright, eds, *Rationality, Religious Belief, and Moral Commitment* (Cornell University Press, 1986).
57. *Ibid.*
58. *Ibid.*
59. Immanual Kant, *Critique of Judgement*, quoted by C. Stephen Evans, *Subjectivity and Religious Belief* (Eerdmans: Grand Rapids, Mi., 1978), p.67.
60. Norman L. Geisler and Paul D. Feinberg, *Introduction to Philosophy* (Baker, 1997), p.275.
61. Albert Camus, *The Myth of Sisyphus*, Justin O'Brien, trans. (Penguin, 1975).
62. *Ibid.*
63. Stephen T. Davies, *God, Reason and Theistic Proofs* (Edinburgh, 1997), p.177.
64. Albert Camus, *op. cit.*, p.46.

65. James W. Sire, *The Universe Next Door*, third edition (IVP, 1997), p.75.

66. Ravi Zacharias, *Can Man Live Without God?* (Word, 1995), p.64.

67. Frederick Nietzsche, A section from *Gay Science* in Walter Kaufmann, ed., *The Portable Nietzsche* (New York: Viking, 1954), p.125, quoted by Ravi Zacharias, *Can Man Live Without God?* (Word, 1995), pp.58–60.

68. Ravi Zacharias, *op. cit.*

69. Martin Heidegger, *Being and Time* (Macmillan, 1967), p.290.

70. William Lane Craig, *op. cit.*, p.58.

71. Stephen T. Davies, *op. cit.*, (Edinburgh, 1997), p.181.

72. These points do not merely apply to secular atheisms such as humanism and communism, but to any atheistic world-view. For example, in Buddhism: our existence is unintended; there is no creator to provide objective purpose; no personal all-good being to ground the existence of objective moral values; human beings therefore have no objective worth; we feel a desire to do the right thing, but there is no objectively right thing to do and ultimate reality, being impersonal, does not desire 'good' over 'evil'; reality does not guarantee the triumph of 'good' over 'evil' except in the sense that Buddhism defines all desire as 'evil'—even the desire for 'good'—and Nivarna will extinguish desire; although each life does not end at death because of reincarnation, the individual does not remember past lives and will eventually attain extinction in Nirvana where the (illusion of the) individual is extinguished. Nirvana was described by Buddha as 'the sphere of nothingness'. Indeed, Nirvana means 'to extinguish'. Therefore, nothing we do, whether as individuals or as a species, has anything but a temporary, subjective value which we subjectively 'ought' not to desire anyway. See: Dean C. Halverson, ed., *The Compact Guide To World Religions* (Bethany House, 1996).

CHAPTER EIGHT

NON-EVIDENTIAL ARGUMENTS—PASCAL'S WAGER AND THE RIGHT TO BELIEVE

'I tell you the truth, he who believes has everlasting life.'

(John 6:47)

Blaise Pascal and William James both defended arguments for believing in the existence of God that did not seek to provide any evidence that God exists. I will examine these arguments in reverse historical order, arguing that both thinkers present sound arguments. Both arguments demonstrate the importance of the question 'Does God exist?', thereby encouraging us to seek answers through reason and openness to religious experience. These arguments lead us to conclude that, in the absence of sufficient reasons *against* God's existence, there is nothing irrational about resolving to believe in God despite a lack of reasons *for* His existence.

In previous chapters I've given arguments which attempt to show, with varying degrees of certainty, that God exists. These arguments are 'evidential arguments', arguments that give evidence for thinking that something is the case. While evidential arguments are arguments for *belief*, they are such only by default. Evidential arguments are primarily arguments for the *truth* of certain propositions. If any evidential argument is to affect me by changing or confirming my beliefs, I must 'buy into' the rules of the logic which underpin it; and this is, of course, something of which the rules of logic cannot persuade me.

To any argument for the truth of a proposition 'P', we must add another 'premise' such as, 'I am going to be rational', to arrive at the conclusion, 'I'm going to believe P', via something like, 'P is the conclusion of a sound argument'. This extra 'premise' is implicit within the fact that an evidential argument is being seriously considered. It is a decision by the person considering the argument to be rational. This means they are committed to submitting to the argument's conclusion if, a) it seems to them to be proven by the argument, or b) it seems to them to be supported by the argument, and there is a lack of evidence of similar or greater strength for the opposing conclusion. If the implicit first premise of an evidential argument ('I am going to be rational') is not acted upon, the argument will not produce belief.

Although to believe 'that P' is to believe that 'P is true' (and vice versa), this depends upon beliefs about the nature of truth. P may be the conclusion of a valid argument using premises I believe to be true, but my belief 'that P' only follows because I believe in the validity of reason (a belief for which I can give no reasons), and because I am committed to being rational.

Logic never caused anyone to believe anything. Logic justifies; love convinces. Someone who loves their desire to do and believe whatever they want more than they love truth will not submit to the conclusion of any argument, however compelling, that goes against the desires of their heart. This point was made forcefully by Pascal, who wrote that 'every man is almost always led to believe not through proof; but through that which is attractive'.[1] William James made a similar point when he wrote that, 'If your heart does not want a world of moral reality, your head will assuredly never make you believe in one.'[2] Peter Kreeft has some wise words to say upon this theme:

> Honesty with oneself is difficult—often much more difficult then honesty with others . . . But unless both sides begin here, with an unqualified 'I will' to honesty and truth, whatever it may turn out to be, there is no hope of really settling this issue, or any other, and debate becomes mere entertainment, a sham.[3]

An evidential argument for belief in the existence of God tries to lead us to the conclusion that the proposition 'God exists' is true. There is another class of argument, called 'non-evidential argument'. This sort of argument does not give evidence for believing that something is true. It argues for belief, not for the truth of that belief. Non-evidential arguments do not try to persuade you to believe something that you know is untrue. Rather, they seek to persuade you to believe something that you presently don't believe, but which you have insufficient reason to think false. Such arguments in no way conflict with the biblical command to use our reason wisely in search of truth (Matthew 22:37; 2 Corinthians 10:5; 1 Thessalonians 5:21), but assume that we have already done our best in this endeavour and remain unconvinced or undecided.[4]

Two prime examples of non-evidential arguments are found in the work of Blaise Pascal and of William James. William James argues that it can be rational to believe that God exists without sufficient evidence for believing that God exists. Pascal argues that the question of God's existence is so important that we ought to pursue it with care, and that in the absence of sufficient reason to believe that God exists we should nevertheless believe in God rather than remain agnostic. Although James lived two centuries after Pascal, his work serves as a neat foundation upon which Pascal's thoughts build, and so I will start with his argument.

William James: the right to believe

I have brought with me tonight something like a sermon on justification by faith to read to you—I mean an essay in justification of faith, a defence of our right to adopt a believing attitude in religious matters, in spite of the fact that our merely logical intellect may not have been coerced.

(William James)[5]

The American philosopher William James (1842–1910), brother of the author Henry James, is known today mainly for his book *The Varieties of Religious Experience*, and for his classic paper 'The Will To Believe'. I first want to show how James' argument in 'The Will To Believe' shows the importance of the question of God's existence.

James begins by giving the name hypothesis 'to anything that may be proposed to our belief', and says that: 'just as the electricians speak of live and dead wires, let us speak of any hypothesis as either live or dead. A live hypothesis is one which appeals as a real possibility to him to whom it is proposed.'[6]

Whatever the hypothesis, it is live if you are willing to consider that it might be true. No one can decide to believe something that they believe to be untrue. If I believe that pigs can't fly, the proposition that 'pigs can fly' will not appeal 'as a real possibility' to me; it will not be a live hypothesis. I may be sceptical about the existence of extraterrestrial life. Yet, if I am willing to consider the hypothesis that aliens exist (admitting that aliens might exist), then the hypothesis that there are extraterrestrials is a live one for me. Similarly, I might be sceptical about the existence of God, but unless believing that He exists is such a silly idea to me that I place God's existence in the same category as flying pigs (or even square circles), then God's existence is a live hypothesis for me.

Next James points out that we face decisions between hypotheses. To face a decision between hypotheses is, says James, to face an option:

> Options may be of several kinds. They may be—1, living or dead; 2, forced or avoidable; 3, momentous or trivial; and for our purposes we may call an option a genuine option when it is of the forced, living, and momentous kind . . . A living option is one in which both hypotheses are live ones . . . each hypothesis makes some appeal, however small, to your belief.[7]

If someone is wondering whether or not God exists, then believing in His existence is clearly a live hypothesis for them and they face a live option. A forced option is one where you must choose one of the two hypotheses presented to you:

> If I say to you . . . 'Choose between going out with your umbrella or without it', I do not offer you a genuine option, for it is not forced. You can easily avoid it by not going out at all . . . But if I say 'either accept this truth or go without it', I put on you a forced option, for there is no standing place outside of the alternative . . . We cannot

escape the issue by remaining sceptical and waiting for more light, because, although we do avoid error in that way if religion be untrue, we lose the good, if it be true, just as certainly as if we positively chose to disbelieve.[8]

Believing in God's existence is a forced option because you either believe that God exists, or not. Believing in God is a forced option because you either believe in Him, or you don't. A momentous option is one involving a unique, significant or irreversible decision:

if I were [an explorer] and proposed to you to join my North Pole expedition, your option would be momentous; for this would probably be your only similar opportunity, and your choice now would either exclude you from the North Pole sort of immortality altogether or put at least the chance of it into your hands. He who refuses to embrace a unique opportunity loses the prize as surely as if he tried and failed. [On the other hand] the option is trivial when the opportunity is not unique, when the stakes are insignificant, or when the decision is reversible if it later proved unwise.[9]

The decision to believe in the existence of God (though one cannot believe merely by an act of will) is a momentous decision, because significant consequences follow from God's existence or non-existence. For example, believing that God exists is linked to the decision whether or not to believe in God, a decision that could have serious moral and practical consequences.

For anyone prepared to admit that God might exist, the hypothesis that God exists is therefore a genuine option. To believe or disbelieve in the existence of God is a choice we all have to make; it is a forced option. Our choice between these rival hypotheses is momentous in that significant consequences follow from whichever option we believe, consequences that will affect our entire world-view. It will affect the way we see ourselves, other people, and the universe around us. Clearly then, the question 'Does God exist?' is among the most important questions we must seek to answer.

Follow your heart

James goes on to argue that, in facing a genuine option, it need not be an irrational act to allow our 'passional nature'[10] to move us towards one belief or the other. By 'passional nature' James means our inclinations and hunches that can't be set out as formal reasons for belief or disbelief, but which nevertheless draw us towards this or that belief: 'differences in judgement are typically affected by what William James called our "willing" or "passional" nature—our temperament, needs, concerns, fears, hopes, passions, and "divinations".'[11]

James says this is a legitimate use of the passions for several reasons. Firstly, because a genuine option is a choice we cannot escape making: it is a forced option. Secondly, unlike the choice between believing in the existence of extraterrestrials or not, the choice between believing in the existence of God or not is a momentous choice that we therefore cannot afford to put off. Lastly, it is because a genuine option is a choice between two rival live hypotheses: 'Each hypothesis makes some appeal, however small, to your belief.'[12] Neither option falls under that category of hypotheses which so repel your belief that you call them daft or preposterous. To neither suggestion ('God exists' or 'God does not exist') are you tempted to reply with scornful derision, 'Yes, and pigs can fly!' You have not made up your mind, but you must decide. Yet you either have no reasons for either option, or are not convinced one way or the other by the reasons you do have. The decision is urgent. Much hangs on it. You must act. It is highly unlikely that each hypothesis is equally 'live' to you. One will appeal more than the other. One may strike you with a force of one hundred metaphorical volts, and the other with one hundred and two. What you should do in such a circumstance, argues James, is follow your heart. Allow your passional nature to decide for you. Take the plunge and, since you must dive one way or the other but cannot decide upon evidential grounds which way to go, dive in the direction you feel happiest about: 'Our passional nature not only lawfully may, but must, decide an option between propositions, whenever it is a genuine option that cannot by its nature be decided on intellectual grounds.'[13]

What James is saying is that, if you are inclined to believe in God, then there is nothing unreasonable in following this inclination so long as there is an absence of convincing reasons to believe the contrary (that God does not exist), even if you have no convincing reasons in favour of the belief towards which you are inclined.[14] (Of course, this cuts both ways in that someone might be inclined to believe that there is no God, and, being unconvinced by the evidence to the contrary, may follow their inclination without doing reason an injustice, even in the absence of any convincing arguments against God's existence.)

James v. Clifford

James argued this point against a philosopher called William Clifford who thought that: 'It is wrong always, everywhere and for everyone to believe anything upon insufficient evidence.'[15] Clifford thought that we should have an evidential argument in favour of everything we believe. James countered Clifford by pointing out that we cannot provide a reason for believing in reason without arguing in a circle. If Clifford held his view consistently he would end up with the self-contradictory belief that it is wrong to believe his own belief! Our belief in the power of reason is an act of faith, and if that faith is well placed, then Clifford must be wrong. On the other hand, if our faith in reason is not well placed, reason is unreasonable and Clifford cannot be right. It's heads William James wins, tails Clifford loses. Pascal made the same point as James: 'We know the truth not only by means of the reason but also by means of the heart. It is through the heart that we know the first principles.'[16] In arguing against Clifford, James places himself in this same tradition:

> If, for example, I am unable to doubt that I now exist before you, that two is less than three, or that all men are mortal then I am mortal too, it is because these things illumine my intellect irresistibly . . . Of some things we feel that we are certain: we know, and we know that we do know. There is something that gives a click inside us, a bell that strikes twelve, when the hands of our mental clock have swept the dial and meet over the meridian hour.[17]

(Pascal and James both echo the thoughts of the French philosopher René Descartes on this matter. See Descartes' '4th Discourse On Method' and 'The Meditations'.) This does not mean that we simply decide what to believe on the basis of our passional nature and thereafter ignore any evidence or argument relevant to our belief. In the interest of intellectual honesty we must always be prepared, if necessary, to revise our beliefs in the light of new information, or even to change one belief for another. James concedes that 'we are all such absolutists by instinct',[18] but says that he lives, 'to be sure, by the practical faith that we must go on experiencing and thinking over our experience, for only thus can our opinions grow more true'.[19] But where we cannot avoid making a decision that we cannot decide intellectually, we have no alternative but to follow our heart. (Indeed, this is what we do; James merely argues that our behaviour in these matters is not irrational.) As Pascal wrote, 'Le Coeur a ses raisons.'[20] The heart has its reasons.

Pascal's wager arguments (If at first you don't believe, try, try again)

> If the wager stimulates us at least to seek, then it will at least stimulate us to be reasonable. And if the promise Jesus makes is true, all who seek will find (Mt. 7:7–8), and thus will be happy.[21]

Blaise Pascal (1623–1662) was a French philosopher, mathematician, scientist and author. Although he never went to school, and was taught by his father, he gave mathematics a new theorem at the age of sixteen. Before he was twenty Pascal constructed the first computer, despite being in constant pain after the age of eighteen. His sister Gilberte wrote that the years he spent constructing his computer permanently ruined his health: 'Pascal combined a brilliant understanding, a lively imagination and an acute critical capacity with a boundless urge to work . . . He knew that he had little time to fulfil what he saw as his task. He died at the age of thirty-nine.'[22]

Pascal is famous today due mainly to his non-evidential argument for religious belief, an argument that has been dubbed 'Pascal's wager'. Perhaps I should have said infamous rather than famous, because Pascal has suffered much criticism on account of his wager. For example, Voltaire called Pascal's wager 'indecent and puerile'.[23]

The wager is found in a collection of notes Pascal made in preparation for a never-completed defence of Christian belief. We will never prove whether or not Pascal would have included the wager in the projected volume, nor in what guise he would have presented it. The unfinalised nature of these notes is something to bear in mind in assessing its contents or passing judgement upon its author, for as Ian Hacking writes, 'this is one thought from a book of thoughts'.[24] This collection of notes was published after Pascal's death as the appropriately named *Pensées* (Thoughts), from which the following thoughts are taken:

(1) I should be much more frightened of being wrong and finding out that Christian religion was true than of not being wrong in believing it to be true. (*Pensées* 6)
(2) According to the odds, you must take the trouble to seek the truth, because if you die without worshipping the true principle you are lost. 'But,' you say, 'if he had wanted me to adore him, he would

have left some signs of his will.' And so he has, but you have ignored them. So look for them, it is worth your while. (*Pensées* 190)

(3) There are only three kinds of people: those who serve God having found him; others who spend their time seeking him who have not found him, and the rest who live without seeking him nor having found him. The first are reasonable and happy, the last are lunatic and unhappy, those in the middle are unhappy and reasonable. (*Pensées* 192)

(4) 'God is or He is not.' But to which side shall we incline? Reason can decide nothing here . . . A game is being played . . . where heads or tails will turn up. What will you wager? According to reason, you can do neither the one thing nor the other; according to reason, you can defend neither of the propositions. Do not then reprove for error those who have made a choice; for you know nothing about it. 'No, but I blame them for having made, not this choice, but a choice; for again both he who chooses heads and he who chooses tails are equally at fault, they are both in the wrong. The true course is not to wager at all.' Yes; but you must wager. It is not optional. You are embarked. Which will you choose then? Let us see. Since you must choose, let us see which interests you least. You have two things to lose, the true and the good; and two things at stake, your reason and your will, your knowledge and your happiness; and your nature has two things to shun, error and misery. Your reason is no more shocked in choosing one rather than the other, since you must of necessity choose. This is one point settled. But your happiness? Let us weigh the gain and the loss in wagering that God is. Let us estimate these two chances. If you gain, you gain all; if you lose, you lose nothing. Wager then, without hesitation that He is. (*Pensées* 680)

The wager is clearly not an argument for the existence of God. Dr Ravi Zacharias is quite right when he writes that 'Pascal's argument should never be offered as a proof for God's existence or as a reason for belief in Him. This was never Pascal's intention.'[25] The whole point of the wager is that it is an argument offered to those who are unconvinced by evidential arguments: 'The argument is directed at the sort of person who, not being convinced of the proofs of religion, and still less by the arguments of atheists, remains suspended between a state of faith and one of unbelief.'[26]

The wager is not a single argument, but a form or class of argument. There are three types of wager argument in the *Pensées*. For example, *Pensées* 6 argues for belief in the 'Christian religion', including, of course, God's existence. *Pensées* 190 and 192 are arguments for seeking the truth in the matter of God's existence. *Pensées* 680 is an argument for believing that God exists, and for believing in him if you believe that he exists. Again, these are not arguments for the *truth* of anything, but an argument for *believing* something to be true.

The importance of searching for God

At its most basic the wager says that 1) If a proposed belief is of type X you should think long and hard before rejecting it, 2) the proposition 'God exists' is a proposed belief of type X, 3) and so you should think long and hard before rejecting the proposition 'God exists'. Such an argument is perhaps best summarised by Wittgenstein's remark, 'Go on, believe! It does no harm.'[27] 'It' is an urged belief. The claim that 'It does no harm' means that the believer has less to lose by believing wrongly than by disbelieving wrongly. As Nigel Warburton says, 'the Gambler's Argument provides no evidence whatsoever to convince me that God does exist: it merely tells me that . . . I would be well-advised to bring myself to believe this to be so.'[28] Proposed beliefs are of the relevant type if the potential losses in mistaken disbelief outweigh the potential losses of mistaken belief. This will be so where the potential gains in true belief outweigh the potential gains of true belief in the contrary of the proposed belief.

This is not to say that those who, like Pascal, use non-evidential arguments, have no interest in truth. Certainly this is not the case with Pascal, whose *Pensées* 'as a whole constitutes a forceful defence of the truth of Christianity'.[29] As William Lane

Craig writes, 'Pascal does believe that there is a way ... to determine how one should bet, namely, the proofs of Scripture of miracle and prophecy, which he discusses in the second half of his work.'[30] Pascal urges the nonbeliever to search for evidence of God (*Pensées* 190), and even gives a cosmological argument (*Pensées* 167).

Pascal is surely right that the question of God's existence or non-existence is important enough, not just theoretically but pragmatically, that we would be well advised to actively pursue the issue for ourselves. Ravi Zacharias concludes that:

> All judgements bring with them a margin of error. But no judgement ought to carry with it the potential for so irretrievable a loss that every possible gain is unworthy of merit. The atheist makes precisely such a hazardous judgement. It is an all-or-nothing gamble of himself, thrust into the slot machine of life. It is a faith beyond the scope of reason.[31]

Seeking God

Pascal views his suggestions to the nonbeliever of *Pensées* 680—who realises that their disbelief is an unjustified disposition of the heart which is both pragmatically and morally risky—to take holy water, have masses said and so on, not as an enticement to self-manipulation, but as a 'medicine' to bring them to their right mind:

> So concentrate not on convincing yourself by increasing the number of proofs of God but on diminishing your passions. You want to find faith and you do not know the way? You want to cure yourself of unbelief and you ask for the remedies? Learn from those who have been bound like you, and who now wager all they have. They are people who know the road you want to follow and have been cured of the affliction of which you want to be cured. Follow the way by which they began: by behaving just as if they believed, taking holy water, having masses said, etc. That will make you behave quite

naturally . . . because it diminishes the passions, which are your great stumbling-blocks.[32]

It is pointless, says Pascal, to examine evidential arguments if you have an entrenched disposition of disbelief: 'Hence our estrangement from consenting to the truths of the Christian religion which are quite contrary to our pleasures.'[33] Such an entrenched but unconfirmed disbeliever must somehow be brought to place a greater value upon truth than they place upon their autonomy. The result of proposing evidential arguments to someone with an entrenched passional disbelief would merely be to cause them to reject the premises of every argument presented to them, even to the point of nihilism. This is a theology of apologetics quite as much as it is a psychology of apologetics:

> God sows his illumination in people's minds only after quelling the rebellion of will by a totally heavenly sweetness which delights and overwhelms it . . . It is then that there is an uncertain balance between truth and pleasure, and the knowledge of the one and the feeling of the other creates a contest whose outcome is very uncertain, since, in order to judge it, we would need to know everything that happens in the deepest interior of a human being . . . From this it appears that, whatever it is one wants to persuade people of, we must take into consideration the person with whom we are concerned, of whom we know the mind and heart, the principles admitted, and the things loved; and then we must take note, in the matter concerned, of the relationship it has with admitted truths or of the objects of delight through the charms we attribute to them. So the art of persuasion consists as much in pleasing as it does in convincing, humanity being so much more governed by whim than by reason.[34]

Pascal is not proposing that apologetics should be carried out by making belief appealing at the detriment of reason. He is pointing out that apologetics must be addressed to the whole person, heart and mind, and that the mind will never convince the heart until the heart loves truth more than it loves its own rebellion against its maker. Pascal's 'holy water' prescription is not a charter for self-manipulation, but for placing oneself in circumstances favourable to the operation of God's Spirit of love upon the heart held back by sin.

If it is not reason that is an obstacle to belief (we are here assuming that intellectual considerations are unable to settle the question either way in the agnostic's mind), the obstacle must lie in the 'passions'. Pascal suggests that someone in this position should attempt to put themselves in a frame of mind wherein they can most easily find faith. If we find ourselves wishing that we could believe in God, and we lack conclusive evidence either for or against his existence, it seems rational to give ourselves the best possible chance of coming to believe. We can attempt to do this by praying, going to church, listening to appropriate music, watching films with a Christian theme, spending time with believers, reading the Bible and books written by believers.[35] Several thinkers have found this suggestion objectionable, but only, I think, because they have misunderstood Pascal's intention. J.J.C. Smart lambastes Pascal, saying: 'The argument of the wager purports to prove that one should by a sort of brain washing, going to masses, using holy water, and so on, induce belief in the Catholic religion.'[36] J.L. Mackie similarly objects that:

> No doubt Pascal is right about this; but it goes against his earlier claim that to bet one way or the other about God will do no injury to your reason. Deliberately to make oneself believe, by such techniques as he suggests—essentially by playing tricks on oneself that are found by experience to work upon people's passions and to give rise to belief in non-rational ways—is to do violence to one's reason and understanding.[37]

Mackie even quotes Pascal on this point: 'As Pascal himself says, 'cela . . . vous abetira': it will make you stupid.'[38] However, this translation is debatable. Ian Hacking gives the translation that the life of religious observance is intended to 'stupefy one' into belief.[39] Pascal's prescription is intended to stupefy the unreasonable disposition of disbelief so that the non-believer may 'behave quite naturally'.[40] Mackie's reading of 'cela . . . vous abetira' is a misreading that goes against the grain both of Pascal's intention in *Pensées* 680, and his underlying theology of apologetics as seen in 'The Art of Persuasion'.

Pascal's suggestion is better taken as the advice to remain as open as possible to religious experience in the realisation that the only barrier to belief for someone in the imagined position lies in their passional nature (as William James would put it). It is in the nonbeliever's interest to earnestly seek after that which they doubt, not in order to brainwash themselves into belief because it is to their advantage, but because the importance of the question as analysed by the wager behoves them to acknowledge that they have no justification for not making such an effort. Here the moral formulation of the wager emerges as implicit within its more mercenary cousin. If God exists, someone who knows they lack justification for not seeking Him, but who nevertheless evades the issue, will surely have more to answer for than the person who genuinely thinks that belief in the existence of God is unreasonable.

I do not see that even the self-interested search for belief in God's existence (and from thence belief in God) 'is to do violence to one's reason and understanding', as Mackie protests. If a person's intellect cannot decide either for or against the existence of God, how can anything they do to alter their state of mind from disbelief to belief be an action against their intellect? Indeed, the wager shows that, if a theist who could not intellectually resolve the question of God's existence sought to alter his or her belief to disbelief, this could only be done for doubtful motives and against his or her own interests. Perhaps, having grown up with a belief they cannot justify to their satisfaction, and wishing to partake of the much overrated 'worldly pleasures', they decide to push aside second-hand belief, suppress inherited qualms, and embark upon a life of sex, drugs and rock 'n' roll. Such a person's action would be against reason and morality. For someone in the opposite position to attempt to alter their belief, on the other hand, may be both morally motivated and rationally neutral.

An unconfirmed atheist may acknowledge the moral claim God would have upon them if He exists, and might therefore take measures to alter their self-enclosed passional nature in order to reduce the risk of offending their possibly existent creator. This could be done without going against any rational precept whatsoever. Perhaps they might even have themselves hypnotised into the firm conviction that God exists! Such a measure would be unreasonable only if such a person had not exhausted to the best of their ability every avenue offering evidential reasons for belief. But the situation we are imagining is one in which this exhaustion of evidential considerations is assumed: 'Your reason is no more shocked in choosing one rather than the other,' says Pascal, 'since you must of necessity choose.'[41]

I think it would be fair to say that most people agree with Pascal's conclusions in weighing up the consequences of belief in God versus the consequences of disbelief in God if Christianity is true. As J.L. Mackie admits: 'It is clear that, given his assumptions, the argument goes through.'[42] This may provide motivation for what Christian apologists call 'the sceptic's prayer' along the lines of, 'God, if you exist, please show me.' However, most people go on to say that the wager seems both morally deficient and unable to produce religious conviction. As Nigel Warburton says: 'We can't simply decide to believe something. I can't decide tomorrow to believe that pigs can fly, that London is the capital of Egypt, or that an all-powerful, all-knowing, and all-good God exists.'[43] Warburton has chosen examples suggesting that we cannot decide to believe that which we already believe to be false (implying that belief in God is like belief in flying pigs), rather than examples to show that we cannot simply decide to believe something by an act of will; but the point is taken. The 'method of tenacity' as Charles Peirce called the resolution to believe 'any answer to a question, which we may fancy'[44] without any regard to evidence, is a road to ruin. However, Pascal does not recommend the 'method of tenacity', since he also recommends evidential arguments. He would not countenance the dogged determination to believe something however strong the evidence against it, just because you wanted to.

The moral reformulation of Pascal's wager

William James comments in 'The Will To Believe' about the moral aspects of the wager, saying: 'if we ourselves were in the place of the Deity, we should probably take particular pleasure in cutting off believers of this pattern from their infinite reward.' Peter Kreeft and Ronald Tacelli take note of this moral criticism of the wager, and offer an alternative formulation: 'The wager can seem . . . purely selfish . . . but it can be reformulated to appeal to a higher moral motive: If there is a God of infinite goodness, and he justly deserves my allegiance and faith, I risk doing the greatest injustice by not acknowledging him.'[45] This version of the wager does indeed appear to be morally superior. If God as traditionally conceived within Christian theism exists, then we ought to worship Him. If there is the slightest possibility that such a God exists, then it would seem that our minimal moral duty would be to demonstrate a willingness to render what we genuinely intend to be acceptable worship to our creator, to put a reasonable amount of effort into seeking to know Him through prayer, looking with an open mind at purported revelation, engaging with arguments for His existence, and so on. It seems that the force of this argument was felt by the Athenians to whom St Paul preached:

> Men of Athens! I see that in every way you are very religious. For as I walked around and looked carefully at your objects of worship, I

even found an altar with this inscription: TO AN UNKNOWN
GOD. Now what you worship as something unknown I am going to
proclaim to you. (Acts 17:22–23)

Paul saw that the Athenians felt a moral duty to honour a god
whom they did not know, and who might not exist (the altar was
not inscribed 'to an un-named god', but 'to an unknown god').
This dual admission of ignorance and duty provided a golden
opportunity to gain a hearing for Christianity. Each form of the
wager can motivate the quest for truth in the matter of God's
existence by showing the importance of the issue. It is this quest
that may or may not produce religious conviction. In other
words, we should see Pascal's wager not as a form of argumentation for belief in the existence of God or the truth of a theology, but as a form of argument for considering arguments for the
existence of God and for the moral necessity of believing in Him
if we believe that He exists. The moral formulation of the wager
is particularly important in that it is an argument in support of
the implicit moral 'ought to believe' within evidential arguments. The wagers are non-evidential arguments for belief in
God in that, by highlighting the pragmatic and moral importance of the question of Christian belief, they seek to promote a
disposition wherein arguments for the truth of Christianity will
be considered with due seriousness: 'The whole wager-argument
is obviously an *argumentum ad hominem* [argument against the
person], a device to move the sceptic to abandon his attitude of
indifference and to do what he can to put himself in that condition in which faith becomes a real possibility.'[46] The wager is, as
William James said, 'a last desperate snatch at a weapon against
the hardness of the unbelieving heart'.[47]

Warburton's wager

To gamble that God does exist because we thereby gain the chance
of everlasting life, and then to trick ourselves into an actual belief in

God because of the prize we win if we are correct, seems an inappropriate attitude to take to the question of God's existence.[48]

Few books introducing philosophy to the general reader or the new student are sympathetic to belief in the existence of God. *Philosophy The Basics* (second edition) by Nigel Warburton is no different in this respect, though it is among the best of such volumes. A mark of its superiority is that it includes a discussion of Pascal's wager.

Warburton introduces the wager after his discussion of evidential arguments for and against God's existence, and rightly says that, while such arguments aim to settle the question of God's existence or non-existence, 'Pascal's wager is a very different kettle of fish. Its aim is not to provide proof. [The aim of the wager is] to show that a sensible gambler would be well-advised to "bet" that God exists.' This, as we have seen, is only one of several interpretations of what Pascal says through this form of argument. Warburton presents his own 'summary' of the wager. This summary is really another formulation of the 'gambler's argument', as must be all such 'summaries', since there is no single wager argument to be summarised, but rather one form of argument in several guises. Warburton likens someone who cannot decide upon the basis of evidence whether or not God exists to a gambler laying a bet before a race is run:

> We must . . . calculate the odds. But to the agnostic it may seem just as likely that God exists as that he or she doesn't. The agnostic's course of action is . . . not making a decision . . . The Gambler's Argument . . . says that the most rational thing to do is to aim to have a chance of winning as great a prize as possible, whilst keeping our chance of losing as small as possible [and] the best way to do this is to believe in God . . . If we bet on the existence of God and win . . . then we gain eternal life . . . What we lose if we bet on this option and it turns out that God doesn't exist is not great when compared with the possibility of eternal life: we may miss out on certain

worldly pleasures, waste many hours praying, and live out lives under an illusion. However, if we choose to bet on the option that God doesn't exist, and we win . . . then we live a life without illusion . . . and feel free to indulge in the pleasures of this life without fear of divine punishment. But if we bet on this option and lose . . . then we at least miss the chance of eternal life, and . . . run the risk of eternal damnation . . . If we gamble that God exists and are wrong we do not stand to lose as much as if we chose to believe that God doesn't exist and are wrong. So, if we want to maximise our possible gains and minimise our possible losses, then we ought to believe in God's existence.

One might be forgiven for suspecting that Mr Warburton has set up what philosophers call 'a straw-man'. A straw-man is an easy-to-knock-down target that does not fairly represent the supposed object of discussion. It's like the big bad wolf blowing down the three little pigs' straw house and trying to convince an audience that he has blown away the three little pigs' brick house. This is certainly a very weak formulation of Pascal's wager, although it is quite close to that given by Pascal in *Pensées* 680. I am aware that the charge of straw-man knocking might be levelled against my good self for attacking a critique of Pascal's wager given by an introductory textbook. However, Warburton's rendition of the wager is symptomatic of a common unsympathetic reading of Pascal's intent with the wager, a reading not limited to writers with the excuse of necessary brevity and simplicity. For example, atheist Antony Flew thinks that 'Pascal's Wager is . . . primarily and essentially an appeal to the prudent calculation of individual self-interest.'[49]

Warburton's formulation falls foul of the objection that anyone who believed because of this argument might be considered to have done so for an immoral reason (and are therefore unlikely to receive their reward in heaven since they would be seeking only to use God).

This formulation also seems to overplay the negative results of belief in God if God does not exist. We may readily agree that if someone believes that God exists and are wrong, then they are living a deluded life 'under an illusion'. However, even if God does not exist it can hardly be maintained that prayer is a total loss. Prayer, like the writing of poetry, is proven to be of use in coping with the stresses and strains of life. Although the non-theist will 'feel free to indulge in the pleasures of this life without fear of divine punishment', this does not necessarily mean that they will feel free to take advantage of those 'worldly pleasures' denied to the Christian believer (sex outside of marriage, alcohol and drug abuse, etc.), because they may adopt a moral code similar to that of the believer. The precepts of morality differ very little from religion to religion. Someone who disbelieves in the existence of God might well be a Buddhist, for example. Many atheists agree with traditionally Christian moral values (though they naturally disagree about the status and basis of these values), and would therefore be no 'worse off' in this department by becoming believers. No one likes a cheat or a child molester. Pascal's answer to Warburton's objection is that: 'It is of course, true; you will not take part in corrupt pleasure, in glory, in the pleasures of high living. But will you not have others?'[50] The advantages of life without religious commitment are overrated. Jean-Paul Sartre, for instance, was deeply distressed and disturbed by his conclusion that the universe was meaningless because God did not exist; and would therefore have lived a happier life had he believed that God existed.

If those (such as myself) who make a necessary link between the existence of God and of objective right and wrong are correct, then there would be nothing morally wrong in believing in God despite the (alleged) fact of His non-existence. This point would carry weight with atheists, such as Sartre, who believe that a world without God is a world without objective moral standards. 'Surely,' you might object, 'such a belief would be false'; and so it would be. I have just said as much. 'But then,' I would reply, 'what is wrong with holding a false belief if there is no such thing as right and wrong? You certainly couldn't say that I ought not to hold false beliefs; so why shouldn't I believe that God exists, even if it is the case that God does not exist?' 'Why should you,' Nietzsche asked, 'pay attention to the truth?' The atheist would be forced to concede that there could be nothing morally wrong in my continuing to believe in God. There could only be something factually wrong in such a belief.

'But why,' I would ask, 'desire factually accurate, true beliefs? The desire for truth cannot be rationally justified since it is a presupposition of the rational enterprise. Neither can faith in the rational enterprise be justified without begging the question. Nor can you say that truth morally ought to be believed in preference to falsehood, or that we morally ought to be rational and play by the rules of logic (even if, as a matter of fact, we cannot do otherwise), for you admit that without God there is no objective moral ought. If the existence of objective moral values depends upon the existence of God, and God does not exist, then your desire to be rational and to believe truly rather than falsely, is merely a rationally and morally indefensible component of your passional nature.' The theist's desire for truth, and faith in reason, is likewise rationally indefensible (by which I mean 'not-justifiable'); but it is morally required by, and implicit within, faith in God.

'Now,' I might continue, 'the desire to smoke carries with it a high risk of developing certain fatal conditions, and so, if you smoke, you would be well advised to give up smoking, whatever the strength of your addiction. Similarly, because your desire to believe the truth concerning God's existence or non-existence falls on the side of disbelief, it carries with it a grave practical risk should you be wrong. This is because the decision to believe in God (according to Christian theism) carries with it certain eternal advantages. Since your ability to make such a decision depends upon your having a belief in the existence of God, your disbelief in God's existence prevents you from believing in God, and you therefore risk losing those eternal advantages. Therefore, you would be well advised to change your belief, however strong your desire to believe the conclusion that God does not exist. You have no reason not to simply change your belief. The change might go against your reason; but why be reasonable in a universe without moral oughts? The only non-moral answers are passional. Having become a theist you would believe that you genuinely and objectively ought to be reasonable, and might be tempted back into disbelief, were it not for the fact that such a move would be self-contradictory, being predicated on God's existence.' In this manner it seems to me to be possible to push Pascal's argument even further into the heart of atheism.

It might be objected that if God exists, then He might take exception to self-interested belief, which would therefore be self-defeating. True; but we have shown the disbelief of such an atheist to be, from their point of view, nothing more than a passion. So long as the atheist does not think that they possess a knock-down disproof of God's existence, change might be accomplished, as Pascal suggested, by fostering an open and seeking attitude towards God (should He exist), motivated by the creditable desire not to offend God (should He exist). If you can try to give up smoking because it is risky, you can certainly try to give up atheism for the same reason. Given that morality depends upon God, the unconfirmed atheist has no justification, moral or evidential, for their disbelief, and good reason, both moral and practical, to be extremely thorough in seeking their maker should he exist.

Warburton's formulation of the 'gambler's argument' slides between belief in the existence of God, and belief in God. Warburton says that: 'If we bet on the existence of God and win . . . then we gain eternal life.' At best this is open to misinterpretation, at worst it is a theological distortion. The Bible says that, 'even the demons believe, and tremble' (James 2:19), the point being that belief in God's existence is not the same thing as belief in God. It is perfectly possible to believe *that* God exists without having the belief *in* God necessary for eternal life (1 Timothy 1:16). As Pascal put it: 'There is a great difference between the knowledge and the love of God.'

What is more, any formulation of the wager which confuses 'belief in' with 'belief that' in this manner falls foul of James' criticism that a faith adopted for such self-seeking reasons 'would lack the inner soul of faith's reality',[51] and may be thought liable to incur God's displeasure in a self-defeating example of cosmic irony.

There *is* a connection between these two types of belief. Belief in God is impossible without at least an implicit belief that God exists, that the object of belief is there to be believed in. This is why I said that 'the decision to believe in God carries with it certain eternal advantages. Since your ability to make such a decision depends upon your having a belief in the existence of God, your disbelief in God's existence prevents you from believing in God, and you therefore risk losing those eternal advantages', rather than repeating Warburton's mistake. The argument would be better if it read that 'if we bet on the existence of God and place our faith in him or her and we win, then we gain eternal life'.

Winnowing the argument

Warburton's wager is but a pale imitation of Pascal's argument. However, he makes some valid criticisms of this weaker wager from which we can learn in assessing which form of wager is the strongest. I suggest that the best form of the wager:

1. Highlights the importance of the question of God's existence in both pragmatic and moral terms when linked to the decision to believe or disbelieve in Him.
2. Encourages the realisation that agnosticism is not a viable position with respect to this important issue.

3. Promotes the acknowledgement that purely passional reasons keep the unconfirmed nonbeliever from belief.

4. Consequently seeks to engender in the nonbeliever the resolution to keep an open mind, doing everything in their power to find out the truth, both through openness to religious experience acting to alter their antireligious passional nature, and through the serious examination of evidential arguments.

Such a formulation of Pascal's wager would not be open to the charge that it provided an unworthy (and therefore possibly self-defeating) motivation for seeking God, or to the charge that it recommended self-deception as a path to faith.

It is clear that someone who leans towards belief in God's existence has no duty to seek to alter their belief in the absence of convincing evidential reasons for disbelief, even without evidence in favour of His existence. It is equally clear that someone with a leaning towards disbelief who lacks evidential justification for their disbelief does have a duty to seek to alter their belief. It is always right to seek to minimise the risk of wrongdoing where such minimisation does not preclude the doing of some positive right. This must be so because it is always right to minimise wrongdoing where this doesn't negate some compensating good, and a good way to minimise wrongdoing is to minimise the risk of wrongdoing. What possible good does the atheist risk not doing by seeking to minimise the risk that they are doing the very great wrong of refusing to seek their maker without even the excuse of a genuinely, albeit mistakenly held evidential justification for their disbelief? Such a wrong would be an offence both against God and against their own nature:

> With absolute sincerity we may simply find it impossible to believe. But a settled attitude of scepticism from the outset would preclude any possibility of belief, even if there is a God. So trust is prior here, in the sense of an openness to the possibility of there being a wise and loving power. In this sense faith . . . is natural.[52]

Conclusion: the importance of the issue: heart and mind, faith and reason

Pascal and William James both demonstrate the importance of the question 'Does God exist?', while Pascal emphasises that the decision to believe or disbelieve in the existence of God (as well as the decision whether or not to believe in God) is unavoidable. Even atheist Antony Flew agrees, 'from the mere fact of being alive the placing of a bet becomes inescapable. Try to refuse and your pretended disengagement amounts in effect to a bet against the existence of God.'[53] As James says:

> moral questions immediately present themselves as questions whose solution cannot wait for sensible [ie empirical] proof; 'you must choose,' says Pascal, 'you must wager. It is not optional. You are embarked. Which will you choose then?'[54]

James also emphasises that the decision is an unavoidable one. In the terms of his sophisticated analysis of decision-making it is a 'forced option': 'We cannot escape the issue by remaining sceptical and waiting for more light, because, although we do avoid error in that way if religion be untrue, we lose the good, if it be true, just as certainly as if we positively chose to disbelieve.'[55]

Both James and Pascal take particular note of the role played by the heart, as well as by the mind, in belief. James demonstrates that it is not irrational to allow non-evidential reasons to motivate belief when faced with a genuine option: 'the postulate that there is truth, and that it is the destiny of our minds to attain it, we are deliberately resolving to make, though the sceptic will not make it.'[56] 'The Will To Believe' is then an unambitious but highly effective piece of apologetics, addressed to those who already have a disposition favourable to religious belief, but who hold back due to concerns about the legitimacy of believing anything in the absence of rational justification.

Pascal goes further than James, proving that there is good reason to seek an alteration of balance between 'live options' in the case of theistic religious belief in favour of belief, and that this may be done from the best of motives, without injury to reason, and without self-deception involving the 'method of tenacity' as some have alleged.

Underlying the thoughts of Pascal and James upon the role of the passions in decision-making is the 'faith seeking understanding' tradition which rightly points out that our reliance upon reason is ultimately an act of faith: 'the postulate that there is truth, and that it is the destiny of our minds to attain it, we are deliberately resolving to make, though the sceptic will not make it.' [57]

Pascal's arguments are best addressed to the nonbeliever who is unsure of their disbelief, though they may be addressed with profit to the confirmed atheist as well. Discussing Pascal's wager, F.C. Copleston says that:

It appears to be addressed to a particular class of person, namely, to those who are not yet convinced of the truth of the Christian religion, though they are also unconvinced by the arguments of sceptics and atheists, and who consequently remain in a state of suspended judgement . . . What he seems to have in mind is . . . the preparation of their minds and the production of dispositions favourable to belief, dispositions which are hindered by the passions and by attachment to things of this world.[58]

William James shows that the question of God's existence is both unavoidable and important, and that in the absence of evidence for the non-existence of God, it is rational to allow our 'passional nature' to make up our minds for or against God's existence. Pascal gives good reason for the agnostic or atheist to reconsider the reasons of their heart as well as their mind.

Recommended reading

Pascal's wager

Blaise Pascal, Honor Levi, trans. *Pensées and The Art of Persuasion* (Oxford, 1995). (3)

F.C. Copleston, *A History of Philosophy*, volume 4 (Image Books, 1963). (3)

William Lane Craig, *Reasonable Faith*, revised edition (Crossway Books, 1996). (2)

Stephen T. Davies, *God, Reason and Theistic Proofs* (Edinburgh, 1997). (3)

Peter Kreeft and Ronald Tacelli, *Handbook of Christian Apologetics* (Monarch, 1995). (1)

J.P. Moreland, *Scaling the Secular City*, (Baker, 1987), pp.131–132. (2)

J.J.C. Smart and J.J. Haldane, *Atheism and Theism* (Blackwells, 1996). (4)

Peter S. Williams: 'The Right to Believe' in *The Philosophers' Magazine*, issue 1, winter 1997, which introduces a reprint of James' 'The Will To Believe' with reference to Pascal's Wager arguments. (1)

Ravi Zacharias, *A Shattered Image, The Real Face of Atheism* (Baker), pp.165–166. (1)

The right to believe

Stephen T. Davies, *God, Reason and Theistic Proofs* (Edinburgh, 1997). (3)

C. Stephen Evans, *Subjectivity and Religious Belief* (Eerdmans: Grand Rapids Mi., 1978). (4)

Martin Gardner, 'Proofs of God' in *The Night Is Large— Collected Essays 1938–1995* (Penguin, 1997). (2)

William James, 'The Will To Believe'—in H.S. Thayer, ed., *Pragmatism—The Classic Writings*, (Hackett, 1982). (2)

M. Peterson *et al*, *Philosophy of Religion, Selected Readings*

(Oxford, 1996): Pascal, 'The Wager', William Clifford, 'The Ethics of Belief', and William James, 'The Will To Believe'. (2)

Peter S. Williams: 'The Right to Believe' in *The Philosophers' Magazine*, issue 1, winter 1997 (Introduces a reprint of 'The Will To Believe'). (1)

Notes

1. Blaise Pascal, 'The Art of Persuasion' in Honor Levi, trans., *Pensées and other writings*, (Oxford, 1995).
2. William James, 'The Will To Believe' in H.S. Thayer, ed., *Pragmatism—The Classic Writings*, (Hackett, 1982).
3. Peter Kreeft, *Does God Exist? The Debate Between Theists and Atheists* (Prometheus Books, 1993), p.287.
4. My thanks to Mr. David Bacon (BA—MSci, Jesus College, Cambridge) for drawing my attention to the importance of making this point.
5. William James, *op. cit.*
6. *Ibid.*
7. *Ibid.*
8. *Ibid.*
9. *Ibid.*
10. *Ibid.*
11. William J. Wainwright—'The Nature of Reason' in Alan G. Padgett, ed., *Reason and the Christian Religion*.
12. William James, *op. cit.*
13. *Ibid.*
14. It might be argued that the term 'Reasons' encompasses the term 'evidence', but not vice versa. If it were argued that a lack of sufficient *evidence* against God's existence was enough to render theistic belief rational, it might therefore be objected that one may nevertheless have *reason* to refrain from belief. For example, Occam's razor would compel us to choose the simpler option, and since not believing in God

is simpler than believing, we should not believe. Issues of comparative adequacy would be redundant in the envisaged situation, as it posits neither option possessing sufficient evidence to allow choice on evidential grounds alone. Occam's razor is not itself a piece of evidence, but a methodological principle that can count as a reason for or against a belief. By stipulating a lack of sufficient *reason* rather than evidence this objection can be met by pointing out that in the envisaged situation the disincentive to belief offered by Occam's razor must be balanced by reasons in favour of theism which are nevertheless insufficient to resolve the option in favour of theism on evidential or methodological grounds. James' argument only applies to a situation where a genuine option cannot be decided on the grounds of evidence or methodological principles. (Thanks are due once again to Mr David Bacon for a useful conversation on this theme.)

15. Quoted by James, *op. cit.*
16. Blaise Pascal, *op. cit.*, *Pensées* 142.
17. William James, *op. cit.*
18. *Ibid.*
19. *Ibid.*
20. Blaise Pascal, *op. cit.*
21. Peter Kreeft and Ronald Tacelli, *Handbook of Christian Apologetics* (Monarch, 1995), p.86.
22. A. Van den Beukel, *More Things in Heaven and Earth*, p.76.
23. Voltaire, quoted by Ian Hacking, *The Emergence of Probability*, p.72.
24. Ian Hacking, *op cit.*, p.66.
25. Ravi Zacharias, *A Shattered Visage—The Real Face of Atheism* (Baker, 1995), p.165.
26. Ian Hacking, *op cit.*, pp.64–66.
27. Ludwig Wittgenstein, 'Lecture on Ethics, Culture and Value'.
28. Nigel Warburton, *Philosophy The Basics*, second edition (Routledge).

29. Michael Peterson *et al*, *Philosophy of Religion, Selected Readings* (Oxford, 1996), p.63.
30. William Lane Craig, *Reasonable Faith*, revised edition (Crossway, 1994), p.54.
31. Ravi Zacharias, *op. cit.*, p.166.
32. Blaise Pascal, *op. cit.*, *Pensées* 680.
33. Blaise Pascal, 'The Art of Persuasion', *op cit*.
34. *Ibid*.
35. Your local Christian book shop (eg SPCK or CLC) should provide a range of contemporary Christian music. My own favourites include: Adrian Snell's *The Passion* (KCD308), everything by Larry Norman (eg *In Another Land* CD-SK 7771), everything by the excellent Celtic rock group Iona (*Iona, The book of Kells, Beyond these shores, Journey into the morn* and *Iona Live*), and Rich Mullins' *a liturgy, a legacy and a ragamuffin band* (Reunion Records 7010087725). Christian themes sometimes percolate through the music of otherwise 'secular' bands. In particular see Marillion's *Brave* (EMI, 1994) and the apocalyptic Genesis track 'Supper's Ready' first aired on the album *Foxtrot* (Virgin, 1972—but rereleased on CD). In the 'classical' music vein there are a great many works to choose from, but as good a place to start as any is Mozart's *Requiem*. Films with a Christian theme include *Ben Hur, Jesus of Nazareth, Chariots of Fire, The Mission, Dead Man Walking* and *Shadowlands*. Aside from reading the Bible and works of apologetics, readers may wish to read autobiographies such as those by C.S. Lewis and Richard Wurmbrand (who was tortured under Communism for his faith). In the fiction category readers may enjoy C.S. Lewis' classic children's fantasy series *The Narnia Chronicles* (Collins Boxed Set, 1995), or the adult science fiction of Lewis' *Cosmic Trilogy* (Pan Books, 1989). A fine collection of Christian poetry can be found in *The Lion Christian Poetry Collection* (Lion, 1995). See also C. S.Lewis' *Poems*

(Fount, 1994) and *The Works of G.K. Chesterton* (The Wordsworth Poetry Library, 1995).

36. J.J.C. Smart, *Atheism and Theism* (Blackwells, 1996), p.51.
37. J.L. Mackie, *op. cit.*
38. *Ibid.*
39. Ian Hacking, *op. cit*, p.66.
40. Blaise Pascal, *op. cit.*, *Pensées* 680.
41. *Ibid.*
42. J.L. Mackie, *op. cit.*
43. Nigel Warburton, *op. cit.*
44. Charles Pierce, 'The Fixation of Belief' in H.S. Thayer, ed., *Pragmatism, The Classic Writings* (Hackett, 1982).
45. Peter Kreeft and Ronald Tacelli, *op cit.*
46. F.C. Copleston, *op. cit.*
47. William James, *op. cit.*
48. Nigel Warburton, *op. cit.*, p.32.
49. Antony Flew, 'Is Pascal's Wager The Only Safe Bet?'
50. Blaise Pascal, *op. cit.*, *Pensées* 680.
51. William James, *op. cit.*
52. Richard Harries, *The Real God*, p.17.
53. Antony Flew, *op. cit.*
54. William James, *op. cit.*
55. *Ibid.*
56. *Ibid.*
57. *Ibid.*
58. F.C. Copleston, *op. cit.*, pp.176–177.

THE MEANING OF IT ALL

Where you go I will go, and where you stay I will stay. Your people will be my people and your God my God' (Ruth 1:16).

Taken together, the arguments presented in this book, I claim, provide good reason to believe in the existence of God. Successful theistic arguments are simply logical codifications of facts that can be intuitively known. Because God exists, human existence is not absurd. Because God exists, miracles are possible and God might be expected to involve himself in human history as well as the lives of individuals. This means that we should seriously consider the claims of purported divine revelations. Although philosophical debate goes on and on, we do not. We must make an honest decision for or against belief in God, based upon the evidence we have, while keeping an open mind about any further evidence we may come across. If we conclude that God exists, we cannot treat this belief like the answer to a trivia quiz—it demands a personal response.

I have done my best to champion belief in the existence of God. I am well aware of objections to belief in God's existence that I have not had the space to consider here. I can only note, having dealt with the prime argument for atheism (the 'problem of evil'), that I think every other objection is answerable. There are also arguments for the existence of God that I have not considered. Readers who want to broaden their search for answers must fend for themselves among the recommended reading material.[1]

The debate about God's existence has been going on for thousands of years, and will continue unless the death of the universe, or the birth of the 'new heavens and the new earth', finally proves one side or the other right. Of course, if the atheist is right, no one will be around to find out; but that takes us back to Pascal's wager.

The matter is clearly important enough to merit serious contemplation, but 'Of making many books there is no end, and much study wearies the body' (Ecclesiastes 12:12). As Richard Swinburne says, 'Argument and counter-argument, qualification and amplification, can go on forever ... But life is short and we have to act on the basis of what such evidence as we have had time to investigate shows on balance to be probably true.'[2]

There comes a time when debate must end (at least for the time being), but personal allegiances remain. Not to decide is to decide by default (Pascal again!). We must draw some conclusions and live with them, while remaining open to the need to 'test everything' (1 Thessalonians 5:21) so that we are always 'prepared to give an answer to everyone who asks [us] to give the reason for the hope that [we] have [or do not have, as the case may be]' (1 Peter 3:15).

Where does the evidence point? If the arguments point to the existence of God, what do they tell us about the nature of God? And what has the answer to these questions have to do with us?

Signals of transcendence

In his book *Why Believe? Reason and Mystery As Pointers To God*, C. Stephen Evans points to the existence of three mysteries that infuse human experience:

> The mystery of cosmic wonder is felt in the strange way humans experience the universe as a 'might-never-have-been'. The mystery of purposive order is felt as we perceive the value produced by the order of nature and strongly suggests that there is a mind at the root of the universe. The mystery of a moral order, felt in the experience of 'oughtness', conveys to us an objectively real order of rightness and wrongness.[3]

Evans sees these mysteries as what Peter Berger calls 'signals of transcendence within the . . . human condition'[4] which 'can plausibly be seen as clues pointing to the reality of a being with many of the characteristics of the Christian God'.[5] In Christianity, God is both the creator of the universe and 'the mind who provides the order and structure that pervades the physical universe'.[6] And for the Christian, God is 'the supreme person, who provides a moral order to that same universe by creating persons in his image'.[7] Evans suggests that these clues all have exactly the character we would expect from the calling-cards of divinity. That is, they are available to everyone, young and old, bright and not so bright: 'Nevertheless, they are in no way coercive. A person must have a certain degree of sensitivity and openness to God to read and interpret the clues.'[8]

The arguments for God's existence are not strange and exotic philosophical tricks. They are the logical setting out of 'calling cards' that are a part of our everyday experience. God has reason not to be 'blatantly obvious', to preserve our freedom of action and belief; but he also has reason not to 'hide' too well. There is, as Pascal put it, enough light for those who will seek Him, and enough darkness for those who would rather not. Our obtaining that light does not depend upon great intelligence or philosophical sophistication. That would be unfair. The arguments for God's existence are simply the explicit logical unveiling of real connections between God and His creation; but these connections can be perceived without the aid of philosophical argument. As Paul wrote to the church in Rome, 'For since the creation of the world God's invisible qualities—his eternal power and divine nature—have been clearly seen, being understood from what has been made' (Romans 1:20). From the theist's point of view, 'God has so constructed us that we naturally form the belief in his existence under appropriate circumstances.'[9]

Set out as arguments these connections have a different impact on the mind capable of grasping them; but they are all-of-a-kind with the presentments of religious experience. Our recognition of objective values and our feelings of moral obligation find logical formulation in the argument from objective moral values. Our feeling of dependence upon something greater than ourselves finds a logical explanation in cosmological argument. Our wonder at the intelligibility and order of the universe finds justification in the design arguments:

> The cosmological argument strongly suggests that there exists a necessary being, a being that if it exists is not dependent upon other

beings for its existence. The teleological argument indicates that such a being . . . acts purposively and so has conscious intelligence and will. The moral argument suggests that this being has some relation to the moral law, and that it is reasonable to conceive of the moral law as somehow grounded in it and manifested in the order of its creation.[10]

This is not a case of transforming mere feelings into 'rationalisations'. If these feelings were without foundation (being merely caused by impersonal natural forces) we would be unable to formalise them soundly into the language of rationality. No, the arguments for God's existence reveal that these 'calling cards' truly come from God. They are not delusions. They can be trusted. God exists.

All-together now

The arguments for God's existence should be considered *en masse* as well as individually. Although the arguments can each stand alone, together they build up a mutually re-enforcing case for God's existence, and a deeper picture of what God is like. It is sometimes thought that the arguments for God's existence are like leaky buckets. Adding more and more leaky buckets together still won't produce something that holds water. Similarly, if you add several weak arguments for God's existence together, you still don't have a case that holds water. But this claim is wide of the mark. For one thing, I have tried to show that there are good arguments for God's existence that can hold at least some 'water' on their own. Furthermore, even if each argument did fail to convince on its own, they may still be convincing when taken together. In a court of law, isolated pieces of evidence may not be enough to warrant a conviction, but a conviction may be warranted when all the evidence is taken into account together. J.P. Moreland argues that the 'leaky bucket' metaphor is wrongheaded and that a better analogy is to liken the arguments to strands in a rope: 'Just as several strands make a rope stronger than just a few strands, so the many-stranded case for God is made stronger than would be the case with only a few strands of evidence.'[11]

The existence of God is the cornerstone of the theistic world-view. In my opinion, the theistic world-view (and the world-view of Christian theism in particular) forms the most adequate interpretation of existence. Indeed, I hold that Christian theism is pre-eminently true, being true in all that it requires to be the case in agreement with any other world-view, and true in all that it requires to be the case in disagreement with any other world-view. The reason that I believe in God is because the theistic world-view seems to me to make the best sense of reality as I perceive it through personal experience and the tools of reason.

The following thoughts are an attempt to think through a little of what God's existence means for us here and now:

What sort of God?

If we were to make a list of the attributes God would have if he exists, the following would surely be among them: all-good, all-powerful, all-knowing, independent or un-caused, eternal (either in the sense of being timeless or everlasting), personal, and the creator of the universe. When we look at the being to whom the arguments of preceding chapters point, we find someone all-good, all-powerful, knowing (and possibly all-knowing), independent and un-caused, eternal (at least in the sense of an everlasting being who has always existed), personal, and the creative designer who made and sustains the cosmos. The match between these lists means that the arguments (if they are sound) prove the existence of 'God' as traditionally under-stood within the monotheistic religions of the world.

Some of these attributes have received more proof than others, and no argument has been advanced for God being all-knowing. However, it seems likely that a personal being capable of designing, creating and sustaining in existence an entire universe would know that universe rather well.

God is eternal

The argument from objective moral values shows that God exists without having come into being (the moral law cannot be created since that implies the existence of a more fundamental moral standard). Having no beginning, God can't have an end—because nothing can end if it hasn't begun. God is. The cosmological argument shows that God does not depend upon anything for his existence. God is the un-caused cause of everything other than himself. Since God depends upon nothing, there are no necessary conditions of His existence that must be fulfilled before He can exist, and so He has always existed and always will.

God is infinite

Being the independent ultimate reality, God is unlimited by anything beyond his own character: God is infinite (unlimited): 'as theists use it, the term ['infinite'] doesn't really specify any attribute of God at all but is rather a catch-all term, qualifying all God's most theologically important attributes.'[12]

> Apart from himself, God has created everything there is to be known and sustains it in being. So is it conceivable that there is something he could not know or not have power over? It is impossible to think of something as thwarting God's [antecedent] will, unless God himself [consequently] allows the thwarting—as in the human free choice to sin.[13]

God is all-powerful and all-knowing.[14]

This is entailed by God's status as creator confirmed by the cosmological and design arguments, the argument from objective moral values, common consent, authority and the religious experience of dependency upon a numinous, transcendent 'other'. Although God is beyond and independent of the universe, He knows everything about it, and can act within it in ways other than are described by the laws of science. God's almightiness means that He can act within history. Given God's existence, the occurrence of miracles can be seen as a distinct possibility, requiring only that God has reason to bring about such events. In other words, God is both transcendent and immanent. Although He is the creative power 'behind' the cosmos, God is 'close' enough to relate with us in a personal way.

That God does in fact relate to humans in a personal way is supported by the arguments from desire and absurdity (why would we have the need to relate to God if we cannot?), by the arguments from religious experience (where the best explanation of religious experience was seen to be that people genuinely experience relationship with God), common consent and authority: '[Our] desire is a desire for God, not simply for knowledge about God.'[15] This is the reason for our existence.

It is futile to seek to 'put one over' on God, whether through force or by deception. God knows everything about us. God knows the secrets of our hearts. He knows our deepest, most secret selves. He knows us better than we know ourselves. Our own self-understanding is limited because we are finite. God's understanding, being the understanding of an infinite mind, is complete.

God is our creator

The cosmological and design arguments, supported by the moral argument, the religious experience of dependency, common consent and authority all show this. We owe God all that we are, all that we have, and all that we experience:

> God has given us life and all the good things it contains . . . great gratitude to God is abundantly appropriate. We should express it in worship and in helping to forward his purposes—which involves,

as a preliminary step, making some effort to find out what they are . . . [16]

God is personal

The moral argument, the cosmological argument, the design arguments, the arguments from desire and absurdity (how could anything less than a personal God satisfy our desire for steadfast love?), and the common consent of religious experience and authority all support this conclusion:

> God is not a mere force or energy . . . God has personality. Personality requires two basic characteristics: (1) self-reflection and (2) self-determination. In other words, God is personal in that he knows himself to be (he is self-conscious) and he possesses the characteristics of self-determination (he 'thinks' and 'acts').[17]

That we are the creations of a personal God implies that we must be made, to some extent, in His likeness. We are personal because He is personal, rational because He is rational, valuable because He is valuable. This also implies that God is neither exclusively male nor exclusively female, but encompasses both in unique wholeness. As Genesis puts it, 'God created man in his own image, in the image of God he created him; male and female he created them' (Genesis 1:27).

The existence of God gives human existence a purpose, and therefore meaning, because God created the universe for a reason, of which we are a part. The anthropic teleological argument strongly suggests that the universe is, at least in part, a means to the end of creating persons. The arguments from desire and absurdity strongly imply that the human *telos* is relationship with God. The existence of God saves us from the bleak, meaningless world of Russell's 'unyielding despair': 'It is our knowledge of His being personal that saves us from frigid and barren reflection on the infinitude and absolute sovereignty of God.'[18]

God is good

This is shown by the moral argument, by the cosmological and design arguments (as the source of our moral intuitions we cannot self-consistently use those intuitions to condemn God), by the arguments from desire and absurdity (only an all-good God can satisfy our desire to worship and guarantee the defeat of evil) and by the common consent of religious experience and authority:

> As being is the essence of his nature, goodness is the essence of his character . . . God's goodness means . . . that there is an absolute standard of righteousness (it is found in God's character) and . . . that there is hope for humanity (because God is love [love being the prime good] and will not abandon his creation).[19]

It is because God is personal (and thus intelligent) that there is the possibility of our deepest needs being met in relationship with God. However, there would seem to be two obstacles to this relationship in that God is totally good, and we are anything but. To relate to God we must overcome our 'fallenness', and to relate to us God must justify our existence and His relationship with us. As the 'problem of evil' demonstrated, God's goodness means that He could not enter into relationship with such 'fallen' creatures as ourselves unless to do so allowed some good which justified Him in creating and relating with us:

> God in his perfect goodness will want to make the best of us . . . give us deep understanding of himself (the all-good source of being), and help us to interact with him . . . But God respects us; he will not force these things on us—we can choose whether to seek them or not.[20]

If we do seek to do God's will, says Swinburne, there are obvious obstacles in our way. These obstacles ensure that our commitment is genuine. 'But God has every reason in due course to remove those obstacles—to allow us to become the good people we seek to be, to give us the vision of himself—forever.'[21]

Evil cannot be allowed to triumph through endless existence in God's universe, and yet humans as we know them are infested with evil. If God wants to have a personal relationship with us long term, He must preserve our identity without preserving our 'sin', and this alteration must be permitted by our own free choice.

The Christian revelation claim

The Christian understanding of how God can create and relate to beings who know the moral demands of God's character but who fail to 'make the grade', centres upon the figure of Jesus Christ.

We find clues to God's reality in the moral order, in nature and in human nature. These clues make it possible for people to know about God in a general way. Such 'knowing about' has value in the right context. But that context is not knowing more about God, but in knowing God Himself. As C. Stephen Evans says, even for us to know about God, He had to plant the clues and make us able to see them for what they are:

> How much more will we be dependent on God if we are to know him and not just know about him! How could we possibly have a personal relationship with God if God himself did not take the initiative? It is the stupendous claim of Christianity that God has done just that.[22]

Consideration of this claimed divine self-revelation forms yet another argument for the existence of God. I think it easiest, for apologetic reasons, to approach Jesus with the belief that God exists in hand. However, even if you are unconvinced by arguments for God's existence, all is not necessarily lost. Providing that you admit that no argument against the existence of God is conclusive, it is still worth while to press forward to consider Jesus. Consideration of the complex range of phenomena which surrounds the advent of Christianity can form a basis for belief in God:

> This complex ranges from Christ's unique personal character and His claims to be the Revelation of God and, indeed, the Son of God, to His resurrection and the birth of the church through the preaching of the resurrection. This is a many sided argument, seeking to vindicate the New Testament account of these phenomena, drawing out their logical implications, and demonstrating that their only coherent explanation lies in the fact of divine activity in and through Jesus Christ.[23]

The meaningfulness of it all

Following on from the discussion of nihilism in Chapter Seven, we can say that the existence of God means that human existence is not absurd. We are meant to be here. We have an objective purpose. Objective moral values exist. Ultimate reality both shares with us the goal of realising the *summum bonum* and guarantees its eventual attainment. Human beings have objective worth. Human individuals, and humanity as a whole, can have eternal significance and value. The most important component of human existence is to relate correctly with God; for as Jesus said, 'Seek first [God's] kingdom and his righteousness [the *summum bonum*], and all these things [the *totum bonum*] will be given to you as well' (Matthew 6:33).

Making your mind up

I hope that this book has helped you to clarify your thoughts. I hope that it has highlighted the importance of the question before us and the inescapableness of your allegiance falling on one side or the other.

If my response to the central argument raised against the existence of God (the problem of evil) satisfies you, then you might
consider the non-evidential arguments of Pascal and James. Do
you have a leaning towards belief in the existence of God that
was being restrained by arguments like those of A.J. Ayer,
Richard Dawkins, J.L. Mackie, Robin Le Poidevin and Bertrand
Russell? Were you unsure of the legitimacy of believing that
God exists in the absence of convincing evidence? If the arguments I have brought to your attention have convinced you that
God *could* exist, then, as William James showed, you should feel
free to follow that call of your heart, that desire for God which
has brought you this far, by taking a step of believing faith in
God's existence.

If you find yourself agreeing with my defence of the *possibility* of God's existence, but are nevertheless reluctant to make
your mind up to the belief that God exists, then Pascal would
ask you to realise that your disbelief is an unjustified passion of
the heart with grave practical and moral risks. The quest for
God is not a search for a comfortable spirituality. Many people
are understandably at home with an impersonal god, a sort of
Star Wars force that we can tap into for help but which can never
condemn us or make demands of us. Belief in the living God of
the Bible requires the dedication of self to the ultimate personal
other, rather than the subservience of the impersonal other to
the ultimate self. The discovery that 'god' is alive can be discon-
certing, and the temptation is to draw back before this discovery is made. As C.S. Lewis said: 'There comes a moment when
people who have been dabbling in religion . . . suddenly draw
back. Supposing we really found Him? We never meant it to
come to that! Worse still, supposing He found us?'[24]

Pascal's thoughts might encourage you to seek to alter such a
disposition. The recognition of your position is a first step of
not-to-be-underestimated importance. You can try opening
yourself to encountering God. I do not mean to recommend a
self-induced delusion. I mean to recommend the fostering of an

open-minded attitude towards the possibility of genuine encounter with God.

You can pray, even if it is only the prayer of a sceptic: 'God, I don't know if you are there or not, but if you do I declare that I dedicate myself to seeking the truth about you whatever it is. If you are there, help me in this quest.'

Peter Kreeft suggests an interesting 'thought experiment', whereby you try out the difference between theism and atheism by trying to live in the light of each world-view for a day.[25]

I would also suggest that a good place to look for an experience of God is in a place where millions of ordinary humans have found what you are looking for. That 'place' is a person. In a debate on the existence of God at the University of Mississippi, the American philosopher J.P. Moreland gave the following personal testimony:

> As a university student in 1968, I met Jesus Christ personally . . . He has given me power for life that I did not know before, and I have had personal experiences of Him . . . When one tries Christianity based upon these rational considerations, he can put Jesus Christ to the test and see if Christianity works out in his own personal life . . . This is an argument from religious experience that has meant a lot to me intellectually and personally, and I recommend it to you.[26]

Approach the arguments for God's existence with a determination to play by the rules and to submit to the conclusions if they seem warranted. We *ought* to be as rational as we can be. As Boethius wrote:

> if someone thinks a particular conclusion hard to accept, he ought to show either that some false assumption has preceded it or that the way the arguments have been marshalled does not necessarily produce the conclusion. Otherwise, provided he agrees to what has preceded, there is absolutely no ground for arguing about the conclusion.[27]

If you believe that God does exist that is not the end of the matter. You cannot simply file away the belief 'God exists' as merely another piece of information to be hidden away with all those beliefs you come out with when playing trivial pursuit . . . 'When was the battle of Hastings?' '1066.' 'Does God exist?' 'Yes.' 'Where is the world's largest ball of string?' 'Oh, it's in America somewhere isn't it?' That surely won't do! Such a belief fails to comprehend the importance of its subject matter, which has guided or deluded more lives and art and philosophy than anything else:

> How could anyone be indifferent to this question? If God equals only Santa for adults, who in his right mind would want to believe in such a myth all his life? If God equals the heavenly Father, who in his right mind would want to disbelieve in his own father?[28]

To react with indifference to the existence of God would be as if someone told you that they loved you and you said 'Oh yes?' and popped the kettle on for 'a nice cup of tea'; not as if nothing had happened exactly, but as if it were something unimportant and trivial. What could be more important or less trivial than the existence of God? The existence of God does not just face us with something to be believed or rejected, but someone to be accepted or rejected.

Recommended reading

What is God like?

The Bible.

Norman L. Geisler and Paul D. Feinberg, *Introduction to Philosophy* (Baker, 1997). (1)

Peter Kreeft and Ronald Tacelli, *Handbook of Christian Apologetics* (Monarch, 1995). (1)

Thomas V. Morris, *Our Idea of God* (IVP, 1991). (4)

H.P. Owen, *Concepts of Deity* (Macmillan, 1971). (3)

H.P. Owen, *Christian Theism* (TT Clark, 1984). (3)

Michael Peterson *et al, Reason and Religious Belief* (Oxford, 1991). (3)

Michael Peterson *et al, Philosophy of Religion—Selected Readings* (Oxford, 1996). (3)

Clark H. Pinnock et al, *The Openness of God* (IVP). (1)

John Polkinghorne, *Science and Christian Belief* (SPCK, 1994). (3)

Richard Swinburne, *Is There a God?* (Oxford, 1996). (3)

Richard Swinburne, *The Coherence of Theism* (Oxford, 1979). (4)

Richard Swinburne, *The Christian God* (Oxford, 1994). (4)

The meaning of God's existence

Stephen T. Davies, *God, Reason and Theistic Proofs*, conclusion (Edinburgh, 1997). (3)

C. Stephen Evans, *Why Believe?* chapter thirteen 'Making a Commitment' (IVP, 1996). (1)

Peter Kreeft, *The Journey* (IVP, 1996). (1)

J.P. Moreland, *Scaling the Secular City* (Baker, 1987). (3)

J.P. Moreland *et al, Does God Exist? The debate between Theists and Atheists* (Prometheus Books, 1993). (3)

Blaise Pascal, Honor Levi, trans. *Pensées and other writings* (Oxford, 1995). (2)

Francis A. Shaeffer, *Trilogy* (IVP). (1)

William Lane Craig, *Reasonable Faith*, revised edition (Crossway Books, 1994). (3)

James W. Sire, *The Universe Next Door*, third edition (IVP, 1997). (1)

Ravi Zacharias, *A Shattered Visage—The Real Face of Atheism* (Baker, 1995). (1)

Ravi Zacharias, *Can Man Live Without God?* (Word, 1995). (1)

Notes

1. Peter Kreeft lists most of the arguments for and against God's existence in his introduction to *Does God Exist? The*

Debate between Theists and Atheists (Prometheus Books, 1993). For an introduction to twenty arguments for the existence of God, see Peter Kreeft and Ronald Tacelli's *Handbook of Christian Apologetics* (Monarch, 1995).

2. Richard Swinburne, *Is There A God?* (Oxford, 1996).

3. C. Stephen Evans, *Why Believe?* (IVP, 1996).

4. *Ibid.*

5. *Ibid.*

6. *Ibid.*

7. *Ibid.*

8. *Ibid.*

9. William Lane Craig, *Reasonable Faith*, revised edition (Crossway, 1994).

10. Michael Peterson *et al, Reason and Religious Belief* (Oxford, 1991), p.87.

11. J.P. Moreland, *Does God Exist? The Debate Between Theists and Atheists* (Prometheus Books, 1993).

12. William Lane Craig, in J.P. Moreland, *op. cit.*, p.154.

13. Peter Kreeft and Ronald Tacelli, *Handbook of Christian Apologetics* (Monarch, 1995).

14. That God can be all-knowing is shown by the following argument. Either there can exist an actually infinite number of things, or not. If there can exist an actually infinite number of things, then even if the universe contains an actually infinite number of facts, God can know all of them, providing only that he has a mind capable of knowing an actually infinite number of things. If there can be an actually infinite number of things, what is there to stop God having an actually infinite number of true beliefs about the universe? On the other hand, if there cannot exist an actually infinite number of things, then God cannot have an actually infinite number of true beliefs about the universe. But if there cannot exist an actually infinite number of things, God does not need to have an actually infinite number of true beliefs in order to know everything, because

there cannot be an actually infinite number of facts to be known. If an actual infinite cannot exist, God can know everything providing only that He has a finite but very great number of true beliefs (ie the same number of true beliefs as there are facts). Either way, it is logically possible that God knows everything.

15. C. Stephen Evans, *op. cit.*
16. Richard Swinburne, *op. cit.*, p.141.
17. James W. Sire, *The Universe Next Door*, third edition (IVP, 1997).
18. T.C.Hammond and David F. Wright, *In Understanding Be Men* (IVP).
19. James W. Sire, *op. cit.*, p.28.
20. Richard Swinburne, *op. cit.*, p.141.
21. *Ibid.*
22. C. Stephen Evans, *op. cit.*, pp.62–63
23. T.C. Hammond and David F.Wright, *op. cit.*, p.43.
24. C.S. Lewis, *Miracles* (Fount, 1974), pp.97–98.
25. Peter Kreeft in *Does God Exist? The Debate Between Theists and Atheists* (Prometheus Books, 1993), p.288.
26. J.P. Moreland in *Does God Exist? The Debate Between Theists and Atheists* (Prometheus Books, 1993), p.74.
27. Boethius, *The Consolation of Philosophy* (Penguin, 1969), p.128.
28. J.P. Moreland *op. cit.*, pp.11–12.

RESOURCES LIBRARY

One of the best all-round Christian apologetics is Peter Kreeft and Ronald Tacelli's *Handbook of Christian Apologetics* (Monarch, 1995). This accessible introduction to the subject covers a wide range of questions and contains an excellent bibliography for those who want to delve deeper. Fine general apologetics are also provided by Peter Kreeft's *Yes or No?—Straight Answers to Tough Questions about Christianity* (Ignatius, 1991). Clark H. Pinnock's *Reason Enough* (Paternoster Press, 1980) and C. Stephen Evans' *Why Believe?* (IVP, 1996). However, C.S. Lewis' *Mere Christianity* (Fount, 1986) stands out as *the* classic general apologetic of the twentieth century. I highly recommend Lewis' other writings as well, especially *Miracles* (Fount, 1974), *The Problem of Pain* (Fount, 1977), *The Abolition of Man* (Fount, 1978), *The Great Divorce* (Fount, 1991), and the essays collected in *God in the Dock* (Fount, 1979) and *Christian Reflections* (Fount, 1991). For an introduction to, and assessment of, world-views, see Dr James W. Sire's *The Universe Next Door* (IVP, 1997), now in its third edition. Of the books by Dr Ravi Zacharias, *Can Man Live Without God?* (Word, 1995) is undoubtedly the best. Comparing theism and atheism at an existential level, Zacharias provides a penetrating analysis of atheism set against the backdrop of the history of ideas and popular culture. The high value appendices provide a transcript of Dr Zacharias answering questions at Harvard University, an introduction to the theistic arguments of Norman

L. Geisler's *Christian Apologetics* (Baker, 1995), and Dallas Willard's contribution to *Does God Exist? The Debate between Theists and Atheists* (Prometheus Books, 1993), as well as a brief critical introduction to several 'Mentors to the Sceptic'. Also available, from Word Audio (1994), is a double-cassette box-set entitled *Can Man Live Without God?* that reproduces the lectures upon which the book of the same name is closely based.

At a more scholarly level, Stephen T. Davies' *God, Reason and Theistic Proofs* (Edinburgh, 1997) covers a lot of ground. Richard Swinburne is one of the most influential contemporary defenders of theism—his slim *Is There A God?* (Oxford, 1996) recasts the arguments of his noted *The Existence of God* (revised edition, Oxford, 1991) in a form easier for those unacquainted with the probability calculus of the latter to follow. Norman L. Geisler's previously mentioned *Christian Apologetics* (Baker, 1995) is a thorough three-stage defence of Christianity. Beginning with the question of how to choose a world-view, Geisler critiques several world-views before concluding that theism is true and defending Christian theism in particular. William Lane Craig's *Reasonable Faith—Christian Truth And Apologetics*, revised edition (Crossway, 1994), presents the material Craig teaches graduate students in seminary, including his defence of the Kalam argument. J.P. Moreland's *Scaling the Secular City—A Defense of Christianity* (Baker, 1987), is particularly strong on the arguments for God's existence. I consider his presentation of the design argument in particular to be one of the best around. Also of note is his chapter on 'God and the Meaning of Life'.

Moreland is one of the main contributors to *Does God Exist? The Debate between Theists and Atheists* (Prometheus, 1993). While the approaches taken by Moreland and his main opponent, Kai Nielson, are so different that little meeting of minds takes place, there is a good exchange over the status of ethics, and good contributions from William Lane Craig and (especially) Dallas Willard on the theist's side, and from Antony Flew and (especially) Keith Parsons on the atheist's side. However, the making of the book, in my opinion, are the introductory and concluding chapters from Peter Kreeft.

For a Christian introduction to Philosophy see Norman L. Geisler & Paul D. Feinberg's *Introduction to Philosophy—A Christian Perspective* (Baker, 1997). For collections of papers in the Philosophy of Religion I recommend the following volumes: *Contemporary Perspectives on Religious Epistemology* ed. R. Douglas Geivett & Brendan Sweetman (Oxford, 1992), *Philosophy of Religion—Selected Readings* ed. Michael Peterson et al (Oxford, 1996), *Philosophy of Religion: The Big Questions* ed. Eleonore Stump & Michael J. Murray (Blackwells, 1999), and *Faith & Reason* ed. Paul Helm (Oxford, 1999), which contains a wider than normal selection of shorter than normal extracts.

On science and Christian belief I suggest the writings of John Polkinghorne, especially *quarks, chaos and Christianity* (Triangle, 1994); *Serious Talk—Science and Religion in Dialogue* (SCM, 1996); *Science and Christian Belief* (SPCK, 1994), and *Belief in God in an Age of Science* (Yale University Press, 1998). See also Keith Ward's devastating critique of the 'new materialism' in *God, Chance and Necessity* (OneWorld, 1996).

Kreeft and Tacelli, Geisler, Craig and Moreland provide first-rate summaries of the evidence and arguments pertaining to Christian beliefs about Jesus. See also: Stephen T. Davies, *Risen Indeed—Making Sense of the Resurrection* (SPCK, 1993); R. Douglas Geivett and Gary R. Habermas, eds, *In Defence of Miracles—A Comprehensive Case for God's Action in History* (Apollos, 1997); Gary R. Habermas and Antony Flew, *Did Jesus Rise from the Dead?* (Harper and Row, 1987); Richard Swinburne, *The Christian God* (Oxford, 1994); Peter Kreeft, *Between Heaven and Hell* (IVP, 1982), and Michael J. Wilkins and J.P. Moreland, eds, *Jesus Under Fire—Modern Scholarship Reinvents the Historical Jesus* (Paternoster Press, 1996).

Web-site addresses

The American *Leadership University* site is jam packed with articles, conference reports, and interviews. Includes articles from *Truth Journal*: http://www.leaderu.com/menus/apologetics.html, and *First Things Journal*: http://www.firstthings.com

William Lane Craig has an excellent Home Page with articles on the existence of God, divine Eternity and Omniscience, together with transcripts of several debates on God's existence, a resources catalogue, and Craig's engagement diary: http://www.leaderu.com/offices/billcraig/menus/index.html

Find a host of Theistic Philosophers on the Web @ http://www.accessone.com~pmartin/theistic.html

Writings from a dozen Christian Philosophers, including William P. Alston, Stephen T. Davies, Peter van Inwagen, Alvin Plantinga and Richard Swinburne, can be accessed @ http://www.faithquest.com/philosophers/

Norman L. Geisler's fundamentalist IMPACT organisation has a site @: http://www.usinterpage.com/impact

Ravi Zacharias heads up a site @ http://www.gospelcom.net/rzim/

Wheaton College has a project to put classic Christian books online @ http://www.ccel.wheaton.edu
  The site includes such great works as Aquinas' *Summa Theologica*, and G.K. Chesterton's *Orthodoxy*.

Christians in Science have a site @ http://www.cis.org.uk/ and their site includes a link to *Christian Students in Science*.

The *American Scientific Affiliation* relates Christianity and Science @ http://asa.calvin.edu/ASA/index.html

The *Access Research Network* promotes Intelligent Design theory @: http://www.arn.org

Another site that focuses on scientific issues is *Reasons to Believe* @ http://www.reasons.org

The Philosophers Web Magazine often includes Philosophy of Religion, and can be found @ http://www.philosophers. co.uk

The Atheistic *Internet Infidels* are to be found @ http://www. infidels.org

American Atheists have a site @ http://www.atheists.org/

Another Atheist Web-Site is *The Fearsome Webzine* @ http:// fearsome.net/

Publications

Dialogue—A Journal For Sixth-Form Religious Studies, 4 Shelly Close, Abingdon, Oxon., OX14 1PP.

Philosophia Christi, is the Journal of the Evangelical Philosophical Society. To subscribe or join, write to Dr W. Gary Philips, Bryan College, P.O. Box 7708, Dayton, TN 37321, or e-mail: phillips@volstate.net

Faith and Philosophy is produced by the *Society of Christian Philosophers*, c/o Department of Philosophy, Asbury College, Wilmore, KY 40390, USA.

Science and Christian Belief is a journal produced jointly by Christians in Science and The Victoria Institute: Paternoster Press, Paternoster House, 3 Mount Radford Crescent, Exeter EX2 4JW, United Kingdom.

The Philosophers' Magazine, The Philosophers' Magazine Subscriptions, 43 Milharbour, London E14 9TR.

And finally, Norman L. Geisler sells his books, tapes and videos through IMPACT, P.O. Box 471974, Charlotte, NC 28247. Or Fax: (704) 845-1979.

INDEX OF NAMES AND SUBJECTS